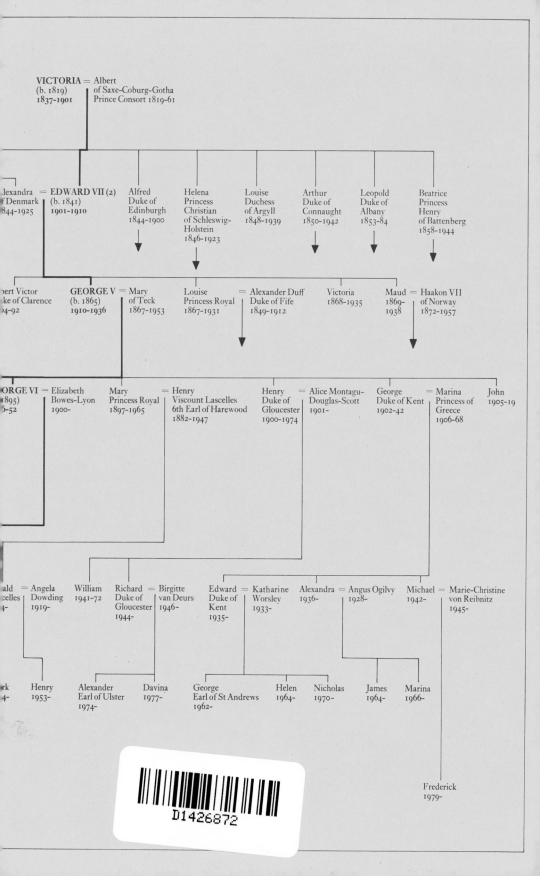

VICTORIA = Albert
(b. 1819)   of Saxe-Coburg-Gotha
1837–1901   Prince Consort 1819–61

Alexandra = EDWARD VII (2)   Alfred   Helena   Louise   Arthur   Leopold   Beatrice
of Denmark   (b. 1841)   Duke of   Princess   Duchess   Duke of   Duke of   Princess
1844–1925   1901–1910   Edinburgh   Christian   of Argyll   Connaught   Albany   Henry
                              1844–1900   of Schleswig-   1848–1939   1850–1942   1853–84   of Battenberg
                                               Holstein   1858–1944
                                               1846–1923

Albert Victor   GEORGE V = Mary   Louise   = Alexander Duff   Victoria   Maud = Haakon VII
Duke of Clarence (b. 1865) of Teck   Princess Royal   Duke of Fife   1868–1935   1869–   of Norway
1864–92   1910–1936 1867–1953   1867–1931   1849–1912   1938   1872–1957

GEORGE VI = Elizabeth   Mary   = Henry   Henry   = Alice Montagu-   George   = Marina   John
(b. 1895)   Bowes-Lyon   Princess Royal   Viscount Lascelles Duke of   Douglas-Scott   Duke of Kent Princess of 1905–19
1895–52   1900–   1897–1965   6th Earl of Harewood Gloucester   1901–   1902–42   Greece
                                           1882–1947   1900–1974   1906–68

Gerald = Angela   William   Richard = Birgitte   Edward = Katharine   Alexandra = Angus Ogilvy   Michael = Marie-Christine
Lascelles Dowding   1941–72   Duke of   van Deurs   Duke of   Worsley   1936–   1928–   1942–   von Reibnitz
1924–   1919–   Gloucester 1946–   Kent   1933–   1945–
                              1944–   1935–

Mark   Henry   Alexander   Davina   George   Helen   Nicholas   James   Marina
1964–   1953–   Earl of Ulster 1977–   Earl of St Andrews 1964–   1970–   1964–   1966–
                    1974–   1962–

                                                                                                      Frederick
                                                                                                      1979–

D1426872

CHARLES, PRINCE OF WALES

ANTHONY HOLDEN

Charles
PRINCE OF WALES

BOOK CLUB ASSOCIATES
LONDON

This edition published 1979 by
Book Club Associates
by arrangement with Weidenfeld and Nicolson

Copyright © Anthony Holden 1979

First published in Great Britain by
Weidenfeld and Nicolson
91 Clapham High Street, London SW4 7TA

Printed and bound in Great Britain by
Butler & Tanner Ltd, Frome and London

For Sam, Joe and Ben

CONTENTS

CONTENTS

Part V: King Charles III

ILLUSTRATIONS

'All hail, Macbeth, that shalt be King hereafter!' (*Press Association*)

Two undergraduate Princes of Wales: the future King Edward VII at Oxford, 1859, and the future King Charles III at Cambridge 110 years later (*Mary Evans Picture Library; Council of Photographic News Agencies*)

The actor manqué: three scenes from the Trinity revue (*Peter Dunne; Keystone; Peter Dunne*)

Two Princes of Wales invested at Caernarvon: Prince Charles, 1969, and Prince Edward (later King Edward VIII and Duke of Windsor), 1911 (*Syndication International; Radio Times Hulton Picture Library*)

At the Castle gate: presented to the people of Wales (*Popperfoto*)

The contemporary monarchy: go-karting with five-year-old Prince Edward (*Fox Photos*)

Degree day: the first heir apparent in British history to win university honours (*photo: Les Wilson, Camera Press*)

High seriousness: an unconventional twenty-first birthday portrait (*Syndication International*)

Between pages 234 and 235

The cadet: receiving his wings at Cranwell (*Syndication International*)

In the passing-out parade at Dartmouth, 1971 (*Syndication International*)

'Bat' in hand: guiding a helicopter aboard HMS *Jupiter* (*Keystone*)

Butterflies: the first royal in history to make a parachute jump (*Fox Photos*)

Sub-Lieutenant the Prince of Wales shows his mother round HMS *Norfolk* (*Syndication International*)

The bearded commander of HMS *Bronington* (*Rex Features*)

Last day in the Navy: farewell to *Bronington*, with a lavatory seat slung round his neck (*Syndication International*)

An unhappy visit: the Nixon White House, 1970 (*Camera Press*)

Paired off with Tricia Nixon at a baseball game in Washington (*Syndication International*)

On safari: Kenya, 1971 (*Rex Features*)

Naba Charles Mampasa, honorary Ghanaian chieftain (*Terry Fincher © Photographers International*)

An occupational hazard in Fiji (*Serge Lemoine*)

Children dance for the Prince in the Ivory Coast (*Terry Fincher © Photographers International*)

One day an Indian chieftain, the next a rodeo cowpoke: with Prince Andrew in Canada, 1977 (*Paul Harris © Photographers International*)

FOREWORD

THIS IS NOT an official or authorized biography, despite assorted newspaper reports to that effect while I was writing it. It would be most unusual for such a book to be commissioned about an heir to the throne, and prospective King of England, in his own lifetime. Such books, moreover, tend to be written by historians rather than journalists.

There are those at Buckingham Palace who would have preferred this book to have been written by a historian. 'You have deliberately adopted an unhistorical, journalist's approach,' I was told by one member of the Prince of Wales's staff who had – at my request – read some of the manuscript. I decided to take the remark as a compliment.

Journalists are, in their modest way, contemporary historians, even if on occasions such as this they decide to dispense with the academic impedimenta of footnotes and source references. Half this book is an account of the Prince of Wales's life so far, to a point just beyond his thirtieth birthday; the other half is an analysis of his life, work and personality today, with a brief glance towards the future. That seemed to me the correct balance in a book about a man whose career has only just begun in earnest, but who has been a focus of the world's attention since the moment it was announced that his mother was pregnant.

If that process involves comparing the present Prince of Wales with his recent predecessors, and making some general observations about their office, the author nevertheless lays no claim to being a professional historian. The only claim I would make, as a professional journalist, is that I have aspired to factual accuracy in a field where this is extremely difficult to achieve. When you write about the Royal Family, most journalistic rules are inverted. The more sources you have for a story, the less likely it is to be true. The more conscientiously you allow your subject to comment on the factual matter of your work, the more obfuscated those facts become. The irony is that there is no subject in the world less likely to answer back were you just to sit down and make the whole thing up.

As this last is a process not unknown in the chronicling of our Royal Family, I have attempted to pursue the most rigorous journalistic practices in the gathering and checking of material. I have spent a good deal of time amid the Prince's entourage, and enjoyed many a casual (and off-the-record) chat with him. I have talked to most of the senior – and some junior –

members of his staff, to his friends and acquaintances, to people who have passed through his life or played some role in it. Most of them, for fear of endangering their relationship with the Royal Family, requested that their contributions be off-the-record, so the acknowledgements which follow simply list some of the names of those to whom I have reason to be grateful, without detailing the nature of their assistance. Many requested complete anonymity, so their names do not appear at all.

The Prince of Wales's staff assisted me patiently while I was researching and writing the book in 1978-79, though – again because of newspaper comment – they have since asked me to say here that 'the facilities were the same that would be given to any serious writer'. A number of people inside the Palace read a draft manuscript comprising three-quarters of the book as it now stands, and gave me their comments on it, in whole or in part. They did so at my request, as the only method of sorting fact from fiction in those areas where no other source or sources could be relied upon. Nothing they have done, however, should be taken to imply acceptance or approval by Buckingham Palace, or any of its occupants, of the book's contents. There were disagreements of fact and emphasis between us, some resolved, some not. No editorial control was ever given to anyone at the Palace, or indeed sought by anyone there. The responsibility for the finished product remains entirely mine.

As the book has no direct source attributions, for reasons I have explained, I should also like to record here that a number of individual chapters have been read for factual accuracy by other interested parties. Chapter 7, for instance, was read by Colonel Henry Townend, headmaster of Hill House School; chapter 9 by Peter Beck, headmaster of Cheam School during Prince Charles's time there; chapters 10 and 11 by Robert Waddell, the only Gordonstoun master still at the school who was there throughout Prince Charles's time; chapter 12 by Dr Denis Marrian, Senior Tutor of Trinity College, Cambridge, while the Prince was an undergraduate there, by Lord Butler, then Master of Trinity, and by Edward Millward, the Prince's tutor in Welsh language and literature at the University College of Wales, Aberystwyth. Other chapters have been read by other protagonists who made a specific request for anonymity.

In alphabetical order, therefore, for assistance great or small, I would like to express my thanks to: Ronald Allison, Robin Baring, Dr Tony Barker, Julian Barnes, Beth Barrington-Haynes, Sir Cecil Beaton, Peter Beck, Basil Boothroyd, Humphrey Burton, Lord Butler, Helen Cathcart, Geoffrey Chandler, David Checketts, Jane Cousins, George Darby, Frances Donaldson, Sally Emerson, Oliver Everett, David Frost, Sir Ian Gourlay, John Grigg, Harold Hayward, Sally Head, John Heilpern, Derek Homer, Anwar

Hussein, Susan Jeffreys, Hywel Jones, Sir Emmanuel Kaye, John Kempe, Mary Kenny, Robert Lacey, Serge Lemoine, Magnus Linklater, Sir Tom McCaffrey, John Maclean, Sir Philip Magnus, Jack de Manio, Dr Denis Marrian, Helen Martin, Dickie Miller, Edward Millward, Sir Iain Moncreiffe of that Ilk, Cliff Morgan, David Niven, Richard Nixon, Paul Officer, Lord Olivier, George Pratt, Dr Anil Seal, Lord Snowdon, Nicholas Soames, Norman Stone, David Taylor, George Thomas MP, Colonel Henry Townend, Hugo Vickers, Robert Waddell, Sir Brian Warren, Michael Wheeler, James Whitaker, Alastair Wilson, Sir Harold Wilson, the Rt Rev. Robert Woods, Bishop of Worcester, Hugo Young.

I would also like to thank the Master and Fellows of Trinity College, Cambridge (one of the perks of my researches was an invitation to their Candlemas Feast); British Rail; the staff of Caernarvon Castle; Lewisham Police; the Welsh Office; the staff of the Prince's Trust, the Prince of Wales's Committee, the Royal Jubilee Trusts and the United World Colleges; the Queen's Flight; the librarians of Islington public library, *The Guardian, The Times* and especially of *The Sunday Times*; and, for their hospitality, Her Majesty's Ambassadors to Brazil, Venezuela and Yugoslavia. Lynda Poley carried out the picture research and Jackie Pyle typed the manuscript.

For their friendship, encouragement and professional advice, and for between them having had the idea that I should write this book, I thank John Curtis, Hilary Rubinstein and Godfrey Smith. Linda Osband's editing has led to many an improvement. The editors of *The Sunday Times* and *The Observer*, Harold Evans and Donald Trelford, were most understanding about my requests to be freed from newspaper duties at the beginning and end, respectively, of my work on the book. Nor could it ever have been written without the help and support of my wife Amanda, not least in her heroic efforts to keep its dedicatees out of the way.

Above all I am deeply indebted to John Dauth, assistant press secretary to the Queen, and his secretary, Sarah Brennan, for time, effort and Buckingham Palace notepaper expended far beyond the call of duty; and to the Prince of Wales himself for authorizing his staff to assist me, giving certain of his friends clearance to talk to me, and for tolerating my shadow around the world for some eighteen months. Any criticisms contained in the resulting work he knows to be levelled with the best intentions, by one his own age who does not envy him his job.

Not that he envies me mine. He once said to me: 'It must be such hell writing a book. They're so *long*, aren't they?' I couldn't agree more.

All the world and the glory of it, whatever is most attractive, whatever is most seductive, has always been offered to the Prince of Wales of the day, and always will be. It is not rational to expect the best virtue where temptation is applied in the most trying form at the frailest time of human life.

Walter Bagehot, THE ENGLISH CONSTITUTION

PROLOGUE

WE ARE ALL the victims of our parents' genes, but none more so than Charles Philip Arthur George Mountbatten-Windsor, heir to the loftiest position on earth still determined solely by heredity. The odds against being born to his fate are incalculable. He was the first child to be born in direct line of succession to the British throne since his great-uncle, the future King Edward VIII and Duke of Windsor, fifty-four years earlier. Princess Elizabeth was only the fourth heiress presumptive in British history to give birth to a male child – and only one of those children, Henry II, subsequently became King. Queen Elizabeth II has herself talked of 'the uncertainty of human life'; but should her son in due time become King Charles III, Britain will have to go back seven hundred years to the Plantagenets to find six successive generations of unbroken descent down a family tree.

He is the twenty-first English Prince of Wales, but the first in direct descent from both the great Welsh princes, Owen Glendower and Llewelyn-ap-Gruffydd, the last native Prince of all Wales. He is descended from all the British monarchs save his namesake Charles I and his sons, and from every royal house of Europe. His ancestors include Charlemagne and Genghis Khan, El Cid and George Washington, Shakespeare and Count Dracula. He is thirty-ninth in descent from King Alfred the Great, thirty-second from William the Conqueror, fifth from Queen Victoria, and eighth from a London plumber called John Walsh.

He is the first Prince of Wales in British history to have gone to school; the first to have won a university degree; the first to have captained his own ship and led a national sports team; the first to fly helicopters and supersonic jets; the first to train as a frogman and a commando; the first to make a parachute jump. He and the Duke of Windsor are the only two Princes of Wales in history to have been invested at Caernarvon Castle, symbol of the English usurpation of Welsh sovereignty, and the only two Princes of Wales since James Stuart, the Old Pretender, to have reached the age of thirty unmarried.

He is Earl of Chester, Duke of Cornwall, Duke of Rothesay, Earl of Carrick and Baron Renfrew, Lord of the Isles and Great Steward of Scotland, Knight of the Most Noble Order of the Garter, Knight of the Most Ancient and Most Noble Order of the Thistle, Great Master and Principal Knight

Grand Cross of the Most Honourable Order of the Bath. He is Personal
Aide-de-Camp to Queen Elizabeth II, Commander Royal Navy, Wing Commander Royal Air Force, Colonel-in-Chief of ten regiments, member of a
dozen international orders of chivalry, president, patron or member of some
200 clubs, charities, committees and learned organizations.

A thousand years of history merge in this diffident, self-conscious, deeply
vulnerable, desperately well-meaning man, a bachelor still living with his
parents in his thirties, embarrassed about his jug ears and weak chin, vain
enough to try to hide an incipient bald patch. He enjoys his ex-officio sex
appeal, and is jealous of his younger brother's better looks. He hates, yet
shares, the obsession of the British press and people about whom he will
marry; he talks to friends these days of little else. He has a quick wit, a
talent for mimicry, a sharp tongue and a good seat on a horse. He paints
water colours, plays polo, listens to opera, hunts foxes, shoots pheasants,
loves babies, dances with as much rhythm as abandon, skis with more reck-
lessness than skill. He is a countryman at heart, but would rather like to
have been an actor. He is proud, ambitious, romantic, and anxious to carve
himself a place in history.

Unless you're a member of his family, you call him 'Sir'. 'Your Royal
Highness' is equally correct, but a bit of a mouthful; if you follow it with
'I humbly crave to submit ...' he will soon be stifling a yawn. If you call
him 'Your Majesty' he will giggle and correct you. If you call him 'Wales'
to his face, he will probably never speak to you again. He is not a pompous
man, but it is tempting at times to say he gets ideas above his station. He
expects the deference due to his office, takes its pomp and circumstance very
seriously, enjoys the archaic rituals of royal ceremonial. He is more intelligent than most of his predecessors, which only makes him more confused
about his destiny. He is often bored and more often lonely. He has few
friends, and can arrive nowhere unannounced. He has spent most of his
life in a world of older people.

He usually breakfasts alone, and has seven homes in which to do it. His
birthright provides incomparable material comfort and international respect, adulation, even awe. Government departments look after various
aspects of his business and pay people to tidy up after him. On his birthday
flags fly, guns sound and judges don their scarlet robes; when he becomes
King he will have *two* birthdays, one an official one whose date he can choose
for himself. All red lights turn green for him. He will never have to queue,
do his own washing-up, service his own car, muck out his own polo ponies,
worry about losing his job, change his children's nappies or fret about their
education. He does not handle money, or, with an unearned income of some
£125,000 a year after tax, much have to worry about it. He is landlord of

a 130,000-acre property company, and heir to one of the greatest private fortunes in the world.

He carries out about a thousand public engagements a year, planting trees, unveiling plaques, inspecting soldiers, launching ships, making after-dinner speeches, receiving honorary honours, distributing political honours, declaring things open, declaring things closed. Every word he speaks is remembered or written down. His presence unnerves people; they snigger, they lose the power of speech, they are astonished to find that he is human, they fight to touch him as if he were divine.

He cannot walk down a street without several months of preparation by a large number of people. This is not a fate he has sought, or earned, or to which he has fought for election. He was born to it; it has been, for him, ever thus. Yet he enjoys his privilege, and is rarely resentful of all it denies him. It is a comfortable form of inherited imprisonment.

PART I

HRH

1

The People's Prince

Were it not for my ability to see the funny side of my life,
I would have been committed to an institution long ago.

IT IS AN icy, blizzardy Friday in February, and we are a thousand feet above
snowclad Hampshire in a tiny twin-engined de Havilland Otter, the Prince
of Wales at the controls. For thirty minutes our fragile aircraft has been
buffeted by strong winds, rendering the Prince's assistant private secretary
a colour similar to that of the landscape beneath. In the cockpit our pilot's
headphones sit incongruously above his pin-striped City suit; he resembles
nothing so much as a hardened, if harassed, international businessman –
which, in a way, is precisely what he is. This is the only time he has sat
down all day. Behind him lies a fact-finding tour of a light industry plant,
followed by a stand-up lunch with fawning executives; ahead lies another
welcoming committee and another speech.

Every so often the gold, three-feathered signet ring on his left little finger
catches the light as he reaches for the flap controls. It reminds his handful
of passengers in whose hands they have placed their lives. The Prince's private secretary, his detective and the deputy captain of the Queen's Flight
have seen it all before, but the clutch of local worthies giggle nervously.
Every dip of the wings, every change in the engine note will be something
to tell their grandchildren. Beneath us, the Royal Rolls cruises along the
M3 motorway to meet our descent. Ahead, the runway lights of Farnborough
beckon.

We are losing height. In the foothills just outside the airfield's perimeter
we pass over a squad of Army personnel on tank exercises. They are also
on discreet guard duty, we can tell, as they snap to a salute in our direction.
Two minor bumps, and the Otter is down. The passengers gird their loins
for the ceremonies ahead, but suddenly the engine note rises again. There

is just time for a quick glance to the cockpit, where our pilot is pulling back hard on the throttle, before we are airborne again. The Prince of Wales is enjoying himself.

His private secretary is not. There is a low moan from his direction as we bank steeply to circle the Royal Aircraft Establishment. On the ground, outside hangar P72, the expectant crowd radiates astonishment. The Prince looks down with a grin, then chats cheerfully with his co-pilot. A look at his watch tells him he is still five minutes ahead of his scheduled arrival time. He's going to do it again.

Back over the startled military detachment, who snap to attention again; down, this time rather more bumpily, and up again, even more sharply.

Before we took off, the Prince had been warned of icy runways at both ends of his journey. The deputy captain of the Queen's Flight, Group Captain Derek Homer, had suggested, tentatively, that His Royal Highness might be content to take the co-pilot's seat, and leave the take-off and landing to the Otter's regular pilot. There was a curl of the royal lip, rather like that of the spoilt child deprived of a cherished toy. There was a look of mingled frustration and annoyance, then a few sharp words too staccato to overhear. Wing Commander the Prince of Wales had pulled rank. After he had climbed aboard, his head briefly reappeared through the hatch to assure his private secretary of the abundance of air-sickness bags. Now he is extracting his revenge on protocol for attempting to cheat him of his day's best moment. He is taking six icy risks for the price of two.

For the third time we are saluted, and (for the third time) we are down – this time, it seems, to stay. The Prince taxis slowly – it is still one minute to three – towards the arrival area, where we jolt gently to a halt twenty yards from the assembled dignitaries and journalists. They peer curiously through our windows. Instinctively, they are smiling.

In the tiny, cramped fuselage we sit tight. Protocol decrees that the Prince of Wales must be first out of the aircraft, and there is only room for one stooped figure in the aisle. An appreciative pat of the dashboard and the stooped Prince joins us, now the airline captain asking if we've enjoyed the flight. He braces himself to remember where we are: at an exhibition of the British Transglobe Expedition, of which he has graciously consented to be patron. It's now exactly 3 p.m. 'How long are we here?' he asks his private secretary, who stoically conceals his continuing discomfort. 'Until 4.25, sir.' '*That* long?' There is a sudden cold draught behind us, and the sound of cheering.

15.00 His Royal Highness alights from the aircraft and is met by Group Captain G.W.F. Charles, Commanding Officer, Experimental Flying, Royal Aircraft Establishment, representing the Director of the Royal Aircraft

Establishment, who welcomes HRH to RAE. Sir Ranulph Fiennes, leader of the Transglobe Expedition, will then introduce to His Royal Highness the following:

> The Right Honourable the Lord Hayter
> Sir Vivian Fuchs
> Brigadier Wingate Gray.

15.10 Captain Giles Kershaw, Expedition Pilot, and Sir Edmund Irving, Chairman of the Executive Committee, remain with His Royal Highness for two or three minutes for press photographs. Sir Edmund will then invite His Royal Highness to enter the hangar, where Sir Ranulph will introduce to the Patron certain Expedition Committee members.

15.15–15.45 His Royal Highness inspects the exhibitions.

15.45 The training film will be shown.

16.15 Presentation to His Royal Highness by Sir Edmund Irving on behalf of the Expedition of a commemorative crystal chalice.

16.20 His Royal Highness speaks about the Expedition.

16.25 His Royal Highness the Prince of Wales departs.

All standing up. In the space of seventy-five minutes the Prince of Wales shakes some three hundred hands and talks to perhaps half their owners. The expedition, at least, is something which gets his adrenalin going again. It is the kind of thing he would like to have done himself if he were not a Prince. He examines the tents, the water shoes, the prefabricated Tri-Wall huts, the skis, the snow-cats, the canoes, the maps and the tins of baked beans as closely as if he *were* going on the expedition.

When the time comes for the formalities, he inspects the commemorative crystal chalice minutely, then passes it deftly backwards, where it disappears with an aide. He is supporting the expedition, he says, 'because it is a mad and splendidly British enterprise'. He will hope, he goes on in a fit of enthusiasm, to drop in on it 'somewhere in the world in the next three years – if it can be arranged'. His staff shoot each other morose glances.

The exhibitors applaud, and the journalists drink, as the Prince conscientiously lists those trade names generously giving financial assistance.

At 16.25 (precisely) the Prince of Wales departs. At 16.30 (or thereabouts) the vast hangar is suddenly deserted.

It is his complexion that first strikes you: the ruddy, weathered face of the countryman, its rosy cheeks offset by tired and deeply bagged blue eyes. You can see that he once broke his nose playing rugger. He lets his sideburns advance, wedge-shaped, across his cheeks. When talking to him, it is hard to take your eyes off them.

In private, the automatic public gestures remain. The wringing of the hands, for want of being able to put them in his pockets. (Offstage, when he suddenly realizes he is no longer on display, he will sink his hands deep into his trouser pockets.) The nervous smile, the apprehensive frown whenever the conversation takes an unexpected and possibly undesired direction. He inclines his head, like a child, and looks at you through his eyebrows, wondering what you're after. His guard is never down.

Onstage or off, he lives on his nerves. He grinds his signet ring around his little finger, he licks his lips, he strokes the contours of his nose. His mouth has an involuntary tic, which drags its corner down towards his chin, unhappily giving an impression of disapproval. He can get so wrapped in his own thoughts, remembering what he must do next, guarding against the unexpected, that he can appear unduly solemn: he forgets to laugh at people's jokes, lets glowing compliments pass by without his practised, graceful smile.

His voice has the unmistakable huskiness of his father's, but his vowel sounds remain his mother's. Whatever he is saying, however ponderous or flippant, those vowel sounds remain in danger of undermining it. They are not of the real world. They pigeon-hole his every pronouncement in some remote eyrie of inherited privilege. It is as well people read, rather than hear, most of what he says.

And yet it is not; he has an excellent line in repartee, which falls limply on the printed page. His comic eye is for the absurd, and he is both quick and remorseless with puns. Meanwhile, he has his own ways of amusing himself. The tiniest detail, he knows, can create an enormous effect. He will occasionally substitute 'My mother...' for the more correct 'The Queen...', to insert a calculated *frisson* into the conversation. It helps him take control.

At five foot ten he is slightly shorter than you expect; his eleven-stone frame wears its fitness and strength lightly, its slight shoulders and trunk settled on generous hips. His waist, thanks to constant exercise, remains a trim thirty-one inches, but his chest a rather disappointing thirty-seven. His movements are sudden and awkward – he has a tendency to knock things over – but furiously ever onward. Wherever he is in the world, he is the focal point of an ebb tide flowing this way and that on the tightest of schedules. The pace in his company is exhausting. When he stops for a conversation his eyes keep moving, working out where to go next, unable to ignore the frantic activity around him.

It is all the more of a shock, in quieter moments, to be fixed by his eye and held by it while you talk. You have to spend some time in his company, sort out the face in front of you from the icon, before you can concentrate on what he is saying. You can be talking to him on the terrace of Buckingham Palace, on a bright, clear summer's day, watching a gleaming red helicopter cross the sun. Gradually you realize it is heading towards you, and you watch with awe as it lands noisily, gigantically, fifty yards away on the lawn.

'Who's that for?' you ask with wide eyes.

'Well,' he says with some diffidence, 'me, actually,' and starts towards it. 'I've got to go to Wales and open a hospital they've named after me.'

Will it ever be possible, you wonder, to talk straight to this man? As you watch him fly himself off over London, you go over the conversation you've just been having: it was relaxed, insubstantial, quite amusing, nothing special. Yet you can't stop remembering that once, the previous year, in a remote corner of western Africa, more than a million people travelled hundreds of miles to fight for a glimpse of him.

2

The Private Prince

The children soon discover that it's much safer to unburden
yourself to a member of the family than just to a friend....
You see, you're never quite sure ... the pressures are a bit
... a small indiscretion can lead to all sorts of difficulties ....

Prince Philip

IF INVITED TO visit the Prince of Wales at home, you present yourself at
the South Centre Gate of Buckingham Palace, where the policeman on duty
will be expecting you. He will point you to the Privy Purse Entrance, some
fifty yards ahead, towards which you scrunch across the gravel of the Palace
forecourt. The eyes of a thousand tourists bore into your back, wondering
who you are. Sentries will snap to attention, march across your path, even
present arms; they are most unlikely, alas, to be doing it for you.

The first red carpet you meet is somewhat weather-beaten, for it extends
down the Privy Purse steps into the forecourt itself. The heavy mahogany
door opens as if by its own accord; the policeman has telephoned news of
your approach, and your identity, to the footman on duty. He is an unctuous,
red-waistcoated, brass-buttoned figure who will take your coat, fold it immac-
ulately on a table, and buzz for the secretary to the Prince of Wales's Office
to come and collect you. (If you are a journalist, it will be the press secretary;
if you are a general or a portrait painter, you are treated to the equerry.)
You wait in a small but grand anteroom, garlanded by paintings from the
Queen's collection; on the table lies *The Times* (or, during its non-appear-
ance, the *Daily Telegraph*) and the *Daily Express*, ironically enough the
Prince's least favourite newspaper.

Your escort will take you deeper into the Palace, past a huge portrait in
oils of Elizabeth II's coronation, into a scarlet corridor filled with busts of
Victoria, Albert, Edward VII and their contemporaries. From here you take

a sharp left through the Luggage Door, out into the inner courtyard, across which you are conducted to the Prince of Wales's door. Through this into the secretary's office, where he will check by telephone that the Prince is ready for you. And so into the lift.

On the second floor you take a sharp left past a Lady-in-Waiting's Room, down another red-carpeted corridor, this one with green walls and illuminated display cases. The rooms now on your right are the Prince of Wales's suite, overlooking the Mall and St James's Park. The first door you pass is the Prince's luggage room. The second is his study.

It is a brown, rather sombre room which Prince Charles regards as his most private. Its centrepiece is a large desk, at which he sits with his back to the windows, complaining about the traffic noise (loud enough to render radio and TV interviews impossible). Two walls are book-lined; against the third is a large, glass-fronted display cabinet in which he keeps his prized collection of glass, gold and silverware, much of it modern, most purchased rather than given him; in the evenings, it is rather dramatically illuminated from inside.

You can't sit opposite the Prince's desk. A long sofa is ranged against its front, making with three comfortable chairs a conversation area to which he will motion you. If it's that time of day you'll be offered a drink, though your host will be unlikely to join you. At the end of a long day he can make short work of a stiff gin-and-tonic; with his family, he is happy to share a pre-prandial Martini. Otherwise, he is most likely to drink water. He is particularly averse to red wine.

Past the sofa and the desk, by the windows, is the connecting door to the Prince's sitting-room, about half again as large, blue, and densely cluttered with what his staff call, slightly satirically, 'the boss's *objets*'. The Prince is something of a hoarder. He is presented, of course, with a great many things, of which he must express polite admiration in public. Those which subsequently receive the accolade of a place on display in his sitting-room, lost in a jungle of treasures from all over the world, are a constant source of surprise to his friends.

There are two more large bookcases; beside his window is a table piled high with yet more books, mostly new ones, a large and ever-changing collection. He will turn first to historical biographies and anything by Alexander Solzhenitsyn; anthropology remains an abiding interest, and E.F. Schumacher's *Small Is Beautiful* is something of a bible, but he will fall asleep over a novel. In the far corner is his television set and video cassette recorder, alongside the best stero system that money can buy. In the centre of the room is another suite of sofa and chairs, ranged around a glass-topped coffee table – one of the few expressions of individual taste amid the Prince's furnishings. Most of his suite, originally decorated for him by Lord Mount-batten's son-in-law, David Hicks, is standard Buckingham Palace baroque.

His bedroom, also blue, is dominated by a great four-poster, beside which is a button to be pressed for all requirements or in any emergency. There is a bathroom, hung with his favourite royal cartoons, and that is that. The Prince's London home is much like any other spacious Mayfair or Belgravia flat, with the richly comfortable, rather dated look so characteristic of in-herited wealth. The only difference is that one floor down, 150 yards along a corridor, at the other end of an internal telephone, lives the Queen.

It is here that the Prince begins and ends most of his days. One of his two valets, the only people allowed to see the Prince in bed, enters the bedroom each morning at 7.30 a.m. – as often as not, to find him already up. He takes a cold shower first thing every day; at Buckingham Palace he will have a swim in the pool before breakfast, at Windsor he will jog round the Castle estate. He returns to find clothes laid out for him, fresh from the pressing room across the corridor. Only rarely will the Prince reject the valet's choice. His taste in clothes is too conservative to inspire Bertie Wooster-type dis-agreements.

His valets, Stephen Barry and Ian Armstrong, are men of the Prince's own age who have graduated from being junior footmen. They do all the Prince's shopping for him, though he himself exercises the final choice over his clothes. His sartorial taste is much less daring than that of other Princes of Wales of recent memory. If, however, you have in your time been named as the World's Worst Dressed Man one year and the World's Best Dressed Man the next, there is little incentive to do more than opt for comfort.

Turnbull and Asser, the upper-crust shirtmakers of Jermyn Street, regu-larly send a selection of shirts and ties to the Palace for the Prince's perusal. He dislikes man-made fibres, preferring silk or cotton next to his skin, and is far too hardy to bother with vests. His suits – three or four new ones a year – and most of his uniforms are made by Hawes and Curtis of Dover Street, whose master tailor, Edward Watson, applauds the Prince's con-servatism: 'He likes to dress in the classic style in which we have been making our suits for the past thirty years. He tells me exactly what he wants, the only stipulation being that nothing should be too way out.' At some £300 each, his suits come with waistcoats, which he never wears. They are designed to be worn with braces, which he also refuses to wear; thus, to Mr Watson's chagrin, the Prince's trousers often hang baggily around his ankles.

He owns a pair of jeans, though they have never been seen in public, and a pair of Gucci boots for evening wear. At Balmoral he favours the kilt, of which he owns a large variety, all specially tailored to prevent high winds causing royal embarrassment. His hair is cut once a fortnight, at the Palace, by a barber from Truefitt and Hill of Old Bond Street.

Here, in his Buckingham Palace sitting-room, the Prince of Wales breakfasts alone, with his personal mail and the morning newspapers. If the day ahead is a public one, he will take the lift down to the Prince of Wales's Office to go over the arrangements with his staff. If not, he will spend most of the day in these rooms, his inner sanctum, receiving official guests, writing speeches, going through State papers – and later reading, listening to music, watching video tapes of TV programmes he has missed. In the autumn of 1978 engagements kept him busy during each of the Wednesday evenings on which Thames TV was showing its series about his great-uncle's abdication, *Edward and Mrs Simpson*; Prince Charles got Thames to send him over a set of tapes, which he watched more than once. As a child, his mother complained, the Prince watched too much television, which is why he came late to books. As an adult he still watches his fair share, preferring absurdist comedies such as *Monty Python's Flying Circus* and *The Goodies*, and BBC-2 documentary series such as *Horizon*, *The World About Us* and David Attenborough's *Life On Earth*. Often the television is his only evening companion. In his sitting-room he will dine alone, off a tray brought up in the lift, with a glass of milk or water. It can be a very solitary life.

These are some of the few rooms in Buckingham Palace not frequented by corgis. The Prince prefers labradors – as countryside companions rather than domestic pets. If a posse of corgis does lumber over the threshold, it heralds the arrival a few seconds later of the Queen, who is not likely to drop in without telephoning first. The Prince is very close to his parents, and deeply reliant on them, but it is only at their country homes that they can enjoy anything approaching a normal family life. In London, in the Palace, the Prince of Wales must often make an appointment to see his mother. There is a constant flow of guests, dignitaries, members of staff seeking decisions, which can lead to embarrassing interruptions. Only by looking at each other's daily printed schedules do the members of the family keep track of each other's whereabouts. They are rarely all at home at once; family dinners have to be arranged as much as a week or two in advance.

On the other hand, impromptu moments can become memorable occasions. In February 1979 Prince Charles and the Queen were preparing for a two-month separation; she was to return from a three-week tour of the Gulf states on the same day he flew out on a six-week swing through the Far East, Australia and Canada. The Friday before she left, the phone in his study interrupted a solitary morning's work. Would he like to come and have lunch? When he arrived downstairs, he found the Queen alone with the then Prime Minister, James Callaghan. The three enjoyed a quiet meal together – unusually, no other staff or advisers were present – and the Prince of Wales reckoned he got the better of the PM in one or two exchanges on the small print of recent Cabinet memoranda.

It was the kind of occasion of which posterity might be expected to know more – from the royal diaries made available, posthumously, to an official biographer. But Prince Charles, in a rare break with royal tradition, does not keep a diary. He hates paperwork, of which his job already generates considerable amounts. And he is not the kind of man to clear half an hour for diary writing before retiring at night, like most of his immediate forebears. Apart from anything else, he gets too tired. The Prince has an unfortunate tendency to drop off during the daytime: in the middle of a portrait sitting, a car journey between engagements, even a committee meeting. His first words to many of the people who visit him at the Palace are: 'Now *do* wake me up if I doze off.' An unnerving introduction to the royal presence.

He likes to be in bed by midnight, and to rise later than usual when on holiday. At Buckingham Palace the working day starts soon after 8 a.m.; at Sandringham and Balmoral breakfast is at 9. Following a tradition no one quite understands, the Prince of Wales eats alone in London, but joins his staff at the royal country residences. His taste in food is unpredictable, and subject to passing crazes, often inspired by his foreign travels; at one time his staff had to go to great lengths to lay on ugli fruit for breakfast every day. He does not drink tea or coffee. Buckingham Palace relays this useful information in advance to prospective hosts, who are advised to pro-vide a wide choice of fruit juices; the Prince is capable of then embarrassing everyone by calling for a cuppa. His perennially favourite dish, which he can eat at any time of day or night, is smoked salmon with scrambled eggs. If it is followed by Peach Melba with lashings of whipped cream, washed down by a glass of dry French white wine, the Prince of Wales will be in Elysium.

Spending as much time as he does with his staff, the Prince has come to rely on them for their friendship as much as anything else. The requirements of public office dominate and restrict his private social life. He rarely makes excursions to London clubs or restaurants. He has been known to go dancing at Annabel's, dining at Boulestin or Rules, but only in large parties and after much persuasion. The fuss involved embarrasses him, the gaze of fellow-revellers destroys more than his appetite. He prefers to entertain in the Palace, where the Chinese dining-room or the India Room can stage elegant, formal dinner parties. Very few friends are close enough to share the evening tray in his suite.

And he frequents only a handful of private dining-tables around London, on the strict condition that he knows in advance who the other guests will be. One such belongs to Princess Elizabeth of Yugoslavia, Prince Charles's second cousin. Elizabeth has been married twice; in the 1970s she enjoyed a much publicized romance with Richard Burton, when he was between marriages. Twelve years older than Charles, she is one of several married or once married women on whose friendship the Prince places a special value. Like his great-uncle when young, the Prince of Wales enjoys the 'safeness' of female friends unlikely to provoke marriage rumours; before he met Wallis Simpson, Prince Edward liked to surround himself with surrogate families.

At Princess Elizabeth's Chelsea home early in 1979, Charles listened as a fellow dinner guest, the financier Sir James Goldsmith, waxed lyrical about the delights of being a newspaper proprietor. Already owner of *L'Express*, the French news magazine, he was in the throes of setting up his right-wing English weekly, *Now*; to the other guests it seemed that Goldsmith saw himself as a second Beaverbrook, undisguisedly owning newspapers for propaganda purposes. To the other guests it also seemed that the Prince of Wales was jealous. Here was a man with power, and a naked enjoyment of it, the kind of power a Prince of Wales tastes and sees in action, but can never exercise.

He can talk candidly on such occasions, because his friends protect him with a Berlin Wall of secrecy. They never talk to the press about him, and will rarely gossip elsewhere. The penalty for so doing, they know, is instant excommunication. 'I trust my friends implicitly,' he says. 'And they know it. The more discreet, the more trustworthy they are, the better. Those people who do get drawn into conversation and do natter about me find they get into the papers. But I hear they don't get paid much....'

Thus he has very few friends, and those from a very narrow slice of life. Most are polo players or aristocrats. Others are much older, trusted confidants, friends of his parents, churchmen, specialists in his own areas of interest. There are few to help his view of the world, from behind the lace curtains of his Palace windows, become much more realistic.

They even come and go less than most other people's friends. No friend of Prince Charles will see him much more than once every few months; but once you become a friend, you are likely to remain one. The accolade is to become a fixed point on his annual routine – like Charles and Patti Palmer-Tomkinson, who host his annual skiing trip to Klosters; Lady Jane Wellesley, the most enduring of his girl friends, whose father the Duke of Wellington is the Prince's host on his regular shooting trips to the family estates in Spain; Guy Wildenstein, to play in whose polo team, *Les Diables Bleus*, Prince Charles makes his August visit to Deauville; and the Tryons, whose fishing-lodge on the River Hofsá in north-east Iceland is the setting for an annual late-summer house party.

Lord and Lady Tryon (Tony and Dale) are among the few friends on whom Charles may drop in unheralded. He has been known to turn up un-announced in the middle of a dinner-party, refuse all invitations to stay and slink off home in embarrassment. Lord Tryon, thirty-nine-year-old son of the Queen's late treasurer, is a director of the merchant bankers Lazard Brothers, and chairman of the finance firm English and Scottish Investors Ltd. His financial advice has often proved useful to Charles. Dale, Australian born, is ten years younger than her husband, and another of the married women to whom the Prince is particularly close. She is a vivacious, extrovert woman, in striking contrast to her more sombre and forbidding husband. When she married Tony Tryon in 1973 she gave up her own two passions, riding and skiing, for his, shooting and salmon fishing. Prince Charles occa-sionally joins them for a pheasant shoot on their 700-acre estate in Wiltshire, but all three prefer the solitude of their summer fishing in Iceland.

The Tryons's lodge is near Egilsstadir, a remote and rugged spot where there is no danger of being disturbed. There are no ghillies, as at Balmoral, to help you find the fish; each member of the party goes separate ways, and swaps the day's yarns over dinner that evening. It is *de rigueur* not to boast about, even mention, *numbers* of fish caught, but everyone is expected to have some heroic saga of the one that may or may not have got away.

Guy Wildenstein, a year older than the Prince, is the son of a Parisian art dealer and editor of his own art magazine, *La Gazette des Beaux Arts*. Rich, well-born, physically diminutive and politically ambitious, he had played polo against Prince Charles often before, in the late 1970s, he became his friend. There was many a Palace hoop to jump through before he could achieve his ambition of persuading the heir to the British throne to join his French polo team. They share three passions: polo, art and beautiful women. In the summer of 1978 Guy flew one of the Prince's old flames, Laura Jo Watkins, over to Deauville from her California home – by way of a surprise which was not altogether appreciated. The Deauville week-end is always one of high living: all-night parties, visits to night-clubs, a chance for the Prince to indulge in his passion for dancing. But Charles rarely socializes before or after other polo matches. He will arrive with just enough time to change – at Windsor he will come already kitted out – and drive home immediately after-wards. Very occasionally, after much persuasion, he will have a quick drink in the club-house before leaving. Not all polo players are trusted friends.

There are many who are: notably Mark Vestey, who married the Prince's former girl friend, Rosie Clifton, his brother Lord (Sam) Vestey, head of the family meat firm, and the Prince's polo coach Sinclair Hill, an Australian millionaire who spends only his summers in England. Polo is a brusque, hard-fought business which gives the public one of its few chances to hear royal four-letter words, and Sinclair Hill talks to Prince Charles more directly than most. He can get away with swearing at him – just – so long as he adds the afterthought of 'Sir'. Hill is a stocky and somewhat boorish character. 'It's unlikely', says another polo friend, 'that they spend much time discussing opera.'

Even most of these rather depressingly one-dimensional friends are now drifting off to get married and make their own lives. 'Whenever I give a dinner party these days,' Charles recently confided to one of them, 'more and more of the guests seem to be married.' As he has lost special girl friends, such as Lady Cecil Kerr, to other suitors, so he is losing trusty male confidants. One bachelor chum still devoutly loyal is Nicholas Soames, son of Lord Soames (formerly British Ambassador to Paris and the EEC) and grandson of Winston Churchill. In the early 1970s Soames was constantly at Charles's side as his equerry; now that he has taken himself off into the world of finance, and on a thus far vain quest for a Conservative seat in Parliament, they see rather less of each other. But he is a survivor among a group of early friends Charles has now outgrown, those of the caste satirized by television's Monty Python team as 'Upper-class Twits of the Year', who preserve undergraduate life in aspic. The Prince these days favours more substantial figures such as his barrister friend Richard Beckett, who serves on the committees of one of his trusts, and Hywel Jones, a socialist economist who shared his staircase at Cambridge.

Other married friends include the van Cutsems and the Tollemaches, who, like the Tryons, have provided the Prince with godchildren. (The van Cutsems and the Tryons named their sons after him.) Hugh van Cutsem is the son of Bernard, the late Newmarket horse trainer; his wife Emilie was formerly one of Holland's best women golfers. They dine with Charles in London, but more often entertain him on their Newmarket estate, with its excellent shooting. Lord and Lady Tollemache (Timothy and Alexandra), introduced Charles to his new passion of cross-country riding, and lay on pleasant house parties at their stately home in Suffolk, Helmingham Hall; though heir to the Tollemache and Cobbold brewery fortune, the fifth Baron has recently felt obliged to open Helmingham's gardens to the public.

This safe, small, well-born group provides the Prince of Wales with an occasional escape-hatch; they constitute the only life he has forged himself outside his family's. They are a means to week-end sport and relaxation. But for intellectual companionship he invariably turns to people of his parents' generation or older. He has remained close to Lord Butler, the former Conservative politician, who was Master of his Cambridge college;

he enjoys the company of Sir John Miller, the sixty-year-old Crown Equerry, who first encouraged him to hunt despite the controversy it was bound to cause. His interest in anthropology has led to a friendship with Laurens van der Post, the South-African-born writer now living in London, who has helped develop his strong views on racial prejudice. His religious convictions were first encouraged by the Rt Rev. Robert Woods, when Dean of Windsor and Chaplain to the Queen. Now Bishop of Worcester, Woods is gratified to find the Prince unassailed by doubts. Charles is a regular communicant, and in his speeches even something of an evangelist. As the future head of the Anglican Church he is anxious to use his position to encourage *rapprochement* with Rome. Ecumenism, he feels, is one of the few delicate contemporary issues on which he can speak his mind. In the process he has developed a friendship he especially prizes with Cardinal Basil Hume, Archbishop of Westminster.

The Prince's closest friendships, however, remain within his family, by reason both of his position and his own nature. His mother is the mainstay of his life. Both have inherited the fundamental diffidence of King George VI; both have fought to overcome it, with a conscious effort of will. Neither wholly enjoys their excursions into the outside world, the polite conversation, the strain of eternally correct and decorous behaviour. Both like to slump in a chair afterwards, kick off their shoes, and swap stories about the absurdities of their day, the arch and often ludicrous behaviour of those delegated to escort their respective royal personages. There is a bond between them unlike that between any other members of the family. They have, after all, a unique fate in common.

Prince Charles calls the Queen 'Mother' and Prince Philip 'Papa'. He began life hero-worshipping his father. Throughout his childhood and schooldays, much of Charles's time seemed to be spent emulating the energetic young Prince Philip's achievements. It was always something of an ordeal to follow so closely in his father's footsteps. Charles is a very different type of man: circumspect, gentle and kind-hearted, where his father is often brash, outspoken and occasionally severe. Even now, Philip can lose his temper with his eldest son, chide him for 'monkeying about' in public, for an incautious speech, an ill-guarded aside. The Prince of Wales's respect for his father is almost unbounded, so he tends to lose the arguments. His face will pucker up in surrender, and he will concede the point. Off duty, however, on holiday at Sandringham and Balmoral, they are constant and warm companions in the outdoor life. Philip is pleased that his son has taken up the polo mallet he himself had to lay down in middle age, but disappointed that Charles does not share his love of sailing. He introduced Charles to the contemplative pleasures of water-colour painting, but does not otherwise share his son's love of the arts. He would like Charles to have shown more interest in science and technology, but is happy to see him joining with increasing vigour in his own familiar royal broadsides against British industry, and his campaigns for the conservation of the environment.

In his childhood, Prince Charles was probably closer to his father than his mother; in his adulthood, the roles have been reversed. The one constant has been his special affection for his grandmother, the Queen Mother, perhaps his closest confidante. Queen Elizabeth is said to see more of her late husband, King George VI, in Prince Charles than in any of her other grandchildren. She was a pillar of his childhood, almost a mother-confessor when the requirements his parents made of him seemed too great to sustain. At Balmoral she taught him fly-fishing, at which she was long the family expert. In his parents' lengthy and frequent absences, she nourished in him the gentleness and concern which she now cites as his outstanding qualities. She and his great-uncle, Lord Mountbatten, share the secrets he won't always confide to his parents, notably about affairs of the heart.

Throughout his life he has always revered his 'Uncle Dickie' – Earl Mountbatten, elder statesman of the Royal Family. The two have become something of a mutual admiration society, who go to great lengths to be sure of seeing each other at least once a month. Mountbatten's daughter and son-in-law, Lord and Lady Brabourne, long-standing friends of the Queen and Prince Philip, have now become as close to Charles. He holidays frequently at their home on the Caribbean island of Eleuthera, where their *svelte* young daughters, the Knatchbull girls, play hostess. Their son Norton Knatchbull was at Gordonstoun with the Prince, and remains a regular companion. He works in the film industry like his father, among whose latest productions are two Agatha Christie glossies, *Murder on the Orient Express* and *Death on the Nile*. Occasionally Norton has even persuaded Charles to don the promotional T-shirts of films he has worked on, such as *A Bridge Too Far*. In Royal circles, the Prince's appearance in the shirt at a Windsor polo match was thought a plug too far.

Of the other members of the Royal Family, Charles has remained an apologist for his aunt and godmother, Princess Margaret, through her long years of unpopularity around the nation and occasionally within the family. His own emergence as a fully-fledged public figure, during the Queen's Silver Jubilee Year in 1977, coincided with the height of the Queen's displeasure with her sister, then separated from her husband, Lord Snowdon, and providing the popular press with its most salacious story for years: her friendship, conducted largely on the private Caribbean island of Mustique, with Roddy Llewellyn, a hippy-turned-pop-singer fifteen years her junior. Publicly, Charles's seizure of the popular imagination helped deflect a few

of Margaret's less savoury headlines; privately, he remained sympathetic
and supportive. When finally the marriage ended in divorce, Charles also
went out of his way to maintain his friendship with Tony Snowdon, who
soon remarried. Snowdon's unorthodox, somewhat Bohemian presence in
the royal circle had added a colourful dimension to Charles's teens and
twenties; as Constable of Caernarvon Castle he had also been the master-
mind behind the Prince's investiture in 1969, the most traumatic ordeal of
his life so far.

Throughout their childhood together, Prince Charles's relationship with
his sister, Princess Anne, was always somewhat combustible. Anne was his
complete opposite, as much like their father as Charles was like their mother:
stubborn and strong-willed where Charles was meek and defensive, petulant
and haughty where he was bashful and withdrawn. She has remained so,
to the public dismay; several times in the 1970s she was voted the Royal
Family's least popular member, less popular even than her wayward aunt,
Princess Margaret. In their teens she and her brother grew apart; they had
different interests, different friends, different attitudes to their curious des-
tinies. They pursued largely separate lives. Charles would often despair of
Anne's public outbursts, the rage towards press photographers which was
always so counter-productive.

Once when he was abroad, news of the latest incident between Anne and
her public was relayed to him. She had come up against a group of anti-
blood sports protesters when about to go hunting. An exchange of abuse
climaxed with the Princess saying: 'Who's paying you to do this?' Charles
groaned when he heard it. He knew exactly what was coming next: 'Well,
we're paying *you* to do that,' from angry taxpayers. It is a cardinal royal
sin to fall into such traps; avoiding them requires a cautious and prescient
way with words, which the Prince has long since perfected.

When Anne married Mark Phillips in 1973, on Prince Charles's twenty-
fifth birthday, brother and sister grew even further apart. The Prince found
little in common with his new brother-in-law, whose brainpower does not
always match his horsemanship. But the arrival of Charles's first nephew
– and seventeenth godchild – four years later brought a renaissance. He dotes
on young Peter Phillips, and now visits the family at their Gloucestershire
home much more often than before. As he approached his thirties he was,
like his great-uncle before him, feeling the need for some surrogate children.

To his younger brothers, Andrew and Edward, he is a playful, if occasionally patronizing, companion. As Charles approached thirty, Andrew was
growing to manhood. He was twelve years younger, and was free from the
restraints of heirdom. His dashing good looks began to steal some of
Charles's thunder, wounding his vanity and causing a few acid remarks.

'Ah, the one with the Robert Redford looks?', he would say when asked
about Andrew's progress. In 1978 they teamed up for parachute training
after Charles had become Colonel-in-Chief of the Parachute Regiment;
when Andrew teased him gently about his age – 'You're getting on a bit for
this sort of thing, aren't you?' – Charles would lose his temper, and slap him
down for familiarity in front of outsiders. Prince Edward, sixteen years his
junior, is still as yet a wide-eyed younger brother, in whose company Charles
delights. Fortunate enough to have a few more years of protection from the
public gaze, Edward is reputed to be the most contemplative and artistic
of the royal children.

It is a family large enough to provide a close circle of friends, with a special
understanding of his problems, for a man who cannot afford intimates outside it. Few people beyond the royal entourage can grasp the complexities
of Prince Charles's life, or appreciate the self-doubt and heart-searching they
cause. He is a piece of public property, who must fight for a strangely imper-
sonal form of privacy. He must develop informed views on the ways of the
world, but never express them in public. He is privy to all State secrets
– even his father does not receive 'the boxes' – but cannot discuss them
with anyone but his mother and the Prime Minister. In public he must con-
tain most of his thoughts; in private he must be careful to whom he expresses
them. He must maintain a façade of suave self-confidence while inwardly
riddled with uncertainty and apprehension. He must insist on the deference
due to his office, while regretting the limitations this naturally places on
all friendships.

The result is that he takes the safest option: the company of his own kind,
either sporting, or born to inherited privilege. There is no one in his life
to challenge him, to question his received attitudes, to offset the benign but
deeply conservative influence of his parents. Many who meet him, especially
among those his own age, come away itching to fill this role. They find him
impressionable, receptive, even gullible; his quick-wittedness surprises
them, entrenched as it is in so deep and unquestioning a belief in the *status quo*.

On further acquaintance they find him defensive, vulnerable, and thus
the more appealing. But it is precisely for this reason that they cannot
become his friends. The Prince has had to struggle to master himself, to
understand, accept and believe in the role to which he was born. He is well
aware of its irrationalities, and keenly feels its frustrations. To have them
too intelligently challenged would pose too great a psychological strain. It
would undermine him.

Thus he courts physical rather than intellectual danger. The price of such
thrills and spills is a deep monotony elsewhere in his life. He must be his
own best friend, and guard the while against becoming his own worst enemy.

3

Prince Charles Ltd

Question to the Prime Minister: Will the Royal Family be subject to the Government's pay policy?
Answer: No.

THE PRINCE OF WALES once gave an old joke new life by calling the monarchy 'the oldest profession in the world'. His grandfather, King George VI, used to refer to the Royal Family as 'the firm', and his father, Prince Philip, has talked about living 'over the shop'. Prince Charles's own corner of this capital-intensive spider's web is a network of businesses and charitable trusts managed by a disparate array of hard-headed businessmen and enlightened amateurs. Each is answerable to a chairman who likes to play a very active role. For all his other preoccupations, he is not the delegating type.

Head Office is undoubtedly the Prince of Wales's Office, a corridor of large, university-like rooms straddling the eastern corner of the ground floor of Buckingham Palace. If the Prince is chairman of the parent company, which we might call Prince Charles Ltd, the managing director is his private secretary, backed up by an assistant private secretary. The company secretary, responsible for financial and other administrative matters, is the secretary to the Prince of Wales's Office. There is a public relations officer in the shape of his press secretary, and a succession of equerries to act as personal assistant to the chairman.

This is the group primarily responsible for the day-to-day running of the Prince's affairs. As members of the Royal Household, they lead a pleasant life. They can legitimately complain of being overworked and underpaid, but they have chosen their jobs for other reasons. Lunch is a smart affair; a different royal heirloom, complete with a card detailing its provenance and history, adorns the dining-table each day. Tea – an equally elegant mélange of silver teapots, dainty sandwiches and bone china monogrammed cups – is taken in the equerries' room. The Prince's staff inhabit splendid offices, with double doors, huge desks, sofas, cooking facilities and large wardrobes (to accommodate the many changes of formal clothing required in this line of business). On the press secretary's wall hang a van Dyck and a Franz Hals; the private secretary's French windows open onto the Palace forecourt, where a military band serenades him through the day.

This is the Prince's inner Cabinet. Every six months he chairs a major planning meeting, to chart his diary in outline for a year and more ahead, and in detail for the immediate half-year. In the private secretary's office is a large map of Britain with several overlays of transparent plastic; this records the Prince's recent movements, in different colours for different years, to show which areas of the country he has lately been neglecting. He prefers to know personally of every invitation sent him – up to a hundred a week – and likes to make his own choice, often against his staff's advice. Once the public schedule is agreed, the Prince will fit in his private engagements around it. A trip to his principality in Wales, for instance, will often enable him to stay en route at his sister's manor farm in Gloucestershire. Week-ends, wherever possible, are sacrosanct, and his whereabouts rarely made public.

Every letter written to the Prince – several hundred in an average week, into four figures after a speech or a press speculation – will be answered by a member of his staff. Charles himself signs only official documents and personal letters to family or friends. The schedule must allow time for the enormous amount of paperwork his job generates – the aspect of it all he likes least. His staff cite as his most irritating habit the late return of documents given him for perusal and signature, the last-minute delivery of speeches, statements, letters for typing. (He writes all his own speeches, though a journalist, Byron Rogers, has since 1978 helped with research.)

Also on the strength are his two valets, two (female) grooms and six secretaries, or clerks, all of whom are paid out of the Prince's own pocket. Even less orthodox in a company structure are his two armed detectives, seconded from the Special Branch. Detective Chief Inspectors John Maclean and Paul Officer have both been with the Prince for more than ten years. Only when he is safely at home do they leave his side; the rules insist on the presence of one of them everywhere else – even, for instance, hunched in the back of his sports car when he takes a girl friend out for the evening. Both extremely genial men, capable none the less of turning ugly when circumstances require it, they have developed a satisfactory agreement about the regular overseas perks of their job; Maclean's annual treat is the skiing, Officer's the Caribbean. As the two human beings who have spent more time with Prince Charles than anyone else in his adult life, they are certainly

– especially the more bluff and extrovert Maclean – to be numbered among
the closest of his friends.

It was the aptly-named Officer who perhaps saved the Prince of Wales's
life in the one serious and violent attempt so far made upon it. There are
regular 'incidents' – in 1978 a man was jailed for hitting the Prince with a
bottle thrown through his car window – but nothing to compare with the
events of one dramatic night in April 1974. The Prince, a lieutenant aboard
the frigate HMS *Jupiter*, was taking a shore course on underwater warfare at
Portland, Dorset, and had been installed in regular quarters in the RN bar-
racks. Just after 2 a.m. he was awoken by a noise in his sitting-room. He
got up, opened the connecting door, and was pounced on by an armed assailant. Officer was asleep next door, but the sound of the ensuing struggle
awoke him. He ran in to find the Prince floored in the darkness, and his
attacker about to bring a chair down on his head. Officer seized the man
from behind, and detective and Prince wrestled him to the floor. The assailant turned out to be another lieutenant at the naval base, with a history
of mental illness; following an inquiry, he was committed to a naval hospital.
Prince Charles and his detectives were quick to develop and rehearse a set
of standard procedures to be adopted in the event of any form of attack.

Until the late 1970s, the Prince of Wales's life tended to be run by older
people. (Few company chairmen, indeed, have their mother taking such a
close, if ex-officio, interest in the running of their affairs.) From 1970 until
1 May 1979 his private secretary was Squadron Leader David Checketts,
an urbane, grammar-school-educated public relations man with a distinguished RAF record. Checketts was equerry to the Duke of Edinburgh when
he first entered Prince Charles's life, accompanying him to Australia for his
six months at school there in 1966. He became equerry to the Prince of Wales
the following year, and three years later his first private secretary. He was
a pillar in the young Prince's uncertain public life, rarely more than six feet
from his side, always ready to help him through difficulties and defuse awkward situations. Through the end of his schooldays, his time at Cambridge,
his investiture, and his busy Service career, Prince Charles owed Checketts
a huge debt for the smooth progress of his day-to-day administrative needs,
and the grand strategy of his emergence into full-time public life. As the
uncertain, immature youth, however, grew into a self-possessed, capable
young man, he felt a need to surround himself with people more his own
age.

Born in 1930, Checketts unavoidably became something of a father-figure
to the Prince. When both tried to scotch this, his role remained essentially
avuncular. Checketts would attempt to curb some of the Prince's bolder
ideas, urge against his more forthright public statements, express occasional

disapproval of his private life. With the Prince now very much his own man, a certain friction was bound to set in, and a parting by mutual consent, on the best of terms, became inevitable. After eighteen years' service at the Palace, Checketts anyway found fifty an appropriate age at which to return to more lucrative full-time public relations work.

Checketts's place as private secretary was taken by Edward Adeane, nine years older than the Prince, but a friend of long standing. With his appointment, Adeane's family achieved a century of service to the Royal Family. His great-grandfather, Lord Stamfordham, was appointed assistant private secretary to Queen Victoria in 1880; he became her private secretary, then private secretary to the Duke of York, later Prince of Wales and King George v, and was still in royal harness when he died at the age of eighty-two. Adeane's father, Sir Michael (now Lord) Adeane, was a page of honour to George v, then successively equerry and assistant private secretary to King George vi and to Elizabeth ii, whose principal private secretary he was from her coronation year, 1953, to 1972.

The Hon. Edward Adeane was himself a page to the Queen, and knew the young Prince Charles. A bachelor, he shares the Prince's enthusiasm for shooting and fishing, and has in recent years joined the Tryons's summer party to Iceland. To work for the Prince, he gave up a lucrative practice as a libel barrister, with such disparate clients as Lady Falkender and the Tory party, *The Times* and *Playboy* magazine. Educated at Eton and Cambridge, he was plebiscite supervisor in the Southern Cameroons in 1960–61, and was called to the Bar in 1962.

Though older than the Prince, and indeed a man with a demeanour much older than his years, Adeane is Prince Charles's own appointment, and thus the focal point of the first team the Prince has himself established. By the same token the secretary to the Prince of Wales's Office, Michael Colborne, is fourteen years older than Prince Charles; but he was a shipmate aboard HMS *Norfolk*, whence the Prince inveigled him to look after his financial affairs. His press secretaries come and go, but the most successful has been the present one, John Dauth, a thirty-two-year-old Australian diplomat, whose two-year secondment was extended in 1979. Perhaps the most significant appointment, however, was that in 1978 of a thirty-five-year-old diplomat, Oliver Everett, to be assistant private secretary. Everett's bird-like appearance belies his athletic prowess, notably as a polo player of even more accomplishment than his master; more important, he has organized such initiatives as the Prince of Wales's tour of British industry under the auspices of the National Economic Development Office.

Soon after his thirtieth birthday, therefore, Prince Charles had settled around him a youngish team he had personally chosen. It was the beginning of a not altogether successful attempt to remove himself from beneath the protective wings of older people. Many aspects of his official business were still controlled by mandarin figures, but at least Head Office was now in better shape. And the principal subsidiary company, the Duchy of Cornwall, needed only a light hand on the tiller.

The heir to the throne is automatically Duke of Cornwall. Prince Charles is the twenty-fourth since the Duchy's creation in 1337, when King Edward III bestowed it on the Black Prince. King Edward's charter, still to be seen in the British Museum, specified that the Dukedom should pass to the monarch's 'first-begotten son', so that for about half its long history the Duchy has been without a Duke. Princess Elizabeth, for instance, though first-begotten and heir to the throne, could not inherit the Duchy of Corn-wall; it remained vested in the Crown, thus enabling George VI to guarantee a handsome income to his younger brother, the Duke of Gloucester. Since Prince Albert reformed its ancient and creaking machinery for his son, the future Edward VII, the Duchy of Cornwall has become an extremely wealthy landowning enterprise, which provides the Prince of Wales with his major source of income. Almost as important, it keeps him out of the now annual slanging-match about the Civil List, the quota of public money voted by Parliament to the monarch and her family.

The Duchy owns a total of 131,744 acres in nine counties, which break down impressively: 30,700 in Cornwall, 69,500 on Dartmoor, 3,200 in Devon, 3,700 in Dorset, 1,200 in Gloucestershire, 4,100 in the Scilly Isles, 15,600 in Somerset, 3,700 in Wiltshire and 44 in Kennington, London. This last, though the smallest, is far the most profitable area. For the Prince, as Duke of Cornwall, is landlord not only to thousands of West Country farmers. He controls 850 South London tenancies, with a disparate array of inhabi-tants: at one end there are the grace-and-favour flats settled on such faithful retainers as his former nanny, Helen Lightbody, at the other an influx of MPs of all parties, including the imprisoned John Stonehouse and ex-Prime Minister James Callaghan. Rents are generally lower than elsewhere in Lon-don, and access to a Duchy of Cornwall flat is not always easy.

At the heart of his London estate, the Prince owns the Oval cricket ground, leased to Surrey County Cricket Club. Elsewhere, he is the unlikely pro-prietor of Dartmoor Prison (for which he extracts no rent), and owner of such ancient castles as Tintagel, Launceston, Liskeard, Trematon and Res-tormel, as well as Exeter's mighty fortress, and the rich oyster beds on the River Helford in Cornwall (where he has sub-contracted the marketing rights of some million oysters a year to Mac Fisheries Ltd). He has a 550-acre farm of his own, the Duchy Home Farm at Stoke Climsland in East Cornwall, where he breeds Devon Red Ruby cattle. It is a model farm, pioneering new agricultural techniques; in like fashion the extensive flower-growing industry on the Duchy estates includes laboratories for the study of bulb disease.

By ancient statute the Prince has first rights on any whale or porpoise washed up on the Cornish beaches; this has proved more of a liability than an asset, as it is also incumbent upon him to dispose of the carcass. The cargoes of any ships wrecked on the coast are his, as are the worldly goods of any Cornishman who dies intestate and without next-of-kin (reckoned to be about ten a year). He has the right to extract an annual tithe of 300 puffins from the inhabitants of the Isles of Scilly, though he has yet to exercise it.

The great days of the Stannaries, the Cornish tin-mining areas, are long gone, though one of the Duchy's officials is still known as the Lord Warden of the Stannaries. Other traditions die equally hard: on St George's Day each year the townsfolk of Fordingham in Dorset roast a sheep and despatch its most succulent leg to their landlord.

In November 1973 the Prince took part for the first time in the archaic ritual of receiving his dues as Duke of Cornwall. On a green beside what remains of Launceston Castle, in a ceremony dating back to the Black Prince's hunting expeditions around his domain, Prince Charles was solemnly presented with his seigneurial rights, to wit: a load of firewood, a grey cloak, 100 old shillings, a pound of pepper, a hunting bow, a pair of gilt spurs, a pound of herbs, a salmon spear resembling Neptune's trident, a pair of falconer's gauntlets and two greyhounds. With the exception of the greyhounds – which were returned to their owner, Lieutenant Colonel John Molesworth-St Aubyn – everything was duly put back in the Launceston Museum, ready for the next time. The Prince wished his tenants 'peaceable and quiet seizin' before going off to lunch with some of his tenant farmers.

There is nothing archaic, however, about the Duchy's finances. Its annual turnover runs into several millions of pounds, and a percentage of the profit is ploughed back into development of its properties and estates. The net annual profit goes exclusively to the Duke. In recent years this has averaged some £250,000 (in 1978 it was a bumper £290,605), to which the Prince of Wales has been entitled since he came of age. By this own decision, following a precedent set by the Duke of Windsor when Prince of Wales, Prince Charles gives fifty per cent to the Treasury as a voluntary equivalent of income tax, from which only the sovereign herself is exempt. This leaves him with an annual tax-free income averaging some £125,000 (£145,302.50 in 1978). It has been calculated in answer to parliamentary questions that normal taxation would reduce this to some £10,000; on the other hand, to be left with that kind of income *after* tax would require gross annual earnings in excess of £5 million. (The Duchy's accounting methods are somewhat complex, but in recent years they have guaranteed the Prince an annual income – after the split with the Treasury – of at least £120,000. A pattern has been established whereby he is paid £100,000 a year on account, while awaiting the previous year's figures to be settled and a further sum to be brought forward. In 1977, for instance, he received £100,000 plus £190,605 subseqently brought forward; in 1978 £100,000 plus £151,798 brought forward.)

Before Prince Charles became twenty-one, the major part of the Duchy of Cornwall's profits was used to reduce public liability for the Civil List. The Queen retained one-ninth, some £20,000 a year, for her son's education and other expenses, which was increased to a fixed sum of £30,000 on his eighteenth birthday. During those twenty-one years, any surplus was invested on the young Prince's behalf, accumulating a nest-egg estimated to be worth some £300,000 on his twenty-first birthday; in the same period the Duchy's 'contributions' to the Civil List totalled £2,250,000.

The Duchy of Cornwall is a State-financed government department with a staff of about forty, the current secretary being Anthony Gray, formerly treasurer of Christ Church, Oxford, the university's richest college. Its headquarters is a fine Nash-style building next door to Buckingham Palace, and there are five regional offices. Council members include the Marquess of Lothian (Lord Warden of the Stannaries), Major Sir Rennie Maudslay, the Lords Clinton and Franks, and R.A. Morritt QC, Attorney General to the Prince of Wales. The Receiver General, who oversees the Duchy's finances, is the Hon. John Baring, chairman of the merchant bankers, Baring Brothers; he took over the position in 1974 from his father, Lord Ashburton, who had held it since 1961. Full-time staff include an auditor, a solicitor, an assistant secretary, a deputy receiver and a sheriff.

The Prince of Wales chairs regular Duchy meetings, and likes to be seen as an assiduous and fair-minded landlord. The Duchy is run on much more gentlemanly lines than many another property company of the same scale. Land deals are few and far between, although the Prince did in 1959 become the proud new owner of an entire village, Daglingworth in Gloucestershire, including a private boys' school. Prosecutions tend to concentrate on such offenders as ice-cream vendors who disfigure beauty spots. Officially, the Duchy is immune from payment of rates and the obligation to seek planning permissions; in practice, a sum equivalent to the leviable rate is paid to county and district councils, and any development plans discussed in advance with planning authorities. One of Prince Charles's innovations has been to set up a scholarship to send the son of a Duchy tenant to the sixth form at his old school, Gordonstoun.

'To ask for information about the Royal Duchies is like trying to get information from the KGB,' said the inveterate republican campaigner, W.W. (Willie) Hamilton MP in 1975, when introducing a Bill to take the Duchy and its assets into public ownership. In a heated Commons debate he called Prince Charles, whom he had never met (and still hasn't) 'a young twerp'; he was obliged to withdraw the remark in Parliament, and further apologized in a letter to *The Times*. 'The Oxford Dictionary', he wrote,

does not define the word 'twerp'. Webster's 3rd New International Dictionary defines a 'twerp' or 'twirp' as 'an insignificant or contemptible fellow'. Chambers 20th Century Dictionary says it could mean a 'cad'. And the Penguin English Dictionary says it means 'a silly fool; an unimportant person'....

I do not think any of the above descriptions fit. I therefore take this opportunity of publicly and unreservedly apologising for so describing the Prince in the House of Commons. I believe him to be a sensible, contented, pleasant young man. Who wouldn't be with a guaranteed untaxed annual income of £105,000 ...?

For once, improbably enough, Mr Hamilton was following a Conservative initiative. In 1968 the Bow Group of the Young Conservatives had recommended State ownership, and a separate allowance from the Civil List to be allocated to the heir to the throne. Mr Hamilton's intent was much more drastic: under his scheme Prince Charles would have received 'no more than the Prime Minister earns' – at the time of writing £22,000 p.a. His Bill, which he boldly described as 'relatively non-controversial', failed to get beyond its first reading. (Unhappily, Mr Hamilton refused to discuss these and related matters with the author: 'I am too busy', he wrote on 5 February 1979, 'with more important matters.')

The nation's attitude to the Prince of Wales's tax-free income depends entirely on its attitude to the monarchy. Prince Charles undoubtedly appears to need some £100,000 a year to keep himself in the style to which he has become accustomed – the style, moreover, in which his future subjects have become accustomed to seeing him. When a majority wishes to alter the nature and function of the monarchy, that will be the time to start trimming the monarchy's income. The Prince's only other source of income – which *is* subject to normal taxation – is a portfolio of investments handled on his behalf by a consortium of three City stockbroking firms. Its value and its holdings at any given time are a secret as closely guarded as the Crown Jewels. He has never accepted any other form of personal income, even when entitled to it. During his Service career, for instance, he did not draw the salary due to him in the RAF, and donated his Navy pay to the King George's Fund for Sailors.

When he inherits the throne, Charles will become one of the richest men outside the Arab world. The Queen's fortune has often been declared incalculable, but is certainly among the largest in private hands anywhere in the world. Estimates of the sovereign's personal fortune have varied wildly between £10 million and £70 million. One recent obfuscation came with the Companies Act of 1976, which was hastily revised to exempt the Royal Family from a clause requiring anyone owning more than five per cent of a public company to disclose their holdings. On becoming King, Charles will inherit the Duchy of Lancaster, an even larger property company than the Duchy of Cornwall, with revenues – entirely free from income tax – about twice as large. If he still has no son, he will retain the Duchy of Cornwall as well. Until that heady day, he must pay his staff and personal expenses – including, rather touchingly, a small sum to his mother for board and lodging – out of his Duchy of Cornwall income. One luxury, for instance, is his string of polo ponies, whose upkeep is estimated at around £12,000 a year; his blue convertible Aston Martin V8, on the other hand, is eight years old.

As long as the present system holds good, and until he succeeds to the throne, the Prince of Wales will make no demands upon the Civil List. He reserves the right to alter his present arrangement with the Treasury when he marries, and the Civil List sets aside a theoretical and regularly revised sum, at present £60,000 per annum, for his widow. At this stage of his life, his annual income certainly does exceed his expenditure by some twenty per cent, more than enough to make Mr Micawber happy. But out of the surplus he is, according to the secretary of the Duchy of Cornwall, 'hideously generous' to charities. Until the Royal Family's finances are made publicly accountable, only the bankers of Coutts Ltd – who produce special cheques imprinted with the Prince's coronet, which he signs simply Charles – will know more. For now we will have to make do with the Buckingham Palace *argot*: 'While the amount retained by His Royal Highness is in excess of his current expenses, it is related to what can reasonably be foreseen in the future. .... The excess of income over expenditure will permit the gradual accumulation of a reserve fund to cover expenses and contingencies for which there would otherwise be no provision.'

The Prince's private apartments at Buckingham Palace and Windsor Castle are maintained at State expense. The Duchy of Cornwall, meanwhile, provides him with another tranquil retreat: a three-bedroomed cottage on the Scilly island of St Mary's, where the former Prime Minister, Sir Harold Wilson, is a neighbour. Called Tamarisk after a locally luxuriant shrub, the house is set behind high walls in its own half acre, just down the road from the local Duchy offices, and a few hundred yards from a football pitch convenient for helicopter landings. But he uses this retreat only rarely.

The Prince prefers living at home with his parents – as, unlike most young men, he was still doing on his thirtieth birthday. Only when he marries will etiquette force him, reluctantly, to move (though, like his sister after her marriage, he will retain his own suite in the Palace). Even then he is most unlikely, despite popular belief to the contrary, to move into his country home, Chevening, in Kent. The Prince will be found a London home convenient to Buckingham Palace, where he will retain his office. The most likely candidate – though it is mentioned *sotto voce* in royal circles, for it presupposes the death of the Queen Mother – is Clarence House.

Chevening, which at present he scarcely ever visits, will become a home for country week-ends. This comparative neglect will confirm the fears of those Labour MPs who protested when Prince Charles finally, after several changes of heart, accepted the offer of the house in 1974. It was 'scandalous', said Mrs Renee Short, Labour member for Wolverhampton (North-East), that a bachelor should have exclusive use of a vast and architecturally important estate left to the nation. The only concession Prince Charles has made has been occasionally to open the grounds to the public. In the Queen's Silver Jubilee Year, when he was chairman of the fund-raising appeal, several hundred people paid £400 a head to dine with him there.

Chevening was the ancestral home of the Earls Stanhope, having been bought in the reign of George I for £28,000 by the first Earl, General James Stanhope. General James was instrumental in securing the accession of the Hanoverian monarchs, and his descendants have ever since earned distinguished, if minor, reputations as staunch English patriots. The seventh Earl, who died in 1967 at the age of eighty-six, was no exception. As he was without an heir, he gave Chevening to the nation in 1959, under the Chevening Estate Act, which stipulated that (on his death) the Prime Minister should be given first choice of living there, followed by a Cabinet Minister and thirdly by lineal descendants of King George VI. After meeting Prince Charles in 1965, Stanhope wrote a memorandum to the Prime Minister expressing the hope that, despite the 1959 Act, it would be offered first to the Prince of Wales.

Set in a 3,000-acre estate (2,500 of which are let to neighbouring farmers) with its own four-acre lake, the mansion dates from 1630 and is in part attributed to Inigo Jones. Some three miles from Sevenoaks, amid the lush North Downs of Kent, its Palladian magnificence far outranks Chequers and Dorneywood, the official country residences of the Prime Minister and the Foreign Secretary. With its two pavilions, its colonnaded walkways, its thirty-six reception and state rooms, its Italian plasterwork, Waterford chandeliers and marble floors, Chevening is in the most sumptuous tradition of English country mansions.

There were several provisoes built into the 1959 Act, which was primarily designed to avoid death duties forcing the sale of the house. If no one in the first three categories accepted it by August 1973, Chevening was to be offered to the Canadian High Commissioner or the United States Ambassador. Failing all else, it was to pass to the National Trust. In 1969, two years after Stanhope's death, Prince Charles and the Queen went over the house one gloomy autumn day, and were disappointed by its state of disrepair. Walls had been shored up, the plasterwork had cracked extensively, the roof had come away in places, and the whole house wore a dilapidated, unwelcoming air. They turned the offer down.

But renovations were already under way. By the terms of the Act a substantial trust fund was available to improve and maintain the property. In 1973, when a wing became very comfortably habitable as other work progressed, Prince Charles was again offered first choice, and again turned it down. The Prime Minister, Edward Heath, offered it to the highest-ranking Cabinet minister without an official country residence: the Chancellor of the Exchequer, then Anthony Barber. Chevening would very likely have become a permanent privilege of the Chancellorship, beyond the recall of the Prince of Wales, had not a legal oversight been discovered.

The 1959 Chevening Act had provided that occupation of the house should not give rise to any tax liability whatsoever. But a forgetful draughtsman of the 1963 Finance Act had unintentionally made the occupier liable to income tax on the value of his occupancy – although putative, a not insubstantial sum. To meet Stanhope's original intentions, Barber tabled an amendment to the 1973 Finance Act, but then felt he could not properly benefit from his own alteration of the law. So Chevening passed instead into the hands of the Lord Chancellor, Lord Hailsham.

The Hailshams spent a cosy and contented winter in the new wing before the fall of the Heath Government, in the general election of February 1974, forced them as suddenly out again. That Easter Prince Charles took another look over the house, and found it transformed. More than £250,000 had been spent, and the outside renovation work was now complete. The roof had been completely replaced, and the exterior fabric renewed to weather a good 200 years. Work was proceeding on the interior's thirty-six main rooms, including ten bedrooms and eight bathrooms. The decorations were not all to the Prince's liking, but the Chevening trustees were more than happy to alter them to his specifications – and to install, at his special request, an extensive and sophisticated stereo system. The Prince of Wales changed his mind.

Chevening's lawns, he discovered, were a mere twelve helicopter-minutes from the garden of Buckingham Palace. He flew in and out regularly to inspect the progress of the interior restoration, and even talked of producing a book about the house and its glories, as his parents had done after the restoration of Clarence House for them twenty-five years earlier. But since the mansion has been ready for his use, as it was early in 1975, he has very rarely even looked in. Even the shooting rights on the estate, which might well have been thought to be close to his heart, have been sub-let to a consortium. Local people are very disappointed, even angry.

As he grows older, as a family grows around him, the Prince may come to use Chevening as an alternative to his parents' annual round of Januaries at Sandringham, Easters and Christmases at Windsor and summers at Balmoral. It would be a sad Princess of Wales whose husband compelled her to spend all their holidays with her in-laws. Prince Charles's independence, which he has only begun to assert in his late twenties, will perhaps restore some life to what the late Lady Hailsham called 'this most beautiful of English country houses'. As a junior court gathers around the Prince, Chevening may play host to glittering house parties of a scale to recall the halcyon days when the future King Edward VII was Prince of Wales. Until then it seems likely to remain the object of a magnificent, uniquely royal neglect.

4

God Bless the Prince of Wales

Costly thy habit as thy purse can buy,
But not express'd in fancy; rich, not gaudy;
For the apparel oft proclaims the man...

Shakespeare, HAMLET I, iii

THE PRINCE OF WALES spent Saturday, 3 October 1970, out shooting near Paris with the Soames family: Sir Christopher (now Lord) Soames, then the British Ambassador to France, and his son Nicholas. Their route home at the end of the day took them through the Bois de Boulogne, a reminder to the Prince of the nearby presence of his exiled great-uncle, the Duke of Windsor – King Edward VIII for 325 days in 1936, and his immediate predecessor as Prince of Wales.

On the spur of the moment, the Prince asked Sir Christopher to arrange a visit. There was some humming and hawing. The Duke and Duchess were still on uncertain terms with the Royal Family; besides, it was Saturday evening, the switchboard staff were off duty, and people who have been out shooting all day want nothing so much as to relax in a long hot bath. But Prince Charles was insistent. The telephone wires buzzed for a while and later that evening, after dinner, the three were on their way to the Rue du Champ d'Entrainment.

When they arrived, by one account, the Windsors' drawing-room was 'full of appallingly vulgar Americans'. But Prince Charles and the Duke retreated into a corner together, and talked alone for more than an hour. Their respective investitures at Caernarvon – the Prince's fresh in his mind from the year before, the Duke's nearly sixty years earlier – were one unique mutual ordeal for light-hearted reminiscence. But there were many more, as is to be expected when two of only twenty-one Princes of Wales in more than 650 years get together. Afterwards, the Duke politely called the Prince 'intelligent and perceptive'. They parted rather emotionally. Prince Charles was to see his great-uncle only once more: twenty months later, a week before his death.

Their meeting on foreign soil that night, a genteel courtesy from one heir apparent to a fallen predecessor, was in its way a moment of history. The Duke, even *in absentia*, even in death, has played a larger part than most in the unfolding progress of the next Prince of Wales. Britain is more than forty years on, but through Prince Charles's life echoes still the memorable farewell of King Edward VIII to his people in 1936: 'I have found it impossible to carry the heavy burden of duty, and to discharge my duties as King as I would wish to do, without the help and support of the woman I love.'

Constitutional niceties take little note of social change. The abdication was the British monarchy's greatest trauma this century, and Queen Elizabeth II believes history will remember her for having rebuilt the institution on the foundations laid by her father. December 1936 was a moment of near collapse, when a poll showed that half the British people wanted to seize the chance to do away with the monarchy. The phoenix was not proved risen, to the Queen's mind, until the euphoria of her Silver Jubilee celebrations in 1977 took her completely by surprise. Now more than ever, Prince Edward is held up to the next Prince of Wales as an example of how *not* to become a king.

Prince Charles is a keen student of the history of his office, and equally keen to carve himself a conspicuous niche in the annals of the English Princes of Wales. He knows full well that he will probably pass many more years as Prince than as King. With this in mind, many of the precepts he has adopted for his own behaviour, both private and public, are designed to eradicate the mixed memories left behind them by his two most colourful immediate predecessors as Prince of Wales, the future Kings Edward VII and Edward VIII. When the time comes for a soap opera on the young life of the present Prince of Wales, the TV companies will be stretched to come up with anything approaching their recent *embarras de richesse*.

Two nights before his abdication, King Edward VIII was on his best form at a dinner party at Fort Belvedere, his Windsor retreat. In the words of his brother the Duke of York, about to become King George VI *malgré lui*, he was 'telling the PM [Baldwin] things I am sure he had never heard before about unemployed centres etc (referring to his visit in S. Wales)'. The Duke whispered to his neighbour at table, Walter Monckton, 'And this is the man we are going to lose....'

But Edward as King never quite understood why, on a matter like unemployment, there was nothing he could do to force a government's hand; it would have been as unconstitutional as it had been dishonest of him, a few months before, to promise unemployed Welshmen that 'Something must be done'. To his dying day he never really grasped why his choice of bride made abdication inevitable, why the nation and Commonwealth would not accept a divorcee as its Queen, consort to the Defender of the Faith. His memoirs, written in 1951, distort the histori-cal facts of the abdication, and later in life he grew ever more convinced that it had all been a sinister plot against him by Baldwin and others. In view of the Duke of Windsor's subsequent flirtation with Hitler and the Nazis, it is perhaps as well he did not remain a king with what he thought should be irresistible political influence.

From Edward's reaction to his investiture as Prince of Wales at the age of sixteen – 'I recoiled from anything that tended to set me up as a person requiring homage' – we can see the makings of an unorthodox, probably dis-astrous king. The monarch of all people should find some point in pomp and circumstance. But an excellent prince, as history has often shown, does not necessarily make an excellent king. No epitaph for King Edward VIII is more fitting than that of Tacitus for the Emperor Galba: *capax imperii nisi imperasset* (worthy to rule, had he not ruled). It is as a prince we should remember him.

From the early history of Edward's grandfather, King Edward VII, there are contrasting morals to be drawn. Prince Charles and his parents have always regarded Queen Victoria's son, Prince of Wales for fifty-nine years, as an object-lesson in all that can go wrong for the heir of a monarch who comes to the throne young. Charles may well have to wait in the wings, the sovereign's understudy, quite as long as did Prince Albert Edward ('Bertie' to his family). His brief reign turned out to be both popular and successful; but his long years as an idle prince led him into excess and de-bauchery of a kind which would be anathema to the cosy, domesticated monarchy we have today. Bertie involved the monarchy in gambling and divorce scandals, dragging it down in the popular esteem, making it the butt of some of the cruellest cartooning since Rowlandson and George III. Happily for Prince Charles, the reasons are easy to discern.

Queen Victoria denied her son access to State papers; she refused him any positive role in affairs of State, and even discouraged him from meeting politicians. When the Prime Minister suggested the Prince see Cabinet minutes, the Queen allowed only – and that with reluctance – that he be informed of Cabinet decisions. Gladstone spent two years trying to persuade her to make her son Viceroy of Ireland; it would have given him valuable experience of a quasi-monarchical role, and a royal presence in Dublin might have eased the increasingly turbulent Irish question. Victoria would have none of it. Elizabeth II, by contrast, has encouraged her son from his earliest adulthood to take an active part in the constitutional process; he reads Cabinet papers, and since becoming a Privy Councillor in 1977 meets politicians of all hues on an intimate and confidential footing.

In time, when he is married, he may well spend a period as Governor-General of a Commonwealth country, Australia being the most likely choice because of its importance and, quite simply, his fondness for the place. The idea was mooted several times in the 1970s – ironically enough by Gough Whitlam, the socialist prime minister who did away with the national anthem. But the dismissal in 1975 of the Whitlam government by the then Governor-General, Sir John Kerr, brought the office too close to politics for princely comfort. By the early or mid-1980s, when there is a Princess of Wales to act as a Governor-General's consort, these memories should have healed.

In such ways as this Prince Charles is constantly exploring new routes towards a more positive role. It is not an easy task, fenced in as he is by the strict political taboo on the conduct of a representative monarchy. As the Duke of Windsor himself put it: 'Some Princes bend their characters more easily than others to this rule. It was to be my fate to find it at times irksome because I had been endowed with a questioning, independent mind and I found it difficult ever to take anything for granted, even my own position.'

Prince Charles is endowed with a questioning, if not quite so independent, mind. He no longer finds it difficult to take his position for granted. He is happier than Prince Edward to adapt his own royal conduct to the style established by his parents, just now and then treading gingerly into pastures new.

Royal links with industry, for instance, are traditional. The Queen's Awards for Export are only the most familiar of a number of devices of moral encouragement; Prince Philip's 'Get your fingers out' speeches are another, though less familiar in his mellower middle age. In his early thirties, Prince Charles has begun to extend those links into the virgin royal territory of the trade unions, as befits the times; in 1979 he attended the annual conference of the Iron and Steel Trades Federation, carefully selected as one of the few unions which had then submitted to the Callaghan Government's pay policy. Earlier that year, he too had been telling both sides of British industry to get their fingers out.

By then he had also used – of the pollution of the Welsh countryside – those famous words of the last Prince of Wales: 'Something must be done.' They are generally remembered as the words of a concerned and dynamic Prince of Wales: in fact, when he said them to a group of unemployed-

Welshmen, during a tour of the depressed mining valleys of South Wales in 1936, Prince Edward had lately become King, and already knew of the likelihood of his abdication. They were dangerous words for Prince Charles to revive, standing as they now do for a memorable moment of betrayal. Already he was trying to right the wrongs of recent history, to show that this was one path down which he would never go.

There are many possible views of the abdication: a dereliction of sacred duty, an easy way out of an unfortunate predicament, visible proof that the monarchy's creaking irrationality is finally outmoded. Wherever the truth lies, there can never be any doubt that Edward was a superb Prince of Wales. Glamorous, energetic, debonair, with a liberal dash of raciness and more than his fair share of charm, he genuinely did care about the less privileged of his father's subjects, and was blessed with a flair for showing that he cared. His impatience with the trappings of royalty, his distaste for protocol and ceremonial, only added – and still do – to his appeal. In 1913, called home from Oxford for a State visit by the King and Queen of Denmark, he wrote in his diary: 'We stood about in the picture gallery till 11.15 talking to the guests. . . . What rot & a waste of time, money & energy all these State visits are!! This is my only remark on all this unreal show & ceremony!!'

Compare Prince Charles, more than fifty years later: 'I would change nothing. Besides ceremony being a major and important aspect of monarchy, something that has grown and developed over a thousand years in Britain, I happen to enjoy it enormously.' He is a very different character from his great-uncle – more cautious, more staid, without a trace of the rebel in him – largely because of his much happier family background. Yet he is highly conscious of Prince Edward's young reputation. In 1978, when the TV series about Edward and Mrs Simpson provoked arguments around Buckingham Palace, as around every home in Britain, it was the Prince of Wales who sprang to his predecessor's defence. The series concentrated on the events leading up to the abdication, spending little time on the successes of Edward's earlier years; Prince Charles thought this unfair, and slapped down those of his staff who were critical of television's recalcitrant Prince. At the same time, however, he would in no way condone Edward's ultimate decision to put his private, personal happiness before his public, inherited obligations. It is thus a confused, in many ways paradoxical, example he has to follow.

While emulating Edward's achievements as an industrious, concerned, vivacious Prince of Wales, as much in his private pursuits as his public duties, Prince Charles has gone to some pains to reject the other more colour-ful traits for which Edward is fondly remembered. In such matters as dress, smoking, drinking, late-night cavortings in clubs and casinos – those personal habits which are very much the man – he has studiously fashioned himself into a complete opposite. Style, although these days an overworked word, precisely pinpoints the quality of Prince Edward that Prince Charles so conspicuously lacks. He is aware of it, and not in the least abashed: 'If people think me square,' he has said, deliberately using a dated epithet, 'then I am happy to be thought square.' And again:

I was asked in Australia whether I concentrated on improving my image – as if I was some kind of washing powder, presumably with special blue whitener. I dare say that I could improve it by growing my hair to a more fashionable length, being seen at the Playboy Club at frequent intervals and squeezing myself into excruciatingly tight clothes ... but I intend to go on being myself to the best of my ability.

One hundred and twenty years ago, in 1858, the Prince Consort drew up a confidential memorandum on princely behaviour, designed to equip the hapless Bertie, Prince of Wales, for the position of 'the first gentleman of the country'. All requisite qualities, he argued, would stem from 'outward deportment and manners', which he discussed under three heads (summarized by Sir Philip Magnus in his biography of Edward VII):

1. Appearance, Deportment and Dress
...A gentleman does not indulge in careless self-indulgent lounging ways, such as lolling in armchairs or on sofas, slouching in his gait, or placing himself in unbecoming attitudes with his hands in his pockets.... He will borrow nothing from the fashions of the groom or the gamekeeper, and whilst avoiding the frivolity and foolish vanity of dandyism, will take care that his clothes are of the best quality....

2. Manners and Conduct towards Others
The manners and conduct of a gentleman towards others are founded on the basis of kindness, consideration and the absence of selfishness. [A Prince must always be scrupulously courteous, attentive, punctual and on guard against the temptation to use harsh, rude or bantering expressions.] Anything approaching a *practical joke* [would be impermissible].

3. The Power to Acquit Himself Creditably in Conversation, or whatever May Be the Occupation of Society
[Gossip, cards, billiards were to be regarded as useless; but] some knowledge of those studies and pursuits which adorn society and make it interesting [was essential. The Prince of Wales must be induced] by persevering example ... to devote some of his leisure time to music, to the fine arts, either drawing or looking over drawings, engravings, etc., to hearing poetry, amusing books or good plays read aloud; in short to anything that whilst it amuses may gently exercise the mind....

The memo did not produce the desired effect. So disappointed was Prince Albert with his son's progress that he wrote to his daughter, Bertie's sister: 'Bertie has remarkable social talent ... but usually his intellect is of no more use than a pistol packed in the bottom of a trunk if one were attacked in the robber-infested Appenines.' The Prince Consort would scarcely have derived more satisfaction from the subsequent career of his great-grandson, King Edward VIII. In his great-great-great-grandson, Prince Charles, Albert has at last found a convert – apart, perhaps, from the practical jokes.

One hundred and twenty years too late? Prince Charles does not think so:

> I dare say many of my views and beliefs would be considered old-fashioned and out of date, but that doesn't worry me. ... Fashion, by its very definition, is transitory; human nature being what it is, what was old-fashioned at length becomes in fashion, and thus the whole process continues.

Recent Princes of Wales have tended to be leaders of sartorial fashion. Edward VII, patron of the dinner jacket and the grey topper, champion of side-creased trousers and the Tyrolean hat, received a continuous flow of advice on the subject from his parents. Prince Albert despaired of his son: 'Unfortunately', he told the Princess Royal, 'he takes no interest in anything but clothes, and again clothes. Even when out shooting he is more occupied with his trousers than with the game.' Queen Victoria took a more fundamental view, and wrote to her son:

> Dress is a trifling matter, but it gives also the outward sign from which people in general can and often do judge upon the *inward* state of mind and feeling of a person. ... We do not wish to control your tastes and fancies, which, on the contrary, we wish you to indulge and develop, but we do *expect* that you will never wear anything *extravagant* or *slang*, not because we don't like it, but because it would prove a want of self-respect and be an offence against decency, leading – as it has often done in others – to an indifference to what is morally wrong.

The Queen must have spun in her grave forty-six years later, in the second year of Edward VII's reign, when the King arrived at Marienbad station wearing a green cap, a pink tie and white gloves, with knee-breeches, grey slippers and a brown overcoat with loud checks. 'Loyal subjects must sincerely hope', commented the *Tailor and Cutter*, guardian to this day of British sartorial standards, 'that His Majesty has not brought this outfit home.'

The Duke of Windsor, himself an international leader of fashion, quoted his great-grandmother's homily with approval. He had often wondered, he said, whether to 'certain sections of the Press, I was not more of a glorified clothes-peg than the heir apparent'. The sentiment, like many in his writ-

ings, is retrospective and self-justifying. At Oxford Prince Edward popu-
larized plus-fours and trouser turn-ups. ('Is it raining in *here?*' exclaimed
George V on seeing his son and heir wearing turn-ups around the Palace;
thereafter, the Duke recalled, 'I always kept a pair of old trousers without
turn-ups, which I could slip on before I went to see him.') Over dinner one
night at La Croe, near Antibes, he happened to wear a tartan suit of the
kind his father had been wearing in private for fifty years. 'One of our guests
mentioned the fact to a friend in the men's fashion trade, who immediately
cabled the news to America. Within a few months tartan had become a popular material for every sort of masculine garment, from dinner jackets and
cummerbunds to swimming trunks and beach shorts. Later the craze even
extended to luggage.' Later in life the Windsors' secretary, Diana Hood,
recalled him in the garden of their home in the South of France one day
wearing crimson trousers with a blue shirt and red-and-white shoes, and
the next bright blue trousers with a canary yellow shirt and blue shoes.

Partly because of recent history's cautionary tales, Prince Charles's sartorial tastes are almost defiantly conservative. In matters of *haute couture*
he is the despair of the *Tailor and Cutter*, one of the less likely symbols
of the continuity of the British Royal Family. A century ago Bertie, Prince
of Wales, earned the magazine's scorn for helping to popularize the bowler
hat – 'an abomination in head gear' 'a good friend to the tailors of Savile
Row, consolidating the position of London as the sartorial shrine for
men.... When he visited Marienbad, tailors from Paris, Vienna and all
parts of the Continent used to gather and to follow him around, surrep-
titiously photographing him and jotting down notes on his clothes.'

In our own times the *Tailor and Cutter* at first tried to encourage Prince
Charles to become a leader of fashion, by voting him one of the World's
Top Ten Best Dressed Men at the age of four; twenty years later, having
received little return on its investment (a Prince of Wales can be very good
for business), it denounced his 'cult of studied shabbiness'. Soon after, invited to be guest of honour at the annual dinner of the Master Tailors' Ben-
evolent Association, the Prince rose to the insult by arriving in an old tweed
jacket somewhat the worse for wear. After whisking it off to reveal impec-
cable evening dress, he treated them to one of his better after-dinner jokes:
'I am often asked whether it is because of some generic trait that I stand
with my hands behind my back, like my father. The answer is that we both
have the same tailor. He makes our sleeves so tight that we can't get our
hands in front.'

Prince Charles looks immensely dashing in any of his numerous uniforms
– hats, especially military-style peaked caps, seem to add strength to the
shape of his face – but his civilian suits are generally of a style favoured

by an older generation. His polished toecaps are those of a man steeped beyond his years in Service traditions (and lucky enough to have an industrious valet). His refusal even to reflect fashions, let alone to lead them, betokens a man with higher-minded priorities. Dress, as Queen Victoria said, may be a 'trifling matter', but it remains an index of character and personality. In Prince Charles's case, it is an outward sign, perhaps deliberate, of his adherence to the values of his parents' generation rather than his own. And it is a conscious rejection of the dilettantism of recent Princes of Wales.

If one cannot require the present Prince to be a sartorial trend-setter, no more can one wish alcohol or nicotine poisoning upon him. But he belongs to a generation which looks for chinks in its contemporaries' armour, in his case for some loophole in an otherwise flawless public regime of mental, physical and spiritual fitness. The Duke of Windsor, himself a lover of manly pursuits, made a pleasant confession about his eighteenth birthday; the fact that he was now eligible to ascend the throne in his own right, without need of a Regency, meant rather less to him than 'a tangible and satisfying privilege this birthday brought me. Now that I was eighteen my father lifted the ban on my smoking. . . .'

A year later he was reassuring his father, in a letter from Oxford, that 'I never smoke more than ten cigarettes a day, generally not as many, and then only in the evenings after dinner, with never more than two before tea.' If the Prince appears to be protesting too much, he subsequently confessed so himself. In another undergraduate letter to his father, he had described the antics of a university dining society, the Bullingdon Club: 'Most of them got rather excited and I came back early. There was a good deal of champagne drunk and that accounted for it. It is interesting for me to see the various forms of amusements that undergraduates indulge in.' Nearly fifty years later, in his memoirs, he owned up: 'I now recall with some shame that the real reason for my early departure . . . was that I was no longer so steady on my feet or so clear in my speech as I was when we sat down to dinner. I hasten to add that this was an unusual occurrence, prompted only by the unwritten law of the Bullingdon Club that the new members should be forced to drink themselves into oblivion.'

When offered a cigar by President Tito during his visit to Yugoslavia in 1978, Prince Charles joked that he gave up smoking at school. He is a militant non-smoker, and will drink only at the end of a trying day or when politeness requires it of him. The boldest escapade on record from his university days is a midnight bicycle chase around a courtyard with some rumbustious friends, which earned a complaint about the noise from his director of studies. All his life he has aspired to sober standards of conduct, believing that his office requires him to set a moral example. As he has grown older, and more self-conscious about his role, he has not hesitated to inflict these standards on others. In November 1975, at an anniversary dinner of the Lord's Taverners, the Prince found himself being asked to propose the Loyal Toast half-way through the meal, so that the 1,350 hard-pressed sports and show-business guests could begin smoking.

'Do we have to do this now?' he asked the toastmaster, Bryn Williams, as he placed the microphone in front of him. 'Why do we have the Loyal Toast so early? Is this a modern trend?'

'I'm afraid so, sir.'

'Well, I don't agree with it. We will have the Loyal Toast at the right time – after the sweet.'

The Prince has proved himself a great defender of royal dignity. In July 1973, while captaining Nassau polo team against Freeport, his game was not improved by the remarks of the commentator over Nassau Racecourse's loudspeaker system. 'Now who's he?' laboured Tom Oxley, something of a local wag, when the Prince got the ball. 'He's the son of ... let's see ... oh yes, it's Queen Elizabeth, isn't it? And now who's the other one? Why, isn't it old Philip, Duke of Edinburgh?' Oxley had just told the crowd that his father and brother had recently played in an American polo team which had beaten an English side including Prince Philip. Charles rode over to the commentary box and strode up its steps. His angry reprimand was broadcast over the loudspeakers to the appalled crowd. 'Less of the wisecracks and stick to the commentary. You're turning the match into a barn dance.' The club president, who promptly removed Oxley from the microphone, then recalled that the same man had been commentating at an earlier polo prizegiving, when he had referred to the Prince as 'Queen Elizabeth's little boy'. Charles, it seemed, had remembered the voice.

His sense of humour does not extend to *lèse-majesté*. In private he can be delightfully witty, with his quick repartee and his gift for mimicry, but he will not gladly suffer any undue familiarity he may inspire. Very rarely can he relax out of his role. He has imposed on himself the sternest obligations of his office.

His public reputation, for a curious combination of bravado and drollery, misses this high seriousness. Yet it is one of the Prince's strongest characteristics. If he brings humour to his job, he also brings an inheritance of dour regal solemnity. The Prince of Wales wishes to improve on the records of his immediate predecessors, to avoid their vagaries, their half-truths, their surrenders to the temptations so vividly conjured up by Walter Bagehot:

All the world and the glory of it, whatever is most attractive, whatever is most seductive, has always been offered to the Prince of Wales of the day, and always will be. It is not rational to expect the best virtue where temptation is applied in the most trying form at the frailest time of human life.

Not rational perhaps, but nor is the institution of monarchy. By taking a different path from his predecessors, this Prince of Wales aims to give purpose to his irrational birthright, and by so doing to reassure himself and his future subjects that the monarchy still works, that a hereditary system can maintain a stable and responsible influence over the affairs of a modern nation. The accident of his birth has indeed laid all the world and its glory at his feet; he is heir to a thousand years of inherited privilege. In return it demands duties which are arduous, monotonous, unavoidable, and often hard to endow with any practical significance.

To take them as seriously as he does is simply to have accepted his fate. The future Edward VII was a Prince of Wales whose enforced idleness left him freer to indulge the perks of his position. The future Edward VIII was a Prince who found the price too high; after a gallant attempt, he set a greater value on his personal happiness. Both were by nature more wayward characters, but both were reacting violently to more austere childhoods. Each was taught from birth to accept his role with the utmost gravity, and to conduct himself accordingly.

Prince Charles, by contrast, was eased into the strangeness of royalty. His parents wanted him to enjoy his childhood *despite* his position. It did not always prove possible. But his early life was more carefree, more *laissez-faire* than that of most future kings. He thus grew into his role with equanimity. His solemn awareness of its responsibilities developed late, and so more deeply. All the clues to this curiously convoluted character, with his public braggadocio and his private high seriousness, his sense of self-parody and his insistence on due deference, lie in the tortured decisions made on his behalf throughout his upbringing.

Royal Action Man: skiing at Klosters ...

polo at Windsor ...

Previous page: On parade: the Colonel-in-Chief of the Welsh Guards

wind-surfing off Cowes...

fly-fishing at Balmoral ...

... and commando training with the Royal Marines

Off duty: between chukkas at Windsor

Right: On duty: representing the Queen at the independence celebrations of Papua New Guinea

Stern words from his polo coach, Sinclair Hill, one of the few men allowed to swear at the Prince of Wales

After a fall: royal dignity abandoned

Above: 'I'm happiest with my family': with Princess Anne on her twentieth birthday ...

Right: ... and his close friend Lord Mountbatten, alias great-uncle Dickie

Below: The Royal Family at the Montreal Olympics 1976 – the only time they have ever been gathered together abroad

Left: 1977: at Elizabeth II's Silver Jubilee Thanksgiving Service in St Paul's Cathedral

Below left: 1978: a thirtieth birthday portrait at Balmoral

Below: Working Prince: a day at Number Ten

Overleaf: The hazards of being a Prince: pounced upon in the Indian Ocean in 1979

PART II

Childhood

5

Prince Charles of Edinburgh
1948-52

From his childhood this boy will be surrounded by syco-
phants and flatterers by the score, and will be taught to
believe himself as of a superior creation.

Keir Hardie on the birth of
the future King Edward VIII

THE RUMOURS BEGAN, not for the first or the last time, in Paris. When
Princess Elizabeth, elder daughter of King George VI and heir to the British
throne, paid a visit there in May 1948, those who saw her told each other
she did not seem herself. At Divine Service in the British Church she looked
tired and listless, rarely raising her eyes from the ground. At a British
Embassy reception in her honour that evening, she had met only half the
guests when her husband led her from the room to rest. It was less than
six months since she had married Lieutenant Philip Mountbatten, the
former Prince Philip of Greece, but that was time enough. Paris decided
that twenty-two-year-old Princess Elizabeth was pregnant.

Even in 1948, pregnancy was a word which Buckingham Palace official-
dom could not quite bring itself to utter in public. On 4 June, the eve of
Derby Day, the formal statement simply announced that 'Her Royal Highness the Princess Elizabeth, Duchess of Edinburgh, will undertake no public
engagements after the end of June'. The public, left to draw its own conclusions, remembered that the same wording had last been used eighteen
years earlier of the Duchess of York, four months before she gave birth to
Princess Margaret Rose. No announcement at all had been made during
the Duchess's previous pregnancy; the first the world had known of Princess
Elizabeth Alexandra Mary, whom they then little thought would one day
be Queen of England, was when she entered it by Caesarean section on
21 April 1926.

Official confirmation that an heir to the throne was on the way came later that summer in unexpected form. The King, it was announced, had decided to abolish the ancient custom whereby the Home Secretary of the day attended and verified each royal birth. 'The attendance of a Minister of the Crown at a birth in the Royal Family', said the official statement, 'is not a statutory requirement or a constitutional necessity. It is merely the survival of an archaic custom, and the King feels that it is unnecessary to continue further a practice for which there is no legal requirement.' In 1948 Mr James Chuter-Ede was thus spared the embarrassment of one of his predecessors, Sir James Graham, who in 1841 had waited uneasily at one end of a huge Palace bedchamber while at the other Queen Victoria gave birth to the future King Edward VII. After satisfying himself that all was in order, he approached the bed and intoned: 'I congratulate Your Majesty most warmly. A very fine boy, if I may say so.' From behind the heavy curtains of the four-poster an indignant voice replied: 'A very fine *Prince*, Sir James.'

The origin of this curiously British tradition is disputed, but it seems to have been firmly established since 1688, when James II's wife, Mary of Modena, was accused of offering a changeling as heir to the throne (known to popular history as 'the warming-pan baby') despite the presence of the Lord Chancellor and all available Privy Councillors at the foot of her bed. In more recent times it had led rather to embarrassment and farce. In 1926 William Joynson-Hicks had waited uneasily downstairs at 17 Bruton Street, Mayfair, during the operation that delivered Princess Elizabeth; four years later J. R. Clynes, summoned early to Glamis because of a false alarm, spent two weeks kicking his heels at Airlie Castle and was finally in mid-dash between the two when Princess Margaret was born.

The baby was expected in mid-November. The Princess and her husband were still living at Buckingham Palace while Clarence House was made ready for them, but much of their time was spent at Windlesham Moor, their then country home near Sunningdale, in Berkshire. There were those who suggested this might be the most peaceful place for her *accouchement*, but the Princess herself decided she would like to have her baby at the Palace. On the first floor, overlooking the Mall, a suite centres around the Buhl Room, which Queen Mary had converted into a makeshift Palace surgery. Within a few months, this was to be the scene of the first of King George VI's arterial operations, which saved him the loss of his right leg. During the latter stages of his daughter's pregnancy, the King was for the first time becoming aware of the seriousness of his illness; arteriosclerosis, with a grave danger of gangrene, was diagnosed in the Buhl Room only two days before Prince Charles's birth. But the King gave strict instructions that the Princess was to be told nothing. For the present, therefore, it was for a happy event that the room was converted into a lavishly equipped surgical theatre.

Despite the distractions of his illness, King George soon found himself confronted by another constitutional problem. Under the edict issued by his father George V in 1917, in response to wartime criticisms of the Royal Family's Germanic titles and connections, the title of Prince of the newly established House of Windsor was restricted to the offspring of the sovereign and his sons. As the Royals divested themselves of their German titles, and the House of Saxe-Coburg-Gotha surrendered its name to that of the pleasant Berkshire town where it spent its week-ends, no thought was given to the offspring of the sovereign's *daughters*. Thus it was, less than a week before Elizabeth's baby was due, that the King's private secretary, Sir Alan Lascelles, warned him that his first grandchild would not be entitled to the rank of Prince or Princess.

On becoming engaged to the King's daughter in July 1947, Prince Philip had divested himself of all his Greek and Danish titles, including the rank of Prince, and adopted his mother's name of Battenberg, which had been anglicized to Mountbatten. In exchange, this member of the Danish Royal House of Schleswig-Holstein-Sonderburg-Glücksburg had received from his future father-in-law the style of Royal Highness, the Order of the Garter and elevation to the peerage as Baron Greenwich, Earl of Merioneth and Duke of Edinburgh. 'It is a great deal to give a man all at once,' the King had written to his mother, Queen Mary, 'but I know Philip understands his new responsibilities on his marriage to Lilibet.'

According to strict rule, Philip was not reaccorded the title of Prince, although George VI always referred to him as Prince Philip, and went to his grave believing the rank was automatically conferred with the style of Royal Highness. (In fact, Philip was not formally granted the style and titular dignity of Prince of the United Kingdom until 22 February 1957, when his wife bestowed it on him in recognition of his ten years of service to the country.) Thus his and Princess Elizabeth's child, which showed signs of arriving any day, would have to struggle with the help of the Garter King of Arms for a name befitting the King's first grandchild. If it were a boy, the baby would be known simply as Charles Mountbatten, salvaging his infant dignity with the courtesy use of his father's second title: Charles Mountbatten, Earl of Merioneth. If the baby were a girl, she would be known as Lady Anne Mountbatten. And these were the very names with which the genealogists juggled, for Princess Elizabeth and her husband had already decided upon them, although they were to remain a closely guarded secret for another month.

On 9 November, less than a week before the child's birth, the King issued

Letters Patent under the Great Seal ordaining that any children born to the Duke and Duchess of Edinburgh would have the title of Prince or Princess and the style of Royal Highness. In the process, he put paid to another fevered argument among historians and constitutionalists: that on his death, Princess Margaret would have as strong a claim to the throne as her elder sister. The view was based on the legislature's discriminatory failure to establish any rule of primogeniture among females; strictly interpreted, the law as it stood found all daughters of equal rank in the division of inheritance. By placing Princess Elizabeth on the same footing as the sovereign's eldest son, the King had secured her position as his heir and staunched the doubts of worried genealogists the nation over.

Against this heady background, Princess Elizabeth was enjoying a pregnancy so trouble-free she was able to continue an active and varied social life. In October she attended the wedding of her lady-in-waiting, Lady Margaret Egerton, to her private secretary, John Colville, and felt sufficiently well to go on to the crowded reception at Londonderry House afterwards. Despite her doctor's predictions, she rather hoped the baby might not arrive until her first wedding anniversary on 20 November. On 12 November, less than forty-eight hours before that hope was to be proved vain, she was still going out in the evenings, on this occasion to dinner with close friends, the Brabournes, in Chester Street. The royal midwife, Miss Helen Rowe, was already installed in the new Buckingham Palace nursery; but it was only when Sir William Gilliatt, president of the Royal College of Obstetricians and Gynaecologists, spent the following night at the Palace that the British public knew the waiting was nearly over. Still rationed, still hard-pressed, still surrounded by the physical and spiritual aftermath of war, they had followed their Princess's pregnancy with an anticipation unusual even for royal births. The doctor's presence was enough to draw a crowd of 1,500 to the Palace gates that night.

November 14 was a Sunday, and by early morning the throng outside Buckingham Palace had grown to several thousands. The lack of news all day did little to dampen their ardour, despite the dull, chill weather. In the late afternoon expectations were revived by the sudden arrival of a posse of cars containing medical men; assisting Gilliatt and Sir John Weir, the King's physician, were Mr (now Sir) John Peel, the obstetrician, and Dr Vernon Hall, the anaesthetist. But there was still no word. Inside the Palace, the expectant father grew characteristically impatient. He took off his private secretary and close friend, Lieutenant-Commander Michael Parker, for a game of squash in the Palace court. After a swim in the adjacent pool, they were still playing at a quarter past nine when the King's private secretary, Sir Alan Lascelles, ran in with the news that a prince had been born.

Philip took the stairs three at a time. He rushed into the Buhl Room to find his wife still under anaesthetic; it had been a forceps delivery. After speaking with the doctors, he was taken to the nursery to behold his infant son, and to share a handshake and an embrace with his parents-in-law. When the Princess awoke, her husband was at her side with a bouquet of carnations and roses. In an outer room, he had already been opening bottles of champagne for the medical and household staff. By this time the Palace post office was hard at work: pre-prepared telegrams, the word 'Prince' written into their blank spaces, were being despatched around the world to kings and presidents, governors and ambassadors – the first, by another 'archaic custom', carried by the rather less archaic means of motor-cycle despatch rider to the Lord Mayor of London.

Mr Chuter Ede, though not at the bedside, was waiting by the telephone, for he it was who had to sign the notices to be posted outside the Home Office in Whitehall and the Mansion House in the City. The wording was the same as in that secured to the Palace railings by the Colville cousins: Sir John ('Jock'), private secretary to Princess Elizabeth (and previously to Neville Chamberlain, Winston Churchill and Clement Attlee at 10 Downing Street), and Commander Richard, press secretary to the King (and later to Elizabeth II). Richard Colville had proudly written the announcement in his own hand: 'Her Royal Highness the Princess Elizabeth, Duchess of Edinburgh, was safely delivered of a Prince at 9.14 o'clock this evening. Her Royal Highness and the infant Prince are both doing well.'

By that time, however, the news had already drawn Londoners from their homes, their restaurants, and their night clubs to swell the crowd outside Buckingham Palace. John Snagge, the BBC Home Service announcer, had in his excitement offered the nation's 'royal' rather than 'loyal' greetings; the version now in the BBC archives was re-recorded for posterity two days later. It had been nicely timed, however, to launch closing-time celebrations in pubs all round the country, to start guns firing and bonfires blazing, to turn the fountains in Trafalgar Square blue for a boy (as they stayed for a week), and to draw 4,000 telegrams of congratulation to the Palace post office that night.

The first the growing crowd outside the Palace knew of it was very soon after the event itself, when those who had climbed to the top of the Victoria Memorial saw a blue-liveried Palace footman emerge to whisper into the ear of a policeman – one of the many trying to protect the Palace guard, then still on the pavement outside the railings, from being trampled underfoot. 'It's a boy!' bawled this privileged officer, and the cry was taken up around the Mall, growing to a roar which lasted several hours, punctuated by occasional chants for 'For he's a jolly good fellow', 'We want Philip' and, from the prescient Welsh contingent, 'Land of our Fathers'.

Every car going in and out was fiercely scrutinized, none more so than that of the King's mother, eighty-one-year-old Queen Mary, who arrived at 11 p.m. to inspect her first great-grandchild. Despite the after-effects of a bout of influenza, the old lady stayed until after midnight, by which time the crowd outside had grown larger and noisier than ever. Up on the first floor of the Palace, on the Mall frontage, was a young woman exhilarated by the birth of her first child and the enthusiasm of her family, but in need of sleep. The well-wishers outside were keeping her awake. At the Princess's behest, therefore, Michael Parker and a colleague walked across the fore-court to try and quieten them. As they struggled to make themselves heard over the hubbub, the first recipient of the Princess's message was none other than David Niven, already at that time a well-known and eminently recognizable figure. 'I was pinned against the railings and, being unable to move, I was the recipient of the message hissed in my ear by the man from the Palace. I had my coat collar turned up and was huddled inside the garment, hoping not to be recognized and asked for autographs on that par-ticular location. However, I turned round and did my best to shush those nearest to me, which did little good as everyone was far too excited and happy.' Police loudspeaker vans had to be called in to disperse the crowd. Thus did the Princess fall asleep to the strangest of lullabies.

The 7 lb. 6 oz. infant so warmly welcomed was the first royal child to be born at Buckingham Palace for sixty-two years (the last being the daughter of Arthur, Duke of Connaught, and so niece of Edward VII), and the first royal baby in direct succession to the throne since the birth of the future King Edward VIII in 1894. Princess Elizabeth was only the fourth heiress presumptive in British history to have given birth to a male child. In 1133 Matilda, daughter of King Henry I, bore the future King Henry II; in 1566 Mary Queen of Scots (the undeclared heiress presumptive) bore Prince James; and Queen Anne had a number of children, none of whom survived childhood.

The Prince, as yet unnamed, could be declared fifth in descent from Queen Victoria, thirty-second from William the Conqueror and thirty-ninth from Alfred the Great. He was described as the most Scottish prince since Charles I and the most English since Henry VIII; eleventh in descent from the Electress Sophia, through whom the present Royal Family's claim to the throne is established under the Act of Settlement, he could claim descent from the Yorkist kings through William I and the Lancastrian kings through John of Gaunt. Thirteenth in descent from James I and VI, his Scottish ancestry included Robert the Bruce and St Mary of Scotland through

James's mother, Mary Queen of Scots; through Henry Tudor, his Welsh ancestry could be traced back to Llewelyn-ap-Gruffydd, the last native Prince of all Wales. Through his maternal grandmother, he was the first potential Prince of Wales ever to be a direct descendant of Owen Glendower; through his father, he had the blood of Harold, last of the Anglo-Saxon kings. Genealogists stretched the line almost to the crack of doom: on one side Charlemagne, Cadwallader and Musa ibn Naseir, an Arab sheikh born in Mecca in 660, on the other plainer names such as John Smith, Frances Webb, Mary Browne and Peter Checke, a sixteenth-century Essex innkeeper (see Appendix C, pp. 284–88).

Next morning, the world acknowledged the news. The British fleet, wherever it happened to be, was dressed overall; in Australia, the Melbourne town hall carillon somewhat prematurely played 'God Bless the Prince of Wales'; forty-one gun salutes and peals of bells awoke New Zealand and South Africa; in Kenya, the news was broadcast in seven native languages; from Key West, Florida, President Truman sent a telegram of congratulations, and from South Africa, Premier Jan Smuts cabled: 'We pray that the Prince will be a blessing to our Commonwealth and to the world.' In republican New York the *Herald Tribune* declared that freedom in Britain had 'grown and been safeguarded under the ancient institution of the monarchy'. In Athens, where it was not forgotten that Philip had been a Prince of Greece, hundreds of his compatriots carried their greetings to the British Embassy; on the island of Tinos, where she was engaged on charitable work, Philip's mother, Princess Andrew of Greece, was roused from her sleep by the arrival of her telegram.

In London there was special pageantry as the King's Troop, Royal Horse Artillery, rode in full dress from St John's Wood to Hyde Park, drawing six guns to fire a forty-one-salvo salute. The bells of St Paul's pealed almost without interruption from 9 a.m.; those of Westminster Abbey took three hours to complete a peal of 5,000 changes, then did it all again. On the Thames, barges and small craft were gaily festooned with flags and bunting; at the top of the Mall, cars and taxis passing the Palace kept up a constant hooting of horns; at Plymouth, the US warships *Columbus* and *Hamel* joined with the battleship *Vanguard* in a twenty-one-gun salute; guns were fired in Edinburgh and Rosyth, Cardiff and Windsor; beacons were lit along the Welsh mountains. In towns the length and breadth of the kingdom, the day was marked by the constant firing of guns and pealing of bells. By evening, another crowd had gathered outside the Palace gates, this time to sing a succession of somewhat raucous lullabies.

Inside the Palace, the cause of it all slept in the same cradle used by his mother and aunt in their infancy. His cot, trimmed in advance in ambiguous yellow, was a splendid cast-iron four-poster used by the King's family for more than a hundred years. The Palace nursery was of course affected, if less than many others, by post-war austerity; silk and lace had been dug out of old trunks at Windsor to be re-used, and Prince Philip even came up with some of his own baby clothes for repair. Unlike most other homes, however, the Palace had received an avalanche of gifts from around the world, notably a ton and a half of nappies from the United States, which were distributed from a special operations room to other expectant mothers around the country. The Linen and Woollen Drapers Institution, of which the Princess was patron, had presented a layette of fifty-five garments, produced by the cottage industry of twenty-five retired dressmakers; within a few weeks, the Prince was earning his first dollars for Britain as replicas of his baby clothes sold in US stores. It was within his first few hours of life, however, that he received his first family gift: an ivory-handled rattle from his grandmother, the Queen, which she had once given her own first child, and since kept in hope of this day.

Next day, the BBC marked the occasion by commissioning 'Music for a Prince' from three prominent British composers, Gordon Jacob, Herbert Howells and Michael Tippett, to be performed at a special Albert Hall concert two months later. No less speedy in his inspiration was the Poet Laureate, John Masefield, whose quatrain 'A Hope for the Newly Born' had the Laureateship's authentic limp:

> May destiny, allotting what befalls,
>   Grant to the newly-born this saving grace,
> A guard more sure than ships and fortress-walls,
>   The loyal love and service of a race.

A week after Charles's birth Palace staff were allowed in to coo over him in groups of five, as shortly afterwards were select members of the Privy Council. His mother had already begun breast-feeding him, as she did for several weeks. The Princess did not leave her bed for the first ten days, but her son was soon being walked in a second-generation pram, which Elizabeth had sought out in Royal Lodge, her parents' Windsor retreat. It was so enormous that Charles claims he can remember to this day lying in its vastness, overshadowed by its high sides.

Information as to his looks was at a premium. His mother's first day out of doors, 29 November, was to have been the occasion for a newsreel film of her wheeling him around the Palace gardens, to be shown at the Royal Command Performance. But fog ruled this out. So the first word came from the Queen's sister, Countess Granville, who told a convention of Girl Guides in Northern Ireland that 'he could not be more angelic looking. He is golden

haired and has the most beautiful complexion, as well as amazingly delicate
features for so young a baby.... The Queen says that she thinks the baby
is like his mother, but the Duke is quite certain that the baby is very like
himself.' Princess Elizabeth, whom the Countess described as 'wonderfully
well and radiantly happy', soon wrote to a friend:

> Don't you think he is quite adorable? I still can't believe he is really mine,
> but perhaps that happens to new parents. Anyway, this particular boy's
> parents couldn't be more proud of him. It's wonderful to think, isn't it, that
> his arrival could give a bit of happiness to so many people, besides ourselves,
> at this time?

To her former music teacher, Miss Mabel Lander (known to the Princess
as 'Goosey' Lander), she wrote:

> The baby is very sweet and we are enormously proud of him. He has an inter-
> esting pair of hands for a baby. They are rather large, but fine with long
> fingers – quite unlike mine and certainly unlike his father's. It will be interest-
> ing to see what they will become. I still find it hard to believe I have a baby
> of my own!

Visiting the Palace to take the first official photographs, Cecil Beaton was
also struck by the child's 'remarkable long and pointed fingers'. His eyes,
Beaton told the world, were like his mother's, and he had a tuft of fair hair:
'He looks like Queen Mary.' Queen Mary herself, looking through an old
family album, decided the baby looked remarkably like his great-great-great-
grandfather Albert, the Prince Consort. Princess Elizabeth herself began
to tell friends he had his father's smile; his father told *his* friends the baby
resembled nothing so much as a plum pudding.

Such tiny morsels were eagerly snapped up because no pictures of the
child were released, nor was any announcement made of his name, until
the day of his christening, 15 December. The unusual delay prompted some
criticism – in fact it was the first of his parents' many moves to protect him
from undue publicity – which quickly turned to surprise when the names
were finally made known. All the pundits had been proved wrong, especially
those who believed that Elizabeth and Philip would not be the first royal
generation in a hundred years to defy Queen Victoria's wish that all her
descendants should bear her or her husband's name. (They remedied the
matter in 1960 by christening their second son Andrew Albert Christian
Edward.)

The choice of Charles Philip Arthur George, with the emphasis on
Charles, was said by the Palace to have been made by the baby's parents
for 'personal and private reasons'. The surprise about Charles was that the
two English Kings who had borne the name had had such miserable reigns

that it had been abandoned by the Royal Family for nigh on 300 years; its only other royal holder, Bonnie Prince Charlie, was notorious for his insurrection against the House of Hanover. It was widely interpreted, especially when the Prince's younger sister was christened Anne almost two years later, as a deliberate revival of the names of the royal Stuarts; the only immediate explanation was that it was in tribute to the baby's godfather, King Haakon of Norway, who had been Prince Charles of Denmark until he acceded to the Norwegian throne in 1905. In truth even this had scarcely occurred to Elizabeth and Philip; they had called their son Charles simply because it was the male forename they like best. Another of the Prince's godparents, Princess Margaret, greeted the news with a surprised 'I suppose I'll now be known as Charley's Aunt.'

He was named Philip, of course, after his father, and George after his grandfather, who also bore the name Arthur. But Arthur is one of the most traditional royal names. Apart from its romantic associations with the Arthurian legend, it has been borne by many heirs to the throne: for instance the eldest son of Henry VII, Arthur, Prince of Wales, whose premature death led to the succession of Henry VIII and deprived England of its first post-Conquest King Arthur. It was also chosen for a closer family association: Princess Elizabeth's godfather had been Arthur, Duke of Connaught, third son of Queen Victoria, who had in turn been named after his own godfather, the then elderly Arthur Wellesley, first Duke of Wellington.

The names were duly registered by Prince Philip with Mr Stanley Clare, senior registrar of Caxton Hall in the City of Westminster, who called at the Palace on the morning of the christening. The ceremony that afternoon would have been held at Windsor, where all such family occasions usually take place, had it not been for the King's health. As it was, the Palace chapel had been destroyed by Nazi bombers in September 1940, so the baptism was performed in the white and gold Music Room, whose great crimson-curtained bow window looked out onto a wintry Palace garden.

The Archbishop of Canterbury, Dr Geoffrey Fisher, officiated, assisted by the Precentor of the Chapels Royal, the Rev. Maurice Foxell. The golden Lily Font designed by Prince Albert for the christening of his and Victoria's children had been brought up from Windsor for the occasion. By Dr Fisher's account the infant Prince, dressed in a robe of Honiton lace and white silk again used by all Victoria's children, remained 'as quiet as a mouse' as he was bathed in water specially brought from the River Jordan, a royal tradition dating back to the Crusades. The baby was held by his youngest godparent, Princess Margaret. His other sponsors were the King and Queen; the Queen's brother, David Bowes-Lyon; the King of Norway; the Duke of Edinburgh's grandmother, the Dowager Marchioness of Milford Haven;

his uncle, Prince George of Greece; and his cousin, Earl Mountbatten's elder daughter, Lady Brabourne. Of the eight, only King Haakon and Prince George, both in their late seventies, were unable to be present. By Charles's thirtieth birthday in 1978, indeed, only three of his godparents – the Queen Mother, Princess Margaret and Lady Brabourne – were still alive.

The half-hour ceremony, which began with a piano rendition of Handel's Water Music by the organist of the Chapel Royal, was attended by the closest circle of the Royal Family. So the room contained four grand-daughters of Queen Victoria – the Dowager Marchioness of Milford Haven, Princess Marie Louise, Princess Alice, Countess of Athlone, and Lady Patricia Ramsay – all of whom had themselves worn the same christening robes. But the Princess had not forgotten others close to her. As the two magnificent crystal chandeliers glinted in the firelight, lighting up the golden splendour of Prince Albert's font, watching between the Music Room's massive purple pillars were the Princess's own nurserymaid, Margaret MacDonald ('Bobo', since 1952 the Queen's dresser), and the domestic staff from Windlesham Moor, including the cook, Mrs Barnes. She had baked one of the three christening cakes which afterwards graced the party in the White Drawing Room, where the guests presented their lavish array of christening presents. Queen Mary's seems to have stolen the show; that night she noted in her diary: 'I gave the baby a silver gilt cup and cover which George III had given to a godson in 1780, so that I gave a present from my great-grandfather to my great-grandson 168 years later.'

Thus Prince Charles of Edinburgh formally entered the Protestant Church of England, a solemn prerequisite for one day ascending the British throne. At the same time, being a newborn post-war baby, he received his ration card and milk allowance. Sister Rowe's work complete, she yielded her place in the nursery to two Scottish-born nurses, Helen Lightbody and Mabel Anderson. Miss Lightbody had been 'passed on' to the Princess by her aunt, the Duchess of Gloucester, whose two sons she had brought up; as the senior of the two Palace nurses, she was given the courtesy title of 'Mrs'. Miss Anderson, the young daughter of a policeman killed in the Liverpool blitz, had placed an advertisement in the 'Situations Wanted' column of a nursing magazine, and been pleasantly surprised to find herself summoned to Buckingham Palace for an interview with the Princess. In time, she was to find herself in charge of Anne, Andrew and Edward as well; now she is nanny to Princess Anne's son, Peter Phillips.

Five days after the christening, Dr Jacob Snowman of Hampstead, London, then in his eighties, visited the Palace to circumcise the baby. It was the week before Christmas, and a festive tree adorned the dressing-table of Charles's first nursery, a converted guest-room to which he had now been moved from his mother's dressing-room. Though no one could predict it then, the baby's first Christmas and New Year was the last for several years that he would spend with both his parents at his side. The family was, for the first time in many years, to spend Christmas in London, as the King's doctors had advised against the seasonal journey to Windsor. Only two days after the birth, in fact, they had insisted that the King announce the cancellation of a Commonwealth tour through Australia, New Zealand and Canada. It had been the first his daughter knew of the extent of his illness, and it cast the only shadow over the annual celebrations.

Early in January, however, the King was sufficiently recovered to lead a family expedition to Norfolk, and by 18 January was out shooting on his beloved Sandringham estate. Miss Lightbody was back in familiar territory, having spent many hours in the country nursery with Prince William and Prince Richard. Suddenly she found herself more than ever in sole charge of Charles, as his mother contracted measles and was not allowed near her month-old baby for three weeks.

By March the family was back in London, and the Princess able to resume public engagements. For the King, however, the prognosis was much more dispiriting. Since the November diagnosis, he had led the life of a virtual invalid; his doctors now advised that he must always continue to do so, or face an immediate operation to ease blood constriction in his right leg. For a man of his temperament, there was no choice. The operation, performed in the Buhl Room on 12 March, was so successful that he was able to hold a Privy Council meeting by 29 March, to be undertaking public duties again by May and to attend the Trooping of the Colour in June. But he and his wife had already realized that he could not have long to live.

By July, when her father seemed in much better spirits after a week's rest at Balmoral, Princess Elizabeth was at last able to move with her husband and child into their first family home. The renovation of Clarence House had dragged on much longer than expected, and it was a great relief to leave the lonely vastness of the Palace for a more compact, centrally heated home with all mod cons. Clarence House, just across the Mall from the Palace, had been the home of the Duke of Clarence before his accession as William IV in 1830. Later it had been the London home of the Princess's godfather, the Duke of Connaught, until his death in 1942 (although in old age he rarely used it). During the Second World War, George VI had given it to the British Red Cross as office space. Now it housed a chintz-curtained nursery, with white walls and blue-for-a-boy mouldings, which looked out across its own walled and private garden beyond the Mall to St James's Park. The family moved in on 4 July – as Prince Philip aptly pointed out, 'Independence Day'.

From Clarence House the two nurses could wheel the baby round the park with little fear of recognition. The only identifying features, which sometimes drew the curious to peer into the pram, were the private detectives following discreetly behind and the Edinburghs' noisy little terrier, Shandy. The infant Prince Charles's daily routine has been described in meticulous detail, but it comes down to an unsurprising round of playpens, teddy bears, torn-up books and regally soiled nappies. One of its few distinguishing features was that the enormous pram would sometimes be wheeled to nearby Marlborough House, where visits to Queen Mary (whom her great-grandson called 'Gan Gan', as Edward VIII had Queen Victoria) provide another of Charles's earliest memories. He has a vivid picture of the dignified old lady sitting bolt upright, her legs culminating on a footstool, surrounded by the array of precious objects which formed her famous collection. History relates that the previous generation of royal infants, the Princesses Elizabeth and Margaret, were never allowed to go near the jade, the silver, the crystal in their magnificent display cabinets, whereas young Charles was permitted to play around with whatever priceless object took his fancy. Since the Princesses' infancy, however, Queen Mary had lived through the deaths of her husband and two of her sons, and had seen another abandon the throne for an American divorcee. Now another son, she knew, was dying. In the child by her footstool lay the future of the dynasty of which she was matriarch.

Charles's first year of life had been one of royal indulgences: his mother had been spared all but a few royal duties, and his father had been based at the Admiralty in London rather than on active Naval Service. By his first birthday that November, however, the normal working life of what George VI called 'the firm' had been resumed. Princess Elizabeth gave a small tea-party at Clarence House, and Prince Philip flew in a present from Malta, where he was serving as a lieutenant aboard HMS *Chequers*. Before joining her husband out there for their second wedding anniversary the following week, the Princess authorized the release to the press of the latest Charles statistics: age one year, weight 24 lb, hair gold and shiny, teeth six and pearly. Already he was taking his first steps, with the aid of Jumbo, a much-loved fluffy blue elephant on wheels.

His father was also away for Christmas, which was spent with the King and Queen at Sandringham. Cinema audiences at the festive season enjoyed the first newsreel film of the happy young Royals, playing with their baby in the garden of Windlesham Moor. The public had been taken further into the family's domestic life with the publication of a book illustrating the renovations at Clarence House. That Christmas, however, there was another secret of which they were to know nothing until a Palace announcement the following May. During her anniversary visit to Malta, spent with her husband in the seclusion of the Mountbattens' Villa Guardamangia, Princess Elizabeth had conceived her second child.

Princess Anne was born at Clarence House on 15 August 1950 – just before midday, in midsummer, in the mid-year of the century. Prince Charles was one year and nine months old. His father, who had returned from Malta for the event at the end of July, told him over lunch that Monday that he had a baby sister, and most unusually allowed him to get down from the table to go and take a look at her. Photographs of the period quickly show the tiny signs of bewilderment on the face of a young child no longer the epicentre of his parents' attention. Charles could scarcely yet have been aware that straits and islands around the world had been named after him, though he took more than a usual childly interest in the sheets of stamps which bore his face. He was too young to know that the visitor for whom he had been taught to say 'Bonjour' the previous March was the President of France. But his young world was already, as it was to remain throughout his childhood, one much more of adults than of children his own age; and it may not have been simply the fondness of his parents that already credited him with a certain maturity, as he took 'a most watchful, protective interest' in his sister from the first.

With two children installed, and their parents' lives again busy and public, the royal nursery settled into a more rigid daily regime than before. Charles and Anne were got up each day at seven sharp, dressed, fed and played with in the nursery until nine, when they enjoyed a statutory half-hour with their mother. Fresh air was the order of every day, and mornings were spent in the park. Lunch, Charles's favourite menu being boiled chicken and rice, was at one, followed by more outings until 4.30, at which time Princess Elizabeth would hope to have cleared two hours in her day. She insisted on bathing the children herself whenever her schedule permitted, and distinguished visitors were rarely allowed to distract her. The man who arrived with a splendid fleet of metal battleships, marvellous on the nursery floor but disappointingly leaden at bathtime, was King Frederick of Denmark. The lady perched on the bathroom chair, wiping splashes of water from her dress, was Queen Louise of Sweden. No one was spared Charles's incessant beating of an old saucepan with a wooden spoon. Only two royal personages insisted on a certain decorum. Even before his third birthday, Charles had learnt to bow before offering his cheek for a peck from 'Gan Gan' Mary, and not to sit down unbidden when in the presence of his grandfather the King.

By Christmas 1950 Prince Philip had his own naval command. Gazetted lieutenant-commander on the day of his daughter's birth, his ship was the frigate *Magpie*, again in Malta, where Elizabeth again flew to spend the holiday with him. Charles and Anne were left in their grandparents' care at Sandringham, with their Aunt Margaret deputizing for their mother at bathtime. The young Prince enjoyed his first experience of constitutional monarchy that Christmas, when the Lord President of the Council, Herbert Morrison, shut the door of a Privy Council meeting in his face. 'Sorry, young fellow-me-lad,' said Morrison, 'but I'm afraid you can't go in there. We've got a meeting with your grandfather, and it's very, very secret. Ever so secret. Some day ... well, you'll learn about that in due course.'

On New Year's Day there was the excitement of a phone call from his mother aboard the *Magpie*. She had received a letter from her father at Sandringham, saying: 'Charles is too sweet, stumping around the room. We shall love having him at Sandringham. He is the fifth generation to live there, and I hope he will get to like the place.'

Charles was visibly happier when the domestic routine settled back to normal at Clarence House that spring. And so might the Princess's happy family life have continued, as she dearly hoped, for another ten or fifteen years before being blighted by the burden of monarchy. But the King's health was growing worse. His wife and daughter knew, though as yet he did not, that he had cancer. In July, an increase in the young couple's royal duties on the monarch's behalf forced Prince Philip to give up his one, brief naval command. In October, their departure delayed for two weeks by another operation on the King, they left for a tour of North America and Canada. Included in the Princess's luggage was a sealed envelope of documents she would have to sign if her father died during her absence.

So Elizabeth and Philip missed their son's third birthday, which was spent with his grandparents and Aunt Margaret at Buckingham Palace. Charles's one memory of his grandfather dates from this day: an impression of sitting on a sofa with him, this much larger person, while another man dangled something bright and shiny in front of them. Colville, the press secretary, was waving his pocket watch to try to keep the boy still while he had his photograph taken with his grandfather. The resulting picture has since become famous. It stands, and has always stood, on Queen Elizabeth II's desk, uniting one of her last memories of her father with one of her first of her son.

There were more phone calls from his absent parents, one from the White House where they visited President Truman. Three days after his birthday, Charles made one of his first formal public appearances when he was taken to London Airport to greet their return. Control tower staff made his day by allowing him to switch on the runway lights in front of the incoming aircraft. And back at Sandringham, this second long absence was more than compensated for by the cowboy and Indian outfits it bestowed on him. He little knew the significance of a ceremony on 4 December, when the King made the Duke and Duchess of Edinburgh members of the Privy Council. It was all by way of momentous preparation, which to Charles only meant a Christmas rather spoilt by the news that his parents would soon be off travelling again. His mother took him to visit Father Christmas at Harrods, perhaps meditating that a particular wheel had come full circle. At the time of Prince Charles's birth, the King had had to cancel a Commonwealth tour; by Christmas 1950 it had been re-scheduled for early 1952. Now, again because of his health, it was to be undertaken for him by his daughter and her husband.

On 30 January 1952 the King took them to *South Pacific* at Drury Lane theatre, and next morning to London Airport to see them off to the Commonwealth. Charles and Anne had already said their good-byes. The pictures of the King at the airport, a frail and shadowy figure seemingly buffeted by the breeze, were a shock to the nation. It was Elizabeth's last moment on British soil as a Princess. Her life in the wings, protecting her children from the centre-stage spotlight of monarchy, was at an end.

6

Duke of Cornwall
1952-54

... the heir, as long as he is a child, differeth nothing from
a servant...

Galatians iv, 1

THE FIFTH OF February 1952 was 'Keeper's Day' at Sandringham, and
King George VI enjoyed a particularly good day's hare shooting before
spending a late tea-time playing with his grandchildren. As the Queen followed them up to the nursery, to supervise bathtime and hear them say their
prayers, the King sent notes of thanks and congratulation to each of his
keepers, and planned the next day's shooting. He was contented and relaxed
over dinner that evening. After retiring to his room at 10.30, he worked
on papers until midnight, when a watchman saw him close his bedroom
window. In the early hours of 6 February, the King died peacefully in his
sleep.

Charles and his sister were kept unusually late in the nursery that morning. When the boy noticed one of the maids in tears, he asked Nurse Lightbody: 'Why is everybody crying?' Because his grandpa had gone away, he
was told, which made him wonder why his grandpa had not said good-bye.
He asked to see his grandmother, but was told he must wait. When Queen
Elizabeth at last did come to the nursery, she took Charles on her knee and
listened for a while to his chatter, telling him that his mama and papa would
soon be home, sooner than expected. But Charles again asked where his
grandpa had gone, and Queen Elizabeth broke down. When Charles said
gently 'Don't cry, granny,' the nurses too were in tears.

At about that time, 11.45 a.m. in a hunting-lodge called Treetops overlooking the Sagana River in Kenya, Charles's mother learnt that she was
Queen. Michael Parker had taken a phone call from Martin Charteris, the
private secretary, who was in a hotel across the valley. A reporter from the

East African Standard had told him of a news agency wire announcing the King's death. Parker tried to tune in to BBC news bulletins, but could find only solemn music, which seemed confirmation enough. Careful not to be seen by Elizabeth, he signalled the Duke of Edinburgh to step out of the lodge's long sitting-room. Prince Philip himself broke the news to his wife.

As Parker and the Prince worked out the fastest route back to London, Elizabeth calmly set about her first duties as Queen: messages to all the Commonwealth countries she would not be able to visit, the summoning of the traditional Accession Council, and the announcement that she would style herself Queen Elizabeth II. Monarch at twenty-five, she had suddenly lost her already restricted freedom and family life; her father was dead at fifty-six, fourteen years younger than his father George V, and as it was to prove twenty-two years younger than his brother Edward VIII. Even less prepared for accession on this journey than on her last, she left for the urgent flight home in a brightly patterned dress and white hat. As she said good-bye to the grief-stricken servants at the door of the lodge, her chauffeur knelt on all fours to kiss her shoes.

London and the nation, very personally shocked by the suddenness of the King's death, plunged into official and ritual mourning. At the request of the Prime Minister, Winston Churchill, all but a defiant few wore dark clothes for three days and observed a nationwide two minutes' silence on the day of the funeral. Shop window displays were draped in black; a rush-hour crowd emerging from an underground station was observed to divide into two streams, to avoid treading on a fallen newspaper placard saying 'The King Is Dead'.

On 7 February, when the Argonaut *Atalanta* bore the new Queen home to London Airport, the Prime Minister, the Leader of the Opposition (Clement Attlee), and the Foreign Secretary (Anthony Eden) were there to meet her, with other members of the Cabinet and the late King's brother, the Duke of Gloucester. Crowds stood silent along the Mall as the royal motor-cade approached Clarence House, where Queen Mary waited to greet her new sovereign. As the Queen's car drew up, the royal standard was raised on the flagstaff for the first time in Elizabeth II's reign.

Heir apparent at three years old, Prince Charles was now Duke of Corn-wall, Duke of Rothesay, Earl of Carrick and Baron of Renfrew, Lord of the Isles and Great Steward of Scotland. 'That's me, mummy,' he was soon to cry on hearing the Duke of Cornwall's name mentioned in church among the prayers for the Royal Family. Contrary to popular belief, he was not yet Prince of Wales. That is a title the sovereign may bestow on his or her eldest son at whatever moment he or she deems appropriate.

From his point of view, of course, little had changed. He was scarcely aware that flags would now fly throughout the land on his birthday. His family was still living at Clarence House; daily routine was much the same, apart from the absence of his grandfather; he saw no difference in the mother who still supervised his bathtime – to which end the Queen had asked the Prime Minister, Churchill, to put back his weekly appointment with the monarch by one hour. It was Charles's mother who, in time, explained his grandfather's disappearance as far as any Christian parent can to a three-year-old child. Charles was kept strictly away from all the ritual obsequies; he had been taken for a walk to the other side of the Sandringham estate as the funeral cortège left for London, and he was sent back to Sandringham for two days during his grandfather's funeral and burial ceremonies.

Easter was spent, as usual, at Windsor, though with the court still in mourning it was a subdued holiday. When it was over, Charles was confronted with the first outward sign of change. His grandmother and Aunt Margaret had moved into Clarence House, the family home so recently prepared for him and his parents, who in turn moved back into Buckingham Palace. The second-floor nursery suite had been carefully redecorated, to seem as much like the Clarence House nursery as possible. There was his box of toy soldiers, his cuckoo-clock, his ten-foot-high mock-Tudor dolls' house, his toy cupboard (his particular favourite being a model steam-shovel); he had a new, full-size bed, made for him by students of the Royal College of Art, but still the same horse-hair pillow. The only room in the Palace forbidden to him was his mother's study on the floor below.

Passing it one day, Charles urged his mother to come and play. 'If only I could,' said the new Queen, gently closing the door. Forbidding this territory to Charles and Anne – by the childhood of Andrew and Edward, she was sufficiently experienced to relax the rule – was one of the few impositions the Queen allowed her new role to place on her family life at home. But it was a sign of a new era in family monarchy that she refused to allow her children to bow and curtsey to her, as tradition decreed, and as she and her sister had been instructed when their father had unexpectedly become King. Such decorum was still maintained at Marlborough House, where Queen Mary did not altogether approve of these new dispensations. Elizabeth, however, knew how much it had upset her father to see his children suddenly take to performing acts of fealty when they entered the room. It had been Queen Elizabeth, equally reluctantly, who had insisted on it, to help her husband acquire the essential aloofness of sovereignty which was so little in his nature.

As the months went by, Charles had no reason to think his childhood any different from any other little boy's. When he joined his family on the

Palace balcony, or at the Trooping of the Colour, his eyes were those of
an excited member of the crowd, watching the colourful displays. It was
puzzling when some people seemed to prefer to look at him. All the Palace
staff, at the Queen's insistence, called him simply 'Charles'; when he heard
himself referred to as 'Prince Charles', the prefix seemed no different from
that of his friends Master Norton (Knatchbull) or Lady Jane (Wellesley).
He had a penchant for collecting the plastic gifts then given away in cereal
packets, but was dismayed when the Palace butler would open only one
packet at a time. Coming across a valet one day, he said: 'Those are my
daddy's clothes. Where are you taking them?' When he misbehaved, he was
punished, the palm being administered to the royal hindquarters as much
by his nanny as his father. He had to learn to take his toffee out of his mouth
before the royal car stopped, and not – as he once did, to general popular
delight – to press his half-sucked sweet into his mother's hand. Prince Philip
once spanked him for sticking his tongue out at the crowd watching him
drive down the Mall. In such painful ways did Prince Charles begin to learn
about the unusual accident of his birth.

His parents were particularly anxious to ensure that the deference all
around the young Charles should not affect his character. When he omitted
to call the Queen's detective 'Mister', simply using his surname, as he heard
his mother and father do all the time, he was rebuked and told to apologize.
When he slipped an ice-cube down a footman's neck, he was punished. Once,
when he left a door open and a footman rushed to shut it, Philip stopped
the servant, saying: 'Leave it alone, man. The boy's got hands.' His father
also once found Charles pelting a Sandringham policeman with snowballs,
while the hapless officer took his punishment, unsure whether to reply in
kind. 'Don't just stand there,' shouted the Duke of Edinburgh. 'Throw some
back.' Also at Sandringham the Queen once sent Charles back out of the
house, not to return until he had found a dog lead he had lost in the grounds.
'Dog leads', she told him, 'cost money.'

Such was the pattern throughout his childhood. But in the later months
of 1952, as he began to master the rudiments of the Queen's English, Prince
Charles began almost by accident to discover the meaning of the lavish home
life he otherwise took for granted. Meeting a private secretary in a Palace
corridor, a few weeks before his fourth birthday, Charles asked his usual
question: 'What are you doing here?' 'I'm going to see the Queen,' explained
the secretary. 'Oh yes?' said Prince Charles. 'Who's she?' On being told
the Queen was his mother, Charles appeared extremely puzzled. The
courtier felt a qualm of guilt, 'as if I had given away the secret of Father
Christmas'.

Other outward signs began to impress upon him what he was much later to call 'the ghastly, inexorable' truth. No longer could he ride around London in the back of the family car, with his father at the wheel. These favourite excursions had suddenly stopped, and now – aged three – he had his own car with his own chauffeur. He also had his own footman, an eighteen-year-old Palace servant called Richard Brown (whom he once 'knighted' with his knife when he stooped to pick up some food the young Prince had dropped). 'Why haven't you got a Richard?' asked Charles when out to tea with a friend one day. His friend didn't have a Mister Kelly, either – to be precise, Sergeant Kelly, Charles's newly assigned private detective, the first in a long line who would shadow him for the rest of his life. It was thanks to Kelly that Charles soon met another change of routine. No more could he go for walks through Green Park and St James's Park, across the road from his home. Public curiosity had grown too intense. Instead, Mrs Lightbody took the royal children on excursions to Putney Heath, Richmond Park and Wimbledon Common – with the faithful Kelly discreetly in attendance.

Looking back on all this nearly twenty years later, Prince Charles was unable to pinpoint any particular moment when he realized he had been born to be King. 'I didn't suddenly wake up in my pram one day and say "Yippee". I think it just dawns on you, slowly, that people are interested ... and slowly you get the idea that you have a certain duty and responsibility. It's better that way, rather than someone suddenly telling you "You must do this" and "You must do that," because of who you are. It's one of those things you grow up in.'

Part of growing up, as Charles's distinctive character began to emerge, was to develop some sort of childish working relationship with his sister. The Queen, looking back, is emphatic that all four of her children showed very different personalities at the earliest of ages, and it was already clear that Charles and Anne were totally unalike. He was much more like their father in appearance, already aping some of his public mannerisms: the hands behind the back, the erect bearing, the habit of looking an interlocutor fixedly in the eyes, often causing a certain uneasiness. She was much more like their father in character: extrovert, self-confident almost to a fault, occasionally temperamental. Charles took after his mother, who in turn took after George VI: instinctively shy and retiring, yet overcoming it with a deliberate effort of will, which in time sowed the seeds of a driving sense of duty. The solemnity on Charles's face in some of those early pictures, contrasting with the evident mischievousness of Anne's, is that of the camera-shy, not of the humourless, child.

It was Anne, the Mall contingents noted, who waved confidently, after the fashion of her mother, long before her elder brother could summon the gall to do the same. It was Charles, by contrast, who kept reminding his sister, often in vain, that she must curtsey when entering Gan-Gan's drawing-room. It was Charles who pulled Anne along the platform to say thank you to the engine driver when the royal train delivered them to Sandringham. But it was Anne who first discovered, and exploited, the wonderful Palace game discovered by her mother before her: if you walked past a sentry, he would make a very satisfying clatter coming to attention and presenting arms. To walk back and forth past a sentry box provided hours of childish entertainment, to the chagrin of the long-suffering guards on duty. Charles, when he discovered that he too was one of the privileged few who could produce this startling effect, steered clear of sentry boxes. It was somehow embarrassing.

Charles's fourth birthday that autumn was the first his father had ever spent with him. It was the occasion for a grand Palace party; marble busts and other ornaments were cleared from the corridors – at 200 feet long, they were ideal for races and games – and the Palace rang with the laughter of young children for the first time since the parties of Queen Victoria's off-spring a century before. Among the guests were his Gloucester cousins; the Knatchbulls (children of the Brabournes, grandchildren of Lord Mountbatten); the Charteris children; James Dawnay, son of the Queen Mother's private secretary; Nicholas and Simon Renton, grandchildren of Sir Alan Lascelles; and Lord Ipswich and Lady Henrietta Fitzroy, children of Lord and Lady Euston. The band of the Grenadier Guards played a selection of nursery rhymes, interspersed with 'Happy Birthday To You' and the young Prince's favourite, 'The Teddy Bear's Picnic'.

The coronation of Elizabeth II was by now set for the following June. The Duke of Cornwall, as senior royal duke and head of the peerage, would be obliged to take an oath of allegiance to the new monarch; but it was the first time in British history, at least since the creation of the Dukedom in 1337, that a sovereign with so young an heir was to be crowned. The Queen was reluctant to put Charles through such an ordeal, and knew that worries about his behaviour would stretch her own already taut nerves. At Sandringham and Balmoral, he had had to be taken out of the parish church for fidgeting during the sermon. As a test, two days after his birthday, the Queen accompanied her son on his first public appearance: to one of Sir Robert Mayer's concerts for children in the Royal Festival Hall. Alas, boredom set in half-way through the programme, and he had to be taken home.

So it was decided to spare Charles the solemn oath of allegiance, and a decision was postponed on whether he would attend the coronation at all. In the meantime, there was much for him and Anne to enjoy in the preparations for the event, marred only by the death of Queen Mary in March, though again the Prince was too young to be touched by his great-grand-mother's sudden disappearance. As June approached, Charles was much amused to find that a part of his mother's magnificent robe was called a train; courtiers and visitors alike were roped into coronation games. Looking out of the window one day Anne declared excitedly that the coronation had begun, only to be informed rather haughtily by her brother that it was just the changing of the guard. Charles remembers a large man with a large hat and a large cigar – Winston Churchill, who had developed a rather emotional affection for his young new Queen – coming and going with great ceremony. He had a ride in the coronation coach as it was put through its trials in the Palace Mews, causing royal commentators to announce excitedly that he had become the first future monarch in history to ride in the coach before his own coronation.

By the day itself, 2 June, a grey summer's day even by London standards, there had been a last-minute change of heart. Prince Charles's name did not appear in the official coronation programme, indicating that the Queen had thought it best to leave him, like Anne, at home. But he begged to be allowed to come. A white satin suit was prepared, his hair was slicked down with brilliantine, and he watched his parents drive through the cheering Mall crowds in the state coach of George III. After the mile-long procession had disappeared, Mrs Lightbody saw him into a plain car, which took a side route to Westminster Abbey. The heir apparent entered holding his nanny's and a Grenadier Guard's hands. Quietly he joined his grandmother and Aunt Margot in the royal box, where he stood on a footstool to watch the solemn coronation rites of his mother.

The ceremony was well under way, and had just reached one of its most splendid moments: the anointing of the sovereign with consecrated oil, as the choir sang Handel's anthem 'Zadok the Priest'. It was a worrying moment for the child: he saw his mother divested of her ornate finery, in the plainest white robe, surrounded by men in extravagant uniforms; four of them, Knights of the Garter, held over her head a canopy of cloth of gold, while the Archbishop of Canterbury prepared to anoint her hands, breast and head with oil. For all her preoccupations, the Queen was seen to look up and give her son a reassuring little smile.

Those eyes that remained on Charles saw him spread his arms wide in admiration of the gold plate on the altar. And, amid his constant questions to the Queen Mother, he kept smoothing his hair with his hand, then offering her his palm so she could smell his new hair oil. Only once did she have to restrain him as he leaned over the balcony for a better view. But he was allowed to stay longer than anticipated, and was ushered out shortly before the peers' oaths of allegiance – which it might anyway have been constitutionally improper for him to attend without taking part. Mrs Lightbody saw him out through a side door and home for lunch.

That afternoon, like the rest of a nation newly equipped with sets for the occasion, Charles watched his parents' triumphant progress through the West End of London on television. When they returned to the Palace, the Queen went out on the balcony alone for a few moments, still wearing her robes and crown. Then Prince Philip led the children forward, to renewed cheering. It was Charles's first experience of mass adulation, which might be thought to have turned the head of a four-and-a-half-year-old child. But scarcely anything of that day has lodged at all vividly in his memory.

For the slightly bewildered young boy, all the coronation really meant was that his parents would soon be going away again – for much longer than ever before. For a few months, the Queen's presence at home was interrupted only by excursions around the country, to show herself to her new subjects. But in late November she and Prince Philip were again to undertake that postponed and interrupted Commonwealth tour, this time in their own right. They would be away for six months.

The days until November passed happily enough. Charles had swimming lessons from his father and Michael Parker in the Palace pool; at Balmoral, he learnt to ride on an old Shetland pony called Fum. In June, the young Duke of Cornwall's five-year-old bull Supreme – just a year older than its owner – was named Supreme Champion at the Bath and West Show. He was always more passionate about animals than things mechanical: the Palace nursery had by now become a veritable menagerie. Apart from his two corgis, there was a hamster named Chi-Chi, a rabbit named Harvey, and two South American love-birds (a gift from his grandmother) which he called David and Annie, after Davy Crockett and Annie Oakley.

The coronation had led to the first full flush of publicity about the royal children, which their mother decided was not in their best interests. They had never been allowed to see too many of the newspapers which carried their photographs; but she now began to impose further restrictions, for her children's own good. In late June, the Palace officially announced that Charles – still only four – would not be undertaking any official engagements. By way of a sign, the Queen cancelled plans for the youngest member of the Duke of Cornwall's Light Infantry to present Charles with a set of model soldiers to mark their 250th anniversary.

For several months following the Trooping the Colour on 11 June no photographs at all were issued of the royal children. There had been criticism that they were already becoming over-exposed to the public's unremitting interest; the *Daily Express* calculated that in the twenty-three weeks of 1953 up to June, it alone had published fifty pages of royal photographs. Nor was there any special celebration of Charles's fifth birthday in November. His parents stayed at Sandringham, finalizing their plans for the tour, whilst Charles spent the day at Windsor with his grandmother and Aunt Margaret. Much of it he passed aping the guards, with the helmet and sword given him by his mother for his birthday. His grandmother, providentially in view of the months ahead in her care, gave him a miniature set of gardening tools.

A week later, however, came the moment of parting. One of Prince Philip's last acts before leaving was to see the nursery staircase at Buckingham Palace safely covered over with netting, so boisterous was Charles growing. The Queen again took herself off to Harrods, returning with a red-white-and-blue glider, and some mud-pie moulds, to be stored away for her son's Christmas presents. Then, on 23 November, they waved good-bye to their children. The royal yacht *Britannia* had only been launched in April, and was still undergoing trials. So they flew to Jamaica to join the converted cruise liner *Gothic*, a cardboard cut-out of which was added to Charles's already voluminous scrapbook. The night before the Queen had tucked her children up, and Charles had spontaneously promised 'to look after Anne'. Once out of the room, Elizabeth II – still feeling inadequate to the role suddenly thrust upon her – melted into tears.

As much as Charles resented these partings, he was already aware of the need for them. 'Mummy has an important job to do,' he told a friend who asked where the Queen was. 'She's down here.' He pointed out Australia on the globe newly installed in the nursery, on which he followed his parents' progress. Letters and phone calls kept them in touch, with a special message from New Zealand on Christmas Day. The Queen had anyway planned to link up with *Britannia* for the leg home from Tobruk. She promised Charles and Anne that they could sail out in the new yacht to join her there.

It was the royal children's first trip abroad, and it remains Charles's earliest memory of his sister. On 5 April Queen Elizabeth took them down to Portsmouth, where she handed them into the care of Mrs Lightbody and Miss Anderson. The Queen Mother was happy to see that the royal crew had risen to the occasion: already installed on deck was a sandpit, a slide and a model of *Britannia* mounted on a pedal car frame. It was a somewhat unorthodox maiden voyage, with the heir to the throne rolling up his corduroy dungarees and swabbing the decks with the four young ratings assigned to keep an eye on him. With films and other entertainments laid on the week's sailing to Malta was quickly over, and Charles was reunited with his favourite uncle, Dickie (Lord Mountbatten), based on the island as Commander-in-Chief of the Mediterranean Fleet. There followed a further week of play and sightseeing, with some crab-fishing in the rock pools of Gozo, punctuated by a day aboard the visiting aircraft-carrier *Eagle*, where Charles was seen to snap to attention and salute with all the gravity of his great-uncle.

Then, on 2 May, the Queen was piped aboard at Tobruk. Only with difficulty was Charles restrained from joining the line of dignitaries waiting to shake hands with her. 'No, not you, dear', were Her Majesty's first words to her son after their six-month parting, before she took him off to the state rooms for a private and very emotional reunion. The young Prince seemed to have grown up beyond recognition during the long separation, and the rest of the voyage was a joyous holiday of rediscovery. The interval at Gibraltar, where Charles encouraged the Barbary apes to jump on his sister's shoulders, but was visibly horrified when they treated Miss Anderson with similarly scant respect, remains one of the family's treasured memories.

At the time, there was a permanent reminder in the shape of a model train set, presented to the royal children by the Gibraltar Garrison. Most of Prince Charles's many unsolicited gifts of toys and games were passed on to children's hospitals, but this one took pride of place back in the Palace, in what had been King George VI's schoolroom. Prince Philip, like all fathers, spent perhaps more time than his son racing it round the papier-mâché rock. For Charles, it came second only to his favourite childhood possession, a powder-blue Austin pedal car, which to this day you still walk past when you take the Queen's Entrance out into the Buckingham Palace garden.

Thanks to Winston Churchill's sense of occasion, the royal yacht sailed home up the Thames to the Pool of London. There the Royal Family transferred to a stately barge and continued their triumphant progress – with the Prime Minister on board – through a wildly enthusiastic throng to Westminster. There were great celebrations at the Palace homecoming that evening, but next morning the prolonged holiday for Prince Charles was finally declared over. It was time for his education to begin in earnest.

7

'Mispy' and Hill House School
1954-57

The difficulty in the education of a Prince, especially of the heir to the throne, is that he is forced too early into life, and that too much is expected of him.

Frederick Waymouth Gibbs,
senior tutor to the future King Edward VII

ON HIS FIFTH birthday the previous November, Prince Charles had reached the age at which the law requires every English child to begin a formal education. The Queen and Prince Philip had already decided, some time before, to alter the traditional patterns of royal tutelage; they wished their children, especially the heir to the throne, to grow up as far as possible like other people's children. The plans they had in mind were in their way revolutionary, but as yet strictly secret. Charles did not seem quite ready to be sent, as some MPs were demanding, to the state primary school around the corner. For a five-year-old, the rather plump little boy was socially mature, as was only to be expected of one living in a world of adult and formal behaviour. But he did not seem particularly bright.

He could write his own name, in carefully etched capital letters, he could count to a hundred, and he could tell the time. His mother herself had taught him that much. But he could scarcely read at all, despite hours of enjoyment being read – and committing to memory – the works of Beatrix Potter and A.A. Milne, and the 'Babar the Elephant' books. He enjoyed his dancing classes, for which a mixed group of young aristocrats joined him at the Palace each week under the instruction of the celebrated Miss Marguerite Vacani; at Windsor, he had graduated to a Welsh pony called William under the instruction of Sybil Smith, who had taught the Queen to ride, but he already showed less enthusiasm than his sister. The Prince attended a London gym class, and had started piano lessons with Miss Hilda Bor. He showed some

musical aptitude, singing nursery rhymes with his mother, and driving some
Palace staff to distraction with his love of military marches, especially 'The
British Grenadiers'. But, thus far, the only other formal instruction he had
received for the arduous royal years ahead was to be made to stand still for
long periods of time.

Before leaving for her Commonwealth tour, the Queen had engaged a
governess for Prince Charles: Miss Catherine Peebles, another Scotswoman
(the nursery staff became known as 'the Scottish Mafia'). A small and spry
woman in her mid forties, 'Mispy' had previously had charge of the widowed
Duchess of Kent's two younger children, Princess Alexandra and Prince
Michael. She had no formal training, no university or college degree, and no
revolutionary ideas on the upbringing of children; but the Queen had noticed
in Miss Peebles a mixture of common sense and kindly strictness which
echoed her own attitudes. The one rule Her Majesty imposed on her son's
governess, knowing the child's uncertainty of himself, was 'No forcing'.

The Queen had considered inviting other children to join Charles's classes,
but decided his temperament urged against it. If his world so far had been
one of adults, it had also been one of female adults – and distinctly genteel
ones at that. Apart from his father, who was so often away, Charles had
spent most of his time with the Queen, the Queen Mother, Princess
Margaret, Mrs Lightbody, Miss Anderson and his sister. The difficulty of
establishing normal dealings with other children just now might distract
him. It was decided that Charles would have his lessons alone. Even Anne
was forbidden to disturb his morning with Miss Peebles in the Palace
schoolroom, where a desk and blackboard had now joined the more familiar
globe.

When the time came for Mispy to teach Charles's three younger siblings,
other children did join the classes. Looking back, the Queen is sure she
judged the difference in Charles correctly.

Miss Peebles became one of the select few to receive a copy of the Queen's
daily engagement card. Each morning, when possible, Charles still spent
half an hour with his mother at 9. Then the day's instruction began, lasting
initially until 11.30, noon when he was a little older. Mispy confirmed the
Queen's concern for Charles as a nervous, over-sensitive child. 'If you raised
your voice to him, he would draw back into his shell and for a time you
would be able to do nothing with him.' Mabel Anderson agreed: 'He was
never as boisterous or noisy as Princess Anne. She had a much stronger,
more extrovert personality. She didn't exactly push him aside, but she was
certainly a more forceful child.' Anne could always find something to amuse
herself with, whilst Charles often needed to be entertained. She was also
better with her hands; Charles was all 'fingers and thumbs'.

Charles's shyness was in part due to some dawning awareness of his position. He knew how to behave, if not yet exactly why. When he visited a
friend's farm, it was noticed that he took a polite interest in everything to
be seen – almost as if he were on a royal visit – rather than showing a child's
quick and selective enthusiasms. At times the spectacle of a little boy so
aware of proprieties became almost pathetic: when encouraging his corgi
or another pet to perform its tricks, he would always add a most polite
'please'.

On a rewards-for-effort system, Miss Peebles began to draw out his special
interests. After beginning each day with a Bible story, Charles was allowed
to indulge his fondness for painting, at which he has since developed some
of his father's skill. Geography was a natural source of fascination; it was
Miss Peebles who installed the globe on which he followed his parents'
travels, and he was soon able to tell visiting ambassadors the precise whereabouts of their country. History was more of a problem when trying to educate a future king to think of himself as a normal child. But Miss Peebles
carefully developed a course she called 'Children in History', in which great
figures were traced right back to their origins, whether regal or humble.
The only subject which completely baffled him, and has done ever since,
was maths. The Queen smiled indulgently, for like her mother she has always
had the same blind spot.

The afternoons were taken up with educational excursions. Down the
Mall to the shipping offices in Cockspur Street, for a talk from Miss Peebles
on the trade routes. Up to Highgate Hill to trace the steps of Dick
Whittington and his cat before a visit to the pantomime. To the Tower,
to be shown round by the beefeaters; to St George's Chapel, Windsor, to
see Winston Churchill installed as a Knight of the Garter; to Madame
Tussauds, to laugh at the wax effigies of his parents.

In that first year, Charles quickly learnt to read, but still had some difficulty with his writing. After Christmas 1955 – celebrated with a party for
forty children at the Palace, and a visit to Harrods to ask Father Christmas
for a bicycle – Charles began to learn French. The afternoon excursions
became more rigorously instructive, with visits to the various London
museums. But by now the press had caught on to the routine, and all too
often the outings had to be abandoned for a straightforward nature walk
through Richmond Park.

The Queen began to doubt whether it was possible for her son to enjoy
a normal education. If the press would not allow him to visit the British
Museum in peace, what chance of privacy would he have at a normal school?
And would his presence disturb the education of his fellow school-children?
Her cherished plans seemed in danger, but she was determined not to

abandon them lightly. On 11 April 1955, her press secretary, Richard
Colville, sent a personal letter to all newspaper editors:

> I am commanded by the Queen to say that Her Majesty and the Duke
> of Edinburgh have decided that their son has reached the stage when he
> should take part in more grown-up educational pursuits with other children.
>
> In consequence, a certain amount of the Duke of Cornwall's instruction
> will take place outside his home; for example, he will visit museums and other
> places of interest. The Queen trusts, therefore, that His Royal Highness will
> be able to enjoy this in the same way as other children without the embar-
> rassment of constant publicity. In this respect, Her Majesty feels it is equally
> important that those in charge of, or sharing in, the instruction should be
> spared undue publicity, which can so seriously interrupt their normal lives.
>
> I would be grateful if you will communicate the above to your members
> and seek their co-operation in this matter, informing them at the same time
> that they are at liberty to publish this letter if they so wish.

The request caused a lull (it was to prove only temporary) in press attention, but had the unwelcome counter-effect of persuading editors to satisfy
the public demand with totally fictitious stories. One popular paper, for instance, had Charles cruising down the Rhine, complete with photograph
(in fact, of the son of a British naval officer). Moved only in the direst straits
to issue denials, the Palace had to put up with it. At least Charles and Mispy
remained comparatively unmolested when they visited London Zoo and the
Planetarium; Charles was soon an expert in recognizing constellations, proof
to his mother that, like her, he was at heart 'a country person'. They even
managed a ride on the underground, Charles apparently passing unrecog-
nized as the son of inconspicuous parents (Mispy and the Prince's detective).
It was to be some years yet, however, before he realized his childhood dream
of riding on a double-decker bus.

Extra-curricular activities included charades, field sports, more riding and
Charles's initiation into the curious rites of his countrymen's national game,
cricket. The first was especially popular: if you happen to be a member of
a family which enjoys dressing up, there can be fewer places with better-
equipped wardrobes than Buckingham Palace and Windsor Castle. At Sandringham, Charles had already helped to round up the hounds before a hunt,
and at Balmoral his Welsh pony had been replaced by an Irish roan. He
played his first game of cricket in the summer of 1956, and that autumn
his first game of soccer; but neither was to prove an abiding interest. Under
the tuition of one of the Balmoral stalkers, Charles meanwhile developed
his lifelong love of fly-fishing. His father had begun to teach him boxing,
but had reluctantly, and with some irritation, abandoned the idea after a
chorus of public protest.

Above: 'Safely delivered of a Prince': the first picture, by Cecil Beaton, November 1948

Above right: Four generations: with his mother, his grandfather, King George VI, and his great-grandmother, Queen Mary, at his christening

Below: The birth certificate

ourteenth ovember, 1948 uckingham Palace	Charles Philip Arthur George	Boy	His Royal Highness Philip, Duke of Edinburgh	Her Royal Highness The Princess Elizabeth Alexandra Mary, Duchess of Edinburgh	His Royal Highness The Duke of Edinburgh (Lieutenant, R.N)	[signature] father Buckingham Palace, S.W.1	Fifteenth December, 1948	I. L. Mare Registrar	

First year: on the lawn at Windlesham Moor

Aged two, at Clarence House

Watching the parade go by: on the garden wall of Clarence House

Third birthday: a walk in the park with Nanny Lightbody

En route for Sandringham: Princess Anne's first public appearance

Duke of Cornwall. The new Queen with her family at Balmoral, September 1952

Above: The favourite pedal car, now a Palace *objet d'art*

Left: With 'Grandpa England': Elizabeth II's favourite portrait of her father and her son, which still stands on her desk at Buckingham Palace

Left: Coronation, 1953: the heir apparent arrives at the Abbey ...

Centre: ... and is kept in order by Grandmama and Aunt Margot

Below: First 'balcony job': enjoying the coronation fly-past

Royal siblings: a study by the future Lord Snowdon

Making new friends at Sandringham ...

... and Windsor

Hill House: the first heir apparent ever to be a schoolboy

Sports Day at Hill House, under the watchful eye of Colonel Townend

One boy who can't be an engine driver when he grows up

'The Duke of Edinburgh', Mabel Anderson recalled, 'was a marvellous father. When the children were younger, he always used to set aside time to read to them, or help them put together those little model toys.' As they grew, he also encouraged practical jokes, something of a family tradition. The last two Princes of Wales, Edward VII and Edward VIII, set the precedents: the one was known for concealing dead birds in guests' beds, the other for once feeding his French tutor, M. Hua, a tadpole sandwich. In time, Charles would develop his own eccentric style – at its height during his Service career. For the present, to his father's delight and Mrs Lightbody's dismay, he contented himself with more traditional pranks such as artificial ink-stains, and a 'whoopee cushion' upon which the Bishop of Norwich once sat while visiting Sandringham.

By the autumn of 1956 the Queen was sufficiently pleased with Prince Charles's progress to take the next major step she had in mind. In October, soon after the start of the school term, Colonel Henry Townend, founder and headmaster of a smart London day-school for boys, was pleasantly surprised to find himself invited to tea with Her Majesty at Buckingham Palace. Hill House, the Colonel's small establishment in Hans Place, just behind Knightsbridge (conveniently near the Palace), had been recommended to Charles's parents by friends and acquaintances who had sent their own sons there. One had particularly pleased Her Majesty by informing her that it was the only school in London outside which the pavement was washed and the railings dusted every day. The school's philosophy is, to this day, trumpeted on the busy notice board beside its front steps, open for inspection to any casual passer-by:

A sense of rivalry has to be encouraged and a boy must be led to discover something in which he can excel. He must be trained to react quickly in an emergency, have a good sense of balance and control, have the strength and ability to extract himself from a dangerous situation – and the urge to win.

Colonel Townend was naturally flattered when the Queen asked him to accept her son as a pupil, but alarmed by the enormous double responsibility, both to the heir to the throne and to his other pupils. It was mutually agreed that, for the present, Charles would join the other boys only for their afternoon recreation.

Lessons with Mispy continued in the mornings, then Charles would don his school uniform and be taken to Hill House to join the crocodile along the King's Road to Chelsea. School games were played in the grounds of Duke of York's Headquarters, the military depot named after that very Duke who marched his men to the top of the hill and marched them down again. Newspaper editors, of course, also marched their men to the top of the playing fields, once the Prince's new afternoon schedule – which had been successfully kept secret for several weeks – was discovered. But one picture of Charles playing soccer looked much like another, especially as he did not join in the game with much enthusiasm, and the novelty soon wore off. As the Queen and Colonel Townend had hoped, he quickly merged into the crowd of schoolboys walking in line down the street, recognizable only when politely raising his school cap to passers-by. It was not as if he were yet a fully-fledged schoolboy.

That, again amid tight security, was being planned for the New Year. Over Christmas, meanwhile, official duties again took Prince Philip abroad, to open the Olympic Games at Melbourne and tour the Antarctic, so it was thought necessary to provide Prince Charles with some male company to offset the petticoat régime. Michael Farebrother, a thirty-six-year-old former Guards officer, and headmaster of St Peter's School, Seaford, joined the Royal Household at Sandringham as 'tutor-companion' to the Prince. They roamed the estate together, visited Brancaster Beach, kicked a rugby ball around the Sandringham gardens, and talked about the great figures of history.

Farebrother's special subjects were Latin and history, but little academic work was done. Charles's favourite occupation that Christmas, according to his new companion, was watching The Lone Ranger and Champion the Wonder Horse on TV.

Farebrother's brief spell coincided with Catherine Peebles's Christmas holiday, but it also marked the end of her supervision of Prince Charles. Though Mispy was to stay at the Palace to take charge of Princess Anne, Charles was to miss her sorely. With the retirement not long after of Helen Lightbody (Miss Anderson also stayed on to look after Anne), he was suddenly deprived of the two main guardians of his childhood, with whom he had spent considerably more time than with his parents. As he moved into a suite of his own in the Palace, Charles kept in close touch with both, writing them long letters, and visiting Miss Lightbody in her grace-and-favour Duchy of Cornwall flat in Kennington. But the shock of their departure drove home the awesome prospect of his first day at school with other children. Although his parents had striven to prepare him for it, he was simply not equipped to be wrenched from his sheltered environment.

Not long before the news of Colonel Townend's establishment was broken to him, Prince Charles had asked the Queen: 'Mummy, what are school-boys?' For all the Queen's thoughtful care, for all the down-to-earth influence of Prince Philip, by no stretch of anyone's imagination was eight-year-old Prince Charles an ordinary child. He had grown up in palaces and castles. Ships and soldiers, objects of fantasy and imagination to other boys his age, were to Charles everyday realities. He had seen his parents, and on occasion himself, treated with awe and reverence. People became nervous and ill-at-ease in the presence of his family. At the ring of a telephone, his nanny – and he had no reason to suppose that all children did not have nannies – would abandon whatever was happening and take him along to see his mother. At the age of four, he had been named one of the world's Top Ten Best Dressed Men. (The citation, in the *Tailor and Cutter* magazine, praised his taste in baby bows, farm stalkers and double-breasted woollies. 'His velvet-collared topcoat also follows a popular current trend.' On the list with Prince Charles were Marshals Tito and Bulganin, General Sir Frank Browning, Billy Graham, Fred Astaire, Charlie Chaplin and Adlai Stevenson. He made the Top Ten again two years later, aged six, along with Harold Macmillan [then Housing Minister], Sir Hartley Shawcross ['easily the best-dressed Socialist'], Rocky Marciano, Stewart Granger and Captain Cecil Boyd-Rochfort, the Queen's racehorse trainer.)

The Prince had never handled money; when eventually he did, it turned out to be puzzling discs of bronze and cupro-nickel bearing a picture of his mother. He had never been shopping. He had never been on a bus. He had never got lost in a crowd. He had never had to fend for himself.

Nevertheless, on 28 January 1957, Prince Charles made British history by becoming the first heir to the throne ever to go to school. At 9.15 a.m. a black Ford Zephyr driven by a Palace chauffeur, with Charles and Miss Peebles in the back, pulled up at the school entrance, where Colonel Townend was waiting to greet him. In the school uniform of cinnamon-coloured jersey and corduroy trousers, Charles ran up to the man he had previously known as a football referee. Inside he hung up his coat – distinctive for the velvet collar so admired by the *Tailor and Cutter* – and plunged straight into the morning's routine.

The new boy was No. 102 on the school roll of 120, the sons of well-to-do professional men, lawyers, doctors, military men and politicians. One fellow pupil was the grandson of the new Prime Minister, Harold Macmillan. There were a number of foreign children, the sons of diplomats stationed in London. It was a school for privileged children, still young and self-confident enough not to be in awe of him. The headmaster had warned them to make no special fuss of the distinguished new face in their midst, but their upbringing anyway equipped them to take Charles's arrival in their stride. All of which was of little more help to him at Hill House than it would have been at Dotheboys Hall.

Opened only five years before, the school very much reflected the personal philosophy of Colonel Townend, a former Gunners officer of forty-seven, who had been an Oxford football blue and England athlete. There was no corporal punishment, and the predominantly female staff taught a syllabus broad by pre-preparatory school standards. It even included elementary anatomy lessons from Mrs Townend, a state-registered nurse who had once been theatre sister at Guy's Hospital to Sir John Weir, Gilliatt's assistant at the Prince's birth. The school doors were equipped with automatic devices to prevent trapped fingers; all the furniture had rounded edges. The fees were £27 a term (lunch 2s 6d a day extra) and the school motto was taken from Plutarch: 'A boy's mind is not a vessel to be filled, but a fire to be kindled.'

Charles's first day began with the school song, for which Townend had chosen a hymn called Schooldays by the little-known composer Jonathan Battishill (1738–1801):

> Help us that with eager mind
> We may learn both fact and rule,
> Patient, diligent and kind
> In the comradeship of school.

Prince Charles to the staff, plain Charles to his fellow-members of Form Six of Middle School, he was given no special escort that first morning, but left to make his own way. Highlight of the day was a visit to the school 'madhouse', a gymnasium with padded walls, for basketball. After lunch – beef and carrots, followed by apple pie – he painted a picture of Tower Bridge, and signed it Charles. At 3.30 it was time to go home, and the black Zephyr was waiting at the door. As the Prince told the Queen all about it that evening, she felt a great sense of relief. The experiment, it seemed, was going to work.

Next morning, however, the crowd outside Hill House was so enormous that she hesitated to let him go. It was not just that the press had set up a constant vigil; local residents who had read of the new recruit in their morning newspapers were all but choking the street. After telephone consultations with Townend the Queen relented, and Charles arrived at school thirty-five minutes late. He had to run a gauntlet of sightseers and photographers to get inside. It was the same when he left.

On the third morning, Townend again telephoned the Palace to warn them of a large crowd. It became clear to both the headmaster and the royal parents that this could not go on. Unless the news-hounds could be called off, the monarchy's experiment in liberal education might have to be abandoned. The Queen kept her son at home, while her press secretary went into action.

A detective reported back to him with the identities of all pressmen waiting outside the school, and the news that they intended to wait all day. Colville then personally telephoned each of the newspaper editors involved, reminding them of the Queen's plea of eighteen months before. Within an hour all the Fleet Street representatives had been recalled, and Charles was able to go to school. Thus might his first term have continued in comparative normality, had he not contracted tonsillitis the following day, and taken to his bed for three weeks.

By the end of February, he had settled back into everyday school routine more smoothly than those watching over him dared to hope. Swimming and wrestling (which took the place of boxing at Hill House) became his favourite pastimes, and he continued to show promise with water colours. In the class-room, he remained something of a plodder.

This worried nobody. The purpose of sending Prince Charles to school was not to sow the seeds of a giant intellect, but to help him meet people his own age, and learn to live among them. More important, perhaps, it was also to help him develop normal relationships with people older than himself – people other than courtiers and aristocrats. In this it succeeded admirably. Charles was, if anything, politer to the staff than most of the other children; if not yet wholly aware of his station in life, he had been sufficiently drilled at home to treat those around him, however deferential, with the utmost respect. Moreover, Townend's philosophy was to instil discipline in a family rather than an institutional context. Though the boys called him 'Sir', and though he did not eat his meals with them, the geography of the cramped, converted six-storey building was such that they constantly ran in and out of his private quarters at will. It all helped Charles to understand status as a functional necessity, not a matter of arbitrary rank and privilege.

To run into the headmaster's dining-room while he was entertaining guests was no crime. To disgrace the school uniform in public, however, was the cardinal sin, meriting the ultimate punishment: the loss of the school tie. Townend allowed healthy chaos to exist behind the school doors, but insisted on utterly correct decorum in public. Charles, he later recalled, was usually to be found in the thick of any high-spirited *mêlée*. But he never lost his tie.

The climax of that first term was the school's Field Day. Townend was insistent that it should not be called Sports Day, as there was less emphasis on competition than on keen participation, in the Olympic tradition. The Queen and Prince Philip attended with Anne, after first making it clear that no fuss was to be made of them. Following a recent school outing to the Royal Tournament, Townend included on the programme the dismantling and re-erection of a military-style field gun. The Prince was practice-perfect at this event, though he did not otherwise shine as an athlete. None the less, he remembers how bucked he was to hear his father's stentorian 'Well done, Charles' ringing across the field. For the Queen, it was a day of great importance. As she watched her son set to with a will, anxiously looking to her every so often for fond maternal approval, she was moved by the apparent success of her initiative. And as Charles gravely introduced her to the members of his class – Andrew Smith, son of an Air Marshal; Michael Carpenter, son of a Westminster canon; William Ladd, son of a diplomat; Edward Lankey, son of a senior Foreign Office civil servant; Andrew Starling, son of an architect; Nicholas Lamb, son of an Army officer – she shook hands with them as earnestly as if they had been the Privy Council. Perhaps the heir to the throne could, after all, grow up like any other little boy from a 'good' family background.

His end-of-term report was certainly ordinary. Hill House made a practice of not sending exam results to parents; they were posted on the board, and could be viewed by those who wished to. The royal parents did not bother, and Charles himself has perhaps conveniently forgotten how he fared. His school report, however, has been preserved for posterity:

Lent 1957, Upper VI
    Reading: very good indeed; good expression.
    Writing: good, firm, clear, well formed.
    Arithmetic: below form average; careful but slow, not very keen.
    Scripture: shows keen interest.
    Geography: good.
    History: loves this subject.
    French: shows promise.
    Latin: made a fair start.
    Art: good, and simply loves drawing and painting.
    Singing: a sweet voice, especially in the lower register.
    Football: enjoying the game.
    Gymnastics: good.

Hidden behind the familiar vernacular of the schoolteacher, anxious not to cause too much trouble at home, was a reassuringly average start.

The summer term began, like the first, with an attack of tonsillitis, but this time the tonsils lost. They were removed in the Buhl Room at the Palace by James Crooks of Great Ormond Street Hospital for Children, and Charles insisted on keeping them in a jar on his bedroom mantelpiece. During a few days' recuperation in Great Ormond Street, he sent a message to the eight-year-old daughter of a hospital porter: 'To Maureen, with love from Charles.' Maureen wrote back, but the romance ended there. Charles was sent to convalesce in Norfolk, at Holkham Hall, home of the Earl of Leicester. It was conveniently near Sandringham and the coastline he knew so well, and he was soon romping in the sandhills with the Leicesters' twelve-year-old daughter, Lady Sarah Coke. In late May he was back at Hill House.

By the end of term the assessment remained much the same: determined but slow. He was, perhaps generously at that stage, credited with 'above average intelligence', and showed signs of a creative bent scarcely evident in either of his parents. Arithmetic was still a major problem, painting his favourite pursuit. At Balmoral that summer, twenty-seven-year-old Mlle Bibiane de Roujoux was imported from Paris on the recommendation of the Queen's former teacher, Madame Untermeyer, to help with his French, which for a while was the only language spoken at the royal dining-table.

By August he was enjoying his first yacht racing at Cowes, though sea-sickness made his first outing with his father in *Bluebottle* something of an ordeal. Once he got over it, however, he shared Prince Philip's exhilaration at the closeness to sea and wind, and the distance from the press. Earlier that summer, his father had stumped up ten shillings after betting Charles he could not swim two lengths of the Palace pool; later that summer he ticked him off for fidgeting at the Highland Games at Braemar, observed by a crowd of 20,000 people. The Prince was wearing his first kilt, of Balmoral tartan – to the Scots a sure sign that he was growing up.

The nation had already received another sign that summer, with the announcement that Prince Charles was to be sent away to a prep school.

PART III

Education

8

The Education of Princes
1841-1957

Poor little Wales,
Sure the saddest of tales
Is the tale of the studies
With which they are cramming thee.

PUNCH on the young Bertie, Prince of Wales

IN THE EARLY years of her reign, Elizabeth II's sense of inadequacy to the task suddenly thrust upon her was capable of reducing her to tears. For the first ten years of her life, after all, there had been no prospect of her becoming Queen of England; she was taught the decorum befitting a King's grand-daughter and niece, not the sophistication and know-how befitting a King's daughter and heir. Even after King George VI's reluctant accession, when his daughter's prayers that he might yet have a son proved vain, her father thought *Punch* magazine the best way of introducing her to political arguments and personalities. Occasionally he would mark an article for her to read in the Palace copy of *The Times*, in those days still a special edition printed on superior paper.

From Elizabeth and Margaret Rose's governess, Miss Marion Crawford ('Crawfie'), we have received a chatty and detailed account of the little princesses' upbringing, which makes it clear that preparations for the burdens of monarchy were the last thing on the Duke and Duchess of York's curriculum for their children. 'I had the feeling', wrote Miss Crawford, 'that the Duke and Duchess, most happy in their own married life, were not over concerned with the higher education of their daughters. They wanted most for them a really happy childhood, with lots of pleasant memories stored up against the days that might come out and, later, happy marriages.' Even their grandfather, King George V, was concerned about nothing so much as their handwriting. 'For goodness sake,' he told Crawfie, 'teach Margaret and Lilibet to write a decent hand, that's all I ask you. None of my children could write properly. They all do it exactly the same way. I like a hand with some character in it.'

Their mother's aspirations for them summed up the princesses' education: 'To spend as long as possible in the open air, to enjoy to the full the pleasures of the country, to be able to dance and draw and appreciate music, to acquire good manners and perfect deportment, and to cultivate all the distinctively feminine graces.' Thus Elizabeth II, not surprisingly, would have preferred to the life of a queen that of 'a lady living in the country with lots of horses and dogs' (which, for somewhat less than half her waking hours, is precisely what she is). But for over twenty-five years and more she has also, after that uncertain start, become the shrewdest and most deft of monarchs, inching the institution closer to its people while preserving the essential, mystical gulf between the two.

Such skills are innate in her; they owe little to the lessons in the constitution which she started at the age of thirteen with Sir Henry Marten, Vice-Provost of Eton, and which became a correspondence course when she was sequestered at royal country residences during the war. Marten religiously imbued the teenage princess with the precepts of Walter Bagehot, on which her grandfather, George V, had been raised, despite the aspersions occasionally cast on his father. Bagehot's definition of the British constitutional monarchy, with its famous summary of the monarch's rights vis-à-vis the Prime Minister, 'to be consulted, to encourage and to warn', remains largely unchallenged. But the representative family monarchy of the later twentieth century, as acclaimed by its people in Silver Jubilee Year, 1977, is much more the personal creation of Elizabeth II.

One uncharted course in which she showed a hand both firm and innovative was the education of her eldest son. In the long and painstaking series of decisions it involved, she relied heavily on the rough-hewn good sense of her husband. If, in retrospect, it seems inevitable that Prince Charles should have gone to the same schools as his father, these were far from foregone conclusions in the first few years of his life. The young Duke of Cornwall showed little of the self-confidence one of his rank would need to survive in the brutal amoral world of young schoolboys away from home. But the Queen and Prince Philip had pooled their own very different experiences, hers the traditionally sheltered royal education at the hands of governesses and tutors, his a disrupted progress through private schools in France, England, Germany and Scotland. They were determined to make a bold departure from the pattern established by their forbears, and their every effort with the young Charles was directed towards it. They wanted the heir to the throne to be educated outside his home, in the company of other boys his own age, from the earliest possible moment.

It had never been attempted before. The education of Princes of Wales has throughout British history provided a forum for argument, experiment and even intrigue, resulting as often as not in unhappiness and failure. From the time of Edward I, who was sent to France to be educated, most monarchs have tried to create super-monarchs in their own image; others, such as the Hanoverians, have been more intent on defusing the threat posed to their own rule by their own heir. But it was the last hundred years which provided the most instructive examples, all too familiar to Queen Victoria's two great-great-grandchildren in the 1950s. Elizabeth II and her consort were above all concerned to learn from the mistakes made by Victoria and hers.

Elizabeth and Philip's supreme good sense was to realize that a contemporary constitutional monarch needs a good, all-round education much more than any form of special training. Since the death of George IV in 1830, when monarchs have reigned rather than ruled, the one essential requirement of a sovereign has been that he command the respect of his people. It would be absurd to expect consistent ability, even competence, of any office passed on by heredity. Given a character which his people can respect, from a distance, any sovereign can survive; without it, the monarchy would be in its nearest danger of collapse, as it was in 1830, and as it would have been in 1936, had not the Duke of York quickly grown into the breach left by the abdication of his elder brother. King George VI was a historic example of a monarch who started out with respect, if few other qualifications, and was subsequently enlarged by his office. Prince Charles himself has said: 'There isn't any power. There can be influence. The influence is in direct ratio to the respect people have for you.'

Of his upbringing he has also said: 'I've learnt the way a monkey learns – by watching its parents.' Prince Philip has always been cogent on this: 'Training isn't necessary. They do on-the-job training, so to speak, and learn the trade, or business, or craft, just from being with us and watching us function, and seeing the whole organization around us. They can't avoid it. What is much more difficult is bringing them up as people.' Victoria and Albert saw things precisely the other way round.

Who Should Educate The Prince Of Wales? was the title of a provocative and anonymous pamphlet published in 1843, when the future King Edward VII was just two years old. His mother, Victoria, was as intent as the pamphleteer and his huge readership on producing a model Prince – ideally, to her, a working model of her beloved husband. The Queen was aware of the inadequacies of her own education, thanks in part to the plain speaking of her uncle, the King of Hanover: 'She was more ignorant on her accession than any girl of her age in the world.' But she was more anxious, as were her subjects, to eradicate the memory of George III's lecherous sons, her other uncles, of whom she shared Shelley's view ('the dregs of their dull race') rather than Lord Melbourne's ('jolly fellows'). The plans she and Albert laid for their son's upbringing, even before he had been born, were partly by way of atonement. More important, they constituted an elaborate effort to secure a shaky and discredited monarchy, and to lay the foundations for its survival into a more democratic age.

The educational treadmill they devised for poor Bertie was founded on a fundamental misreading of history, swallowed wholesale from their over-trusted German confidant, Baron Christian von Stockmar. He persuaded them that the mistakes of George III's sons were caused by their inadequate education, and that this had been largely responsible for the gradual shift of executive power from the monarch to the monarch's ministers. But their education had been excellent: George IV, if not William IV, was one of Britain's most cultivated kings. The alteration in the unwritten constitution owed much more to the industrial revolution, and the nineteenth-century electoral reforms which followed it, than to the character of the sovereign. The growth of diverse political parties, and the alternatives thus available to a more broadly enfranchised nation, forced the monarchy into its now familiar non-political role. The alternative, and the only way to retain executive State powers, was for the King to identify himself with political factions, which would have ensured his downfall with theirs. He could not, as Sir Lewis Namier observed, 'in turn captain opposite teams'.

Victoria was plainly surprised by the limits to her constitutional powers, and constantly attempted to exceed them. Prince Albert was himself a man of considerable ability, whose intellect and imagination were quite the match of most of his wife's ministers. He was, as Lord John Russell put it, 'an informal and potent member of all Cabinets', and he believed that his son would need similar qualities to ensure the monarchy's survival. So, with Stockmar, Prince Albert personally devised a comprehensive programme designed to drum them into him.

At the age of seven, the Prince was handed from the nursery to a formidable team of tutors. Their principal, a thirty-year-old Eton master aptly named Henry Birch, was instructed quite simply to fashion an 'executive Governor of the State ... the repository of all the moral and intellectual qualities by which it is held together, and under the guidance of which it advances in the great path of civilization'. Lessons in the Palace lasted at first six, then seven, hours a day, six days a week. Bertie worked longer hours, and enjoyed shorter holidays, than any of his schoolboy contemporaries. Birch had orders to ensure that he was thoroughly exhausted by the end of each day; among other physical pursuits, he was drilled daily by a drill sergeant to deflect his budding skills at dancing. Even the tutors began to think the régime too demanding. 'You will wear him out too early.... Make him climb trees! Run! Leap! Row!' the French master, Dr Voisin, urged Birch's successor. 'In many things, savages are much better educated than we are.' But Albert and Stockmar would have none of it. The results were disastrous.

Before he was ten, the Prince was on the edge of a nervous breakdown. Days of utter lethargy began to follow a few of intense activity. There were outbursts of destructive rage. He would stand in a corner screaming and stamping, or hurl things against walls and through windows, before falling into a state of complete physical collapse. His father devised a series of punishments for this behaviour, but none, however severe, could curb it.

The young Bertie's world was entirely one of adults. At one stage he was sent to attend meetings of Pop, the Eton debating society, but behaved with such boorishness, and displayed such ignorance, that he was quickly withdrawn from the society of his fellows. When he was finally sent out into the world, to Oxford, his father was insistent that 'his position and life *must* be different from that of other undergraduates'. He wore the distinctive gown and gold-tufted cap of the nobleman; professors came to his home to teach him and six hand-picked aristocrats; students had to rise whenever he entered a lecture hall or common room. Prince Albert at this time dismissed him as 'a thorough and cunning lazybones', and Queen Victoria even told friends that he was mentally deficient. But his tutors found in him powers of application, and qualities of openness and honesty, which his regimented life had all but suppressed.

Thanks to a liberating tour of America in 1860, and a happier time at Cambridge, Bertie gradually began to escape the shadows of his youth and adolescence. He grew from an overweight, oversexed, utterly repressed Prince of Wales into a mature, diplomatic and immensely popular King. For over forty years as the pillar of a glittering London court, he eroded memories of the gambling and marital scandals with which his youth had besmirched the monarchy. On his thirtieth birthday, soon after giving evidence in the Mordaunt divorce case, he lay apparently dying from typhoid; his sudden recovery six weeks later had the nation, surprised at its own fickleness, demanding a day of national rejoicing. His strength of character ensured his security and success, thirty years later, on the throne. Some legacies of his upbringing, notably those fits of rage, never left him. But he was aware of it, and took pains to see that his own sons were spared such suffering.

King Edward VII was a grandfather four years before he acceded to the throne. As Prince of Wales, he had had to cope with his widowed mother's intransigence when setting about the education of his own heir. His initial plan was to send Prince Albert Victor ('Eddy' to his family) to public school and university, and his second son George to Dartmouth and a naval career. But at only seven months Prince Eddy was diagnosed a weak baby, and soon showed himself a backward child. The tutor engaged by their father, the Rev. John Neale Dalton (father of the Labour politician Hugh Dalton), found that only Prince George's company could inspire Eddy's constitutional lethargy to any interest in anything. He advised that they should on no account be separated.

Their grandmother had set her heart on sending Prince Eddy to Wellington, a school with a military slant of which the Prince of Wales was a governor. She was content for George to enter the Navy, but Eddy was to be King, and should not be allowed to acquire the rough habits and nationalistic attitudes of Service life. It took all her son's and Dalton's ingenuity to dissuade her; the Palace memos that flew on this subject are themselves full of cautionary tales for anyone contemplating the education of a monarch. The Prince of Wales's first concern was that his sons should grow up, unlike him, with people rather than books, out of doors more than in classrooms, left to find their own levels rather than programmed for perfection. But thanks to Dalton, he was now even more intent on keeping them together. Victoria was coaxed into permitting them both to attend Dartmouth 'as an experiment'.

King George v later recalled:

> It never did me any good to be a prince, I can tell you, and many was the time I wished I hadn't been. [Dartmouth] was a pretty tough place and, so far from making allowance for our disadvantages, the other boys made a point of taking it out of us, on the grounds that they'd never be able to do it later on. There was a lot of fighting among the cadets, and the rule was that if challenged you had to accept. So they used to make me go up and challenge the bigger boys – I was awfully small then – and I'd get a hiding time and again. . . .

It may have made a man of George, but it just about destroyed poor Eddy. Dalton reported to the Prince of Wales that Eddy 'fails not in one or two subjects, but in all'. His 'abnormally dormant' disposition made it impossible for him 'to fix his attention to any given subject for more than a few minutes consecutively'. And even that was only achieved thanks to the reassuring presence of his younger brother. Plans to part their ways were again abandoned, and Eddy was sent to join George aboard HMS *Bacchante*. Between 1879 and 1892, accompanied by Dalton and a team of tutors specially chosen to assist his backwardness, Eddy accompanied George on three extended world cruises, the one still fading away, the other growing to the full flush of manhood. Those years, wrote King George v's biographer, Harold Nicolson, developed in him 'a quality more forceful than ordinary manliness – a categorical sense of duty ... which became the fly-wheel of his life'.

In 1892 their ways did at last part. After a brief sojourn together in France, Prince George was back in the Navy as a midshipman, while Prince Eddy was being crammed for Cambridge. 'I do not think he can possibly derive much benefit,' the head tutor reported to Dalton. 'He hardly knows the meaning of the words "to read".' After Cambridge, Eddy served a bored term in the Hussars, then began to devote what energies he had to a life of somewhat scandalous dissipation; to this day, theories survive that Prince Eddy was Jack the Ripper. For once, Queen Victoria and the Prince of Wales were agreed: his only chance of salvation was 'a good sensible wife with some considerable character'. She was found in Princess May of Teck, to whom Prince Eddy proposed in December 1891. A month later, aged twenty-seven, he was dead of pneumonia.

For all his lack of promise, Prince Albert Victor in death stirred his family and the nation to paroxysms of grief. His brother George, robbed of the only human being with whom he could enjoy an absolutely equal friendship, was desolated. 'No two brothers could have loved each other more than we did,' he wrote to his mother, Queen Alexandra. 'Alas! It is only now that I have found out how deeply I have loved him.' The Prince's devastation was compounded by the fact that he was now heir to the throne, and would have to abandon his naval career for a study of the constitution. His standard of education, as he himself readily admitted, was 'below that of the average country gentleman educated at a public school'. The Navy had given him a strict sense of duty, orderly habits, a strong instinct for command and obedience and a deep feeling for conservative orthodoxy. But he was woefully ignorant, for instance, of contemporary domestic and foreign politics; his main interests were yachting, shooting, stamp-collecting and the management of the Sandringham estates. Even after falling in love with and marrying his brother's fiancée, Princess May (who later became Queen Mary), he remained emotionally immature.

His father came to the rescue. Edward VII took a great delight in endowing his virtuous son with all the fatherly companionship he himself had been denied. 'We are more like brothers than father and son,' he wrote to him. He made George, created successively Duke of York and Prince of Wales, privy to all State secrets, against a reversal of his own parents' policy, and instructed him in the ways of the world. But he could do nothing about that emotional deficiency. King George V conspicuously failed to recreate this happy and productive relationship with his own children.

George told his friend Lord Derby: 'My father was frightened of his mother, I was frightened of my father, and I am damned well going to see to it that my children are frightened of me.' Throughout his life, he treated his family as if it were a ship's company, of which he was both master and martinet. His eldest son, when Duke of Windsor, recalled in his memoirs:

> We were, in fact, figuratively speaking, always on parade, a fact that he would never allow us to forget. If we appeared before him with our Navy lanyards a fraction of an inch out of place, or with our dirks or our sporrans awry, there would be an outburst worthy of the quarter-deck of a warship. Another greeted the appearance of one of us – it may well have been me – with hands stuffed into trouser pockets. Lala [their nanny] was immediately summoned and ordered to sew up the pockets of our sailor suits, a royal command which, despite some inward reservations, she did not dare to disobey.

The King deeply detested change, and decreed that what had been good enough for him would be good enough for his sons. A senior tutor, H.P. Hansell, was therefore engaged to prepare Prince Edward and Prince Albert (known to their family as David and Bertie, later respectively King Edward VIII and King George VI) for entry to Dartmouth. Hansell urged that they be sent to preparatory school, where, he argued, they would benefit from the stimulus of competition, and gain valuable early experience of community life. 'My brother and I,' George replied, 'never went to preparatory school. The Navy will teach David all he needs to know.'

This time it was the younger brother who lagged behind. Prince Edward, though slight, was physically robust; his natural charm, combined with his quick brain and genuine modesty, ensured easy success. Prince Albert was more diffident, suffered from a stammer, and was invariably bottom of his class. 'One could wish', wrote his tutor to the King, 'that he had more of Prince Edward's keenness and application.' King George VI's biographer, Sir John Wheeler-Bennett, quotes a contemporary's judgement that 'it was like comparing an ugly duckling with a cock pheasant'. Through a characteristic effort of will, however, Bertie later began to make up lost ground, and was to enjoy a happy and successful naval career after his elder brother had been diverted to training for kingship.

Edward was sent to France and Germany, to learn their languages and study their politics, and thence, reluctantly, to Oxford. At Magdalen he insisted on living in his own rooms in college – a happy precedent for Prince Charles – and was soon known around the university as 'the Pragger-Wagger'. He beagled, kept a string of polo ponies, played roulette and frequented the college steward's bar, 'Gunners'. (Gunstone, the steward, was in the habit of inserting a banana in the neck of a bottle filled with burning paper, so that the banana would be pulled inside. This more than anything else impressed the King on his one visit to his son in Oxford. 'By God,' he said, 'that's one of the smartest tricks I've ever seen.') This routine Edward recalled in his memoirs as 'tranquil, sober and serious' days. 'Bookish he will never be,' reported the college president, Sir Herbert Warren, to the King, 'not a "Beauclerk", still less a "British Solomon".' George v was not in the least concerned.

Edward viii, in fact, seemed in later life to think education a positive disadvantage for a prince. Remembering how little he learnt from his tutor, Mr Hansell, and being 'unable to recall anything brilliant or original that he ever said', the Duke of Windsor commented: 'No doubt, in view of the restraints laid upon the Monarchy, this was all for the best. To have put a Prince in the direct line of succession under a bold and opinionated teacher might well have led to the one conflict with which the constitutional system cannot cope.' At least Oxford taught him something of his fellow man. 'All the time', according to Warren's report, 'he was learning more and more every day of men, gauging character, watching its play, getting to know what Englishmen are like, both individually and in the mass....'

This would have stood him in good stead at Dartmouth, where he had been mercilessly ragged. The other cadets were fond of dyeing his hair red, and on one occasion 'guillotined' him in a window-frame to remind him of his heritage. 'Nothing I had ever learnt under Mr Hansell', he wrote, 'seemed to supply a solution' to such problems.

Prince Edward did not risk taking a degree at Oxford. Nor did Prince Albert when he spent a year at Cambridge after the 1914–18 war – in which both saw service, though not as active as either would have wished. In the early 1920s Albert was content to build up a solid reputation at home, particularly in industrial welfare and youth work, while the Prince of Wales scored a series of dazzling personal triumphs overseas. It was this cautious, determined conscientiousness which stood the Duke of York in such good stead in 1936, when his brother's abdication suddenly pitchforked him into a job for which he was totally unprepared.

George vi's daughter and her husband thus had a lengthy chapter of accidents from which to learn. Elizabeth ii also knew that she herself had met few beyond the Palace walls before the age of eighteen, when she had persuaded her father to let her sign on as a second subaltern in the wartime ATS. She and Prince Philip were all too aware of the disadvantages of sequestering their eldest son at home. But they had equal evidence that it was no use expecting him to melt inconspicuously into the life of a boarding-school, like any other child. Simpering royal commentators were cooing in column after column that Charles and Anne were 'ordinary' children being brought up in a 'normal' way, but it was obvious to their parents that this was impossible. No one put the problem better than the Duke of Windsor, whose memoirs were published at this time (1951): 'The pleased incredulity with which the public reacts to the elementary demonstrations on the part of Royalty that they are, after all, like other people is matched by the public's firm refusal to accept them as such.'

The best Elizabeth and Philip could hope for was to guide Charles, by their own fond attentions, into sharing the lives of other children without himself unduly suffering. Prince Philip put this forcefully to his biographer, Basil Boothroyd, when Prince Charles was already at public school.

> People talk about a normal upbringing. What is a normal upbringing? What you really mean is: was I insisting that they should go through all the disadvantages of being brought up in the way other people are brought up? Precisely that – disadvantages. There's always this idea about treating them exactly like other children. In fact it means they're treated much worse, because they're known by name and by association.... It's all very well to say they're treated the same as everybody else, but it's impossible. I think that what is possible, and in fact necessary, is that they should realize they're not anonymous. This has got to come at some stage.

The first step with Prince Charles – and an innovation of more consequence than the common sense behind it suggests – was to treat him exactly the same as his younger sister and brothers. All four were introduced at the earliest ages to the widest possible choice of pastimes: swimming, sailing, shooting, fishing, go-karting, polo. In Charles's case, fishing, shooting and polo became abiding passions, at all of which he in time became more proficient than his father. 'I've always tried to help them master at least one thing,' said Prince Philip, 'because as soon as a child feels self-confidence in one area, it spills over into all the others. You even notice that if they feel they've made a real personal accomplishment of that kind, then this is immediately reflected even in their academic performance.'

He never cared too much, however, about academic prowess. Like any other parent, Prince Philip went through school reports, but there were rarely recriminations. 'I don't really take them frightfully seriously. I say: "Look, I'm only going to bother if you're permanently bottom. I really couldn't care less where you are. Just stay in the middle, that's all I ask."' He has always, anyway, disapproved of the importance attached to examinations.

> Children go through enormous changes. For a time they're in phase with life around them, then they go out of phase and become unlivable with, and

everything they do is wrong and cross-grained and maddening. Then suddenly it all comes right for a bit. Then they go off on another tack. It's impossible at any point to say 'This is what they're going to be like'. The pendulum's got to swing a lot more before it settles down.

Prince Philip is not the strict, disciplinarian parent that has been painted. His idea of a major family crime is dishonesty – 'by which I mean that if you ask them a question, they must give you an honest answer'. Nor has he been an over-inquisitive father: 'There are often questions you'd like to ask, but it's much better not to unless it's really necessary.' His children's behaviour, he told Boothroyd, had been average to good. 'I think they do silly things occasionally, but it's nearly always satisfactorily resolved, more by discussion than anything.'

Thus Prince Charles was consulted about his own education at every stage after his prep school. 'From the beginning,' said his father,

> I was careful not to make a rigid plan – I haven't for any of them – until some sort of foreseeable situation arose. I said 'Well, here are the alternatives: you've seen Eton, you know the place, it's right on our doorstep [at Windsor], you can more or less come home any time you like. Its disadvantages are that every time you hiccup you'll have the whole of the national press on your shoulders. Also, Eton is frequently in the news, and when it is it's going to reflect on you. If you go to the north of Scotland you'll be out of sight, and they're going to think twice about taking an aeroplane to get up there, so it's got to be a major crisis before they'll actually turn up, and you'll be able to get on with things. . . .' And we had a general discussion, and I said 'Well, it's up to you.'

The Prince of Wales has repaid the compliment: 'My parents were marvellous in this way. They'd outline all the possibilities, and in the end it was up to you. My father had a particularly strong influence, and it was very good for me. I had perfect confidence in his judgement.'

Family decisions are still taken on a committee basis, one member, one vote. Again, Elizabeth II and her husband have learnt from their family's recent history. As Prince Philip put it:

> It's no use saying do this, do that, don't do this, don't do that. You can warn them about certain things – that's about the most you can do – or you can say this is the situation you are in, these are the choices, on balance it looks as if this is the sensible one, go away and think it over, and come back and let me know what you think.

There were times, of course, when the children's wishes were overruled. 'It's very easy, when children want something, to say no immediately. I think it's quite important not to give an unequivocal answer at once. Much better to think it over. Then if you do eventually say no, I think they really accept it.'

Prince Philip's free-wheeling nature has also propelled him, of course, into expansive pronouncements on such subjects as education in more general terms. 'The art of education' [he once said]

> is to combine formal training with as wide a variety of experiences as possible, including some which involve a calculated risk. I think education is intended to produce intelligent, morally strong, self-sufficient human beings willing and capable of improving the machinery of living which man has created for his enjoyment.

On a visit to the USA in 1956, he was a little more specific. 'The Queen and I want Charles to go to school with other boys of his generation and learn to live with other children, and to absorb from childhood the discipline imposed by education with others.' The royal couple had already been making a series of visits, private and public, to British boys' schools, and had entertained a number of headmasters socially at Buckingham Palace. But Philip's announcement brought forth a predictable shower of advice.

In the forefront was Lord Altrincham (now John Grigg), whose attack on the monarchy in the August 1957 edition of his journal, the *National and English Review*, had earned him a televised slap in the face and lasting public obloquy. It is generally forgotten that Altrincham was a self-declared monarchist, and that the rest of his review's special edition on the monarchy was devoted to glowing assessments by such passionate loyalists as Dermot Morrah, Prince Charles's previous biographer. Altrincham protested that he made his criticism in the Queen's own interests; there were few, however, who bore this in increasingly apoplectic mind as they read how the monarchy had 'lamentably failed to live with the times' and that the court, unlike the society it was supposed to reflect, remained 'a tight little enclave of English ladies and gentlemen'.

The Queen's already announced decision that Prince Charles would go to a private preparatory school was one topic to which Altrincham addressed himself.

> Will she have the wisdom [he wrote] to give her children an education very different from her own? Will she, above all, see to it that Prince Charles is equipped with all the knowledge he can absorb without injury to his health, and that he mixes during his formative years with children who will one day be bus-drivers, dockers, engineers etc., not merely with future landowners or stockbrokers?

A minority of socialist MPs joined him in the cry that the heir to the throne should attend a state school, and mix with the less wealthy and less privileged of his future subjects.

The feeling at the Palace was not that such a course was impossible. Indeed, it had obvious cosmetic advantages at a time when Elizabeth II was concerned to bring the monarchy into closer touch with a broader cross-section of her people. (She had recently introduced Palace luncheon parties with more democratic guest lists, abolished the presentation of debutantes at court, welcomed the introduction of life peerages, and opened part of Buckingham Palace to the public as the Queen's Gallery.) But would not the pupils, perhaps even the staff, at a London secondary or grammar school be even more in awe of the heir to the throne than the sons of the well-to-do? Would not a private boarding-school, enclosed in its own grounds, afford a greater chance of privacy than a school open to the streets of the capital? If Charles were to be the first heir to the throne in British history to be sent away to school so young, might it not be done by degrees, rather than by so abrupt and melodramatic a gesture towards democracy?

If this reads like special pleading, so it was. Apart from any such considerations, the Queen and Prince Philip, like a large proportion of the British public, were convinced that the standards of private education were still higher than those of state schools. They were about to make their son suffer quite enough, they could tell, without risking substandard tuition to undermine his future. And, given a system which permitted freedom of educational choice to the wealthy, they had as much right as any other well-heeled British couple to make their own decision.

A boarding-school, and a private one, it was to be. Prince Charles was too young to be consulted about his first school, and had anyway made it more than clear that – like any other child his age – he was reluctant to leave home at all. But the Queen and Prince Philip had looked over a number of preparatory schools, including the one Philip had himself attended. It had moved since the 1930s, and was scarcely the same school. But it provided everything they were looking for. And, despite himself, Prince Philip found the idea of sending his son to his old school downright satisfying.

9

Cheam
1957-62

He is still a little shy, but very popular ... passionately keen on and promising at games ... academically, a good average....

Prince Charles's first end-of-term
report from Cheam

JUST BEFORE THE First World War Prince Louis of Battenberg, then First Sea Lord, had occasion to be impressed by the polished manners of two midshipmen under his command. He asked them where they had been educated. On discovering they were both ex-pupils of Cheam preparatory school, the Duke of Edinburgh's grandfather decreed that henceforth all male members of the Battenberg family would go there.

When Prince Philip enrolled at the school in 1930, it had been established for more than 200 years in the Surrey town from which it takes its name. But the school from which it grew has an even longer history, giving Cheam its claim to be England's oldest prep school. The pupils of the Rev. George Aldritch, founder of a small private establishment in London for the sons of the gentry, can be traced back to the reign of Charles I; the records of Caius College, Cambridge, show one of them matriculating in 1650. The Great Plague of 1665 forced Aldritch out of London to Cheam, where he joined forces with a local school in a house called Whitehall, which still stands (it is now an antique shop) in the High Street. After several further moves within the town limits, Cheam School settled itself in 1719 onto the thirteen-acre site it still occupied on Prince Philip's arrival in 1930. By then, however, a railway station had materialized nearby, and urban London was fast encroaching.

Thus in 1934, the year after Philip's departure, it moved again: to a sixty-five-acre site in the village of Headley, near the Hampshire Downs. Though now in Hampshire, the school's postal address was in Berkshire, and it was still named after a small town in Surrey. The rest of Cheam's pedigree was equally quixotic, thanks particularly to two colourful headmasters among the fourteen the school had had in some 300 years. In 1752, when there were just fifteen pupils on the school roll, Cheam was bought by a reforming young clergyman called William Gilpin, who went on to become Vicar of Boldre and achieve modest renown as the author of a series of illustrated travel books. He is better known to posterity as the original for Dr Syntax, in whose adventures Rowlandson and William Combe parodied Gilpin's literary style. He may also have been the model for Mr Jennings, the school-master in Smollett's *Peregrine Pickle*. At Cheam, he is best remembered for a very un-eighteenth-century aversion to corporal punishment; he intro-duced a system of fines and detentions, firmly enshrined on paper in case his rage got the better of his judgement. An equally eccentric nineteenth-century successor was Robert Stammers Tabor, who took over the school in 1856 (and, like Gilpin, handed it on to his son after him). Tabor, something of a snob, initiated a new system of address for the aristocratic pupils which Cheam always seems to have attracted: a peer was called 'My darling child', the son of a peer 'My dear child', and a commoner 'My child'.

Tabor would have enjoyed working out a new category for the eight-year-old pupil who joined Cheam School on 23 September 1957: Charles, Duke of Cornwall, the first heir apparent to have been sent to a preparatory school in British history. The joint headmasters, Peter Beck and Mark Wheeler, both Cambridge graduates, contented themselves with continuing the Hill House tradition, as requested by the Queen: he would be 'Charles' to his fellow-pupils, 'Prince Charles' to members of staff, whom he in turn would address normally as 'Sir'.

The school's most distinguished old boy was the new recruit's father. Prince Philip's cousin, the Marquess of Milford Haven, had also been there. Among other former pupils were numbered one Prime Minister, Henry Addington (later Viscount Sidmouth); one Speaker of the House of Com-mons, Colonel Douglas Clifton-Brown (later Viscount Ruffside); two Vice-roys of India, Lord Willingdon and Lord Hardinge of Penshurst (friend of Edward VII, and father of the private secretary to Edward VIII and George VI); Sir Iain Hamilton, military commander of the ill-fated Gallipoli expedition; Lord Dunsany, the Irish writer of plays, prose and verse; and Lord Ran-dolph Churchill, father of Sir Winston, who according to his son was 'most kindly treated and quite content' at the school.

Charles had already visited Cheam with his parents and his sister. 'You won't be able to jump up and down on *these* beds,' the Queen told him as he gazed with dismay upon the 200-year-old springless wooden frame and its unyielding hair mattress. Beyond the lily pond was a happier sight: a swimming pool. As the Royal Family roamed the tranquil school grounds, the peace disturbed only by jets from the nearby US air base, they agreed that the sixty-five acres should provide the required insulation from the outside world of sightseers and pressmen; its copious undergrowth, however, would also provide excellent cover for intruders, so it was decided that the young Prince's detective should accompany him, and live in the grounds. Beck and Wheeler further complied with the Queen's wishes by sending a letter to all parents before the beginning of the autumn term:

> It is the wish of the Queen and Prince Philip that there shall be no alteration in the way the school is run and that Prince Charles shall be treated the same as other boys.... It will be a great help if you will explain this. His parents' wishes are that he should be given exactly the same education and upbringing as the other boys at the school.

Once again, however, it was impossible for anyone to expect Charles to merge inconspicuously into the beginning-of-term throng. He remembers those first few days at Cheam as the most miserable of his life. His mother recalls him shuddering with horror as they began the long overnight train journey from Balmoral to London, to be followed by the sixty-mile drive to Headley. On arrival, in his grey school uniform, Charles raised his blue school cap politely to Mr Beck, then watched his parents drive away. A few hours later the maths master, David Munir, who had been detailed to keep a special eye on the Prince, looked out into the school grounds. One small boy, 'very much in need of a haircut', stood conspicuously apart, a solitary and utterly wretched figure. Cheam boys were just that much older than the Prince's fellow-pupils at Hill House; despite – perhaps because of – their parents' urgings, they could not accept the heir to the throne as just another of the twelve new boys. Charles himself had no experience at all of forcing his way into a group of strangers, winning the acceptance of his peers. The Cheam boys couldn't quite believe he was among them. Nor, for that matter, could Prince Charles.

Cheam (fees then £100 a term) had a hundred pupils between the ages of eight and fourteen; Prince Charles's school number was 89. The day began at 7.15 a.m. with the rising bell, followed by prayers at 7.45 and breakfast at 8. For the first time in his life, Charles was sharing an uncarpeted room with other boys, making his own bed, cleaning his own shoes, waiting on others at table, and keeping his clothes in a wicker basket under his bed (known to the boys as 'the dog basket'). Lessons began at 9 and continued, with break, until lunch at 1. There were half-holidays on Wednesdays and

Saturdays; on Sundays there was an extra half-hour in bed before the school parade to the nearby parish church of St Peter's.

Charles happily wrote the compulsory minimum of one letter home per week, and was always among the first to snap up his weekly half-pound allowance of sweets. Though he was losing his puppy fat, the Prince was still a plumpish boy. When the change to a school diet prompted a few stomach upsets, he confided to the first-year teacher, Miss Margaret Cowlishaw, that he wasn't used to 'all this rich food' at home.

No 'tuck' boxes were allowed, as at most such schools, but sweets were 'bought' out of the boys' recommended pocket-money of 25 shillings a term; in fact, the boys did not handle the money themselves, using instead a system of credits. So the young Prince was still denied any experience of coin of the realm, itself enough to render apocryphal one of the first Cheam stories to make the British newspapers. Charles, it went, was kept short of pocket-money by his parents, so had held an auction of his personal belongings to raise money for more sweets. For once, he learnt that newspaper fictions can have their rewards. As the story wended its way into the American press, the Association of Retail Confectioners of America, then in conference in San Francisco, voted to send across a massive food parcel containing everything from bubble gum and jelly beans to peanut butter and tootsie rolls. 'We were told the Prince was short of candy,' said the accompanying note, 'so our committee unanimously passed a resolution to the effect that we ought to pitch in and help him out of a jam.'

It did him no harm in the school popularity stakes. According to Peter Beck, Charles quickly became a good mixer. A special friend was the head-master's daughter, Mary Beck, the only girl at the school. Charles's loneliness, indeed, may have been only in his own mind; he was already aware that other children might befriend him for the wrong reasons. It was often the nicest boys, he recalls, who hung back, not wishing to be seen 'sucking up' to him; those who forced their attentions on him were often those whom he liked least. Throughout his life, he has felt the need to make an extra effort in such company. He knows the heir to the throne is by definition the focal point of any room's attention; to justify that attention, he has to try to appear more than usually interesting. It is a tricky psychological problem, which must account in large degree for the painful shyness of the eight-year-old schoolboy. As he strove to overcome this, his fellows marked him down as a bit of a lone wolf.

At Cheam, furthermore, he began to be haunted by another shadow which has pursued him ever after: that of his father, an outgoing, gregarious man who had never had to cope with such problems. At Cheam, after all, Philip was Prince of Greece and Denmark, not of England or Wales. The press were not pursuing him from bush to bush, and the other boys looked on him with no awe. While academically undistinguished, he had shone on the sports field (first team goalkeeper and captain of the cricket XI) and Charles knew his father was hoping for some such achievement from him.

Charles's lessons at Cheam were of course geared to the Common Entrance Examination taken before admission to most British public schools (although, as it transpired, he was to attend one which did not require it). History remained an abiding interest, not least because he now knew it concerned his ancestors and was already preparing to receive him. In geography he also shone, again because his parents' tours had made the globe a familiar place. Maths remained an utter mystery, closely followed by Latin and Greek. Before the afternoon lessons there were games, about which he remained unenthusiastic (despite evidence to the contrary in his end-of-term reports), or other outdoor activities such as camping or wildlife study, very much modelled on the precepts of Lord Baden-Powell, though the school had no Boy Scout troop as such. As at Hill House, the Cheam gymnasium became one of Charles's favourite haunts, where athletic rough-and-tumble often developed into a mild schoolboy fracas. Charles soon had a reputation for giving as good as he got. He was particularly sensitive to jokes about his plumpness, and took days to recover after hearing the boy beneath him in a collapsed rugby scrum cry 'Oh, do get *off*, Fatty.' The school was visited regularly by a barber from Harrod's, Cecil Cox, who once saw an older boy douse Charles's head under a cold tap; the visitor watched impressed as the Prince filled a bath with cold water, wrestled with his assailant, and finally forced him in fully-clothed – only to be pulled in himself.

This was one of many Cheam anecdotes, some truer than others, which found their way into the press during Charles's first term. 'Even the school barber was in the pay of the newspapers,' snorted Prince Philip. Frequently, and not surprisingly, there had to be complex inquiries before school crimes, apparently to be laid at Charles's door, were found to be the work of others. Within a week of his arrival at the school, for instance, Charles's name had been deeply carved in the back of a pew in the parish church. This was one story the newspapers did get hold of, but Peter Beck made them print corrections when other boys at last admitted their guilt.

In an attempt to head off journalists' intrusions, Beck and Wheeler had held a press visit to the school before term began, and made a special plea to be left thereafter in peace. But of the eighty-eight days of term, there were stories in one newspaper or another on sixty-eight. Again, the effects were unpleasant. Rumours abounded of boys and staff accepting bribes from pressmen. They were never proved true, but a tense atmosphere of mutual suspicion developed. Morale at the school began to suffer. Although the

Prince's detective coped with most intruders, there were occasionally more dramatic incidents. One night he aroused the headmaster after seeing a prowler on the roof of Charles's dormitory; a lengthy search was conducted, but no one found; only much later did a young friend of Charles's, David Daukes, confess to getting back into bed seconds before the search-party arrived. Even schoolboy pranks were becoming worthy of the police incident book. Once again, the Queen decided to safeguard her son's education by direct action.

In the Christmas holidays her press secretary, Richard Colville, invited all newspaper editors to a meeting at Buckingham Palace. Peter Beck told the gathering of the disruption their employees were causing at his school. Bribes had been offered, though none to his knowledge accepted. Everyone felt they were under constant surveillance. The Prince's first term had ended unhappily for all. Recalling the pleas he had made before and during Charles's time at Hill House, Colville spoke plainly to the editors. Either it stopped, and the press printed only those stories of genuine significance, or the Queen would abandon her cherished plan to educate her son at normal schools, and withdraw him behind the Palace walls to the care of tutors – and it would be the fault of the press.

Duly sobered, British editors ensured that Cheam was little more molested during Charles's four years there. Only the foreign photographers persisted, climbing over the newly heightened walls and building hides in the undergrowth; on one occasion Mary Beck, drawing her father's attention to an unseasonal firework display in the garden, unwittingly assisted in the capture of one intruder, who had been using infra-red equipment to take pictures after dark.

Six months later, however, there was a story 'of genuine significance' to be written. It was the summer term of 1958, the end of Charles's first year at Cheam, and the Commonwealth Games were being held in Cardiff. The Queen had been due to perform the closing ceremony at Cardiff Arms Park on 26 July, but a sinusitis operation enforced her absence. The Duke of Edinburgh took her place, and introduced a tape-recorded message from Her Majesty, which was played over the loudspeakers of the packed stadium. Charles and a few friends filed into Peter Beck's study to watch the event on television. After Prince Philip's opening remarks, they heard the Queen's voice say: 'I want to take this opportunity of speaking to all Welsh people, not only in this arena, but wherever they may be. The British Empire and Commonwealth Games in the capital, together with all the activities of the Festival of Wales, have made this a memorable year for the principality. I have therefore decided to mark it further by an act which will, I hope, give as much pleasure to all Welshmen as it does to me.' There was a buzz of anticipation; many in the arena had guessed what she was going to say. 'I intend to create my son Charles Prince of Wales today.'

The tape had to be stopped as an enormous cheer convulsed the stadium, and 36,000 Welsh voices broke into 'God Bless the Prince of Wales'. When the clamour died down, the Queen's voice continued: 'When he is grown up, I will present him to you at Caernarvon.'

The scene in Beck's study at Cheam might have given the Queen a moment's pause. The headmaster, who with Charles had known what was coming, watched a look of dire unease cloud his face as the other boys spontaneously joined in the clapping and cheering. For a mother trying to bring her son up as much like other boys as possible, aware that his own emerging character had still far from mastered its environment, it was an odd piece of timing. The Queen now perhaps numbers this moment among the mistakes she has confessed to having made in Charles's upbringing. His own memory of the occasion is vivid. 'I remember being acutely embarrassed when it was announced. I heard this marvellous great cheer coming from the stadium in Cardiff, and I think for a little boy of nine it was rather bewildering. All the others turned and looked at me in amazement. And it perhaps didn't mean all that much then; later on, as I grew older, it became apparent what it meant.'

In the headmaster's study that afternoon, Charles automatically also became Earl of Chester and Knight Companion of the Most Noble Order of the Garter. They go, as it were, with the job. The Earldom of Chester is the oldest of all the dignities of the heir to the throne, dating from 1254, when it was bestowed on the future Edward I. Since then it has always been conjoined with the title of Prince of Wales – though both, unlike the Dukedom of Cornwall, are life peerages, which merge into the Crown when their holder becomes monarch, to be bestowed at his discretion upon his eldest son. The monarch and the Prince of Wales are the only two ex-officio of the twenty-six Knights of the Garter, Europe's oldest secular order of chivalry; the Prince's stall, by ancient tradition, is the second in rank (though the first on the left) in St George's Chapel at Windsor, but may not be occupied until he has been formally dubbed and installed by the sovereign. The Queen, perhaps having reflected on her son's reaction at the age of nine years and eight months, did not perform this ceremony (which also entitled him to wear the Garter's resplendent robes and insignia) for another ten years. By that time, in June 1968, it was part of the build-up to his investiture at Caernarvon and his emergence into full-time public life.

Those days were still, however, mercifully distant as Charles enjoyed his summer holidays at Balmoral and shrugged off his weighty new honours for the return to another school year at Cheam. In August he had trodden

Welsh soil for the first time since becoming Prince of Wales, at Holyhead, where a plaque now marks the event. But his new honours seemed a slight distinction compared with the year's superiority he could now exercise over the intake of new boys.

His school progress was steady but undistinguished. Peter Beck later summed it up by saying that Charles was above average in intelligence, but only average in attainment. By this he did not mean that the boy was bright but idle; rather, he sought to confirm the natural advantage Charles possessed in general knowledge. He was much better informed about the world, the outside world and its ways, than his contemporaries; he had, after all, by this time met many of the people who ran it, and engaged them in polite conversation. This strange species of maturity, fostered by the formal conduct around him at home, also meant that he spoke and wrote the Queen's English with above-average clarity and style, at times tending to a precocious use of long words. In other ways, he was much less mature than his fellows, and remained so for many years. He joined in their schoolboy crazes – at that time for pogo sticks, hula-hoops and roller skates – with the intense enthusiasm of one unaware of such excitements at home. But the Queen's caution in not providing everything he requested led to embarrassments. When he asked for a boat to sail on the school pond, his was conspicuously the smallest to be seen. At least he had the good sense not to waste his time sharing his friends' love of stamp-collecting; at home, he knew, the collection he would inherit from his great-grandfather, George V, was the finest and most valuable in the world.

He continued his piano lessons, the first steps in a love of music unparalleled in the Royal Family since Prince Albert. He sang in the school choir and piped a clear treble solo in the end-of-term concert attended by the Queen. He continued to show promise at painting, and a passing talent at woodwork; Charles produced a coffee-table which for many years remained one of Princess Anne's most treasured possessions. He dominated one end-of-term exhibition with a grim construction entitled Gallows and Stocks. He also began to join with a will in many of the school entertainments devised and produced by David Munir. Like his mother, who with her sister had starred in the wartime Windsor pantomimes, he seemed to find such enforced public display one way of conquering his shyness. In a way, it was an apt preparation for the many bizarre public roles required of royalty. One such Cheam production certainly was: a Shakespeare compilation under the title 'The Last Baron', which told the tale of the Duke of Gloucester, later Richard III. The time-honoured understudy's dream came true when the boy cast as Richard fell ill; Charles hurriedly took over the part.

In front of an audience of parents, he had to deliver with due gravity such lines as 'And soon may I ascend the throne'. The drama critic of the *Cheam School Chronicle* wrote: 'Prince Charles played the traditional Gloucester with competence and depth; he had a good voice and excellent elocution, and very well conveyed the ambition and bitterness of the twisted hunchback.' His 'traditional Gloucester' was modelled on Laurence Olivier's performance as Richard III; before the Cheam production, the young Prince listened intensely and repeatedly to a recording of the Olivier production. (In 1978, on hearing of this in correspondence with the author, Lord Olivier repaid the compliment: 'I have a great hero-worship of the Prince of Wales and have found him utterly charming and thoughtful in discussion and conversation. It would be delightful, would it not, for Charles III to be the first artistic King since Charles II.')

The star's mother, unusually, was not in the audience, as she had been the previous Christmas for her son's minor role debut in a Munir entertainment called 'Ten Little Cheam Boys'. Her absence that night was soon explained by the headmaster, who interrupted the performance to come onstage and announce that the Queen had given birth to another son (Prince Andrew). It was 19 February 1960. Charles's delight at having a baby brother, and the enthusiasm with which he relayed the latest news from home, impressed on Cheam staff that he would always be much happier in the bosom of his family. As Mabel Anderson had said of Charles: 'He felt family separation very deeply. He dreaded going away to school.' His only link with home was the unlikely figure of his detective, Detective Constable Reg Summers, who provided a reassuring presence around the school grounds and behind the Sunday crocodile to church. The Queen felt the distance equally keenly, and denied herself as well as her son much pleasure by resisting the temptation to call him home for royal occasions. Later that summer, however, a special dispensation was granted for him to attend the wedding in Westminster Abbey of his Aunt Margaret to the photographer Tony Armstrong-Jones. The Earl of Snowdon, as he became the following year, quickly formed an especially warm friendship with Prince Charles, founded as much as anything else on mutual admiration, which lasts to this day.

The Queen was careful to visit her son no more frequently – three times a term – than other parents, and to ask for no special privileges beyond the fact that cameras should be put away in her presence. Princess Anne enjoyed coming for the annual sports day, and always entered the younger sisters' race, unfortunately achieving no higher a position than fourth. She could take comfort in her brother's generally undistinguished record on the sports field. Never much of a team player, he was bored by cricket, although he eventually made the First XI, and not the most mobile of rugger players:

'They always put me in the second row,' he complained, 'the worst place in the scrum.' His reluctant best was soccer, and in his last year he was made captain of the First XI. Unhappily, the team lost every match that season, with a final tally of four goals scored against their opponents' eighty-two. This time, the *Cheam School Chronicle* was not so kind: 'At half', wrote the soccer coach, 'Prince Charles seldom drove himself as hard as his ability and position demanded.'

Looking back, the staff remember Charles fondly for his uncertainty of himself, and for a few little incidents which showed promise of the man in the making. 'Most of the time,' said one of Charles's teachers, 'he was very quiet. He never spoke out of turn. Sometimes his voice was so low that it was difficult to hear him. But he was a boy who preferred action to noise. When there was a task to do, he got on with it quietly. No fuss.' David Munir remembered once catching Charles downstairs, finishing off his daily chores, when he should long since have been in bed. Munir warned him that he would be getting himself into trouble with Matron. 'I can't help that, sir,' the boy replied. 'I must do my duties.'

Charles's extreme gentility was particularly marked on the football field, where he caused general amusement by his habit of apologizing chivalrously to anyone he felled with a perfectly proper tackle. But it was endearing to find him so embarrassed by the standard prayer for the Royal Family, including the Duke of Cornwall, at Sunday morning service in St Peter's. 'I wish,' he said, 'they prayed for the other boys too.' When someone gave Charles a 'doodle-master', a then new-fangled drawing toy, he was happy to lend it around until every other locker had its own. And he took his corporal punishment – the edicts of Gilpin had long since been abandoned – with the maturity beyond his years of one who 'would rather get things over with'.

These are the kind of school details for which the press hunger, but which tend not to emerge for many years – as is illustrated by two parallel father-and-son anecdotes. When Prince Philip visited the school for its tercentenary celebrations in 1947, one of his first public engagements after his betrothal to Princess Elizabeth, he introduced his fiancée to his former headmaster, the Rev. Harold Taylor: 'This is the man who used to cane me.' In 1974, during an Australian tour, Charles met Peter Beck's son Philip, by then a reporter for an Australian newspaper, beneath a canvas shelter deep in a Tasmanian forest. 'I remember your father well,' Charles told him. 'He caned me once – no, twice – for ragging.'

By the end of his time at Cheam, Charles had scored more credits than black marks for his house, Canada (the others, appropriately enough, being Australia, New Zealand and, until recently, South Africa). School life had

been considerably disrupted, most notably in 1959 when Scotland Yard unearthed a plot by an Irish terrorist group, Fianna Uladh, to kidnap Charles
and hold him hostage against a United Ireland; for days, the school grounds
had swarmed with police. But he had emerged at worst an average pupil,
and the obvious benefits of his presence had outweighed the disadvantages.

In the holidays, meanwhile, his parents found that he was growing fast,
and advanced his home education accordingly. Michael Farebrother had
been called in again as companion, and a French-Canadian tutor, twenty-
seven-year-old Lieutenant Jean Lajeunesse, had taken up the work of Mlle
de Roujoux. Father and son had grown ever closer as Charles developed
Philip's enthusiasm for field sports; from taking him out shooting at Sandringham to teaching him to drive a Land-Rover while only twelve, the Duke
of Edinburgh was intent on advancing his son beyond his years. At Christmas 1958 they went off on their first expedition together, to a coot shoot
at Hickling Broad, near Sandringham; it turned into something of an
adventure when their rented bungalow was flooded, and the royal pair shook
the locals by applying for a room at the nearby Pleasure Boat Inn.

That same Christmas, Charles at his own request toured the British Sugar
Corporation plant in King's Lynn – his first look inside a factory, and his
first solo public engagement. His parents were well pleased with his progress.
In the spring of 1962, in the absence abroad of Prince Philip, the Queen
asked Charles to take his father's place as host at one of the luncheon parties
she had introduced as a means of meeting a broader cross-section of her
subjects. The thirteen-year-old Prince held his own quite happily in conversation with a dozen or so guests, including the editor of the *Church Times*,
an industrialist, a choreographer, a trade union leader, and the chairman
of the BBC.

Cheam had also disposed of a number of the other chores of childhood:
Charles's first broken bone (his ankle, falling down the school stairs), measles
(urgent telegrams to his parents in Pakistan), chicken-pox, and his appendix
(which came out at Great Ormond Street Hospital for Children in February
1962). But the school had never quite won his whole-hearted enthusiasm.
The jolt of leaving home left bruises he still nursed. If he had grown accustomed to life away from home, he was still miserably aware that he was not
– and could never be – quite one of the boys. Peter Beck emphasizes that
'the job of a preparatory school is what it says: to prepare, and not to produce
a finished product'. But Charles had only just mastered his new environment
when he was abruptly removed from it. The last thing Cheam had prepared
this particular pupil for, in a way, was the unwelcome translation even
further from home to the chilly wastes of North Scotland, and Gordonstoun.

10

Gordonstoun
1962-65

Question to Prince Philip: How's he getting on?
Answer: Well, at least he hasn't run away yet.

WAS GORDONSTOUN THE RIGHT CHOICE? Those who advised Elizabeth II
on Prince Charles's education, among them the Queen Mother, Lord
Mountbatten and Robert Woods, then Dean of Windsor, are still divided.
The Queen and Prince Philip – and, now it's all over, their son – are
in no doubt that it was. Charles's younger brothers, Andrew and Edward,
went to the school after him, and there is every reason to expect the
Prince of Wales, in time, to send any sons of his own there. The over-
whelming argument in 1962 was that it was Prince Philip's old school, and
that he had been very happy there. But, as we have already seen, bringing
Prince Charles up in Prince Philip's mould was not a logical exercise. Where
Philip was outgoing, Charles was introspective; where Philip gregarious,
Charles awkwardly sociable; and where Philip had been an obscure Euro-
pean prince, of the kind not unfamiliar to many British public schoolboys,
Charles was the heir to the throne, the first in British history to be sent
away to school so young.

The Queen and her mother had favoured Eton – to many commentators,
also, the obvious choice. They had a friend who was a housemaster there,
Giles St Aubyn, younger son of Lord St Levan, occasionally drafted in as
an older childhood companion for Charles. Speculation had been fuelled
in April 1959 when his other childhood companion, Michael Farebrother,
had taken Charles round the school during the Easter holidays at Windsor.
The press assumed, incorrectly, that his name had been put down for Eton
at birth (causing his father much amusement: 'They'd have found it difficult
to turn him down, wouldn't they?'). There was a wave of criticism in the
Sunday opinion columns, much of it from Old Etonians, more of it from

socialist politicians, that it would be positively dangerous for the future King to go to Eton. His fellow-pupils would scarcely be a representative cross-section of his future subjects; and he would probably find, as King, that all his old school chums comprised the Tory Cabinet. (The same argument was applied, this time about a future Labour Cabinet, when Winchester was suggested.) Prince Philip would not hear of Eton, using much the same anti-élitist arguments. It might be happily close to Windsor, he told his wife and her mother, but it was also unhappily close to Fleet Street. The Queen and her husband went on an extended tour of British public schools, visiting among others Repton, Mill Hill, Fettes and Charles's own suggestion, Char-terhouse, where some of his friends were going from Cheam.

But as early as 1959, three years before any announcement was made, Philip was clearly forcing the pace in the family argument. That July, he subscribed £1,000 towards a rebuilding programme at Gordonstoun, saying to his brother-in-law, Prince George of Hanover, a former headmaster of the school's 'twin', Salem, in Germany: 'Wouldn't it be nice if my son could take advantage of all these improvements?' That October Dr Kurt Hahn, Gordonstoun's founder-headmaster, came to London from his Salem head-quarters to address the Parents' National Education Union; the meeting was chaired by Lady Brabourne, Prince Philip's cousin, and the vote of thanks was proposed by Lady Rupert Nevill, one of the Queen's closest friends. Sitting inconspicuously at the back was James Orr, Prince Philip's private secretary – and himself a Gordonstoun old boy.

By Charles's thirteenth birthday in November 1961 it was time for a decision. The Queen, on balance, confessed that the world of boys' schools remained largely a mystery to her, and was happy to be guided by her husband. So Gordonstoun it was, as a Palace statement announced on 23 January 1962, agreement having been reached with the school's warden, Henry Brereton, and the headmaster, Robert Chew, some weeks before.

Chew paid a secret visit to Peter Beck, to find out more about his new pupil. Gordonstoun does not require the Common Entrance Examination, leading some to conclude that Charles was going there because he couldn't pass it. Particularly stung by one suggestion that the school was 'a kind of academic *salon des refusés*', the Queen insisted that her son take a version of Common Entrance anyway, to staunch any self-doubt as much as to silence further criticism. Mr Chew was more than satisfied. Charles, who would start in May, thought the place sounded 'pretty gruesome'. Lord Rudolph Russell, younger son of the Duke of Bedford, had recently run away, declaring: 'Gordonstoun is no place for me.'

The school has been painted as a remote Spartan outpost providing some sort of Germanic assault course towards manhood. Its life is tough, to be sure, with an unusual emphasis on outdoor and physical attainment. But its ways are far from brutish; every item on the school curriculum, every eccentrically named rung up the school status ladder, is based on a rigorous educational code founded in pacifism. It was formulated in the wake of the First World War by Prince Max of Baden, last Chancellor of the Kaiser's Imperial Germany, and refined by his successor and disciple, Kurt Hahn. Gordonstoun parents are well aware what they are letting their sons in for.

The school is modelled on that founded in 1920 by Prince Max in his castle-monastery at Salem, on the north shore of Lake Constance, in southern Germany. The Prince, to whom Hahn was private secretary, had been intimately involved in the collapse of Germany and set himself the personal task of rebuilding his nation's manhood. 'Let us train soldiers,' he said, 'who are at the same time lovers of peace.' Prince Max was given to somewhat grandiose statements which, by appointing his private secretary the school's first headmaster, he expected Hahn to put into effect: 'Build up the imagination of the boy of decision and the will-power of the dreamer, so that in future wise men will have the nerve to lead the way they have shown, and men of action will have the vision to imagine the consequences of their decisions.'

What he really sought, Hahn realized, was the combination of stamina and leadership which had defeated Germany, the very combination bred in the English public schools – of which he had gained some experience when a Rhodes Scholar at Oxford before the war. Hahn's two great influences were Plato (particularly *The Republic*) and Dr Thomas Arnold of Rugby, both of whom he was given to quoting copiously.

I will call the three views of education the Ionian view, the Spartan view, the Platonic view.... Those who hold the first view believe that the individual ought to be nurtured and humoured regardless of the interests of the community.... According to the second view the individual may and should be neglected for the benefit of the State.... The third, the Platonic view, is that any nation is a slovenly guardian of its own interests if it does not do all it can to make the individual citizen discover his own powers: and further, that the individual becomes a cripple from his or her own point of view if he is not qualified by education to serve the community.

The selection process at Salem was quite as élitist as at Eton. Only children from the upper layers of German society were considered; even then, Hahn fiercely scrutinized their strength of character, far more important to him than their academic prowess, before admitting them.

In the Germany of the 1930s, after the death of Prince Max, Hahn was accused of anglicizing German education. He also happened to have been born Jewish. In 1933, when Hitler took power, he was arrested and the school closed. His stand was uncompromising. He wrote to the old boys of Salem: 'It is a question now in Germany of its Christian morality, its reputation, its soldierly honour; Salem cannot remain neutral. I call on all members of the Salem Association who are active in the SA or SS to terminate their allegiance either to Hitler or to Salem.' The rise of Nazism made him feel more urgently 'the need to educate young people in independence of judgement and in strength of purpose when following an unfashionable cause, to teach the protection of the weak, the recognition of the rights of the less fortunate, and the worth of a simple human life'. The children of Germany at that time were surrounded by 'three decays: the decay of adventure and enterprise, of skill and care, and of compassion'.

On his release Hahn fled to England, where he fell ill. An Oxford friend, William Calder, invited him to recuperate on his estate in Morayshire, where he met up again with another university contemporary, Evan Barron, then owner and editor of the *Inverness Courier*. Hahn told them of his plans to recreate the Salem experiment in Britain, and they took him to see the Gordonstoun estate, near Elgin. A lease was available on the eighteenth-century mansion-house, complete with pepperpot turrets and balustrades, and its 300 acres. Hahn took it, and in the summer of 1934 opened the school with a clutch of masters (including Robert Chew) and just thirty boys, one of them Prince Philip.

(The lease lasted until 1947, when the property was purchased from the Gordon Cumming family. By ironic coincidence, Gordonstoun had been the home of Sir William Gordon Cumming, lieutenant-colonel of the Scots Guards, who had involved a previous Prince of Wales, the future Edward VII, in the famous Tranby Croft gambling scandal. Prince Charles's great-great-grandfather had been dealing the cards when Gordon Cumming was accused of cheating at baccarat. He lost the subsequent slander case – in which the Prince of Wales, to Queen Victoria's and the nation's dismay, had to give evidence – and was drummed out of society and the Army in disgrace.)

The Gordonstoun philosophy was based on that of Salem, but Hahn added two important new dimensions. One was to carry across from Germany the altruistic traditions of the Cistercian monks, who had ministered to the vicinity of Salem centuries before. The other was to counteract the scholastic emphasis of other British schools. 'I estimate,' he said, 'that about sixty per cent of boys have their vitality damaged under the conditions of modern boarding schools.' His aim was 'to kindle on the threshold of puberty non-poisonous passions which act as guardians during the dangerous years'.

He was now accused of germanicizing English education, but all Hahn's philosophy came down to was a version, more literal than in most public schools, of Juvenal's *mens sana in corpore sano*. To protect his pupils from their increasingly urbanized home environment, he wanted them to pit their young physical resources against the forces of nature on land and sea. Like Baden-Powell, he aimed to inspire a sense of purpose and self-reliance, aligned with one of duty and service. Boys, said Hahn, should be taught 'to argue without quarrelling, to quarrel without suspecting and to suspect without slandering'. Apart from a special concern for late developers – a boon to its new recruit – Gordonstoun's purpose, enshrined in the school motto, PLUS EST EN VOUS (There is more in you), was not markedly different from the traditional British public-school ideal. But the method was. (So were the fees. The minimum total of £519 a year – higher than Harrow or Eton – was based on a standard fee of £87 per term, plus an assessed fee of not less than £86 per term. Parents were invited to decide this for themselves, placing themselves in one of twelve categories graded according to wealth and income. Another disadvantage, perhaps, of being the Royal Family.)

Physical fitness was something of a cult: it remains so with the Prince of Wales to this day. Boys were frequently despatched on testing expeditions, over land and water, designed to stretch initiative and physique to their limits. Public service was instilled by participation in four local activities: fire-fighting (the school's auxiliary is a recognized branch of the Elgin fire service); manning a coastguard station, complete with rockets and life-saving equipment; a mountain rescue team, which has in its time saved climbers' lives; and an ocean life-saving team. Hahn introduced the Moray Badge as a selective reward for achievement in these fields. It proved the inspiration for the Duke of Edinburgh's own nationwide award scheme, whose silver medal Prince Charles was to win in his last term.

On the day it was announced that Charles would be going to Gordonstoun, Hahn was by coincidence delivering a lecture in Glasgow. 'A sick civilization,' he said, 'is throwing up five kinds of young people: the lawless, the listless, the pleasure and sensation addicts, the angry young men and the honourable sceptics.' The antidotes were 'simple physical training, expedition training and rescue service training'. With garbled versions of Hahn's precepts and the school's strenuous régime appearing in the British press, it was no wonder the thirteen-year-old Prince felt daunted. Again he paid a private visit to the school with his parents, to find conditions even more Spartan than at Cheam: unpainted dormitories with bare floorboards, naked light bulbs and spare wooden bedsteads. Life appeared to be lived in huts, as exposed to the North Sea gales as were the boys' knees in their short trousers. It was a cheerless sight, and Charles was unenthusiastic about what he called his 'imminent incarceration'. He remained unaware of a goodwill gesture from his future fellow-pupils: Radio Luxembourg, then the favourite channel for public-school pop music followers, had played Bobby Darin's 'Goodbye Cruel World' at the request of a group of Gordonstoun boys, 'as a welcome to Prince Charles'. The joke turned sour when the headmaster, Mr Chew, expressed considerable annoyance; the second line of the song, he had been informed, was '. . . I'm off to join the circus'.

Prince Philip flew his son north on the first of May. The locals could tell they were coming: on the school gate stood naval guards with fixed bayonets, and tradesmen (and parents) were required to produce passes to get in. The Queen's consort, not the new boy, was accorded an official welcome by Brereton and Chew, with Captain Iain Tennant, chairman of the governors, and Peter Paice, the head boy. The only privilege accorded Charles was a private lunch with his father and the headmaster before Prince Philip left. He drove back to his aircraft at Lossiemouth, then flew over the school before heading south again, dipping his wings in a farewell salute to his son. Charles watched with sinking heart.

His arrival at Gordonstoun, he remembers, was even more miserable than at Cheam. As he was shown to Windmill Lodge, the asbestos-roofed stone building he was to share with fifty-nine of the four hundred other boys, the prospects seemed even worse than he had expected. Not merely had he been rudely yanked from an environment to which he had just grown accustomed; all his dogged progress up the Cheam hierarchy had now come to naught. He was an unprivileged new boy again, and at a school where the boys' older years altered their attitude to him. Where at Cheam he had found diffidence, at Gordonstoun he came up against adolescent malice. The only boys he knew, apart from Lord Mountbatten's grandson, Norton Knatchbull, were his cousins Prince Welf of Hanover, whom he had visited with his father in Germany earlier that year, and Prince Alexander of Yugoslavia. Even they, for befriending him in his first few days, were labelled 'bloodsucker' and 'sponge' by their contemporaries.

The Gordonstoun day began with the cry of the 'waker' at 7 a.m., followed by a run round the garden in shorts and singlet. Then came the first of the day's two cold showers; Charles and his fifty-nine housemates shared a washroom containing six showers and one bath. He had to make his own bed and clean his own shoes before breakfast.

The rest of the new boys' day, in an official summary prepared for public consumption by Mr Chew (who died in 1970), ran as follows:

8.15 Breakfast and surgery.

8.55 Morning prayers.

9.10 Classwork begins. There are five 40-minute periods in the morning but for every boy one of these, on several days in the week, is a training break (running, jumping, discus-and-javelin-throwing, assault course, etc.) under the Physical Training Master.

1.20 Lunch. After lunch there is a rest period (20 minutes): music or reading aloud to boys relaxing on their backs.

2.30 Afternoon activities. On three days a week there are either games (rugger or hockey in winter; cricket, lawn tennis or athletics in summer), or seamanship, or practical work on the estate. The proportion of time spent on each depends upon a boy's interests and development. One afternoon a week is allocated to the Services: Coast Guard Watchers, Sea Cadets, Army Cadets, Scouts, Fire Service, Mountain Rescue and Surf Life Saving. One afternoon and evening a week are given to work on boys' individual projects which are exhibited and judged at the end of each year. On Saturday afternoons there are matches and opportunities for expeditions.

4.00 Warm wash and cold shower. Change into evening school uniform. Tea. After tea, classes or tutorial periods.

6.20 Supper, followed by preparation in Houses or by 'Societies'.

9.15 Bedtime; silence period of five minutes.

9.30 Lights out.

When not occupied by this formidable schedule, boys were at liberty to wander at will around the countryside and down to the sea, though the town of Elgin was out of bounds. Charles took full advantage of this freedom; visitors noticed that he tended to take them for walks round the countryside rather than show them round the school. He developed nodding acquaintanceships with the fishermen and shopkeepers of the nearby village of Hopeman, and occasionally – but only occasionally, for fear of singling himself out – accepted invitations to Sunday lunch or a day's shooting with Captain Tennant, who was also the Lord-Lieutenant of Morayshire, or the Vice-Lieutenant, Lt-Col. Kenneth Mackessack. It was in the countryside that he preferred to relax; school games he did not much enjoy, and he shunned his peers' illicit activities in Elgin's Pete's Cafe.

But Charles quickly took to all maritime activities. Having already taken the helm of his father's yacht *Bluebottle* at Cowes, and become a proficient swimmer in the Buckingham Palace pool, he was almost more self-confident in the water than on *terra firma*. He and Welf teamed up as a life-saving unit, and they received their proficiency certificates on Charles's fourteenth birthday. One of his earliest exercises, a canoe expedition from Hopeman Beach to Findhorn Bay, turned ugly even by Gordonstoun standards when a storm blew up shortly after they were out to sea. The twelve-mile journey took all day, and the Prince arrived back at school exhausted. In true British public-school spirit, he went out to dinner that night with Captain Tennant and told him he was eager to repeat the adventure.

Other early duties included humping about the school dustbins and tidying up their trail of refuse. By the end of his first term he had qualified for his school uniform, the grey sweater and shorts to which all blue-uniformed new boys aspire. (Upward progress at Gordonstoun is a curious business with which the author, himself baffled, need not too much trouble the reader. Suffice it to say that Prince Charles graduated through all the stages: School Uniform, Junior Training Plan, Senior Training Plan, White Stripe, Colour Bearer Candidate, Colour Bearer, Helper, Guardian. Colour Bearers [prefects] are elected by their fellows; from their number housemasters appoint Helpers [Heads of Houses] and the headmaster appoints the Guardian, or head boy.)

The winning of his school uniform also involved the new boy, by ancient rite, in a ducking in a cold bath, fully clothed. It seems strange that the Gordonstoun boys hesitated over putting the Queen's son through this traditional humiliation; but one pupil, who left soon after to sell his story to a Sunday paper, explained: 'How can you treat a boy as just an ordinary chap when his mother's portrait is on the coins you spend in the school shop, on the stamps you put on your letters home, and when a detective follows him wherever he goes?' He went on: 'Most boys tend to fight shy of friendship with Charles. The result is that he is very lonely. It is this loneliness, rather than the school's toughness, which must be hardest on him.'

It was. 'It's near Balmoral,' his father had told him. 'There's always the Factor there; you can go and stay with him. And your grandmother goes up there to fish. You can go and see her.' Charles did, whenever he could. At Birkhall, her home on the Balmoral estate, the Queen Mother heard from Charles of his homesickness, his loneliness, the impossibility of blending into school life like other boys. She provided a sympathetic shoulder to cry on, literally, and was especially moved by all the qualities of her late husband so evident in her favourite grandchild. More than Charles's parents, perhaps, she understood the ordeal of the quiet, uncertain child in a harsh and alien world. 'He is a very gentle boy, with a very kind heart,' she said, 'which I think is the essence of everything.' But she would not, as he asked, intercede with the Queen and Prince Philip to take him away from Gordonstoun. She would try, she said, to help him through an ordeal he must face. It was another early lesson in duty.

At the end of Charles's first term Mr Chew reported to the Queen that her son was 'well up ... very near the top of his class'. The Christmas holidays, after family festivities at Sandringham, provided the first in a new and traumatic wave of trials by newspaper. It was New Year 1963, and

Charles travelled alone to Bavaria for a winter-sports break with his 'uncle', Prince Ludwig of Hesse, and his family. The crowds of press photographers, which in turn attracted crowds of sightseers, quite simply ruined it. After two or three chaotic days in the resort of Tarasp, he was forced again to retire into an artificial world: the private slopes of the Hesse *schloss*. Even there, he needed a bodyguard of Swiss police, themselves patrolling the property on skis.

His resentment was only forgotten the following summer, when a much greater ordeal overwhelmed him. The Cherry Brandy Incident, now a fondly remembered, amusing milestone in Prince Charles's childhood to most Britons, was much more than that to the boy at the time. It upset him deeply, leaving scars which lasted several years, notably a bewildered mistrust of the press which has never really left him – though it is not now so bewildered.

On his arrival at Gordonstoun, as at Cheam, an appeal had been made to the press to leave him in peace:

> The added strain and burden of publicity upon a young boy of the Prince of Wales's age, on joining a public school for the first time, can readily be understood by all parents. For this reason, Her Majesty and His Royal Highness hope that editors personally will be able to co-operate.... When publicity was reduced at the end of the first term at Cheam School, it became possible for the whole school to function in the normal way, and therefore the Prince of Wales was able to receive a normal education. This was only possible because neither he nor any of the other boys and staff were subjected to publicity, which is most unsettling and which, of course, singles His Royal Highness out as different in the eyes of all other boys of the school....

By his third term at Gordonstoun, press coverage of his progress was minimal. By then, June 1963, he had received the next – and coveted – stage of school promotion, membership of the Junior Training Plan. It entitled him to more freedom of choice over outdoor training activities, one of which was the expedition aboard the school yacht, *Pinta*, which brought him to Stornoway, on the Isle of Lewis, on Monday 17 June. As usual his detective, Donald Green, accompanied the party of Charles and four other boys ashore. Green went off to make arrangements at the local cinema – Jayne Mansfield was to be the Junior Training Plan's subject of study that evening – leaving the boys to wait in the Crown Hotel. A crowd quickly gathered once word of Charles's arrival got around, and the young Prince soon found a sea of faces pressed against the hotel windows, peering and pointing at him.

> I thought 'I can't bear this any more' and went off somewhere else. The only other place was the bar. Having never been into a bar before, the first thing I thought of doing was having a drink, of course. And being terrified, not knowing

what to do, I said the first drink that came into my head, which happened
to be cherry brandy, because I'd drunk it before when it was cold out shooting.
Hardly had I taken a sip when the whole world exploded round my ears.

What had happened, as he took that first sip, was that into the bar had
come Frances Thornton, a twenty-two-year-old freelance journalist, known
ever after to Charles as 'that dreadful woman'. The Prince of Wales was
fourteen, under the legal age for purchasing alcoholic liquor. Within twenty-
four hours, the story had gone round the world. Coming soon after other
recent public criticisms – of Charles shooting his first stag the previous
autumn, of his 'invading the Lord's Day' by skiing in the Cairngorms on
Sundays – it caused uproar. Even the Profumo Affair, then at its height,
could not keep it off the front pages. To make matters worse, Buckingham
Palace at first issued a denial, after misunderstanding Green's telephoned
account of the incident. The following day, after further inquiries, they were
forced to retract it, thus keeping the story bubbling along. There followed
the carpeting of Green by Superintendent Albert Perkins, the Queen's
senior detective (soon after which Green resigned), and the question of
school punishment for Charles. *The Times* itself felt moved to inform its
readers that the headmaster kept a cane for such misdemeanours.

As leading articles called on the Head to act, Charles was summoned to
Mr Chew's study, where after cross-examination he was deprived of his
membership of the Junior Training Plan. It was a punishment much more
devastating than the cane. Reduced to the ranks, he had again had his life
complicated by unwelcome and undue attention. For so trivial an incident
to have had so disproportionate an effect now seems absurd; the Queen was
able to laugh at the episode, later concluding that it was a good lesson in
the necessary restraints of royal conduct. Charles, though to many newspaper readers a more endearing and human figure, was thoroughly unsettled,
and unable to laugh about it at all for several years. When boys made puns
on the name of the school yacht, *Pinta* – 'Drinka Pinta Milka Day' was then
the Milk Marketing Board's popular slogan – he could never see the joke.

As his Gordonstoun life grew more varied and self-confident – a stint at
HMS *Vernon*, the naval training camp at Portsmouth, his first archaeological digs around Morayshire, a bout of pneumonia after one camping
expedition to Balmoral – he won his way back into the Junior Training Plan
and further up the scale. A year later, he proved something to himself and
many others by passing five GCE O-levels, in Latin, French, history,
English language and English literature, though maths and physics still
eluded his grasp. The summer of 1964 passed happily enough, at Balmoral
and Cowes, with the added bonus of an excursion to King Constantine's

wedding in Athens, where he had the satisfaction of ducking a raft-load of prying French photographers. By the time he returned to school that September, he had found a new equilibrium. But life was very quickly to turn sour again.

An exercise book went missing from his classroom. That sort of thing had happened before: forgeries had been hawked around Fleet Street, and one genuine one, culled from a waste-paper basket, had proved to be the work of another boy. Name tags taken from Charles's clothes had proved popular on the school's 'black market', and books inscribed with his name had disappeared. But this time the olive-green book in which Charles wrote his essays had been stolen from the pile on his form-master's desk, and the headmaster issued an appeal for what he called 'a collector's item'. Too late. It had already reached Fleet Street.

The trial proved mildly fascinating. A Gordonstoun boy (he was never identified) was reputed to have got £7 for the book from a Gordonstoun old boy, an officer cadet, who had then sold it to a Scottish journalist for £100. Rumours of offers as high as £5,000 abounded in London for some time until the book was traced to St Helen's, Lancashire, and the offices of Terence Smith of the *Mercury Press*. It had taken Scotland Yard six weeks to get the book back, and Smith promptly sued the Metropolitan Police Commissioner, Sir Joseph Simpson, for the return of 'goods wrongly taken'. As those goods were stolen property, his case didn't get very far.

The police seizure, however, itself prompted the next stage. The German magazine *Der Stern*, who with *Life Magazine* and *Paris-Match* possessed photostats, had been unconvinced about the authenticity of the documents. The police action, it said, 'made it clear they were genuine'; they bought the rights for £1,000 and on 17 November published the essays in full (in German), illustrated by the handwritten text in English – complete with the form-master's comment 'Quite well argued'. Buckingham Palace, biding its time until authenticity was beyond doubt, said: 'If these reports are true, it is highly regrettable that the private essays of a schoolboy should have been published at all in this way.'

So it was; but it could have been a great deal worse. Charles emerged with credit from world-wide exposure which would have daunted any schoolboy. Though published under the headline 'The Confessions of Prince Charles', what little the essays revealed showed the sixteen-year-old Prince a liberal and original thinker, reasonably mature for his age. *Stern* managed to miss the point of the piece about which it got most excited: a dissertation on the corrupting effects of power. Its views were not those of the future King of England but of the nineteenth-century historian

William Lecky, a section of whose *History of England in the Eighteenth Century* the class had been told to précis.

The Times quoted with approval from another piece on the subject of democracy. The Prince professed himself 'troubled by the fact that the voters today tend to go for a particular party and not for the individual candidate, because they vote for the politics of a party'. He thought it wrong, for instance, that a below-par Conservative candidate should win votes simply because he toed the party line against nationalization or the abolition of the public schools. In another, on the press, he emerged from his recent ordeals surprisingly unsoured: a free press, he argued, was essential in democratic society 'to protect people from the government in many ways, to let them know what is going on – perhaps behind their backs'.

A fourth essay was a ten-minute exercise to name the four items he would take to a desert island if evacuated during a nuclear crisis. Charles opted for a tent, a knife, 'lots of rope and string', and a radio, both to keep in touch with developments, and to monitor any hope of rescue. He did add, however, that such an emergency would have him 'in a frightful panic'.

The matter might have ended there, had not *Stern* thought of adding a last, gratuitous paragraph: 'Prince Charles became short of pocket-money at Gordonstoun at the end of August. It then occurred to him that some collectors paid good money for original handwritten manuscripts. He sold the work to a schoolmate for thirty shillings.' *Time* magazine decided to follow up this intriguing tit-bit and the following week published its version of the saga under the headline 'The Princely Pauper'. The Palace now lost patience, and issued one of its extremely rare denials. 'There is no truth whatever', the Queen's press secretary, Colville, wrote to *Time*, 'in the story that Prince Charles had sold his autograph at any time. There is also no truth whatever in the story that he sold his composition book to a classmate. In the first place he is intelligent and old enough to realize how embarrassing this would turn out to be, and second, he is only too conscious of the interest of the press in anything to do with himself and his family. The suggestion that his parents keep him so short of money that he has to find other means to raise it is also a complete invention. Finally, the police would not have attempted to regain the composition book unless they were quite satisfied that it had been obtained illegally.' In their own unique style, *Time*'s editors headlined the letter 'Moneyed Prince Charlie', and added beneath it: 'The Royal Family's press officer mounts a princely defence in his belated offer to clarify the case.'

There was another diversion from that autumn's strains: a mock election, a common practice in many British schools, to coincide with the British general election of October 1964. Charles was to be seen wearing a Scottish

Nationalist Party rosette around Gordonstoun, and speaking vehemently in favour of what has since become known as devolution. When one opponent gently reminded him he was Prince of Wales, he cried 'Independence for Wales, too! That's for the next election!' It is a measure of the breeding of British public schoolboys that the Conservative Party romped home with 140 votes. The Scottish Nationalist Party polled 129; but Labour – with 16 – trailed behind the Liberals and the Irish Independents, at a time when they were winning their first British general election for thirteen years.

The affair of the exercise book dragged on into the Christmas holidays, marked by the delivery of 'beat group' kit – a guitar with amplifier, and an electric organ – to Windsor Castle, to complement Charles's much-worn Beatle wig. After New Year at Sandringham, he and Anne were again dogged by the press on a skiing holiday in Liechtenstein. Through his hosts, Prince Franz Josef and Princess Gina, he reached an accommodation with the photographers – who were mostly foreign: British editors were still attempting to respect the Queen's wishes. They would be welcome on the slopes in the afternoons, if they would leave him alone in the mornings. To everyone's surprise it worked, and he was able to continue his progress towards becoming the proficient skier he is today.

Back at Sandringham it was the usual round of field sports, in unusually severe winter weather. 'The whole family,' said Mabel Anderson, 'goes out in weather most would think mad.'

Prince Charles had become, his family noticed, more contemplative of late, in part because he was due to be confirmed at Easter. He was again aware of his father's shadow. With his sometimes too unquestioning young seriousness, Charles had long since accepted the tenets of Christianity with due solemnity. But he was aware that his father thought sixteen perhaps too young for confirmation, and had had doubts about his own faith. Prince Philip's tortured progress from the Greek Orthodoxy of his childhood through Salem's German Protestantism to the formal Anglicanism of his adopted life had bred a disenchantment, even a cynicism; there had been a time, though he had now in middle age reverted to Anglican orthodoxy, when he had classed himself agnostic, perhaps atheist. Again, Charles was not in the same mould. During his pre-confirmation talks with the Dean of Windsor, Robert Woods, he displayed a sound grasp of his undertakings, and his faith has not since wavered. At Easter 1965, Prince Philip was not quite so sure, and was anyway of the view that the then Archbishop of Canterbury, Michael Ramsey, was a very tiresome preacher. Throughout his son's confirmation service in St George's Chapel, Windsor, Prince Philip conspicuously read a book – his Bible being the nearest to hand.

'Come and have a drink,' said Woods to Ramsey afterwards. 'Thank you,' said the Archbishop. 'Bloody rude, that's what I call it.'

Charles's progress at Gordonstoun had been interrupted by only one recall to London on official duty, earlier that year, for the state funeral of Sir Winston Churchill. He was nearing the end of his fourth year, had moved from Senior Training Plan to Colour Bearer (prefect), and had finally managed to satisfy the O-level examiners of a modest grasp of mathematics. He had graduated from piano to trumpet, and taken part in several concerts in Elgin town hall and St Giles's Cathedral, Edinburgh. He had also had his first taste of two enduring, if contradictory, passions: polo and the cello. He was to crown his last full year at the school with boldness in a field in which his father never shone: for the school play at Christmas 1965, Prince Charles undertook the role of Shakespeare's Macbeth. Thirty years before, Prince Philip had qualified only for the role of an attendant lord, Donalbain.

Charles took the part very seriously, treating his six weeks of research into the character as an expedition into those realms of human nature questioned and explored at the time of his confirmation. A fortnight after their son's seventeenth birthday, the Queen and Prince Philip flew north to see him strut and fret his few hours in front of Gordonstoun's version of Glamis Castle, ancestral home of his grandmother's family, the Bowes-Lyons. A schoolboy's picture of the false-bearded Prince performing the famous dagger soliloquy again went around the world, earning the Gordonstoun photographic society some £500. It raised only this paltry sum because, in deference to the Royal Family, the picture was distributed through the 'normal channels' of the Press Association; had it been sold through an independent agency, according to a contemporary estimate, it would have earned more than £10,000. The Prince looked so convincing that the Gordonstoun thespians were accused of importing London make-up expertise for the occasion. Not so; the royal chin experienced the familiar schoolboy agonies of tufts of crêpe hair stuck on with Copydex glue.

One small amendment was made in Shakespeare's text. For the benefit of the Queen, it was decided to dispense with the stage direction: 'Enter Macduff, with Macbeth's head.' Otherwise, Charles's satanic Thane stoutly endured the eloquent nagging of fourteen-year-old Douglas Campbell as Lady Macbeth, and raised an impromptu buzz in the audience only when the three witches cried: 'All hail, Macbeth, that shalt be King hereafter!' The *Gordonstoun Record* did him proud:

> Prince Charles was at his very best in the quiet poetic soliloquies, the poetry of which he so beautifully brought out, and in the bits which expressed Macbeth's terrible agony of remorse and fear. In the second part of the play, he equally well expressed the degenerative hardening of Macbeth's character,

the assumption of cynicism in an attempt to blunt the underlying and too painful moral sensitivity.

A local triumph, the high point in a year during which school life had become, after those early trials, somewhat monotonous. That Christmas, the question of a university career was already under discussion in the Royal Family. Charles had not yet completed his span at Gordonstoun, but was in the mood for a change, the familiar mood of those young school-leavers who take a year out in the wide world between school and university. He wanted a break. On the condition that he would return to Gordonstoun later, to finish the business he had begun there, the Queen and Prince Philip agreed.

11

Geelong and Gordonstoun
1966-67

Australia opened my eyes. Having a title, and being a
member of the upper classes, as often as not militates against
you there.... Australia conquered my shyness.

DURING HER CORONATION TOUR of Australia, Queen Elizabeth II had
undertaken to 'send my eldest son to visit you, too, when he is older'. The
promise seemed long overdue in that autumn of 1965, when a Commonwealth school was one of the suggestions under consideration for Prince
Charles's break from Gordonstoun. The Australian Prime Minister, Sir
Robert Menzies, visited London that autumn, and found himself invited
to spend a week-end at Balmoral, for an intensive grilling on his country's
better schools. Others involved in the consultations included the Dean of
Windsor, Dr Woods, whose brother was Archbishop of Melbourne, and the
then Australian High Commissioner in London, Sir Alexander Downer, an
old boy of Geelong Church of England Grammar School, in Menzies's State
of Victoria.

Between them they decided on Geelong, suggesting that its country outpost, Timbertop, might provide exactly what Prince Charles and his parents
were looking for. Geelong School itself, often described as 'the Eton of Australia', is very near Melbourne, but Timbertop is some 200 miles to the
north, and 2,000 feet above sea level, in remote but accessible countryside
on the slopes of the mountain from which it takes its name. Geelong sent
its boys for an outdoor year of exercise and self-reliance at Timbertop, which
immediately made Charles fear it was simply an Australian Gordonstoun.
Not so; its philosophy is less heavy-handed, more homespun. By self-
reliance, the school meant literally that: there were a handful of masters
in loco parentis, but the boys were mainly younger ones in the charge of
their seniors, who would appeal to the staff only in the event of emergency.

Theirs was a rural life of comparative self-sufficiency, each boy having broad freedom to spend his time as he liked. It was an exercise in getting to know people, from which the young Prince of Wales could only benefit. As he was of the age of the older boys, he would also undertake the responsibility of having a younger group in his direct care. Unlike his fellows, he would have to spend some time working for his GCE A-levels in history and French, scheduled for his return to Gordonstoun, but the rest of the time would be more or less his own, in excellent fishing and walking countryside. Though made famous by Nevil Shute in *The Far Country*, the gum forests around Mount Timbertop were otherwise undiscovered by the rest of humanity.

This was the deciding factor stressed by Menzies on his return home, when a Labour member of the Australian Parliament raised the same questions about Geelong as had English critics over the choice of Cheam and Gordonstoun. Geelong, he charged, was 'generally accepted' as the most exclusive school in Australia. 'Why did the Prime Minister not suggest that Prince Charles, like the great majority of his future subjects, should attend one of the excellent state high schools?'

'It is not difficult for people to understand that a school with a rural branch has attractions in this instance,' replied Menzies. 'I would be very sorry for the young Prince if he were at a school in the middle of a crowded city in Australia, with people gazing at him, with people trying to make him a raree-show. This isn't what he will be here for.'

Charles left for Australia at the end of January 1966. He was just seventeen. Though it was nearly nine years since that first dark day at Cheam, he had still not conquered his fears of new, unknown situations, and again remembers being very apprehensive. It is in this curious respect that he perhaps most resembles his grandfather, George VI, and perhaps other, less likely, royal predecessors. George V, for instance, a man by no means daunted by his role, nevertheless expressed surprise at the warmth of his reception during his Silver Jubilee parade through London in 1935: 'I had no idea they felt like that about me. I'm beginning to think they must really like me for myself.' To Charles, as to his great-grandfather, such warmth remains a surprise. He sees no reason why affection should be spontaneous, unearned. He had heard that Australians were 'critical', and expected a mixed reception. Even more unnerving, this was his first trip abroad without either of his parents.

He did, however, have reassuring company in his detective, Detective Inspector Derek Sharp, and Squadron Leader David Checketts, the then thirty-five-year-old equerry to Prince Philip, and already a familiar figure to Charles. A former public-relations man with a distinguished RAF record,

Checketts was to prove a mainstay of Prince Charles's life for the next thirteen years. In Australia, he set up home with his wife and family at Devon Farm, some 120 miles from Timbertop, and acted as a kind of business manager to the Prince. The farm became a headquarters for dealing with all press and administrative inquiries, and for entertaining Charles over many an Australian week-end. The Prince would muck in like a member of the family, coming down to breakfast in his dressing-gown, making his own bed, doing his share of the household chores, acting as elder brother to the Checketts's young children. It was the beginning of a firm friendship; in time, Checketts was to become his equerry, and later the Prince of Wales's first private secretary.

Checketts has said of those seven months in Australia: 'I went out there with a boy, and returned with a man.' Many others, including Charles himself, have testified that this is the period in which he suddenly shed the burden of 'late development', and grew to manhood.

At first the Australians did, as expected, receive him with caution; there were, of course, the usual official receptions and enthusiastic crowds, but it was the acceptance of his school-fellows he wanted to win. One night at Timbertop, after taking a walk in the rain, he knew he had succeeded. He returned to his dormitory duties carrying a rolled umbrella, and was delighted to hear a chorus of 'Pommy bastard'.

It was the first time for forty-five years that a Prince of Wales had set foot in Australia, and the press were rampant. (Within minutes of his arrival in Canberra, while driving to Government House, the Prince saw the all-too-predictable kangaroo by the roadside; local residents believed enterprising newsmen had 'planted' the animal there for his benefit.) Checketts headed off the threat of constant harassment by arranging an open day when Charles arrived at Timbertop. All day the press followed him around the school and the surrounding countryside, on the strict condition that they then withdrew for the rest of the term. And so they did. Checketts fielded myriad telephone calls at Devon Farm, releasing what information he chose. But even he, not noted for his love of the press gangs around the Prince, saluted the Australian newspapers' behaviour as 'wonderful'.

Timbertop boys live together in a compound of nine huts, each containing about fifteen, and each supervised by an elder boy described as 'a sort of NCO'. One such was Charles, who shared a room in the masters' quarters with a sheep-farmer's son named Stuart Macgregor, a former head boy of Geelong who had come out to Timbertop to study in peace for his university entrance. Here Charles, too, worked by himself for his A-levels. He did not attend what few classes there were at Timbertop, but had to spend some of his time supervising the younger boys in such chores as woodcutting, boiler-stoking and (again) dustbin-emptying. He joined with a will in the strenuous hikes and cross-country runs which were compulsory most after-noons and at week-ends; on one occasion, David Checketts gamely joined in a sixty-mile hike across arduous mountain terrain. Charles earned popu-larity by rather neglecting his studies for the life of the outback; a familiar figure silhouetted against the horizon with his fishing rod, he was occasion-ally late with the essays he took down to supervisors at Geelong. His Australian hosts were introducing him, quite deliberately, to a university style of tuition, not knowing whether he would ever again have the chance to enjoy this type of academic life.

Excursions further afield became more exotic: sheep-shearing and pig-swilling, gem-hunting and panning for gold. Charles felled trees, took part in a scheme to help war widows, and was introduced to the exotic local ornithology. He was thoroughly enjoying himself. Timbertop, he found, was as stimulating as Gordonstoun had become monotonous. He was popular among his fellows for himself, not for his rank, and he had never known such freedom to wander the great outdoors unobserved. He had originally come to Australia for one term, but the Queen had privately directed that he might stay on for a second if he wished. The choice was to be left entirely to him. He decided, without hesitation, to stay.

Charles's enjoyment of Timbertop is best expressed in his own words, written under the heading 'Timbertop: or Beating about the bush' for the *Gordonstoun Record*. With boyish enthusiasm, he chronicles the delights of each busy day:

> Almost everyone, master and boys, enjoy themselves up here. One never seems to stop running here and there for one minute of the day, from 7.30 a.m. breakfast – and no morning run, though there's worse to follow – until the lights go out at 9.15 p.m., having had tea at the unearthly hour of 5.30. If you have done a cross-country at 4.45 p.m. and arrived back at 5.05 p.m., it's difficult to persuade your stomach to accept food....

Wood-chopping was

> essential as the boys' boilers have to be stoked with logs and the kitchen uses a huge number. The first week I was here I was made to go out and chop up logs on a hillside in boiling hot weather. I could hardly see my hands for blisters.... Each afternoon after classes, which end at three o'clock, there are jobs which ... involve chopping and splitting wood, feeding the pigs, cleaning out fly-traps (which are revolting glass bowls seething with flies and very ancient meat), or picking up bits of paper round the school....

Of weekend expeditions into the bush, he wrote:

> You can't see anything but gum-tree upon gum-tree, which tends to become

rather monotonous. . . . You virtually have to inspect every inch of the ground you hope to put your tent on in case there are any ants or other ghastly creatures. There is one species of ant called Bull Ants which are three-quarters of an inch long, and they bite like mad! Some boys manage to walk fantastic distances over a week-end of four days or less, and do 130 or even 200 miles. The furthest I've been is 60–70 miles in three days, climbing about five peaks on the way. At the camp site the cooking is done on an open fire in a trench. You have to be very careful in hot weather that you don't start a bush fire, and at the beginning of this term there was a total ban in force, so that you ate all the tinned food cold.

Each Wednesday, there was a tug o' war 'or, if it's hot, there is swimming, or perhaps someone is feeling sufficiently cruel to organize a race that involves carrying half a tree for a certain distance'. If those boys who returned from week-end hikes were indulging in a little royal leg-pulling with their claims of '130 or even 200 miles', Charles was evidently able to give as good as he got. 'I almost convinced one or two Australians outside the school that we rustled kangaroos at Timbertop, and that we performed this art by creeping up on them behind, grabbing them by the tail and flicking them over on their backs, where you had them at your mercy.' Rather more authentic was his account of a sheep-shearing expedition: 'I made rather a mess of it, and left a somewhat shredded sheep.'

A pleasant interruption to the Prince's first term at Timbertop was an Australian visit by the Queen Mother. Charles received an exeat to go and meet his grandmother in Canberra, and they spent two days together in a cabin in the Snowy Mountains. Queen Elizabeth was delighted to hear, and to see for herself, how much happier Charles was than during those early days at Gordonstoun. She was able to return home with news, and snapshots, to reassure the Queen that a second term at Timbertop was in Prince Charles's best interests.

An unexpectedly important moment in the Prince's life came at the end of that first term, when he joined a party of thirty boys making Geelong's annual visit to the missionary stations in Papua and New Guinea. With the headmaster, Thomas Garnett, they flew over Prince of Wales Island to Port Moresby, after a refuelling stop near Brisbane. It was here that a vast and unexpected crowd had gathered on the tarmac to see the Prince, who had never before confronted such a throng in his own right. His instinct was to stay on the aircraft and hope it took off again as soon as possible. But David Checketts urged him to go and talk to them. Checketts, as both remember it, had more or less to kick the Prince off the plane; Charles walked across the tarmac to the ecstatic assembly with very mixed feelings. Once he reached them, however, and found how easy it was to talk to people even in such difficult circumstances, he began to enjoy the experience. Since that day, he says, he has never been nervous of big crowds.

The final stage of the journey was by launch across Goodenough Bay to the village of Wedau, near Dogura Cathedral. There was a reception committee of thousands, Australian and Papuan, in school uniforms, nuns' habits, grass skirts and feather head-dresses; as the southern sun set over the beach, it was an intensely dramatic sight. The Bishop, Dr John Chisholm, led Charles forward, and there was a huge chorus of 'Egualau' – Wedauan for 'welcome'.

For four days Charles and his friends toured the area, seeing the mission's schools, hospitals, churches and charitable outposts. Again he wrote his own account, this time for the Geelong school magazine, in which it is possible to read the dawning of his interest in anthropology:

> I can't help feeling that less and less interest is being taken by the younger Papuans in the customs and skills of their parents and grandparents, because they feel that they have to live up to European standards, and that these things belong to the past and have no relevance to the present or future. This may be a completely false impression, but I was given one or two presents by young people, and when I asked if they had made them, they said their mothers or aunts had. No doubt, however, in the years to come, when there are new generations of Papuans, they will consider these ancient skills of use. . . .

One evening he watched dancers 'in magnificent head-dresses of bird-of-paradise feathers, cassowary feathers, hornbill beaks and chicken feathers', and then joined in the dancing, himself leading 'a somewhat hilarious reel'. In the year following his confirmation, however, it was the work of the Anglican mission, in the middle of nowhere, which most caught his young and reflective imagination:

> I would like to mention how fresh and sincere I found the Church at Dogura. Everyone was so eager to take part in the services, and the singing was almost deafening. One felt that it might almost be the original Church. Where Christianity is new, it must be much easier to enter into the whole spirit of it whole-heartedly. . . .

He spent the rest of that holiday exploring the east coast of Australia with David Checketts, bobbing from one friend's house to the next, fishing, playing polo, and at Eidsvold in Queensland driving twenty head of cattle back and forth through the stockyard gates – for the benefit of the press, who had by now caught up again. At the Malanda reserve near Cairns, he met seventy-year-old Davey Douglas, an aborigine, the oldest living man to have been convicted of cannibalism (in the 1920s). 'I kept my hands behind my back,' wrote Charles, 'but he assured me he has lost his taste for humans.' At Sydney he had his first sight of surfing, at North Bondi, but conditions were too hazardous for beginners. He has since more than made up for this first disappointment.

After visiting the Outward Bound School on the Hawkesbury River, it was back for a few days to Devon Farm, during which brief visit Mrs Checketts gave birth to another daughter. Charles was delighted; he has always been rather soft about babies. (After the early childhood of his two young brothers, there was only his increasing collection of godchildren to coo over, until the birth in 1977 of Princess Anne's son.)

Then back to Timbertop, where life had changed only with the seasons. It was now June, the Victorian midwinter, which gave him a chance for some skiing. But his main preoccupation was still with the A-levels looming on his return to Gordonstoun. In the course of his history studies, more urgent than his French, he decided to give his fellow-pupils a lecture on the subject of King Charles I. This 'saddest of all Kings' was a particularly vivid figure to Charles, who had made a special study of his two historical namesakes, and had grown up with Van Dyck's portraits around him on the familiar walls of the state apartments of Buckingham Palace. Later, he was to find Cromwell a more impressive figure: 'I realized that Charles I was not entirely splendid and innocent, as I had always thought.'

Charles and Checketts returned to England by way of Tahiti, Mexico City and Jamaica, where they joined Prince Philip and Princess Anne at the Commonwealth Games – always, to Prince Charles, the anniversary of his creation as Prince of Wales. Before he left Australia, Geelong's headmaster, Mr Garnett, had said of him:

> Leaving aside the question of Royalty, we have really enjoyed having Prince Charles at the school. Before his visit, most Australians had very hazy and possibly erroneous ideas of him, if they had any ideas at all. They probably thought of him as just a distant, uninteresting figurehead. In future most of them will know him as a friendly, intelligent natural boy with a good sense of humour, someone who by no means has an easy task ahead of him in life.

Charles insisted on repaying the compliment. His six months in Australia had been 'the most wonderful period of my life', and he was himself aware of the self-confidence and maturity he had developed. The freshness and directness of the people had excited him; there was little of the servility or sycophancy to which he had grown so used at home. 'In Australia you are judged on how people see you and feel about you. There are no assumptions. You have to fend for yourself.' He was to make a point of returning to Australia (and Geelong) whenever possible, and has always regarded it as his favourite home from home.

Before leaving, the Prince wrote a few sentences which he asked David Checketts to read aloud to the reporters and well-wishers gathered at the airport:

> It would be difficult to leave without saying how much I have enjoyed and appreciated my stay in Australia and how touched I have been by the kindness of so many people in making these six months such a worthwhile experience. The most wonderful part was the opportunity to travel and see at least some of the country (I hope I shall be able to come back and see the rest) and also the chance to meet so many people, which completes the link with a country I am very sad to be leaving. And yet I shall now be able to visualize Australia in the most vivid terms, after such a marvellous visit.

Three terms back at Gordonstoun seemed an unwelcome fag-end to the Prince's schooldays, but they were to provide new opportunities of some moment. His arrival back at the school was considerably more impressive than his first appearance there, on his father's coat-tails, four years earlier; this time Prince Philip sat in the back as Charles drove himself up to the school gates, six-year-old Prince Andrew at his side in the front passenger seat. (His father's presence in the car was legally required because Charles had only a provisional licence; he passed his driving test in his mother's Rover 2000 the following April.)

His fellows at Windmill Lodge had elected him 'Helper', or Head of House, and the following term Charles was chosen as Guardian. In becoming head boy, he had followed his father in one role close to both their hearts; Prince Philip had been Guardian in 1938–9. The job was really a matter of liaison between the headmaster and the boys. There was no power to inflict corporal punishment, only to urge or advise the headmaster in administrative or disciplinary matters – not unlike the relationship, as defined by Walter Bagehot, between monarch and prime minister. Prince Charles on one occasion exercised his rights by trying to persuade Mr Chew not to expel two boys caught in a serious misdemeanour; his advice was listened to, but not acted upon. Though it failed, his stand was respected by headmaster and fellow-pupils alike. Basil Boothroyd, the Duke of Edinburgh's biographer, made the mistake of suggesting to the Dean of Windsor that Charles's appointment as Guardian was a 'put-up job'. 'No, no,' came the reply, 'he was streets ahead of the lot of them.'

As Helper, Charles had graduated to his own individual study, which set him more than ever apart from his fellows in Windmill Lodge. As Guardian, he moved out to a small bed-sitting-room in the flat of Bob Waddell, the

Gordonstoun art master (who had also directed the Prince as Macbeth). Waddell was relieved to find that the music blasting through the communal wall was, for once, more classical than pop. He had been gratified that the Prince had chosen one of his subjects, pottery, as his special project through-out his time at Gordonstoun. The master and the Prince became close friends, and still remain in touch.

Prince Charles's eighteenth birthday that November was spent carrying out his duties and preparing for his A-levels. As he gave a small tea-party in the Guardian's room, bells tolled in London and judges at the Old Bailey wore their finest scarlet robes in honour of the occasion. The day carried a special significance of which the Prince was well aware. He had now reached the age at which he could reign as King in his own right. If any disablement befell the sovereign, there would no longer be the need for a Regent to act in his place. For the first twelve months of Elizabeth II's reign, any such Regency would have passed to Princess Margaret; by the Regency Act of 1953, however, Parliament, at the sovereign's request, transferred the powers to the Duke of Edinburgh. Had any mischance befallen the Queen before her son's eighteenth birthday, Prince Philip would have reigned in her place.

The Regency, like the Monarchy, had traditionally been a hereditary privilege. In King George VI's reign, under the Regency Act of 1937, the Duke of Gloucester would have acted as Regent until Princess Elizabeth's eighteenth birthday. The reason for this departure from tradition in 1953, given that Prince Philip was well down the line of succession, was quite simply to implement a father's right to be responsible for the upbringing of his son. This was made clear in the Queen's message to Parliament, read by the Home Secretary, Sir David Maxwell Fyfe:

> The uncertainty of human life leads me to put you in mind of the possibility that a child of myself and my dear husband may succeed to the throne whilst under the age of eighteen years. And I would recommend to your considera-tion whether it be no expediency to provide that, in that event and also in the event of a Regency becoming necessary during my lifetime, whilst there is no child or grandchild of ours who can be the Regent, my husband should be the Regent and be charged with the guardianship of the person of the Sovereign.

That day, moreover, Prince Charles qualified to act as the senior Coun-cillor of State in the Queen's absence abroad. The following July, he was named as one of four such Councillors (the others being the Queen Mother, Princess Margaret and the Duke of Gloucester) empowered to act during the Queen's and Prince Philip's six-day visit to Canada. Had there been any urgent legislative business, he could have conducted a Privy Council meeting or given the royal assent to parliamentary Bills. He could have made peace or declared war. Perhaps to the disappointment of one preparing for exams, there was no such emergency to call him away from Gordonstoun.

To his own satisfaction more than anyone else's, that summer brought the news that Prince Charles had satisfied the A-level examiners. He was awarded a Grade C in French, and a B in history, with a distinction in the optional special paper (thus giving him an S-level). Prince Charles had proved that he could win a university place in his own right, unlike any other heir to the throne before him. His own delight was exceeded perhaps only by that of Mr R.M. Todd, secretary of the Oxford and Cambridge Schools Examinations Board, who got quite carried away when discussing the results in *The Times*. The optional paper, he said, was 'the one which marks out the high-flier as regards judgement, initiative and historical acumen. If a boy has done well in this paper – and the Prince got a distinction – it is a very good guide to university prospects.' Only six per cent of the 4,000 candidates had gained such distinctions. 'I consider that his perform-ance was extraordinary, especially when you consider that he was digging about in Australia and that kind of thing beforehand. He has so many things to do, he must have worked like a demon. I should hesitate to take the paper myself. . . .'

In his last days at Gordonstoun, Prince Charles also developed his skills on the cello, explored the music of Bach and Mozart, and followed his suc-cess as Macbeth by singing the Pirate King in Gilbert and Sullivan's *Pirates of Penzance*. Again, in the presence of his parents, there was an unfortunate line: 'We yield at once, with humble mien. . . . Because with all our faults we love the Queen.' As before, he was graduating to a major role from a minor; he had played the Duke of Exeter in *Henry V* before taking on Mac-beth, and he had sung a guardsman in Gilbert and Sullivan's *Patience*. But it was the musical element which most appealed to him – quite apart from his being, against theatrical tradition, the Prince who wanted to play a clown. Music was becoming a passion. A good sight-reader, he had sung in Benja-min Britten's St Nicholas, in Elgar's Dream of Gerontius, in Bach's B Minor Mass. He was playing the cello quite well – better, for sure, than he had the trumpet. 'There was a wonderful German lady who had been there for years; she was there when my father was there [Frau Lachmann, a refugee from Nazi Germany whom Hahn had helped to a job]. She kept turning round in the middle of the orchestra and saying: "Ach ze trumpet, I cannot stand ze trumpet." So I decided to give it up.' Inspired by hearing Jacqueline du Pré play the Dvořák concerto in the Royal Festival Hall, the Prince took cello lessons for several years, though pressure on his time eventually forced him to give it up.

I'm glad I went to Gordonstoun [he said later]. The toughness of the place is too much exaggerated by report. It was the character of the general education there – Kurt Hahn's principles; an education which tried to balance the physical and mental with the emphasis on self-reliance to develop a rounded human being. I did not enjoy school as much as I might have, but that was because I am happier at home than anywhere else. But Gordonstoun developed my will-power and self-control, helped me to discipline myself, and I think that discipline, not in the sense of making you bath in cold water, but in the Latin sense – giving shape and form and tidiness to your life – is the most important thing your education can do.

In this last year, curiously perhaps, Gordonstoun had developed more than anything else Charles's growing fondness for the arts. Other *penchants* were becoming clearer. Unlike his father, he showed no interest in matters scientific or technological; his preoccupations seemed to lie in the past rather than the future, and the time he had spent in the caves of Morayshire, bats fluttering around his head, was to be followed up in a close study of archaeology at Cambridge and thereafter. He had played his last team games – apart from polo, much more an individualist's sport anyway – and had only a broken nose to show for his time on the rugger field. His natural introspection had much more to feed on.

At home, too, he had made significant advances. On becoming eighteen, he had attended his first meeting of the Duchy of Cornwall. He had taken part in his first full-scale public engagement with his parents: a large garden-party at Holyroodhouse in Edinburgh, prompting a headline special to the *New York Times*: 'Prince Charles A Social Success: He's Just A Chip Off The Old Block'. He had been granted his own coat of arms, and thus his own ensign. And a date had now been announced for his investiture as Prince of Wales at Caernarvon: 1 July 1969. He had just two more years before his emergence, fully fledged and much trumpeted, into public life.

He was to spend them enjoying a brief taste of a unique kind of freedom, the freedom of university life, which to most who have known it retains a distinctive flavour throughout all their subsequent metamorphoses. Charles was more than ready for it. He may have been pleased he went to Gordonstoun, but he was even more pleased to leave. 'He's looking forward to leaving school,' said his father. 'There comes a time when you've had enough of it.'

12

Trinity and Aberystwyth 1967-69

I'm one of those stupid bums who never went to university
... and I don't think it's done me any harm.

Prince Philip

ON 22 DECEMBER 1965, the Queen and Prince Philip held a dinner-party at Buckingham Palace with the express purpose of discussing the Prince of Wales's future. Gathered around the table were the Prime Minister (Harold Wilson), the Archbishop of Canterbury (Michael Ramsey), Earl Mountbatten (representing the Services, as Admiral of the Fleet), the Dean of Windsor, the chairman of the Committee of University Vice-Chancellors (Sir Charles Wilson), and the Queen's private secretary, Sir Michael Adeane. Adeane had briefed all the guests beforehand on the subject for discussion – who was not himself invited.

Over breakfast next morning, Prince Charles learned from his parents that the conversation had continued into the small hours. He had already indicated his own wish to go to university, and the dinner-party had gone right through the pros and cons of ancient, 'redbrick' and modern. These in turn were weighed against the Services: Dartmouth, Cranwell, Sandhurst. Soft drinks and beer were served after dinner, plus a brandy for the Prime Minister, who urged Mountbatten to speak his mind. 'Trinity College,' said Charles's great-uncle Dickie, 'like his grandfather; Dartmouth like his father and grandfather; and then to sea in the Royal Navy, ending up with a command of his own.' The pattern was hard to resist.

But there would again be innovations. If he were to go to university, Charles was insistent on living in college – like Edward VIII at Oxford, but unlike Edward VII and George VI at Cambridge, both of whom had lived in large town houses, their tutors travelling to them. None of the three had stayed at university the full three years, or taken a degree. This remained a matter of debate between the Prince and his parents, who postponed a decision. Charles himself was at first in favour of a multi-disciplinary course of study, perhaps including a dabble in medicine and other such curiosities, which would have made a final examination impossible. Prince Philip kept his son's options open for him: 'I don't think his course should be constrained by the absolute need to take a degree.' Some advisers supported this view, telling his parents: 'For God's sake, don't let him risk exams.'

Prince Charles himself opted for Cambridge, preferring the old to the new wherever possible, and valuing his family's links with the University. Edward VIII had been the only Prince of Wales to go to Oxford, where he had won a reputation as a gay blade. The more academically-minded Charles had no such aspiration: he wanted to seize the chance for some peace and quiet, and to devote his last years free from royal duties to the kind of studies for which he would never again have time. Besides, Cambridge was closer to Sandringham, where he now had his own home. An old grey-stone cottage on the estate, known locally as 'Dr Ansell's House' because it had for years been the home of the Queen's Sandringham physician, had been converted for the Prince's use and re-christened Wood Farm. It would make the ideal week-end retreat.

The choice of college took slightly longer. The Dean of Windsor, Dr Woods, was asked by the Queen to look at the possibilities, and travelled to Cambridge for discussions with a number of heads of colleges. He delivered a written report to Her Majesty outlining the merits and demerits of a short-list of five, but finally opting for Trinity, his own college, where his elder son Robert (whom the Prince knew) was already an undergraduate, and his younger son Edward would be a contemporaneous freshman. The Royal Family was pleased. Trinity was the college of the Queen's father, King George VI, and his brother the Duke of Gloucester, of King Edward VII and his ill-fated son Prince Eddy, Duke of Clarence, quite apart from Bacon and Dryden, Marvell and Thackeray, Byron and Tennyson, Newton and Rutherford, Balfour and Baldwin, Melbourne, Grey and Campbell-Bannerman and the composer Ralph Vaughan Williams. King George V had visited the college when its Master had been Henry Montagu Butler, great-uncle of the recently installed Master, the newly ennobled Lord Butler of Saffron Walden. As R.A. ('Rab') Butler, the Conservative Chancellor, Foreign Secretary and Home Secretary, often described as 'the greatest Prime Minister we never had', he had been much involved with the Royal Family over the years, and was a valued and trusted friend.

Over Christmas 1966 Charles invited Butler to tea at Buckingham Palace, and told him of his interest in archaeology and anthropology. The Master suggested he pursue the subjects at Trinity. Against some urgings, Butler saw no point in the young Prince spending his youth trying to master the British constitution. There would be plenty of time for that. Let him study something he was genuinely interested in; if it gave him some understanding of the structure of society, perhaps even of the ritual adulation offered a monarchy by its people, so much the better.

Early in the New Year, Charles and his father returned the visit, driving over from Sandringham to meet Trinity's Senior Tutor, Dr Denis Marrian, who was also to be the Prince's individual tutor. Marrian conducted a standard entrance interview, and made the assessment that 'he was capable enough and interested enough to take an Honours Degree'. Marrian explained that a special course could be arranged, but could not lead to a degree of any kind. If the Prince spent his first year studying for the Part One Tripos, in archaeology and physical and social anthropology, he would then have three options: continue to the Part Two exams, switch to another subject for Part Two, or abandon the idea of taking a degree – and dabble. If he started out on a specially tailored course of studies, there would be no chance to turn back to a degree syllabus. Partly because of this, because he might be thought to be avoiding public assessment, the Prince opted for the 'ark and anth' degree course, reserving the option to switch to history for Part Two. He was thus embarked upon the hazardous course of attempting to become the first heir to the throne ever to win university honours.

That day, the Prince and his father inspected his 'set' of rooms, number six on Staircase E of New Court, a quiet corner of the college beside the River Cam and the Cambridge 'backs'. The Queen later paid a private visit herself, and had a long chat in her son's rooms with forty-seven-year-old Mrs Florence Moore, 'Mrs M' to the students, who was to be Prince Charles's 'bedder' (room-cleaner). She also had a look at the College sick-bay and met its overseer, Sister Custerson. Behind Her Majesty came a train of Sandringham workmen, bearing carpets and curtains for the new royal abode. At Butler's suggestion, the Prince was to allow himself the luxury of a telephone and a small kitchen area in his rooms; Trinity meanwhile protested that a new bathroom suite installed on the staircase that year had anyway long been scheduled. The Prince's set was on the first floor, to prevent inquisitive noses pressing against his window, and gave easy access to Cambridge's river walks and, in summer, punting. As Charles walked back through the Grand Gate with his father, past the statue of the boy Prince Charles (the First), he relished the prospect of a temporarily cloistered life. It would be 'marvellous to have three years when you are not bound by anything, and not married, and haven't got any particular job'.

His arrival as a freshman that October, in David Checketts's red Mini, was chaotic. He was twelve minutes late, thanks to city-centre traffic jams, leaving Lord Butler and Dr Marrian standing outside the College entrance with the huge crowd which had gathered to greet him. All he could see from the Mini on arrival were 'serried ranks of variously trousered legs, from which I had to distinguish those of the Master and the Senior Tutor'. His most vivid memory of that day is of 'several burly, bowler-hatted gentlemen [the College porters] dragging shut those magnificent wooden gates to prevent the crowd from following in. It was like a scene from the French Revolution.'

Someone in the crowd shouted 'Good luck!' 'Thanks,' Charles shouted back, 'I'll need it.' That evening, Robert Woods showed him round the College, and he dined in Hall with the first sitting of freshmen. But Lord Butler had perhaps been prescient in suggesting that Charles have his own kitchen. He had intended to dine in college with his fellow-students as often as possible, but it soon became something of an ordeal. As at Cheam and Gordonstoun, people tended to hang back, even to avoid him; at Cambridge, moreover, in the era of 1968 and all that, it was not always fashionable to be seen in the company of Princes. On one occasion, Charles found himself locked out of the College late at night, along with another nervous young freshman; together they had to ring the porter to let them in. It was the kind of modest adventure which sometimes sparks undergraduate friendships. Next night in Hall, however, as Charles wandered down the aisle looking for someone to sit with, he saw the face of his co-conspirator turn away in sheer embarrassment. Nobody wanted to be thought too anxious to become his friend.

If he did strike up any pleasant acquaintanceships it was hard to follow them up, as people tended to disappear into their own corner of university life for days or weeks on end. There were, at least, his Gloucester cousins to visit. But rather to Butler's disappointment, Charles tended to befriend such groups as the polo-playing fraternity (he quickly won his half-blue) or public-school-educated boys from the country gentry (with some of whom he founded an all-male dining club called the Wapiti Society), rather than the grammar-school products who comprised three-quarters of the College's population.

Butler proved himself a staunch ally and counsellor. He turned a blind eye when Charles went off in his detective's Land-Rover to collect his new MGB, complete with bull horn, from the city outskirts; undergraduates were not allowed cars in their first year, and even after that were forbidden to drive them within the city limits. More important, he cleared forty-five minutes before dinner each evening, and gave Charles his own key to a side entrance to the Master's Lodge, which led by way of what he liked to call 'my secret staircase' directly into the Master's study. He found Charles

Balmoral: last days of holiday freedom before ...

Cheam School: the Sunday crocodile to church

1958: created Prince of Wales at
nine years old

President Eisenhower learns the
royal walk

1960: returning with the Queen and the Queen Mother from Princess
Margaret's wedding to Tony Armstrong-Jones

The new arrival at Gordonstoun meets his headmaster, Robert Chew

Left: 1962: first steps at polo

Above: 1963: a skiing holiday, and a first taste of pursuit by the press

1966: leaving London Airport for school in Australia. Between Prince Philip and Prince Charles is David Checketts

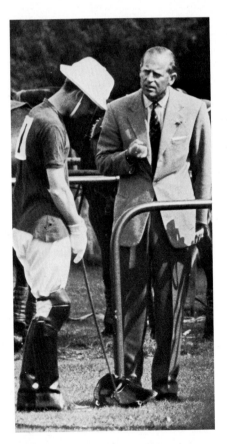

In the heir apparent's seat beside the throne at his first State Opening of Parliament, October 1967

Left: In his father's footsteps: 'He's taught me a great deal'

'All hail, Macbeth, that shalt be King hereafter!'

Two undergraduate Princes of Wales: the future King Edward VII at Oxford, 1859, and the future King Charles III at Cambridge 110 years later

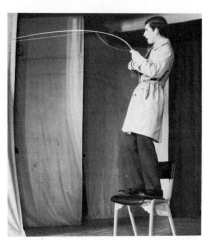

The actor manqué: scenes from the Trinity revue

Two Princes of Wales invested at Caernarvon: Prince Charles, 1969, and Prince Edward (later King Edward VIII and Duke of Windsor), 1911

At the Castle gate: presented to the people of Wales (and a television audience of 500 million)

The contemporary monarchy: go-karting with five-year-old Prince Edward

Left: Degree day: the first heir apparent in British history to win university honours

Above: High seriousness: an unconventional twenty-first birthday portrait

'talented – which is a different word from clever, and a different word from bright'. Though still a plodder academically, the Prince had a relentless curiosity about the ways of the world, which the Master was more than qualified to gratify. 'He grew,' says Butler. 'When he arrived he was boyish, rather immature, and perhaps too susceptible to the influence of his family.' Those evening chats, over Charles's three years at Trinity, were among the most important he had ever had in broadening his experience and understanding of his fellow-men.

They were not, however, without their tricky moments. Charles arrived one evening to tell Butler of a long chat he had with Hywel Jones, an economics student from Cardiff with rooms on the same staircase. Jones had read Marx at fourteen; an eloquent socialist, he was destined to become president of the Trinity student union. 'Do you think it would be all right if I joined the University Labour Club?' Charles asked the Master. 'Hell, no,' said Butler, and patiently explained that he must never show allegiance to any individual political party. But he urged the Prince to pursue his political arguments with Jones, in private, and both Prince and republican now believe they modified each other's views. Any brief flirtation with the Left was anyway, perhaps, only a product of Charles's immaturity, his susceptibility to ideas he had never before heard cogently argued; in his twenties, living at home again with his parents, he quickly reverted to their orthodox conservative attitudes.

Before the Prince's arrival at Trinity, Marrian had met both the local and national press, who had agreed to leave Charles in peace as much as public demand would allow. But happily for a Prince of Wales, the town of Cambridge anyway makes a point of treating celebrities with scant ceremony. He was able to bicycle around the town at will, those who recognized him letting him go on his way with a knowing grin, though a Land-Rover bearing his detective ('Oddjob' to the students) was never far behind. He could, for once in his life, go shopping: he was a familiar figure at the vegetable market, and on one occasion complained (correctly) that he had been short-changed. Without attracting crowds, he could visit the coffee house opposite Trinity, the Whim-at-Eleven, soon rechristened by its clients the 'Him-at-Eleven'. With Robert Woods he joined the college Madrigal Society, and played his cello in a public concert. He went to a club showing of the Marx Brothers in *A Night At The Opera*, signing himself in as Charlie Chester – which, as Charles, Earl of Chester, he had every right to do. He even joined adult education classes in pottery, one evening a week, at the Cambridge College of Arts and Technology.

Cambridge did, however, prompt the Prince of Wales to don a disguise, to avoid public recognition, for the first and only time in his life: he wanted to attend a student demonstration 'to see what they were like'. He came away unimpressed. 'I do try and understand what they're getting at, but I can't help feeling that a lot of it is purely for the sake of change, and for the sake of doing something to change things – which, from my point of view, is pointless.' The Prince also disapproved of less fundamental revolutions. 'Change for the sake of change' was his verdict on Trinity's relaxation of its 'gate laws'. Traditionally, the college door had been closed at eleven and guests had to leave by midnight; the times were now put back two hours. 'It was a great challenge to climb in over the wall,' said the disappointed Prince. 'Half the fun of university life is breaking the rules.'

Charles's first year at Cambridge saw the twenty-first birthday of *Varsity*, the undergraduate newspaper, and he agreed to a request from its then editor, David Taylor (now deputy editor of *Punch*) to contribute. For him, he wrote, life at Trinity meant 'every modulation of light and weather, like the orange-pink glow from the stone of the Wren Library in the last rays from a wintry sun'; it meant 'the everlasting splashing of the Great Court fountain' and the everlasting sound 'of photographers' boots ringing on the cobbles'. In the early morning, there was also the noise of the world coming to life beneath his window. 'This is something I find hard to accustom myself to, particularly the grinding note of an Urban District Council dust lorry's engine rising and falling in spasmodic energy at seven o'clock in the morning, accompanied by the monotonous jovial dustman's refrain of "O Come All Ye Faithful" and the headsplitting clang of the dustbins.' Some have greatness thrust upon them: within a few days the singing dustman in question, an ex-Coldstream Guards sergeant called Frank Clarke, was a national celebrity, and had been signed up by a record company. And – the perks of being a Prince – the UDC put back the collection time of Trinity dustbins to 9 a.m.

On Charles's nineteenth birthday that November, the bells of the University Church of Great St Mary's pealed, as usual, in honour of the occasion; this year, for once, the Prince of Wales climbed the 123 steps to the belfry to thank the twelve ringers. Otherwise, Prince Charles was not much in evidence around Cambridge, as he was taking his work rather seriously. He was keen to endow his anthropology studies with practical significance: 'If more people can be assisted to appreciate and understand their own social behaviour, the better and more healthy our society will be.' His director of studies, Dr John Coles, reported to Dr Marrian: 'He writes useful and thoughtful essays, although sometimes they are a little rushed. He is interested in discussion, and likes to draw parallels between the peoples we study and ourselves.' His archaeology, supervised by Dr Glyn Daniel of modest television renown, took him in the spring to the Dordogne region of France. A few members of the Cambridge Archaeological Society, with Cole, Daniel and David Checketts, had the rare privilege of being flown to France in a Heron of the Queen's Flight, with the Duke of Edinburgh at the controls. From the primitive cave paintings of Les Eyzies, the party travelled north through the Loire to Brittany, and thence to Jersey, where the expedition climaxed in a week-end under canvas. 'Believe me,' said Charles's long-suffering detective, 'this was no holiday. It's one of the hardest few days I've ever spent. I'd like to lie in the sun for a week to recover.'

At the end of the following term, enthusiasm and diligence had their reward: a place in Division I of Class II in the first-year Tripos Exams. When Charles had gone to Cambridge, the National Union of Students had debated a motion of protest at his admission on only two A-levels; others, ran the counter argument, may have been better qualified, but a Prince of Wales is entitled to benefit from the best of British education, and this one was at least trying to win his academic spurs. Now Prince Charles had conspicuously won himself an above-average result, on merit. That June he was formally invested as a Knight of the Garter; after the ceremony in Windsor Castle he walked in public procession, plumed and robed, with such figures as Mountbatten, Alexander and Montgomery. Photographs of the occasion show a new strength in his features: the hard-won self-confidence of a Prince who for the first time has placed himself in open competition with his fellows, and not been found wanting.

For his remaining two years, Prince Charles decided to turn his attention to history. 'Why?' asked Butler. 'If you stick to archaeology or anthropology, you might get a First.' But Charles was determined: Trinity had partly been chosen because of its strong history side, and he had always found it as much a pleasure as a duty to inform himself about his ancestors. He also wanted to begin a study of the British Constitution.

'Why?' asked Butler again.

'Because I'm probably going to be King,' replied Charles.

Butler was disappointed. 'You've got years for all that. Enjoy yourself while you can.' But the Prince was not to be budged. He had some months before attended his first State Opening of Parliament, supreme moment of the monarch's majesty, and for the first time taken the heir's traditional place on the sovereign's right. His sense of history was high in his mind, as intimations of the royal duties ahead began to crowd in on him.

There were, in the meantime, other pleasures to be sought. During one of their pre-prandial chats, Butler encouraged Charles to take part in the activities of the Dryden Society, Trinity's drama club. The Prince had displayed a taste for the stage at school, and now the Master advised him that more experience would prove invaluable for all kinds of royal public occasions, notably appearances on television. Thus it was, at the beginning of Charles's second year in the autumn of 1968, that the nation thrilled to the sight of the Prince of Wales having a custard pie thrust in his face. He had auditioned for (mime, improvisation, prepared speech), and secured the part of, the padre in Joe Orton's *Erpingham Camp*. The production, for which he borrowed the Dean's 'dog-collar', also required him at one point to be pelted with pork pies.

Trinity's modest amateur production received fuller (and more fulsome) reviews than any West End opening that week. Charles was evidently good box office, and three months later he was making his debut in satirical revue. His love of the Goons (a long-running anarchic radio comedy series starring Spike Milligan, Peter Sellers, Michael Bentine and Harry Secombe) was evidence of rather childish sense of humour, but then undergraduate comedy is scarcely of the most mature. His talent for Goonish funny voices, beloved of so many products of the British public schools, wowed the journalists at a special press preview, and had the black market in four shilling tickets active in Paris and Germany. Prince Charles took part in fourteen of the forty sketches in *Revulution*; impersonating the Duke of Wellington, mimicking Lord Butler, and declaring beneath an umbrella: 'I lead a sheltered life.' Most popular moment, perhaps, was his appearance in a Sherlock Holmes sketch as Sir Cummerbund Overspill; the Prince of Wales escorted a young lady offstage, a lascivious look in his eye: 'I like to give myself heirs.' The best remembered image, however, is that of the Prince of Wales sitting in a dustbin. Dustbins seemed to have become a recurring feature of his young life. In the role of 'Reg Sprott, Singing Dustman', the Prince charged £5 for interviews with the press, and rendered his chart-topping version of 'O Come All Ye Faithful'. The final Sunday performance had to be cancelled – the disadvantages of being a Prince – because of protests from the Lord's Day Observance Society. 'Very silly,' said Charles, rather daringly. 'It made me very angry.'

He was beginning to take an interest in wine – an extra-curricular topic of discussion with his tutor. Seeing Dr Marrian climbing out of the iron grating above his wine cellar one day, bottles in hand, Charles said: 'I've always wondered where the Senior Tutor lived.' In his Trinity rooms, meanwhile, he was developing something of a reputation as a homespun chef, entertaining the Butlers more than once to his speciality, goulash, and roasting a chicken for a private dinner with the Queen. His history studies were progressing under a new director of studies, Dr Anil Seal, a modern historian specializing in India and other non-European countries. One vacation saw the first of the Prince's now familiar whistle-stop tours around government and industry – a call on Barbara Castle at the Department of Employment, down a coal-mine, round a newspaper, over a power station – where he met another Trinity student doing a vacation job. 'That,' said Charles, 'makes two of us.'

But other royal duties were increasingly intruding into Cambridge life and work, to the considerable annoyance of Lord Butler, who referred to them scathingly as 'balcony jobs'. The approach of Charles's investiture at Caernarvon made its own demands: on a visit to the Welsh Office in Cardiff, he had a foretaste of the animosities in store – eggs, smoke-bombs, and shouts of 'Go home, Charlie'. Confessing afterwards to 'slight butterflies', he approached the demonstrators to seek their complaints, only to be roundly abused. 'You're not too brilliant, are you?' declared one national-ist (later fined for throwing a smoke-bomb). 'You got into university on just two A-levels.' Charles remembered: 'This chap was holding a placard in Welsh, and I asked him what it meant. I hadn't learnt much Welsh then. He just hurled abuse, so after more questions I gave up. There was no point.'

Back at Trinity, there was a knock at the door of his rooms one evening, and he thought he must be disturbing someone with his cello practice. On opening the door, however, he found two scruffy and menacing individuals, and feared for a moment it might be a kidnap attempt. They turned out to be two students from Aberystwyth University. 'We were in Cambridge collecting for our rag week, and we thought we'd come and see what you were like.' The Prince invited them in, gave them a contribution, and let them take a look at him. They returned home converts.

The occasion for such strange visitations was the announcement, on 1 November 1967, that the Prince of Wales would spend the summer term of 1969 – immediately prior to his investiture – studying Welsh at the University College of Wales, Aberystwyth. There had been a chorus of protest from Welsh Nationalists, then growing in strength, and they had not been alone; such Englishmen as A.J.P. Taylor, the historian, complained of 'this sordid plot to exploit Prince Charles', saying: 'The move is being made for political reasons, and what is worse, for reasons of party.... Mr Wilson is imposing on Prince Charles a sacrifice which he would not dream of imposing on his own son.'

Charles himself was not entirely happy about the move. Like Lord Butler, who was furious, he regarded it as an unwelcome interruption to his Cam-bridge studies, which were still going well. But he could see the need for it. He knew well, as few others did, that in the two years since the date of the investiture had been announced, his life had been geared for these last few months before his emergence as a public figure. He had made his first public speech (on 10 December 1968, as chairman of the 'Countryside in 1970' Conference, in Cardiff); he had attended his first Buckingham Palace garden-party; he had now attended his second State Opening of Parliament – to listen, ironically enough, to a Queen's Speech proposing the abolition of hereditary honours.

He had held two cocktail-parties for journalists, on 24 and 25 June 1968, after the Palace had requested each newspaper to assign one of its staff to take an interest in him. (They dubbed themselves the FOPCs, Followers of Prince Charles, and scarcely rose to their task: Mary Kenny of the London *Evening Standard* emerged from the Palace calling Charles 'a sweet virgin boy'.) He had given his first radio interview, to Jack de Manio for the Today programme, on St David's Day, 1969, and was limbering up for his first TV and newspaper interviews. The BBC–ITV joint production, *Royal Family*, was already well under way, and David Frost had been assigned to make a cinema film about Charles for investiture time.

The entire programme was being carefully organized from Buckingham Palace by two men: William Heseltine, then the Queen's press secretary (today her deputy private secretary), and David Checketts. In consultation with the Queen, Prince Philip and Prince Charles, they intended to use the investiture as an appropriate moment to 're-launch' the monarchy, as well as to launch Charles. Aberystwyth was part of the plan.

Heseltine, an Australian, had originally come to London in 1960, to join the Palace staff as an assistant information officer. Returning to Australia two years later (where he moved from the Prime Minister's to the Governor General's office), he was struck by the difference between the reserved, almost sullen monarch in the popular mind, and the jaunty, witty lady he had got to know. Returning to the Palace in 1965, Heseltine determined to do something about it. Checketts, who had experience of public relations as a director of Neilson McCarthy, was at the same time pondering the problem of sending Charles forth into society. The Jack de Manio interview was less of a calculated risk than is popularly thought; de Manio was also a director of Neilson McCarthy, and had long been a friend of Checketts's. Its success, however, surprised them all. The Prince talked naturally and easily about his schooldays, about Australia, about his parents and his early life, and did some of his funny voices from *Revolution*, then in production. When the television companies subsequently applied for an interview with Brian Connell and Cliff Michelmore, permission was granted warily but the success repeated. Charles was even prepared, to Connell's delight, to answer an unscheduled question about his thoughts on the subject of marriage.

Had this deliberate packaging of the Prince of Wales been more widely perceived early in 1969, as he prepared to brave the wrath of his reluctant principality, protest might have been yet more vociferous. Even as it was, bomb attacks on public buildings began. The Queen told her Prime Minister, Harold Wilson, that she feared for her son's safety. Thus the Home Office held a conference of police chiefs, chaired by the Chief Inspector of Constabulary, Sir Eric St Johnston, who called in a number of Welsh officers and the head of the Special Branch, Commander Ferguson Smith. It was decided to set up an intensive security operation to guard the Prince throughout his period in Wales that year, and Detective Superintendent Jock Wilson was promoted Chief Superintendent to command it. Then head of the Brixton CID, he was transferred to the Special Branch, and set up an operational headquarters in Shrewsbury.

This merely inflamed the controversy. It was argued that the unit should have been commanded by a Welshman, and based in Wales. Many Welsh-born police officers loyal to the Crown were disappointed, and even more dismayed when heavy security blankets descended somewhat crudely on Aberystwyth and Caernarvon, turning them into what the Nationalists could and did call 'garrison towns'. Another mistake, it seemed at the time, was in the very choice of Aberystwyth, whose dowdy mid-Victorian architecture had come to symbolize the unwelcome English invasion. Cardiff or Swansea Universities, neither so fiercely Welsh, would have provided quite as good a grounding in ethnic language and culture in a much less hostile atmosphere. There would have been no need to cause further resentment, as the security unit soon did, by billeting some seventy police officers in the town's hotels and infiltrating under-cover men into the University as kitchen staff, cleaners and even as students.

Furthermore, the choice of Aberystwyth meant that Prince Charles's tutor would be Edward Millward, lecturer in Welsh language and literature, who was also vice-president of Plaid Cymru, the Welsh Nationalist Party, which had declared itself opposed in principle to the investiture. When four Aberystwyth students went on a week's hunger strike in protest against the Prince's imminent arrival at the University, Mr Millward congratulated them.

It was not an enviable prospect. When Charles paid an advance visit to the campus with David Checketts on 1 April, the university bookshop was selling copies of a satirical poster of him captioned 'Arwr, Sant Carlo' (Hero, Saint Charles). Carlo, a common Welsh name for a dog, had become a popular derogatory nickname for the Prince. In that spring of 1969, the leader of the Welsh Language Society, Dafydd Iwan, had risen to the top of the Welsh charts with a song entitled Carlo, which ran:

> I have a friend who lives in Buckingham Palace,
> And Carlo Windsor is his name.

The last time I went round to his house
His mother answered the door and said:
'Carlo, Carlo, Carlo is playing polo today,
Carlo is playing polo with his Daddy.'
So come all ye serfs of Wales
And join in the chorus:
At last you have a Prince in this land of song.

'We don't need a royal circus,' said Dafydd Iwan. 'We need roads, industry, schools, indoor lavatories and water laid on.' Said one of the hunger strikers: 'We have nothing against Charles personally. But we are protesting against the political machine which is using him as a pawn.' Even the English-born president of the Aberystwyth student union declared: 'The investiture is a cheap shoddy political gesture, and if I were Welsh I would feel incensed.' Strong opposition to the English Prince of Wales, it was calculated, was confined to some 300 of the 1,000 Welsh students at Aberystwyth, themselves less than half the total student population. But it was the voice of protest, unsurprisingly, which made the running.

Around the Welsh hills, gelignite and machine-guns were unearthed by Jock Wilson's men. But a time-bomb destroyed an RAF radio post near Aberystwyth. On the day of the Prince's arrival, 20 April, young Welsh bloods attempted to saw the head off the statue of another Prince of Wales, the future Edward VIII, on the town's promenade. To make matters worse, the security team had dictated that the Prince could not live in Ceredigion Hall, the seafront hostel for students of Welsh; instead, he was given Room 95 in Pantycelyn, a modern hall of residence for English students. That first day Windsor, C., as he was in the University register, disarmed all protest by wandering openly around the town on a shopping expedition for coat-hangers and picture-hooks. He had taken the precaution of learning a few words of Welsh during his vacation, from the then Secretary of State for Wales, George Thomas, and he sprinkled them liberally among the crowd who followed his every move. Even more sensibly, he thereafter confined himself conscientiously to the University language laboratory; he knew he had only eight weeks before a major speech in Welsh at an Eisteddfod – quite apart from another a month later, at his investiture, before a television audience of 500 million.

The prospect concentrated the Prince's mind wonderfully, and the crowds soon melted away from the entrance to Pantycelyn. His fellow-students there, on one occasion, dispersed a group of noisy nationalist demonstrators by emptying buckets of water over their heads. But the weeks, on the whole, passed quietly, as he had anticipated in his St David's Day broadcast: 'Once I have been there for eight weeks, things might improve.'

They did. It was a lonely time – 'I haven't many friends, there haven't been many parties' – and it had begun apprehensively: 'Naturally, misgivings had built up, but one had an exaggerated view of the situation.' He turned down an invitation to meet nationalist students in the local milk bar, saying he would choose his own location, but from Millward he learnt 'a great deal about nationalist ideas and aims and policies'. During his television interview, he declared his sympathy: 'If I've learnt anything in the last eight weeks, it's been about Wales in particular, and its problems, and what these people feel about Wales. They're depressed about what might happen if they don't try and preserve the language and culture, which is unique and special to Wales. And if something is unique and special, I think it's well worth preserving.' One measure of his acceptance by fellow-students is that a continental magazine found no takers for its offer of £5,000 for a photograph of the Prince of Wales being slapped in the face by a Welsh Nationalist. After he left, the number of students applying for places at Aberystwyth rose by twenty-five per cent.

When he met the Mayor of Llanelli, Charles was able to 'fill his eye with saliva' by pronouncing the name of his town correctly. His ingenuous charm, and his evident eagerness to please, had won most Welsh hearts. To the majority he was 'Carlo bach' – a term of endearment as significant in Wales as 'pommy bastard' had been in Australia. It was a not immodest personal success, much admired by his father – 'He came, saw and conquered the Welsh,' Prince Philip confided to a friend – and a source of great relief to David Checketts, whose admiration of his young master grew by the day. As Checketts's plans for the 'unveiling' of Charles neared fruition, he had one great source of strength: by hitherto protecting the Prince as far as possible from personal publicity, he had also concealed the fact that this young man was more than equal to the tasks ahead of him. He was alert, shrewd and solemnly aware of his role. All of which would come as something of a surprise to the great British public, who in the Palace's view could have been forgiven for thinking – after the Cherry Brandy Incident, the Goonish theatricals and the initial inability to handle Welsh protest – that the Prince was just another upper-class half-wit.

But if Charles had defused Aberystwyth, he knew that he had as yet won less than half the battle. Just before going there, he had honestly – if foolishly – asked a banner-carrying Welsh Nationalist who Llewelyn was, candidly confessing that he didn't yet know much Welsh history. Now he did. Llewe-lyn-ap-Gruffydd, he knew only too well, was the last Welsh Prince of Wales, killed in 1282 by the English invader, Edward I. The following year, after, for good measure, having hanged, beheaded, disembowelled and quartered Llewelyn's brother David, Edward had captured Caernarvon Castle. There, in 1284, he had declared his infant son the first English Prince of Wales. And there, the following month, Charles was to undergo the private and public ordeal of investiture as the twenty-first English Prince of Wales, but only the second in nearly 700 years to be invested at Caernarvon.

He hadn't conquered Wales yet.

13

Investiture
1967-69

Your friends will understand that as a Prince you are obliged
to do things which may seem a little silly.

Queen Mary to her son Edward, Prince of
Wales, before his investiture at Caernarvon
in 1911

DURING THE SUMMER OF 1969, while Prince Charles was weathering the
storm at Aberystwyth, Welshmen slightly further north were enjoying
another unusual glimpse of their monarchy in action. Out in Caernarvon
Bay the Queen's brother-in-law, the first Earl of Snowdon, was living in
a handsome launch lent to him by a Welsh industrialist. With him were two
friends, both designers: Carl Toms, already well known for his work in
theatre, ballet and film design, and John Pound of the Ministry of Works
design team. At six each morning Snowdon would go water-skiing around
the bay, then breakfast with his colleagues in the morning sunshine, discussing the problems of the day ahead. Charles's investiture as Prince of Wales,
they were determined, was not going to be just another piece of predictable
royal pageantry. The new materials developed in the sixties, the chic new
aesthetic brought into middle-class homes by Sunday colour supplements,
the role Snowdon had won himself as a champion of industrial and commercial design (he had recently provided London Zoo with its controversial
aviary) – all were going to play a part. Above all, Snowdon argued, he was
designing a television production for 500 million viewers. With his theatric-
ally-minded team ranged against Garter King of Arms's traditional protocol
experts, and the Duke of Norfolk acting the genial referee, Caernarvon
Castle was staging another in its long history of Welsh–English battles royal.

Snowdon is, of course, a Welshman himself. The young Tony Armstrong-
Jones grew up only three miles from Caernarvon at Plas Dinas, his father's

home in the village of Bontnewydd, and as a boy had often played in the castle grounds. He had not lost touch when his London career as a photographer began to flourish in the 1950s; among many memorable royal studies was Prince Charles's official seventh birthday portrait in 1955. So when he married the Queen's sister in 1960, it seemed logical that he should take his title from his homeland – and that three years later, following the death of Lord Harlech, the Queen should invite him to become Constable of Caernarvon Castle.

When creating her son Prince of Wales in 1958, Elizabeth II had promised the Welsh people that she would one day 'present him to you at Caernarvon'. There were times she subsequently regretted the commitment; the decline of the British economy, the rise of Welsh nationalism and the advent of an era of violent protest all conspired to make such a ceremony seem at best a political blunder, at worst a positive danger to its protagonist's life. So there was much discussion as to timing, the approach of Charles's twenty-first birthday being balanced against the depressed mood of late-sixties Britain. Five years after the initial announcement, with Snowdon's appointment as Constable, interested parties thought he must know the date the Queen had in mind. He did not. She had not yet decided herself. No announcement was to be forthcoming for another four years.

In the meantime, Snowdon took his new job very seriously. Some 230,000 tourists visited Caernarvon Castle each year in those pre-investiture days (the number has since doubled), and he wanted it looking its best. Down came all those ugly green signs pointing people to the car park and the toilets, and up went the Perspex of which Snowdon was to prove so fond. Floodlighting was introduced. Sightlines were improved. And out went all the relics of the only previous investiture at Caernarvon, that of the last Prince of Wales, the future King Edward VIII, in 1911.

It was David Lloyd George, then Chancellor of the Exchequer, who had foisted this flagrantly political device on King George V less than a year after he had ascended the throne. Alfred Edwards, Bishop of St Asaph (and later the first Archbishop of Wales), had told Lloyd George of his vain attempts to persuade Queen Victoria and Edward VII of the need for some ceremony demonstrating Anglo-Welsh unity, during the painful days of the disestablishment of the Welsh Church. As MP for Caernarvon, Constable of the Castle, and a born opportunist, Lloyd George talked the King into mounting a ceremony which could only enhance his own political prestige and appease the opponents of his constant assaults on inherited privilege. The Duke of Windsor himself recalled how shocked George V and his family had been 'only a few years before' by Lloyd George's famous Limehouse speech.

History has embalmed the myth that Edward I displayed his infant son to the Welsh barons at Caernarvon in 1284, thus creating the long line of English Princes of Wales. The story seems to be pure invention, but it provided the only 'precedent' for the 1911 ceremony. For more than 600 years, monarchs had been content to invest their eldest sons in Parliament, in royal palaces or in English towns. Caernarvon, to the Welsh, remained the symbol of English usurpation of their sovereignty. None the less, the King decided that such a spectacle would provide a fitting climax to his nationwide coronation tour. Lloyd George had his way, and scored a momentous political triumph. To this day he stands in aggressive bronze splendour in the Castle Square, his back turned on the ancient battlements – 'the alternative, I suppose,' as Charles himself pointed out, 'to turning his back on the people'.

For the future Edward VIII, then a seventeen-year-old naval cadet at Dartmouth, popular enough to be nicknamed 'Sardine' by his fellow-midshipmen, it was an appalling prospect.

> The ceremony I had to go through, with the speech I had to make, the Welsh I had to speak, were, I thought, a sufficient ordeal for anyone. But when a tailor appeared to measure me for a fantastic costume designed for the occasion, consisting of white satin breeches and a mantle and surcoat of purple velvet edged with ermine, I decided things had gone too far.

As Lord Anglesey supervised the restoration of the ruined castle, using stone from the same quarries mined six hundred years before, the young Prince refused to wear the 'preposterous rig'. There ensued what he called 'a family blow-up'. He complained that he would become a laughing-stock to his friends in the Navy, but his mother talked him into acquiescence: 'It will be only for this once.'

His memories of that sweltering July day, nevertheless, remained miserable.

> Within the vast ruin of Caernarvon Castle, with Winston Churchill as Home Secretary mellifluously proclaiming my titles (he told me afterwards that he rehearsed them on the golf course), my father invested me as Prince of Wales. Upon my head he put a coronet cap as token of principality, and into my hand the gold verge of government, and on the middle finger the gold ring of responsibility. Then leading me by the hand through an archway to one of the towers of the battlements, he presented me to the people of Wales. Half fainting with heat and nervousness, I delivered the Welsh sentences that Mr Lloyd George, standing close by in the ancient garb of Constable, had taught me.

In his diary that night, the King recorded: 'The dear boy did it all remarkably well and looked so nice.' But the Prince wrote: 'I got the impression that if I did what was asked of me, it would help Papa in his dealings with the difficult Mr Lloyd George.'

These memories were all revived in the summer of 1967, during Prince Charles's last term at Gordonstoun, when it was announced that his investure would be held at Caernarvon two years later. By autumn, the date had hardened to 1 July 1969, and the scale of the operation had become frighteningly apparent. When Charles attended the first meeting of the Investiture Committee at St James's Palace on 26 October, he was astonished to find around the vast mahogany table no fewer than fifty-three members, ranging from Lord Cobbold, the Lord Chamberlain, via the chairman of the Welsh Tourist Board to the Rev. E. Gwyndaf Evans, Archdruid of Wales. The chairman was, of course, Bernard, Duke of Norfolk, who as hereditary Earl Marshal and Chief Butler of England was a past master of state ceremonial, his finest hour having been the stage-management of Elizabeth II's coronation in 1953. His two most vociferous lieutenants were Snowdon and the Secretary of State for Wales, Cledwyn Hughes (succeeded the following year by George Thomas). Charles was relieved to see the reassuring presence of David Checketts.

With a budget provisionally fixed by the Government at £200,000, an office for the investiture was established in Northumberland Avenue. Sub-committees began to proliferate, discussing music, protocol, heraldry, the religious service, and of course design. Snowdon conceived and chaired one of his own, under the auspices of the Council of Industrial Design, to vet all official souvenirs for the occasion. Over the next eighteen months, 166 out of 450 designs submitted – goblets and cruets, pendants and paper-weights, dolls, rugs and even pie-funnels – were approved by a team including Mary Quant, the fashion designer. Strict rules were laid down for the marketing of approved souvenirs: none were to be sold before 31 January 1969, or manufactured after 31 December 1969, and all heraldic devices were to be based on a choice of fifty officially made available to industry by the College of Arms.

Protests began at once. Emrys Hughes MP, a Welsh republican representing a Scottish seat, launched a sustained House of Commons campaign by denouncing the entire 'mini-coronation'. It was quite inappropriate, he told the House, to hold a ceremony 'in a castle built by Welsh slave labour under the orders of the intruder, the conqueror'. The 40,000-member Welsh Nationalist Party, Plaid Cymru, had one MP – its president, Gwynfor Evans, who two years earlier had won Carmarthen from Labour (in the shape, ironically enough, of David Lloyd George's daughter Megan). 'Not unnaturally,' said Evans, 'I am unenthusiastic about this. The situation would be quite different if Wales had Commonwealth status, in which case the Queen of England would be Queen of Wales, as she is the Queen of Canada, Australia and New Zealand when she goes to those countries.'

Plaid Cymru dissociated itself from what it called 'a piece of English trickery', and began a long campaign of peaceful protest. The more extreme Welsh Language Society, claiming 800 members, took to the roads. English-language traffic signs all over Wales were defaced; Welsh, and occasionally revolutionary, slogans appeared on roads and bridges. But both groups also dissociated themselves from the sterner forms of protest which began on 17 November. As Lord Snowdon and the Secretary for Wales were arriving in Cardiff for a planning meeting with 450 Welsh delegates, a time-bomb exploded in the building, unhappily named the Temple of Peace. There was extensive damage, but no one was hurt. It was the first of a succession of fifteen bomb attacks on government and military buildings, post offices and pipelines, which would culminate on the morning of the investiture itself. 'If this doesn't stop, someone is going to get killed,' said Cardiff's chief constable, and he was to be proved right.

For the time being, however, there was the financial battle to be waged. In Parliament that Christmas, another Welsh Labour MP, Elystan Morgan, suggested that the true cost would be closer to two-and-a-half million pounds. For the first time it was publicly made clear that the Queen herself had asked for every economy to be made, offering to save expense by fore-going her own elaborate procession to the Castle with the Windsor greys, and personally vetoing the originally proposed estimate of £500,000. This never deterred Emrys Hughes, who in his subsequent book *The Prince, The Crown and The Cash*, wrote:

> Although the Secretary for Wales took the view that the main purpose of the investiture was to boost the Welsh tourist industry, there was another view: that it would give a boost to the Prince, and Royalty, preparatory to a campaign for an increase in the Civil List.

At a time of national austerity, confusion reigned as to exactly what the cost would be. The Minister for Public Buildings and Works, Robert Mellish, insisted that it was a maximum of £200,000, and the Duke of Norfolk explained the misunderstandings in a letter of apology to the Prime Minister, Harold Wilson. 'It was meant to be a help, not a hindrance. I said that from what I'd heard it might come to more than £200,000, and we may have to have – what's the phrase – a supplementary estimate.' Throughout the disputations, Norfolk preserved an endearing line in no-nonsense banter. He moaned about the limited funds, saying that £1 million would have given his brainchild 'a spot of glamour', and he insisted that all the rehearsals were held in London 'because Caernarvon is such a hell of a place to get to'.

To defuse the growing chorus of protest, it was thought prudent for Charles to begin a series of meetings with Welshmen, and Cledwyn Hughes hosted a luncheon in his honour for Welsh academics, politicians, rugby players, opera singers, actors and Goons. The next target, however, was the £55,000 budget set aside for the preparation of the Castle, £7,650 of which was allotted to Snowdon's design team. Emrys Hughes suggested in the Commons that the money might be better spent on housing and education in the principality. Had he known what Lord Snowdon and his friends were planning, he might have adopted even more acerbic tones.

Attempting to ignore the protest campaign, Snowdon took himself off to Caernarvon with his Aston Martin, his motorbike and his speedboat, and mused upon the Victorian motto which has always been his artistic creed: 'Never construct decoration; only decorate construction.' The Castle, in other words, was to be left as spare and uncluttered as possible. Whatever constructions and embellishments were necessary would be kept classically simple and elegant. By rejecting the serried array of heraldic banners prepared by the College of Arms, in favour of a simplified Carl Toms motif repeated around the towers and battlements, Snowdon deprived the College of considerable revenue and further distanced himself from Garter King of Arms and his traditionalists.

Toms, aesthetically, was a romantic, Pound a modernist. Sitting between them on train rides to and from Caernarvon, Snowdon had to find a balance. When the three had finally agreed in principle on a massive Perspex canopy over the central royal dais, Pound suggested that it should be held aloft by balloons. Snowdon pointed out that it needed only one Welsh Nationalist marksman, or even a mischievous child with an air rifle, to bring the whole edifice down on the royal heads beneath. He opted for giant steel pillars, raked slightly outwards to give the canopy the look of a medieval tent. A model of the structure was tested in the British Aircraft Corporation's wind tunnel, for resistance to 60 m.p.h. gales, which had already caused havoc with some of the Toms heraldic banners. Wind was one of Snowdon's constant worries.

Another was rain. He had further enraged 'Garter' (Sir Anthony Wagner) by refusing to countenance any red carpets, making the revolutionary suggestion that the Queen should walk across grass. Garter pointed out that if it rained, her heels would sink into the fifty tons of specially laid turf; so Snowdon consulted Her Majesty, who happily agreed to avoid stilettos. Had there been any rain in the few days before the ceremony, however, he was well aware that the royal procession would have got bogged down. Even the grass itself caused another disagreement, this time happily settled by compromise. The traditionalists wanted it one inch proud of the paved walkways; Snowdon's team wanted it flush. When the turf was laid, it was slightly proud, contoured down at the edges to meet the paving stones.

Furthermore, Snowdon had insisted to the television, radio and press representatives that he did not want cameras filming each other. Positions were allocated so that no one got in each other's frames; television cranes were reluctantly persuaded to descend out of view between shots. With the enthusiastic support of the TV crews, Snowdon overruled plans for striped awnings to protect the royal party as it processed to its central position. With only the Perspex canopy rising above ground level, the cameras had clear views of the ceremony from every possible angle. The cameramen appreciated having a photographer in charge: light-meter readings were constant all over the site.

Snowdon's aesthetic also called for as few microphones as possible obscuring the Queen and the Prince as the various speeches were delivered. Snowdon decided on a maximum of two, concealed behind an elegant pillar of Welsh slate and fed by underground wires. Again rain, and the failure of either microphone, could have deprived the watching world of sound with its pictures. For aesthetic reasons, Snowdon was taking quite a lot of risks. He was also, to Garter's further horror, refusing any kind of shelter to the VIP guests. In this, as in all, Norfolk gave him invaluable support. 'What happens if it rains?' Charles himself asked the Duke one day. 'We get wet,' replied the Earl Marshal.

In 1911 the central investiture ritual had taken place in a striped yellow crusader tent, so that few of the 11,000 notables present could see a thing. Snowdon's theatrical design eased that problem, but he caused further consternation by insisting that the audience be reduced to 4,000, so that they presented a decorous, well-behaved assemblage for the cameras. Even so, there were some whose view of the proceedings would be obscured by a Castle wall. Snowdon installed close-circuit TV, but it proved invisible in sunlight. So he commissioned a series of giant plastic mirrors to reflect the scene. When they were in place, he realized he had made a fundamental error: they worked for only one vertical segment of the audience. So he took them down again, and installed them as cheery décor in the waiting-room – a converted dungeon – he was making ready for the Prince. He then designed a series of convex plastic balloon mirrors to reflect the scene to the unsighted, and on investiture morning he got the royal trumpeters to blow them up.

Pound and Snowdon then began to think about the design of the 4,000 guests' chairs. They again flouted convention by refusing to accord different styles of seat to different grades of guest, and rejecting Garter's request for specially designed, very costly chairs for VIPs. So it was that royalty entered the era of the utility throne. Made of Welsh slate, those of Prince Philip and Prince Charles were backless, for the benefit of the TV cameras, while the Queen's had a low back for reasons of status rather than comfort. Each throne was tailored to its occupant's every ergonomic need. For the rest, it was to be a simple, elegant chair of laminated plywood, painted scarlet, the seat covered in red Welsh tweed. With their detachable legs, they were among the first 'knock-down' (collapsible) furniture seen in Britain. The majority were positioned, legless, on the scaffolding ranged across the Castle parapets, with the front row alone sufficiently privileged to enjoy attached legs. Adhering to his policy that every material and manufacturer should be Welsh, Snowdon commissioned Remploy Ltd (who employed only disabled people) to produce them so economically that they could afterwards be sold to their occupants for £12 each. Thus they would be self-financing, like many items on his design budget (which after the event came close to breaking even). By the morning of the investiture, Remploy had sold just six chairs – all to Lord Snowdon, the dining-room of whose country home they still adorn. By the end of the day, they could have sold twice the 4,000 they had made, but Snowdon vetoed any profiteering. There was also, however, a brisk trade in £1.50 red tweed cushions, emblazoned with the Prince of Wales's insignia, for those outside the Castle itself.

ICI meanwhile began the manufacture of the giant Perspex canopy. Twenty-five feet wide at the front, tapering downwards to nine feet six inches, and weighing over a ton, it was the largest Perspex object ever made. It had to be transported to the Castle in three separate units, each crate weighing more than two tons, and enjoying a clearance of just three-quarters of an inch through the Castle gates. The moat had to be specially bridged: Snowdon's original scheme to fly the canopy in by helicopter was vetoed by the security team. Like everything else, the canopy was destroyed after the ceremony, at Snowdon's insistence, so fearful was he of a shoddy souvenir hunt. But he himself kept a small chunk which stands to this day in the studio of his home. Over the years the glue welding the three main sections, each more than an inch thick, has cracked and disfigured, making its designer more than ever thankful that he did not leave it in place for posterity. All that remains is the central, circular dais of Welsh slate, which has since been used, to Snowdon's delight, for military ceremonies 'in the round'.

He had decided to attach a giant version of the Prince of Wales's three-feather insignia, moulded in expanded polystyrene and painted gold, to the canopy's underbelly. But he could not find, from all the many available versions, a design combining the simplicity and sophistication he sought. Regular drinkers at the Prince of Wales pub in Notting Hill Gate, London, were surprised one evening to find the Queen's brother-in-law taking minutely detailed photographs of the pub's Victorian windows. The feathers were delicately etched, but still (he thought) rather bland. Then in Caernarvon Castle itself, in the regimental museum of the Royal Welch Fusiliers, he found a Cader Idris belt-buckle with exactly what he was looking for. The right-hand feather sloped elegantly back, and the ICH DIEN scrolled motto curled gently from feather to feather. Large photographic reproductions were made, and the nine-foot polystyrene version hand carved. It was the dominant motif of the day.

On 16 July 1968, just under a year before the appointed date, Prince Charles travelled incognito with Snowdon on the overnight train from London to Holyhead. The Constable thought it important that the central figure of the drama should have some feel of the place, and had shrouded their excursion in total secrecy. They motored across Anglesey and joined the tourists in the Castle; as they processed from the Water Gate along the proposed route of the procession to the central dais, news of the royal presence spread around Caernarvon, throwing the borough council into a panic. The Mayor and the town clerk were out of town for the day on business, so their deputies hurried along to offer an official welcome. Then the press caught up, and Snowdon's hopes of a quiet preview for Charles were ruined. He managed to escape by taking the Prince along to meet Evan Lloyd, boatman to his late father, Ronnie Armstrong-Jones, who took them for a trip round the bay on the Harbour Trust Launch, *Cadnant*. At Snowdon's suggestion, the boatman then simply took the Prince home to meet his wife Nellie. Number 3 Balaclava Road, Caernarvon, thus became the first Welsh household in which the Prince of Wales ever set foot.

During the following year, the prospect of Charles's investiture roused both town and principality to fever pitch. When the date had been announced, eighteen months ahead of time, every hotel room and inn in Caernarvon and for twenty miles around was declared booked within forty-eight hours. As much as a year before the day itself, grossly inflated prices offered for accommodation by overseas visitors and desperate journalists were being turned down. The borough council tried to keep control, but Caernarvon knew it was in for a giant one-night spree. Investiture fever soon spread through the rest of Wales, as plans were laid for a week-long programme of celebrations under the title Croeso 69 (Welcome 69). The Welsh Tourist Board was about to receive the greatest boost in its history. Snowdon's hopes of keeping all souvenirs decorous proved, not to his surprise, vain. Visiting Caernarvon on investiture eve, Nicholas Tomalin of the *Sunday Times* wrote of Prince Charles: 'You can sit on him, wear him, stand on him, drink out of him, dry your dishes with him, even hold your oven casseroles with him.' Shopkeepers had decided, however, that plans to put 'God Bless The Prince of Wales' through special sticks of Welsh humbug rock were 'inappropriate'.

Caernarvon council authorized its private householders to take in paying guests during the investiture period, and issued several tons of free paint to its citizens – in carefully selected, non-controversial colours – as an incentive to spruce the place up. A Welsh property-owner did brisk business with Americans when he offered 500,000 foot-square plots of land in Snowdonia for sale at £4 each; their particular attraction was that the Queen owned mineral and sporting rights to the territory, so each lucky purchaser received an illuminated title-deed proving joint ownership with Her Majesty.

The political protests continued. Charles laughed off the suggestion that he was 'a political tool', but the bombing went on. The investiture was giving a brief new lease of life to a thin line of anarchists calling themselves the Free Welsh Army. They claimed close relations with the Provisional IRA, then a year into a renewed campaign of violence in Northern Ireland, but were fortunately much less well organized. (Nine self-confessed members were arrested in February 1969; after a four-month trial which ended on the morning of the investiture, two were sentenced to nineteen months imprisonment.) The Welsh Language Society, organizing a series of anti-investiture rallies, declared that 'Prince Charles has never done anything for Wales, and has no right to call himself its Prince'.

A majority of Plaid Cymru members voted to boycott the ceremony, although the party's initially united opposition had now broken down in an embarrassing public split. The two groups were fairly evenly balanced: on the one side, implacable opponents who viewed the investiture as an English plot to be resisted at all costs; on the other, the more moderate upholders of party policy, which called for an independent Wales under the Crown. The common ground was perhaps the most paradoxical: to oppose the investiture of a Prince who was taking the trouble to learn Welsh seemed illogical in view of the party's official allegiance to the Crown, yet to support the ceremony seemed somehow supine. The consensus eventually reached the undignified posture of ignoring the whole thing, seemingly in the hope that it would go away.

The polls were not much more helpful. After an unofficial one declaring more support for the investiture in Wales (seventy-six per cent) than in England (sixty-seven) or Scotland (sixty-five), Opinion Research Centre came up with some surprising figures for the *Western Mail*, Wales's national morning newspaper. The poll found that forty-four per cent of the Welsh people thought the investiture and its accompanying celebrations 'a waste of money'. The pollsters themselves immediately questioned the figure by explaining that it was the attitude of the young and the extreme nationalists which had made it so high; older people generally regarded the money as well spent. As many as eighty-six per cent, however, believed that the Prince of Wales did not mix informally enough with the Welsh people, and seventy-three per cent wanted him to have an official residence in Wales.

Six months later, defending the Royal Family's decision in a Welsh television interview, the Duke of Edinburgh felt confident enough to say: 'The governing factor was that it was quite obvious that a very large proportion of Welsh opinion favoured having the investiture.' Having agreed that there may well be further terrorism, and thrown in a characteristic side-swipe at student demonstrators, Prince Philip confessed that 'the doubts were not so much about allowing the Prince to take part at all, but perhaps to what extent this sort of virtually medieval revival is relevant'. Charles himself took a more conciliatory tone: 'I don't blame people demonstrating like that. They've never seen me before. They don't know what I'm like. I've hardly been to Wales, and you can't expect people to be over-zealous about the fact of having a so-called English Prince come amongst them and be frightfully excited about it.' He wasn't surprised it had become 'a friction point' for so many people.

He also admitted to sharing his great-uncle's dread of the occasion, pointing out that he himself had the advantage of being three years older. 'It would be unnatural if one didn't feel any apprehension. One always wonders what's going to happen in this sort of thing. But I think if one takes it as it comes, it'll be much easier. . . . As long as I don't get covered too much in egg and tomato, I'll be all right.' He would be glad, he said, when it was over.

Six months before the appointed day, at the height of the bombing and protest campaign, a small but persistent caucus of the Investiture Committee favoured cancellation or postponement. The Secretary of State, George Thomas, called a representative meeting at the Welsh Office in Cardiff, which has remained a closely-guarded secret to this day. The arguments for postponement were reluctant, but there was an irresistible fear that the Prince's life was in genuine danger. Thomas himself had received letters threatening his life, but it was his speech from the chair, the eloquence of a Welshman sharpening the shrewdness of an experienced politician, which swayed the meeting. 'If we postpone the investiture,' he said, 'we will be cancelling it – putting it off for ever. There should be no part of the United Kingdom where the Royal Family cannot go.' He went on: 'It will require great moral courage from that young man, but he has already displayed it in considerable quantities.' He told the meeting of the day he had accompanied Prince Charles through noisy demonstrators to the Welsh Office. Looking out at them through the window, the Prince had said to the Secretary of State: 'I'm going to talk to them.' Thomas had said: 'I would advise against it, sir.' 'I know you would, but I'm going.' 'In that case, sir, I'm coming with you.'

The caucus was persuaded, and the meeting had officially never taken place. Those still in doubt as the investiture approached were mightily cheered three weeks before the event, when Prince Charles himself dramatically changed the atmosphere. His speech in Welsh to Urdd Gobaith Cymru, the Welsh League of Youth, at its Eisteddfod in Aberystwyth, was a triumph. Three hundred well-pronounced, unfluffed words proved that this English Prince of Wales could speak Welsh quite as well as those few Welshmen who could speak any. 'I have found time to read Dafydd ap Gwilym in bed,' he said of an amorous Welsh bard well known to the locals, 'and now I know something of the girls of Llanbadarn.' All that was needed was a promise to fight for the preservation of the language, and his reception was tumultuous. The Plaid Cymru split widened in the moderates' favour, and a majority statement from its executive called for an end to the Welsh graffiti protest campaign. The Welsh Language Society remained undeterred, and announced anti-investiture rallies for the week before the ceremony. But Charles had won Welsh hearts. The token eight weeks in Aberystwyth had more than justified the risks involved; by his own steadfast and cautious efforts, he had converted an apparent political blunder into something of a personal triumph.

The open-hearted Welsh, after all the bluster, realized what an impossible position Charles had been placed in, and what a decorous exit he had made. 'If anybody lays a finger on that lad,' a self-declared nationalist was heard to announce in an Aberystwyth pub, 'they'll swing from the nearest tree.' A mid-Wales trade unionist opined: 'I'm not a royalist. I'm a socialist. But I tell you this: that young man has done more for Wales already than we could dream of.' It was, however, the Mayor of Caernarvon, Ifor Bowen Griffiths, who scaled the true Welsh heights of English hyperbole: 'Charles is the ace in our pack. When he stood up at the Eisteddfod and started to speak in Welsh, he wasn't just a boy. He was a Prince. You could have put a suit of armour on that lad and sent him off to Agincourt.'

The Prince found further evidence of his hard-won acceptance later that week in Cardiff. Receiving the freedom of the city on behalf of the newly-formed Royal Regiment of Wales, of which he had just been installed Colonel-in-Chief, he also received a huge and very personal ovation – not least, according to the local paper, for 'speaking better Welsh than the Lord Mayor'. George Thomas added to Charles's kudos by making his own rather endearing Welsh error: by addressing the Lord Mayor as 'Arglwydd Fawr' instead of 'Arglwydd Faer', he had hailed him as God Almighty. (Thomas also noticed a strong strain of nationalism in the Prince's remarks – the influence, he assumed, of Edward Millward at Aberystwyth. Later that year, at a banquet in London to celebrate the centenary of the *Western Mail*, he was relieved to hear him return to more orthodox sympathies.)

In the newly designed Colonel-in-Chief's uniform he wore that day in Cardiff, Prince Charles had chanced upon a welcome alternative to the satin breeches which had so mortified his great-uncle. His investiture regalia was at last decided. But over the military uniform, protocol decreed, he would indeed wear a purple surcoat trimmed with ermine. Snowdon was disappointed. He had designed for himself a sharp tail-suit of military green, zip-fastened to its roll-collar neck, which was trimmed with the three-feathered insignia in mirror images. He had hoped the Prince would wear a similarly simple cloak over his military gear. But he had the consolation after the event that his own outfit, for all its traditional military touches, was perhaps the most satirized item on display.

He did not, however, approve of the coronet to be worn by the Prince. Snowdon, again, had wanted a classically simple band of plain gold around Charles's brow. But this time the College of Arms won the day, and a carefully contemporary version of the Prince of Wales's traditional crown was commissioned from Louis Osman. (Charles was amused to hear that Osman had previously found renown by designing a big top for Billy Smart's circus.) It was the first coronet or crown in history to be made by electro-forming – that is, electro-plated from a wax mould, rather than 'beaten' in time-honoured fashion. The new process made it much lighter, only about three pounds. Like King Charles's traditional coronet, its design included alternate crosses and fleurs-de-lys spanned by an arch and surmounted by an orb and cross. The gold was reinforced with iridium platinum, studded with seventy-five diamonds and twelve emeralds, and set off by a base of ermine and a cap of purple velvet to match the Prince's mantle. It cost £3,600 to make, though that says nothing about its value.

As the goldsmith imprinted his hallmark on the Osman coronet, a tiny flaw was discovered; were it to fall from Charles's head on the big day, it would shatter ominously before the watching millions. So a second gold crown was fashioned, and the seventy-five diamonds and twelve emeralds hastily transferred, the platinum trimming renewed. The finished object was to be worn once before, like Edward VIII's regalia, finding its way into a Welsh museum.

Charles wore his crown around the Palace for a few days, to get used to it. Down the road at Kensington Palace, Lord Snowdon was at much the same time inviting the visitors to try out the three royal thrones sitting waiting in his hallway. He took one of the £12 chairs round to Clarence House for his mother-in-law, Queen Elizabeth, to try. There were other vicarious entertainments for Londoners during those months: those passing Buckingham Palace atop a double-decker bus could see the Royal Family being shunted by the Duke of Norfolk through a rehearsal ground of white markers and measuring tapes. When the Queen congratulated Bernard Norfolk on his plans, he told her he'd had his best ideas in the bath.

The day before the ceremony, a dress rehearsal (without the Royal Family) was held at Caernarvon. Journalists were surprised to find themselves given every courtesy and facility: evidence indeed, as one of them put it, that the monarchy was 'going into overdrive'. A vogue joke in somewhat bad taste – 'What time is it by your bomb?' – was of little consolation to Lord Snowdon that week, as he travelled in his speedboat to an investiture party at the home of Lord Newborough, high above the Menai Straits. He was delighted to see the assembled guests gathered on the cliff-top to greet his arrival, and not displeased when a cannon salute heralded his approach. Several seconds later, however, a cannon-ball whacked into the spray, a yard from his bow. 'What a pity you didn't sink him,' one of the guests told Newborough. 'Think what an honour it would have been for our lifeboat boys to have rescued him.' (This particular eccentricity seems to run in Lord Newborough's family. In 1911 a stray shot from the loyal salute of one of his ancestors nearly sank the royal yacht.)

On investiture eve, the Queen's progress north with her family in the royal train was interrupted for an hour outside Chester. A bomb had been found beneath the bridge which carries the railway across the River Dee. It turned out to be a hoax: three sticks of Plasticine, attached to an alarm clock, in a cardboard box. A few hours later, around dawn on 1 July, two men were attempting to position a real bomb against the wall of a local government office in Abergele, thirty miles from Caernarvon. It exploded as they were priming it, killing them both. In London the previous afternoon Jack de Manio, Denis Marrian and others had foregathered in a BBC television studio to record their personal tributes to the Prince of Wales – to be broadcast in the event of his assassination next day.

The train and its occupants spent the night in a special halt built in the railway siding of Ferodo Ltd near Bangor, close enough to Plâs-Newydd, the Marquess of Anglesey's home, for some convivial hospitality. Next morning the Lord Lieutenant of Caernarvonshire, Sir Michael Duff, escorted the family to Vaynol, his elegant Queen Anne mansion overlooking the Menai Straits. This was the royal rendezvous point. 'Do you realize,' said the Duke of Beaufort, 'that so many royals have never been under one non-royal roof before?'

Charles spent much of the morning wandering nervously around the Duff estate. Each time he returned to the house, he found his television interview being replayed on one or other of the channels. 'It's always me,' he complained. 'I'm getting rather sick of my face.' After lunch, the Queen wished him a slightly tense 'Good luck' as he left with the advance party. George Thomas and David Checketts shared the coach in which he made his triumphal progress through the crowds to the Castle. A loud bang was heard in the near distance, and Charles asked Thomas what it was. Both knew very well it was another bomb. 'Oh, that's a royal salute, sir.' 'Peculiar sort of royal salute.' 'Peculiar sort of people up here,' said the southern Welshman of his northern compatriots. The carriage continued its way through the narrow streets of the city, overhung by many an open window which would have made an assassin's work easy. But the Special Branch had been thorough. Thomas, nevertheless, remembers being much more nervous than the Prince. 'You felt safe once inside the Castle, but far from safe outside its walls.'

The Prince and his companions arrived to see his personal banner unfurled on the battlements, and to hear a deafening rendition of 'God Bless the Prince of Wales'. Thomas joined in, but could not get beyond the first verse. As he lah-lahed his way through the rest of it, the Prince gently chided him. 'You must remember,' Thomas replied, 'the last time I sang this was for your great-uncle.'

He and Checketts accompanied the Prince to the waiting-room, where Snowdon's young children ran into Charles's arms and made him forget his nerves for a while. For twenty minutes, he watched his relatives' arrival on television. On the table was a good-luck note from Lord Snowdon, asking Charles to sign the central table with a felt-tip pen. This he did, and the signature is now immortalized there in stainless steel.

Outside, a boom had been stretched across the harbour entrance, which was patrolled by two minesweepers. Snowdon had wanted *Britannia* to hover dramatically in the estuary, but the naval authorities had calculated that she would probably run aground in the shallows; so the royal yacht waited up the coast off Holyhead, where frogmen regularly checked her hull for limpet mines. Back in Caernarvon, police patrolled the straits in launches and rubber dinghies, helicopters scanned the crowds from 300 feet, and close-circuit TV relayed the watching faces to a police control centre. The town was sealed off from all traffic. Even Princess Margaret was asked for proof of her indentity. As the Queen's carriage approached the Castle, a banana skin was thrown beneath her horses' hooves. Watching police had to extract the offender quickly from the angry crowd, who appeared to be about to lynch him.

The tension surrounding the day ahead had even infused the words of the poet laureate, Cecil Day Lewis, who had made a break with tradition by presenting his celebratory verse to that morning's *Guardian*, rather than *The Times*. *The Times*'s editor, William Rees-Mogg, professed himself 'undismayed', for reasons we can only surmise:

> Today bells ring, bands play, flags are unfurled,
>   Anxieties and feuds lie buried
> Under a ceremonial joy. You, sir, inherit
>   A weight of history in a changing world,
> Its treasured wisdom and its true
>   Aspirings the best birthday gift for you.
>
> Coming of age, you come into a land
>   Of mountain, pasture, cwm, pithead,
> Steelworks. A proud and fiery people, thoroughbred
>   For singing, eloquence, rugby football, stand
> Beneath Caernarvon's battlements
>   To greet and take the measure of their prince.
>
> But can they measure his hard task – to be
>   Both man and symbol? With the man's
> Selfhood the symbol grows in clearer light, or wanes,
>   Your mother's grace, your father's gallantry
> Go with you now to nerve and cheer you
>   Upon the crowded, lonely way before you.
>
> May your integrity silence each tongue
>   That sneers or flatters. May this hour
> Reach through its pageantry to the deep reservoir
>   Whence Britain's heart draws all that is fresh and young.
> Over the tuneful land prevails
>   One song, one prayer – God Bless the Prince of Wales.

Lord Plunket knocked on the Water Gate, which was opened by the Constable, Lord Snowdon, bearing a fifteen-inch key: 'Madam, I surrender the key of this Castle into Your Majesty's hand.' The Queen, in a yellow Norman Hartnell dress and hat, touched it, saying: 'Sir Constable, I return the key of the Castle into your keeping.' The royal party made its way across the central dais (heels not sinking into the grass, though rain threatened). Prince Charles was summoned, and the ceremony was at last under way.

Charles's procession was more splendid than anything he will know again before his own coronation. Flanked by the Secretary of State for Wales, the Welsh Herald Extraordinary and two Lords-in-Waiting, he was followed by five Welsh peers carrying his insignia. Earl Lloyd George of Dwyfor bore the same silver-gilt sword used by the last Prince of Wales, Lord Heycock the golden rod, Lord Maelor the gold ring embellished with two dragons and an amethyst, Lord Harlech the mantle of purple velvet and ermine, and Lord Ogmore the coronet. To Snowdon's horror, a few drops of rain began to fall. At this climactic moment, however, the 4,000 were not to be disturbed. Only one, before the watching millions, disrupted the scene by manoeuvring himself into a raincoat: Mr Jeremy Thorpe, then leader of the Liberal Party.

The Queen handed the Letters Patent to the Home Secretary, James Callaghan, himself by happy chance the member for a Welsh constituency. Almost entirely lacking punctuation, they were something of a mouthful.

Elizabeth the Second by the Grace of God of the United Kingdom of Great Britain and Northern Ireland and of Our other Realms and Territories Queen Head of the Commonwealth Defender of the Faith. To all Lords Spiritual and Temporal and all other Our Subjects whatsoever to whom these Presents shall come Greeting Know ye that we have made and created and by these Our Letters Do make and create our most dear Son Charles Philip Arthur George Prince of the United Kingdom of Great Britain and Northern Ireland Duke of Cornwall and Rothesay Earl of Carrick Baron of Renfrew Lord of the Isles and Great Steward of Scotland Prince of Wales and Earl of Chester And to the same Our most dear Son Charles Philip Arthur George have given and granted and by this Our Present Charter do give grant and confirm the name style title dignity and honour of the same Principality and Earldom And Him Our most dear Son Charles Philip Arthur George as he has been accustomed We do ennoble and invest with the said Principality and Earldom by girding him with a Sword by putting a Coronet on his head and a Gold Ring on his finger and also by delivering a Gold Rod into his hand that he may preside there and may direct and defend those parts To hold to him and his heirs Kings of the United Kingdom of Great Britain and Northern Ireland and of Our other Realms and Territories Heads of the Commonwealth for ever. Wherefore We will and strictly command for us Our heirs and successors that Our most dear Son Charles Philip Arthur George may have the name style title dignity and honour of the Principality of Wales and Earldom of Chester aforesaid unto him and his heirs Kings of the United Kingdom of Great Britain and Northern Ireland and of Our other Realms and Territories Heads of the Commonwealth as is above mentioned. In Witness whereof We have caused these Our Letters to be made Patent. Witness Ourself at Westminster the twenty-sixth day of July in the seventh year of Our Reign.

As Callaghan struggled on, the Queen formally invested Charles with the insignia, and both waited while the Charter was read again in Welsh, this time by George Thomas. Then came the climax of the ceremony. Kneeling before his mother, the Prince of Wales intoned the oath he had been too young to swear at her coronation. Placing his hands between the Queen's, he declared: 'I Charles, Prince of Wales, do become your liege man of life and limb and of earthly worship, and faith and truth I will bear unto you to live and die against all manner of folks.'

At the same moment, across the world, three men were preparing to land on the moon. But this archaic ritual, watched with mixed emotion by the Duke of Windsor in his Paris home, had a vital saving grace. In the week before the investiture, the TV film *Royal Family* had at last been shown, giving the British people an unprecedented peep into the private life of their Royals. The majestic hands now raising Charles to his feet had last been seen wielding a barbecue fork; Prince Philip, watching solemnly in his Field Marshal's uniform, had just rowed a complaining Prince Edward into the Balmoral sunset; Her Majesty's 'liege man of life and limb' had endangered his younger brother's by snapping a cello string in his face. Charles, particularly, had been discovered in every home that week, through interviews and special films, to be every parent's ideal son. The Royals may not have been a family just like any other, but they were a family, who did relatively normal things in relatively normal ways. For once, the pomp and circumstance of royalty in public ceremonial perhaps took second place, in the minds of those watching, to the private family cracking jokes around the breakfast table. Paradoxically, the ancient ritual crystallized a new era of family monarchy, which would reach its climax eight years later in Elizabeth II's Silver Jubilee.

As Charles listened to George Thomas's rolling Welsh phrases, his coronet balanced uncertainly on his head, his left hand encumbered with a Sceptre, he realized, appalled, that he was sitting on his speech. The TV record of the occasion shows him fumbling urgently beneath the folds of his purple mantle, trying to dislodge those vital words of Welsh without at the same time dislodging his crown. Success; a relieved smile; and he launched into a carefully phrased vow to fight for the preservation of all things Welsh – unstuffy enough to number 'a memorable Goon' (Harry Secombe) among them. There followed a short service, a Welsh bible reading, and the Queen was soon presenting her son to his people at three gates of the Castle. Fanfares sounded, the RAF flew past overhead, and all Welsh doubts were staunched in an irresistible tide of loyal emotion.

'Oh, Mr Thomas,' said the Queen to the Secretary of State, 'it's been a wonderful day.' Said the Secretary of State: 'I don't want to be guilty of the Welsh sin of exaggeration, but it was a far greater triumph than we had a right to expect. He really was the Prince Charming. Wales has been in a state of euphoria, and at least half a million dollars came to Caernarvon itself.' George Thomas, a hardened political veteran (now the Speaker of the House of Commons), says he has never known such an overwhelming sense of relief as he felt at the end of that day.

Back at the Ferodo siding Charles bid farewell to his parents, and repaired to the royal yacht for 'an evening's rest' (a high-spirited ball for young friends). For the next four days, as he toured his principality, he could do no wrong. From Conway to Montgomeryshire, from Fishguard to Swansea, from the Rhondda to Newport, and finally to Cardiff, he prompted scenes of rejoicing which belied the past two years. An icon in his own right (the stamps, the commemorative medals, the souvenirs, the TV presence), he baffled people into hysterical submission. 'I touched him' was a familiar cry from teenage girls. 'I *saw* him' was enough for most. The Prince of Wales was himself elated. Only on the final day did a last, ugly outrage turn his week sour: in Caernarvon an eleven-year-old schoolboy playing football set off a booby-trap bomb, and lost his leg. Before leaving for a holiday in Malta, Charles launched a fund for the child; he wanted to visit him, but was told his condition was too grave. The boy recovered, yet Charles's hostess in Malta, Lady Dorman, testifies that the event clouded his few days' respite.

Not a happy ending. But the Prince had, despite it all, conquered Wales.

14

The Services
1970-76

There is no more fitting preparation for a King than to have
been trained in the Navy.

Prince Louis of Battenberg to the future King
George V

PRINCE CHARLES'S twenty-first birthday found him hedged around with
young seriousness. He posed for an official photograph at the controls of
an aircraft, unconventional by royal standards, but in his eyes shone the
uncluttered idealism with which the emotional period of his investiture had
fired him. Early on the morning of his birthday he escorted his grandmother
to the Chapel Royal of St John, in the Tower of London, for a service of
thanksgiving and dedication for his future life. Of ICH DIEN (I Serve), the
motto he had inherited from Edward, the Black Prince, he said: 'It means
just that. It is the basis of one's job: to serve other people. If you have a
sense of duty, and I like to think I have, service means that you give yourself
to people, particularly if they want you, and sometimes if they don't.' He
was soon to put it to practical, and literal, use by a prolonged stint in the
armed services. First, however, he had to finish his university degree.

On the night before 14 November 1969, a group of Trinity students
climbed two eighty-foot towers, the highest points of the dining hall and
the college chapel, to sling between them a 300-foot banner proclaiming
'Happy Birthday, Charles' in gold letters three feet high. Their spectacular
gesture was, alas, in vain, as unknown to them the Prince had already left
for London, where a grand birthday party was to be held at Buckingham
Palace. Again, young seriousness was to the fore: he had asked Yehudi
Menuhin and the Bath Festival Orchestra to play a Mozart violin concerto,
and Maurice Gendron to follow with a Haydn cello concerto. Fireworks
lit the London sky, and four Oxford undergraduates managed to gate-crash

the proceedings, enjoying long chats with the Prime Minister (Harold Wilson), the Leader of the Opposition (Edward Heath) and their 'host' himself before being ejected. Four hundred guests – including the Queen, who kicked off her shoes with gay abandon – danced until a kedgeree breakfast at 3 a.m.

The Royal Warrant Holders Association, that select group of traders entitled to use the 'By Appointment' tag, presented the Prince with a £700 polo pony called Freckles, no doubt to encourage him to start issuing warrants of his own. He decided to postpone this until 1980. But the birthday did prompt another step further forward into the life of what King George VI liked to call 'the firm' – and Prince Charles prefers to call 'the family firm'. On 11 February 1970, with Princesses Anne, Alexandra and Margaret watching from the balcony, and the Lords Mountbatten and Snowdon lending moral support in the chamber, the Prince of Wales was formally introduced into the House of Lords.

Prince Charles had hoped to make an earlier debut in the Lords, and the Queen had asked her staff to investigate the precedents as early as 1964, when he was fifteen. But the Clerk of the Parliaments gave a disappointing reply to her private secretary:

> The question has proved rather more intricate and has involved more research than I expected....
>
> House of Lords Standing Order No 2 says that: 'No Lord under the age of one and twenty years shall be permitted to sit in the House.' This Standing Order dates from 22nd May 1685 and since that date no Prince of Wales has been introduced under the age of twenty-one. It seems, I must say, a little odd that the Prince of Wales could inherit the crown without being subject to a Regency at the age of eighteen and yet does not qualify (if that is the fact) for a seat in the House of Lords. But so far as the precedents since 1685 go, it seems clear that the Prince of Wales has been treated as if the Standing Order applied to him.
>
> There have, in fact, been only six introductions of a Prince of Wales since 1685, four in the eighteenth century, one in the nineteenth and one in the twentieth.... Three out of the six, namely the Princes of Wales who subsequently became George III, George IV and Edward VII, were introduced as Prince of Wales within a few months of becoming twenty-one....

So he had had to wait. But this heady background to the occasion made it the more worth-while. Preceded by his coronet on a velvet cushion, Charles strode into the chamber with such self-confidence that he looked to *The Times* correspondent 'as if he owned the place'. Sponsored by the Duke of Kent and the Duke of Beaufort, he had beforehand stood between them in the full regalia of ermine-collared purple robe, cupping his hands to his mouth to mimic a town crier. Once inside, however, he treated the occasion with due solemnity, even when declaring an oath of loyalty to himself: 'I, Charles, Prince of Wales, do swear by Almighty God that I will be faithful and bear true allegiance to Her Majesty Queen Elizabeth, her heirs and successors, so help me God.' The formalities over, he slipped out again to disrobe, and returned to the chamber in a plain suit to listen, appropriately enough, to a debate on youth and community service.

Back at Cambridge, Charles now had new and grander rooms on Staircase P of Great Court, including a panelled sitting-room dating from the seventeenth century on whose chimney-piece he duly carved his initial. It was to be an interrupted year, he knew, so he largely withdrew from Cambridge society and, in Denis Marrian's words, 'got his head down'. In view of his looming deadline, he even took a course in speed-reading – which has since proved invaluable to one who so dislikes paperwork, yet must get through so much of it. He joined the Cambridge Union, and attended a couple of debates, but his main concern was that his success or failure in the final Tripos exams the following summer would be world-wide public knowledge. A bad degree would be disastrous.

None the less, there were some indulgences he could not resist. In the spring term of 1970 he was back on stage in another revue, this time called *Quiet Flows the Don*. To spare him a repeat of the world-wide interest in *Revulution*, tickets were limited to members of Trinity and their guests. Among these were the Queen and Princess Anne, who dined with the Prince in his rooms before attending one of the five performances. Charles took part in four sketches, notably as a weather forecaster in flippers and gas mask: 'By morning promiscuity will be widespread, but it will lift, and may give way to some hill snog.... As William of Orange said, here come the pips.' At a dress rehearsal, to which the poker-faced press were admitted, the Prince raised the biggest laugh of the evening by forgetting his lines. 'What the hell comes next? It doesn't happen like this on the BBC.'

The Easter vacation, to a long sigh from Lord Butler, took the Prince of Wales on an extended tour of New Zealand and Australia with his parents to celebrate the 200th anniversary of Captain Cook's voyage, and onward to Japan on his own. He returned to Cambridge barely a month before his examinations. The six three-hour papers included such questions as 'How and to what extent did George III exercise control of his ministers before 1784?', 'What role in politics and society was the Prince Consort able to exercise?' and 'Was Winston Churchill an unsuccessful peacetime Prime Minister?' There was a question, appropriately enough, on Machiavelli's *The Prince*, and, almost as close to home, 'In what sense is it true to describe Louis XIV as "King of the Vile Bourgeoisie"?'

The Prince's answers to these and other apposite inquiries will be known to posterity, as his exam papers are already lodged in the Royal Archives at Windsor for an official biographer to inspect after his death. As a last-minute afterthought, Denis Marrian also rescued his file on the Prince's progress from the pulping machine, and placed it in the Trinity archives. For now, all we know is that Prince Charles won a BA honours degree in Class II Divison II. Sandwiched in the list of results between Vaux, J.F.G. (Selwyn College) and Walker, J.N.G. (Caius), Wales, H.R.H. Prince of had made royal history. The fact that it was a 'II,2', an absolutely average result, helped to convince the sceptical that the Prince's papers were written beneath an anonymous number, and did not bear his name.

Lord Butler believes the Prince might have achieved a II,1 had royal duties not intruded so much on his last year's work. He also believes Charles would have stood 'a damn good chance of a First' had he stuck to archaeology or anthropology, and not gone to Aberystwyth. Be all that as it may, the three years had more than satisfied the Prince of Wales. He had successfully emerged as a public figure, ridden the Welsh storm, and at the same time become the first heir apparent in British history to win a university degree. Said Lord Butler: 'I think I can say we have done a good job at Trinity.' And Dr Marrian: 'It is a good thing for the country to be able to see that the heir to the throne is able to start and finish an extremely difficult task like this.'

And so to the final dose of Lord Louis's prescription.

It is pointless and ill-informed to say that I am entering a profession trained in killing. The services in the first place are there for fast, efficient and well-trained action in defence. Surely the Services must attract a large number of duty-conscious people? Otherwise who else would subject themselves to being square-bashed, shouted at by petty officers and made to do ghastly things in Force Ten gales? I am entering the RAF and then the Navy because I believe I can contribute something to this country by so doing. To me it is a worth-while occupation, and one which I am convinced will stand me in good stead for the rest of my life.

It was a week before the Prince of Wales was due to check in as a graduate entrant at RAF Cranwell, and he was thanking the City of London for making him a Freeman. It was scarcely the most solemn of occasions: Charles had enjoyed hearing it proclaimed that he was the son of 'Prince Philip, Duke of Edinburgh, Citizen and Fishmonger of London, and that he was born in lawful wedlock ... his son so reputed and taken to be, and so they all say'. But he had been irritated by suggestions in the press that the Services no longer provide appropriate training for an heir to the throne; he entirely shared the views of his family, both living and of recent memory, that an officer's career in at least two of the three was an indispensable discipline and adventure.

The maritime traditions of his family go back a long way on both sides. Prince Charles's great-uncle, Lord Mountbatten, was a naval cadet at the age of thirteen and a First Sea Lord at fifty-five, having spent the better part of all the intervening years at sea. His father, Prince Louis of Battenberg, was also First Sea Lord in 1914, when the approach of war with Germany forced him to resign his German name and titles, becoming the first Marquess of Milford Haven. And Prince Louis's great-grandson, Prince Philip, Duke of Edinburgh, had taken British citizenship in February 1947 as a means of continuing his career in the Royal Navy – not, as was thought at the time, to smooth his path towards a distinguished marriage. As Prince Philip of Greece, he had already distinguished himself in HMS *Valiant* in 1941; he was mentioned in despatches by his commanding officer, Admiral Cunningham, for his handling of the searchlights at the Battle of Matapan. In time, he had his own command, of the frigate *Magpie* in the Mediterranean in 1950–51 – cut short by the last illness of King George VI, and a call to royal duty. But there were sterner precedents for that.

On his mother's side, Prince Charles's great-grandfather, King George V, had also just enjoyed his first command (of the gunboat *Thrush*) when the death of his elder brother, Prince Eddy, Duke of Clarence, cut short his naval career in 1892. In the words of his son, the Duke of Windsor, the loss of his life at sea affected him deeply. 'He did love the Navy ... and long after he had taken up work ashore, the habits and outlooks he had formed in the Navy continued to regulate his daily routine. He retained a gruff, blue-water approach to all human situations.' The King's other son, George VI, Prince Charles's grandfather, saw active service at the Battle of Jutland when a twenty-one-year-old acting lieutenant. At the time, he too had no thoughts of ascending the throne. After his elder brother's abdication in 1936, the reluctant new King confided to Lord Mountbatten: 'Dickie, this is absolutely terrible. I never wanted this to happen; I'm quite unprepared for it.... I've never seen a State paper. I'm only a Naval officer. It's the only thing I know about.' Mountbatten replied: 'This is a very curious coincidence. My father once told me that, when the Duke of Clarence died, your father came to him and said almost the same things that you have said to me now, and my father answered: "George, you're wrong. There is no more fitting preparation for a King than to have been trained in the Navy."'

With every awareness of this heritage Prince Charles was about to devote to the Navy, and to the naval arm of the RAF, the major part of his next five years, the prime of his young manhood. The nine months since Cambridge had meanwhile taken him round the world again: to Canada and the Arctic, to the Nixon White House in Washington (see chapter 17, pages 224–227), to Fiji and the Gilbert and Ellice Islands, to the 350th anniversary of the Bermudan Parliament and to Kenya, on televised safari with Princess Anne. Nineteen years to the day after his mother's accession to the throne, he had visited the site where she had heard the news of her father's death – to find that the Treetops Lodge had been destroyed by fire, and a modern motel had risen in its place. He had celebrated his twenty-second birthday with another cello concerto (plus a harp concerto performed by Osian Ellis); lunched with the Prime Minister, Edward Heath; and addressed the Institute of Directors at the Royal Albert Hall: 'Whoever invited me exploited my extreme ignorance. I assumed you were a small business organization. Little did I know that I had agreed to speak to five thousand whizz-kids, tycoons, industrial giants....'

Flight Lieutenant the Prince of Wales rather saucily flew himself to RAF Cranwell on 8 March 1971. Having left Windsor by helicopter, he changed at RAF Benson to a twin-engined Basset, in which he had already won his pilot's licence (Grade A) and clocked up some eighty flying hours. Charles had begun flying lessons during his first year at Cambridge, starting in a Chipmunk, as had his father before him. On 13 June 1968, a team of doctors from the RAF Central Medical Establishment visited Buckingham Palace to give him his 'medical', and by the end of the month he had sampled the first of a series of air experience flights at RAF Tangmere in Sussex. A special training unit was meanwhile established under the aegis of the Queen's Flight at RAF Benson, near Oxford; in command was the Captain of the Queen's Flight, Air Commodore A.L. ('Archie') Winskill. Flight Lieutenant (now Squadron Leader) Phillip Pinney, a New Zealander, was assigned from the RAF Central Flying School to see the Prince through to his first solo flight. Six months later, on 14 January 1969, after only fourteen and a half hours instruction in nineteen dual sorties, the big moment had come at RAF Bassingbourn, in Hertfordshire: 'I taxied and took off, wondering whether I could do it, and the moment I was in the air it was absolutely marvellous.... Fortunately, I landed first time. I had visions of myself going round and round until eventually the fuel ran out.'

In the following ten months, the Prince accumulated some sixty flying hours, about twice as many as he would have achieved as a member of an RAF University Air Squadron. On 2 August 1969, he had received his Preliminary Flying Badge from the Air Officer Commanding-in-Chief, RAF Training Command, and was ready to graduate from the Chipmunk to the twin-engined Beagle Basset. With its more advanced controls and communication system, the Basset was an ideal aircraft for the Prince to fly himself to and from official engagements. The RAF made one over to the Queen's Flight on 27 June; the Prince made his first flight in it on 10 October, and has been using it ever since.

The Duke of Edinburgh, though so closely identified with the Navy, says instinct would have taken him into the RAF. For Prince Charles the prospect of a career in both, apart from carrying on a type-cast family tradition, provided the chance of hours of unwonted freedom. To fly an aeroplane is in itself an exhilarating experience, more so if it is one's only chance to escape from a womb of advisers and observers. Similarly, the Prince's time at sea was to prove perhaps the most 'natural' of his life. No press, no sightseers, no private secretaries, no red boxes – even, for the only time in his life, no private detective, as the Navy took over responsibility for security whilst the Prince was off *terra firma*. Added to which, there was the camaraderie of life in the Services, which made him more genuinely than at any other time in his life 'one of the boys'.

He was not pleased, therefore, when his five-month jet conversion course at Cranwell was christened 'Operation Golden Eagle'. To hear the station commander describe him as 'a precious piece of the nation's property', and to know that the two Mark V Jet Provosts set aside for his personal use had been specially modified, was not to his liking. He had specifically asked not to be provided with special privileges or safety systems: the extra warning lights on the Provost control panel and the improved ejector seat beneath him were as irritating as they were reassuring. It was perhaps because of this unfortunate start that he went on to attempt more reckless and dangerous feats quite unnecessarily. 'I'm stupid enough to like trying things. Perhaps I do push myself too hard.'

He has a natural talent for flying, and the five months saw him proceed effortlessly to the winning of his wings, under the expert tuition of Squadron Leader Dick Johns. He shunned the Cranwell revue, preferring to clock up another eighty hours in Provosts, some twenty-four of them solo, as well as going through ejector-seat training, ditching drill and all the irksome paperwork of navigation. He lived in normal Cranwell quarters with three other officer cadets, each with their own private bedroom, but was still uneasy that as Golden Eagle his path had been somehow made smooth. It was not enough to have played a role in operational 'front-line-raids' over the North Sea, and to have co-piloted supersonic Phantom and Nimrod jets, 'attacking' Royal Navy submarines and flying the length and breadth of Britain in eight-hour sorties. Although he was spared parades and drill, because he was completing a twelve-month course in five, it was not enough to have perfected the handling of his aircraft at high, medium and low levels, flying

by day and by night, by instruments and in formation. It was not enough
to have taken courses in aerodynamics, airmanship, meteorology, navigation,
aviation medicine, safety equipment, survival and rescue, and instrumenta-
tion. Before the passing-out parade in August, he announced, he wanted
to make a parachute jump. Needless to say, this too was something no heir
to the throne, indeed no member of the Royal Family, had undertaken before
him.

The Queen was not enthusiastic, but she knew she could not talk him
out of it. Hearts in Whitehall also skipped a few beats as the Prince of Wales
found another way of testing and proving himself. The Gordonstoun ethic
had stuck deep. He had already experienced a 'near miss', ironically enough
whilst co-piloting the modest Basset with his father in 1970; they were three
seconds from collison with a Piper Aztec over Sussex. Now he took himself
off to the RAF Parachute Training School at Abingdon, near Oxford. He
went through all the ground simulation exercises in preparation for the big
day, 28 July 1971 – when, of course, something *did* go wrong.

Twelve hundred feet over Studland Bay in Dorset, the Prince watched
as two senior officers jumped from the Andover ahead of him. 'You're the
chap who pushes me out, I suppose?' he said to Flight Sergeant Ken Kidd
beside him. 'Oh, no, sir,' said Kidd. 'We don't do that. We just help.' Kidd
thought the Prince looked nervous, so he gave him a Polo mint. On the
command Charles jumped, and found the slipstream stronger than he
had expected. It was 6.20 p.m.; at 3 p.m. that afternoon the wind speed
had been recorded at 9 knots, 0.3 above the RAF's maximum strength
permissible for parachute-jump safety. The Prince of Wales flipped over
onto his back, and looked up to see his feet caught in the rigging over his
head.

He recalls the moment with all the nonchalance of Biggles:

It was very odd. Either I've got hollow legs or something. It doesn't often
happen. The first thing I thought was 'They didn't tell me anything about
this'. Fortunately, my feet weren't twisted around the lines, and they came
out very quickly. The Royal Marines were roaring around in little rubber
boats underneath, and I was out of the water within ten seconds.... A rather
hairy experience.

The Prince's Cranwell report just glowed: 'He will make an excellent
fighter pilot at supersonic speeds ... a natural aptitude for flying ... excelled
at aerobatics in jets ... all-round ability.' He had completed the first-year
graduate course in five months, and even managed to leave the characteristic
little memory of which he is so fond. On 1 April the Prince persuaded the
college caretaker, Joe Sylvester, to announce over the loudspeaker system

that all regulation-issue officers' shoes should be handed in as the manufac-turers had found the heels to be faulty. Several dozen shoe-less officer cadets thereupon proved themselves April Fools.

While at Cranwell he travelled around the station on a bicycle, like every-one else. But he had also swapped his MGB for a dark blue Aston Martin DB6 Volante, which whipped him off to polo matches and week-end retreats at Sandringham. Charles had also taken advantage of the anonymity of the RAF uniform, never given a second glance in that corner of Lincolnshire, to indulge in some inconspicuous sightseeing. Two favourite memories: a high-level bombing attack by Vulcan on his unsuspecting future subjects in Doncaster, where he scored a 'direct hit' on the railway yard; and the Philipesque flourish, a week before his parachute jump, of shattering the regal July air over Balmoral as he flew himself by Phantom into the exclusive Ten Ton Club (more than 1,000 m.p.h.). On 20 August the Marshal of the RAF, a proud father indeed, saluted his son before watching him receive his wings from the Air Chief Marshal, Sir Denis Spotswood. The passing-out parade band struck up 'God Bless The Prince of Wales', and Prince Philip told photographers: 'I'll stand on my head if you like.'

A month later Acting Sub-Lieutenant the Prince of Wales took up resi-dence at the Royal Naval College, Dartmouth, attended by his father and grandfather before him. It had been at the Captain's house, now occupied by Captain Allan Tait, that the young Prince Philip of Greece had first met thirteen-year-old Princess Elizabeth, heir presumptive to King George VI, in 1939. That year, Prince Philip had won the King's Dirk as the best cadet, following in the tradition set by his uncle, Lord Mountbatten. Charles had a lot to live up to in six short, intensive weeks of basic training in seamanship, navigation, marine and electrical engineering, administration, man-manage-ment – all the duties of a divisional officer – plus a brief stint at sea aboard the minesweeper *Walkerton*. Even when he treated himself to a week-end off in Cornwall, his companions found him swotting at his naval manuals on the beach.

When he too pulled off a royal coup – top in navigation and in sea-manship: 'all' as Lord Mountbatten declared 'we seamen care about' – his father was in Berlin, and unable to attend the passing-out parade. Mount-batten telephoned Tait: 'I think the family should be represented. I'm flying down.' With proprietorial pride, Uncle Dickie afterwards took his nephew home by helicopter to lunch with the Queen.

At Dartmouth, Charles had lived in Cabin A30, a handsome first-floor room overlooking the River Dart, and shared his brief course with twelve other graduates of his own age. He had worn a naval uniform for the first time, his RAF wings conspicuous on his arm. Now, pausing only to attend a conservation conference in Merthyr Tydfil and the State Opening of Parliament at Westminster, he was off to sea in earnest. The next nine months were to be spent as an officer of Her Majesty's guided-missile destroyer *Norfolk*.

The Services had, for a while, ridden roughshod over the fact of his royalty. There may have been huge holiday crowds on the cliffs near Poole to watch his parachute jump the previous July. But the press had been granted few facilities at Cranwell and Dartmouth, and Charles had achieved proportionately more in a very short time. One of the irritants of being a Prince *had* marked his arrival at the Royal Naval College. He had driven down from Balmoral the previous night to dine with Captain Tait, but because of a large and formal welcoming committee next morning, had had to slip out of a back entrance and pretend to arrive again. 'Sorry I'm late, sir,' he said to Tait, after enjoying his last lie-in for some considerable time. 'I've had a long drive.'

A greater disadvantage soon became apparent when he flew out to join the *Norfolk* in the Mediterranean on 5 November. The 5,600-ton vessel was on routine NATO exercises, of the kind which would help the Prince to his watch-keeping and naval competence certificates – but it happened to be berthed at Gibraltar. As soon as the Prince of Wales set foot there, the Spanish Foreign Minister lodged a note of protest: the Prince's presence, it said, 'caused uncalled-for injury to national sentiment and stirs up Spanish public opinion'. The British Embassy in Madrid countered that His Royal Highness's movements as a serving officer were 'subject to normal operational requirements, and purely a matter for Her Majesty's Government'. The Chief Minister of Gibraltar, Major Robert Peliza, felt moved to write to *The Times* in protest that he had received no advance warning of the Prince's visit. Far from preferring to play down the distinguished arrival, as the press had suggested, he would have considered it 'a profound honour to have been allowed to have received and welcomed Prince Charles in our homeland on behalf of a people who, notwithstanding many years of economic, political and psychological harassment caused by the hostility of the Spanish dictatorial government, almost unanimously resolved in the 1967 referendum to remain under the British crown'. Merely by attempting to carry out his naval duties, the Prince had reopened an old and particularly sore wound. The Ministry of Defence advised the *Norfolk*'s captain not to put in, as planned, at Malta, whose relations with Britain were then at their most strained. Thus did protocol deprive the Prince of a chance to see the Maltese Prime Minister, Dom Mintoff, with whom he had struck up a particularly jaunty friendship in 1969. Thereafter, the course charted by HMS *Norfolk* was always a matter of political nicety for NATO.

Unknown to the Prince, other arguments raged around him in Whitehall. The old naval school thought it demeaning that the heir to the throne should have been posted to a ship as large as *Norfolk*, where the duties of a Sub-Lieutenant carry little responsibility. Behind the move, however, lay the traditional beliefs of the Admiral of the Fleet himself, Earl Mountbatten, who felt that one of the 'capital' ships carried the appropriate status for Charles's first posting. It had already been decided that a year later he would join HMS *Minerva*, a Leander class frigate, with only seventeen officers in the ship's complement as opposed to *Norfolk*'s thirty-three. On *Minerva* he would carry considerable responsibility, including the welfare and, when necessary, punishment of a proportion of the crew. A preparatory year aboard a larger ship would ease him into this unaccustomed and not altogether congenial role.

Cabin 36 on the starboard side of HMS *Norfolk*'s 01 deck was a mere seven foot square, the first of a series of such confined spaces which the Prince of Wales would be calling home. Cramped between its steel wash basin, wardrobes, bunk and desk, Charles had to compile the junior officer's journal as well as continue all the paperwork of the apprentice officer. Life aboard was more mechanized than he had envisaged, more so indeed than either his father or his great-uncle had experienced. The Prince's twenty-third birthday was celebrated off Sardinia, keeping watch in a Force Ten gale. By day, his duties included a humble role in the complex control room, and an assistant's position at the ship's wheel.

After only six weeks he was home for Christmas at Windsor, then quickly back to paperwork – communications, bridgework and gunnery courses – at the shore base, HMS *Dryad*. That January also took in another unenviable royal 'first': underwater escape practice in the 100-foot training tank at HMS *Dolphin*, the Gosport shore base. The Prince of Wales's staff were as apprehensive as the naval top brass, who filmed the whole event for re-cruitment purposes, as Prince Charles made three separate escapes, from 30, 60 and 100 feet. The occasion is preserved in the TV film, *Pilot Royal*, in which the Prince's face provides evidence enough of the genuine dangers involved, and his awareness of them. Though some 5,000 officers and men complete this routine training each year – the Prince of Wales had rejected all suggestions that he should give it a miss – the next two years were to see the death of two ratings in separate underwater escape accidents.

If he was insistent on shirking none of the less pleasant aspects of train-ing, there were other areas in which Prince Charles's wishes were overruled. Later in his Service career, his request to fly Buccaneer strike aircraft at sea would be vetoed as simply too dangerous for the heir to the throne. For the same reason, he never fulfilled his wish to pilot Sea King anti-submarine helicopters. Political considerations prevented him serving aboard Polaris nuclear submarines, their missiles supposedly trained on Moscow. The 1974 defence cuts ruled out the posting he would have then preferred aboard the commando ship *Bulwark*; it was thought unseemly for the Prince of Wales to serve aboard a vessel due to be scrapped within eighteen months. Similarly, he was never allowed to serve aboard the aircraft-carrier *Ark Royal*, as one of his position would be unsuitably submerged in so large a crew; for political reasons, he could never be transferred to any of the frigates patrolling the fishing waters off Iceland during the so-called 'Cod wars', or blockading Beira in the earlier days of economic sanctions against Rhodesia.

In the meantime, the Prince got through quite enough to satisfy the less aspiring. 'I have to try that little bit harder,' he conceded, 'to be as professional as possible, to assimilate all the vast problems rather more quickly.' *Dryad* and *Dolphin* were followed by three weeks aboard the Fleet Air Arm frigate *Hermione*, engaged in mock attacks upon 'Portlandia' (Portland). Back aboard *Norfolk*, May saw the Prince of Wales donning civvies to tour Toulon's red-light district with brother officers, before joining his mother on her state visit to France. With the Queen, Prince Charles spent a night in Provence before returning to Paris, where they went to visit the ailing Duke of Windsor at his home in the Bois de Boulogne. Eight days later, as a reprieved *Norfolk* enjoyed a summer visit to Malta and Dom Mintoff, Charles was called home by news of the Duke's death. It was the Prince of Wales who escorted the Duchess of Windsor, for the first time in her life accorded Buckingham Palace hospitality, to see the body of her husband, his predecessor as Prince of Wales, lying in state at Windsor.

The following month, with *Norfolk* back at Portsmouth, the Queen paid her son a visit aboard 'while I still have the chance'. His nose was embellished by sticking-plaster, after a polo mishap, as Charles showed his mother over the ship before giving her tea in the officers' mess. His watch-keeping and competence certificates secured, he was now embarked on courses at the naval signals school *Mercury*, in Hampshire, and back at *Dryad* for a study of nuclear, biological and chemical weapons. That summer he flew by helicopter with his grandmother to the wedding of his cousin, Prince Richard of Gloucester. Within a month, when it had already been announced that Prince Charles was to return to Cranwell for a Provost refresher course, Richard's brother Prince William was killed in a light aircraft crash.

The Queen's anxieties were again aroused. It was a doubly unhappy coincidence that a Jet Provost Mark 7, of the type her son would be flying, had also crashed a week before. But by now the Prince had an irresistible momentum. At Cranwell he flew the new Hunter jet fighter as well as the

Provost. He then had a brief foretaste of helicopter flight at the Navy's Yeovilton base – to which he would later return with renewed enthusiasm – before returning to Portland for a ten-day course aboard the minesweeper *Glasserton*. And so down to Portsmouth, to join the 2,450-ton *Minerva*.

This hectic routine was interspersed, naturally enough, with calls away on royal duty. That October: to Germany, to visit the Prince of Wales Division (where as a new officer he was required to eat a raw leek and sing an unaccompanied song – he chose the Goons' 'Ying Tong Tiddle-i-po') and to attend a reception in his honour at the West German Senate; to Southern Spain, for a shooting holiday on the Wellington estate. In November, just before going to *Minerva*, Charles organized and hosted a private dinner-party to mark his parents' silver wedding anniversary. At his behest, the English Chamber Orchestra played the Wedding March, and the Bach Choir sang anthems from the service twenty-five years before. The day had begun with a thanksgiving service at St Paul's and a 'walkabout' in the new Barbican development, about whose architecture he was rather rude; it ended with a lively after-dinner speech from Charles, and the four royal children offering a barber-shop quartet's version of *Happy Anniversary* for their delighted parents.

Minerva's first commission took Prince Charles and his crew-mates to the West Indies. In further token of his growing stature, Charles had been encouraged to double diplomatic and naval duties, so that courtesies were exchanged with local dignitaries at each port of call, in many of which he also managed to fit in a game of polo. For his shipmates, this new dimension of life at sea brought welcome perks: everywhere she went, *Minerva* attracted all kinds of welcome attention. In Bermuda the Prince of Wales spent a long evening with the Governor, Sir Richard Sharples; after dinner they took a stroll around the garden, continuing their discussion of the effect on the Caribbean of the Bahamas' imminent independence. Taking the same stroll around the same garden a week later, Sir Richard and a young aide, Captain Hugh Sayers, were assassinated.

At first it was thought that one of the bullets might have been intended for the Prince. His departure from the island might have escaped the gunman's notice, the theory went, and Sayers had been mistaken for Charles. Either way, Sir Richard was an alternative symbol of British imperialism as acceptable to the gunman's purpose. The Prince's visit may well have stirred the growing anti-British feelings of Bermuda's small but militant group of independence fighters. Within a couple of years, rioting and civil disobedience on the island had grown to such a pitch that a Royal Commission under Lord Pitt recommended that independence be granted.

The assassination's immediate effect was that Prince Charles was transferred to the survey ship *Fox*, working out of Antigua. *Minerva* was due to revisit Bermuda for repairs and maintenance work, and no one was going to risk returning the Prince with her. His brief stay on *Fox*, a small hydrographic workhorse, was not uneventful: within a few days, he was involved in her attempts to refloat a 55,000-ton Swedish freighter, *Ariadne*, which had hit a reef while en route from Virginia to Japan. There was a further touch of drama when *Fox* had to withdraw her divers as man-eating sharks moved in.

Back with *Minerva*, now promoted Acting Lieutenant, the Prince as second gunnery officer was responsible for the vessel's 4.5-inch weapons and Seacat missiles. It was the climax of a very happy period. The ship bobbed from one to another of the world's most attractive islands: the Leewards, the Windwards, the Virgins and the Bahamas, in the last of which Charles represented the Queen at the independence ceremonies, taking a delighted ship's company ashore with him for the exotic celebrations. He discovered the pleasures of deep-sea diving, gathering pieces of eight from an old Spanish wreck in an underwater world resembling 'some vast green cathedral filled with shoals of silver fish'. In Nassau, he joined with a will in a spectacular local dance called the *merengue*; in Caracas, he danced in a night-club until 5 a.m. with *Minerva* due to sail again at 6.30.

Relations aboard ship were perhaps the closest he had known. As his father has said: 'At sea you learn to live with people.' Out on the ocean for days on end, with no distractions beyond the calls of naval duty, he was required as much as anyone else to reminisce of life at home. It was part of his job as an officer to take an interest in the crew's welfare, and thus their tales about wives and girl-friends, but he managed to keep his own royal counsel to an extent tantalizing for his companions. The best tit-bit they brought ashore was the gallery of pin-ups ingeniously hidden behind the bulkhead shaft over his bunk; other royal gossip gleaned they none. 'We learned a lot about the Prince,' said one brother officer, 'but nothing about the rest of his family.'

Furthermore, what they did pick up they kept to themselves, in the best naval traditions. There was much talk of practical jokes and other such high jinks, but no detail beyond the Prince of Wales's penchant for cooking his shipmates bread-and-butter pudding, laced with 'lashings of rum'. He was also said to be fond of blowing up balloons for target practice with an air rifle; yet a much-travelled story that one rating slipped in a contraceptive, which the Prince had begun inflating before realizing what it was, may be discounted. It is true, however, that during this period he compiled a German–English phrase book, entitled *A Guide to the Chatting Up of Girls*, for the men of the Royal Regiment of Wales, of which he is Colonel-in-Chief.

In his monthly newsletter, he had received complaints from the squaddies, stationed in Germany, that language difficulties were inhibiting their progress with the local ladies. Charles obligingly drew up a list of useful gambits, which David Checketts helped him translate into German. The resulting two-page dossier is said to have increased the Anglo-German marriage rate during the regiment's tour of duty.

Charles left *Minerva* when it docked at Chatham in September 1973, and had four months before his posting to another frigate, HMS *Jupiter*, in January. He threw himself into his first sustained stint of royal duties, including for the first time the receiving of ambassadors as senior Councillor of State during the Queen's absence in Australia. On one notable day he ended a programme of engagements in Luxembourg by attending a charity dinner for the Lord's Taverners back in London, telling the comedian Jimmy Edwards he had 'always wondered what it was like to do two shows a night'. There was another State Opening of Parliament, by now a familiar occasion, and Princess Anne's wedding. Charles took much care and trouble choosing appropriate gifts: for his sister a spectacular diamond brooch, and for his new brother-in-law, Captain Mark Phillips, a pair of leather gun cases. They were married in Westminster Abbey on 14 November, Prince Charles's twenty-fifth birthday. Captain Phillips, like Tony Armstrong-Jones a commoner marrying into the Royal Family, had been Princess Anne's equestrian friend and team-mate, winner of a gold medal at the 1972 Olympic Games in Munich, but to growing subsequent dismay showed little interest in anything else. It is said to be from soon after his engagement to Princess Anne that Captain Phillips was saddled with the Royal Family's nickname for him: 'fog' – 'because he is thick and wet'. He hit back with a nice stroke of self-parody in November 1977, when Princess Anne gave birth to their first child: 'Well, at least I've done *something* right.'

On 4 January 1974, the Prince of Wales joined the frigate *Jupiter*, which had two things in common with *Minerva*: it belonged to the same Leander class, and it quickly become the most popular ship afloat. The Prince of Wales's presence on board guaranteed enthusiastic receptions wherever *Jupiter* called, which in the first few months of 1974 included Australia, New Zealand, Suva, Samoa, Hawaii, Fiji and California. There was one night of drama at sea, when *Jupiter*'s communications officer, Lieutenant the Prince of Wales, played a central role in the rescue of the crew of the tug *Mediator* which had gone aground in ferocious weather with two heavily laden barges in tow. Otherwise, *Jupiter*'s landfalls were rather more eventful than its progress at sea.

During the ship's stop-over at Brisbane, a member of the Prince of Wales's signals staff, Neil Race, was killed by a hit-and-run motorist. In accordance with naval tradition, the dead man's belongings were auctioned, to benefit his next-of-kin. Neil Race's personal effects raised the astonishing sum of £1,500, thanks largely to the Prince's generosity. He set the bidding standards by paying £100 for a tired old suitcase and £60 for a pair of socks.

While at Brisbane Prince Charles took the chance for some surfing, and made telephone contact with his father, then en route to open the Commonwealth Games at Christchurch, New Zealand. When *Jupiter* docked in Christchurch on 29 January, its communications officer could be seen sprinting along the dock to the royal yacht, *Britannia*, six berths away; it was barely dawn, and Charles was anxious to surprise his father by carrying in his breakfast. The following day the Queen and the young newly-weds, Anne and Mark, joined them after flying from London via the Cook Islands.

Their ways soon parted again, the royal yacht to the New Hebrides, and Charles in *Jupiter* to San Diego, where he played a (for him) rare game of golf with the then US Ambassador to London, Walter Annenberg. In Hollywood he took tea with Barbra Streisand, who professed herself bowled over by 'this real English gentleman', and at San Diego yacht club he met an admiral's daughter named Laura Jo Watkins, who was to occupy his attentions for several months.

It was during this shore leave, on 20 March, that he heard by telephone of the attempt to kidnap Princess Anne in the Mall. The Princess and her husband, just back from the royal tour, were returning to Buckingham Palace from an equestrian charity film show when a Ford Escort swerved across the path of their car, forcing it to a halt. Its driver (subsequently found to be mentally ill, and ordered by the Lord Chief Justice to be detained 'without limit of time') shot and wounded the Princess's detective and chauffeur, plus another policeman and a passer-by, in his attempt to abduct her. At one point, after Captain Phillips had closed the car door on the assailant, he fired straight at the Princess; but her detective, James Beaton, already shot in the stomach, put his hand over the muzzle of the gun and deflected the bullet. Beaton was later awarded the George Cross.

During the phone call, Prince Charles was at first intent on flying straight home. But his sister reassured him that she was recovered, if shaken. She would hear none of it. At her behest, Charles continued to enjoy himself. When a posse of photographers arrived on the quay in pursuit of him, they shouted their inquiries to a scruffy, unshaven sailor leaning over the ship's side. 'Prince Charles?' he shouted back. 'Oh, he won't see you. He's a pretty nasty piece of work, you know.' The newshounds departed reluctantly, little knowing they had been talking to their prey.

The long voyage home gave the Prince a chance for some painting, some reading (Solzhenitsyn and Cecil Woodham-Smith's biography of Queen Victoria) and time to plan another practical joke. His brother officers had normally known how to conduct themselves towards the royal heir in their midst; occasionally, and inevitably during a 46,000-mile round-the-world voyage, they had overstepped the bounds of familiarity. Attempting on one occasion to 'debag' him, they removed his trousers to find another pair beneath; after removing those to find a third, they gave up. Not so much on his dignity at sea, Charles had responded by threatening them with the Tower. 'I can send you there, you know. It's quite within my power.' When *Jupiter* docked at Devonport that April, a black naval mini-bus waited on the quayside; emblazoned on its side in nine-inch letters was 'HM Tower of London for officers of HMS Jupiter'. The communications officer, it appeared, had been radioing ahead.

One of the Prince's duties on *Jupiter*'s home voyage, as flight deck officer, had been supervising the landing and take-off of Fleet Air Arm helicopters. At Devonport he waved his 'ping-pong bats' for the benefit of the press, excited by the prospect of his next posting: to master helicopter flight himself, back at Yeovilton. Prince Philip had gained his helicopter licence at the age of thirty-five; Charles was now intent on winning his ten years younger. Again it involved an intensive, truncated course: 105 hours instruction in forty-five days, comprising fifty hours of ground instruction, forty of flight training in dual-control aircraft, and a minimum of fifteen of solo flight.

Endowed with another somewhat melodramatic call sign, Red Dragon, the Prince undertook all the emergency training procedures – including landing damaged and blazing helicopters – and awkward routine operations such as carrying heavy loads. He also went to the Royal Marine School at Lympstone for a fearsome commando training programme, on the theory that helicopter pilots should familiarize themselves with the skills of the marine commandos they support. In camouflage gear, his face blacked, he was asked by one press photographer 'When does His Nibs arrive?'

It was 'very exciting, very rewarding, very stimulating and sometimes bloody terrifying'. But he had found his true metier. 'I adore flying, and I personally can't think of a better combination than naval flying – being at sea and being able to fly.' In an introduction to a history of the Fleet Air Arm, he wrote:

> Pride swells in my heart when I recall the part played by my great-grand-father, Prince Louis of Battenberg, in the formation of the Royal Naval Air Service in 1914. Without his interest and enthusiasm, and his determined support of the aeroplane versus the airship, the Naval Air Service might quite literally have had great difficulty in getting off the ground.

During his forty-five days at Yeovilton, spread over the last three months of 1974 and much interrupted by royal duties, Charles managed to complete 105 flying hours, twenty-six of them solo, in his Wessex V helicopter code-named Whisky Alpha.

On 12 December he passed out as a fully qualified pilot winning the Double Diamond award for the trainee who had made the most progress. It was 707 Squadron's tenth anniversary, and the Prince led a celebratory fly-past, his personal standard streaming from the winch-wire beneath his aircraft. His fellow officers, who had enjoyed his company on pub crawls around Somerset in search of 'scrumpy', the powerful West Country cider, presented him with a pen-stand made from a piece of helicopter rotor blade: one of his most valued possessions, it still sits on his desk at Buckingham Palace.

If Charles had at last discovered his favourite Service activity, he was well aware that it had been one of the most dangerous, and that his position might prevent him keeping it up. 'I hope and pray there'll be a chance for me to continue,' he told his fellow Red Dragons in a farewell speech, 'but we shall have to wait and see.' He was also aware that special precautions had again surrounded his training; throughout his solo flying time, he had been shadowed by an auxiliary machine with fire-fighting and other emergency equipment. Just as well: in his twenty-six hours aloft, the Prince was forced to make three emergency landings, due respectively to computer failure, engine failure, and a broken fragment of engine cover lodging in his engine. Shudders passed between Whitehall and Buckingham Palace, but the Ministry of Defence, still keen to use the Prince as a recruiting agent, mentioned only 'precautionary landings' in its press statements. Through it all, Charles was still resentful that the most hazardous thrills aloft, in Buccaneers and other supersonic jets, were implacably denied him: 'If you're living dangerously,' he declared, 'it tends to make you appreciate your life that much more, and to really want to live it to its fullest.'

His enthusiasm did, however, win him a postponement of his return to shore studies at Greenwich. Instead he joined 845 Naval Air Support Squadron aboard the aircraft-carrier *Hermes*, bound for NATO exercises in the Atlantic, en route for the West Indies. In April he was called away to royal duties in Canada, but seized the chance to travel north and sample the ice-bound life of the North-West Territories. The pressmen ever at the Prince's heels were beginning to feel the strains of following so insatiable an adventurer, and life in the Arctic brought Prince and press unusually close together. For those who had lugged their cameras that far, however, he turned in a princely *tour de force* after diving beneath the North Polar ice

EDUCATION

with Dr Joe Macinnis, a young scientist based at the underwater research station at Resolute Bay.

The ice had closed over their heads as soon as they disappeared beneath it: in a temperature of 28.5 degrees Fahrenheit, it was six feet thick, over water only thirty feet deep. Returning to the surface after half an hour under water, Charles inflated his orange diving suit with compressed air until he looked 'like a Michelin Man', then let it deflate again until he was merely 'an orange walrus'. As he bowed to the ecstatic TV cameras, he knew the whole scene would be enjoyed by his family back home.

Hermes then took him to a month's helicopter training with the Royal Canadian Air Force at the inaptly named Blissville, New Brunswick, where he shared two weeks of life under canvas in sub-zero temperatures. The cameras followed him even to this desolate spot, where Charles felt sufficiently remote and at ease to give on-camera interviews unshaven – on his way, as it transpired, to a 'full set'. The beard, which reminded many of that of the young Duke of York, his grandfather, is preserved for posterity in the TV film *Pilot Royal*. Charles directed his own sequence at Blissville, in a sepia parody of silent films in which he at last takes his revenge on his instructor, Lieutenant Commander Alan MacGregor. Still to be seen in *Pilot Royal*, the royal film alternates between faintly embarrassing Goonery and a passing imitation of Laurel and Hardy.

The beard became even more famous when it flew home with its owner for his installation as a Great Master of the Order of the Bath, ranking third to the Garter and the Thistle among British knighthoods. In the car home from Heathrow with David Checketts, Charles joked about returning from a bathless month under canvas to receive that particular dignity. He also wondered what his mother would say about his beard. That was clear next morning. The beard had gone, and Prince Charles sported only a moustache as he processed with his mother through Westminster Abbey and vowed 'to defend maidens, widows and orphans'. Even the moustache had gone by the following morning, when he flew back to *Hermes*; naval regulations stipulate a 'full set' or nothing. But the beard is a fond memory. The only jarring note was a *vox populi* exercise in one of the popular newspapers, in which a loyal subject declared that she liked the Prince's beard 'because it hid his rather weak chin'. Of all the many millions of words written about him, that remark has always stuck in Prince Charles's mind. It rankles still.

His Service career was to end in style, with a command of his own. On 9 February 1976, after completing captaincy courses at Greenwich and Portsmouth, the Prince of Wales took command of the minehunter HMS *Bronington*, at 193 feet and 360 tons one of the Navy's smallest ships, with a complement of four officers and thirty-three ratings. The wooden-hulled vessel – named, appropriately enough, after a Welsh village – was built in the 1950s, and based on Rosyth. Its new commander was just twenty-seven years old, two years younger than his father had been when given command of the frigate *Magpie* in 1950.

Bronington was not renowned as a particularly stable vessel. Her outgoing captain, Lieutenant Commander Harry Bates, said she rolled 'even on wet grass'. Known in the Navy as 'Old Quarter Past Eleven' – her pennant number was 1115 – she had a young crew: the first officer, Lieutenant Roy Clare, was twenty-five, and the ratings' average age just nineteen-and-a-half. The captain's cabin, nine feet by ten, with a folding bunk, a desk, chair and faded green carpet, was situated next to the ship's deep freeze. In rough weather, the best lunch available was stew from a pot tied to the galley stove.

For ten months, Prince Charles and *Bronington* patrolled the North Sea locating mines and assisting naval divers to dispose of them. Not an immensely exciting schedule, and not immensely pleasant in a ship so much at the weather's mercy. Charles later confessed that command had 'aged' him – and that, after five years in the Navy, *Bronington* was the first ship aboard which he had been sea-sick.

On *Bronington*'s return to Rosyth, its commander proudly welcomed the Admiral of the Fleet, his father, on board, and entertained him to tea and cucumber sandwiches in the cramped wardroom. But his finest hour came in mid-November, when he sailed his ship into the Pool of London just in time to be home for his twenty-eighth birthday. He was to enjoy just one more month on the bridge. Queen Elizabeth II's Silver Jubilee in 1977, in which the Prince of Wales was to play a central role, loomed large. On 14 December he jumped two ranks in both the Services in which he had served, promoted Wing Commander in the RAF (skipping David Checketts's rank of Squadron Leader) and Commander (skipping Lieutenant Commander) in the Royal Navy. The following day, his crew 'pushed' him back into Civvy Street in a wheelchair, a lavatory seat slung like a laurel wreath around his neck. 'See you behave yourself, lads,' were the commander's parting words, to which 'Doc' Kevin Ryan, *Bronington*'s medical assistant, countered, 'See you keep your bowels open, sir.' An inelegant farewell, but one in keeping with the Navy's cherished traditions (previous Captains had been hoisted aloft on cranes to mark their departure), and boorish enough to appeal to the broader side of the Prince's sense of humour.

The Services had proved a successful, if conventional, end to twenty-four years of royal education. Elizabeth II and her consort had long since realized that their gamble had paid handsome dividends. Their son had had opportunities unprecedented for an heir to the throne to share the life of his fellow men. He had been allowed to go much further in hazardous personal adventure. What had started for him as a bad dream had developed into a glimpse of a freer world he was reluctant to leave.

But, as his father reminded him, duty called. And the Duke of Edinburgh added a compliment which touched his son: 'What a great relief it is when you find that you've actually brought up a reasonable and civilized human being.'

PART IV

I've Danced with a Man Who's Danced with a Girl Who's Danced with the Prince of Wales

My word, I've had a party,
My word, I've had a spree!
Believe me or believe me not,
It's all the same to me!
I'm wild with exaltation,
I'm dizzy with success,
For I've danced with a man who –
Well, you'll never guess!

I've danced with a man who's danced with a girl
Who's danced with the Prince of Wales!
I'm crazy with excitement,
Completely off the rails!
And when he said to me what she said to him
The Prince remark'd to her,
It was simply grand!
He said, 'Topping band!'
And she said, 'Delightful, sir!'
Glory, glory hallelujah,
I'm the luckiest of females,
For I've danced with a man who's danced with a girl
Who's danced with the Prince of Wales!

*Popular song by Herbert Farjeon
and Harold Scott, 1928*
(reproduced by kind permission of
Ascherberg, Hopwood & Crew Ltd;
Chappell Music Ltd)

15

The World's Most Eligible Bachelor

I have not yet met the girl I want to marry.
*The Prince of Wales on 17 June 1977, the
day the* DAILY EXPRESS '*officially' announced
his engagement to Princess Marie-Astrid of
Luxembourg*

IN AUGUST 1861 Bertie, Prince of Wales, the future King Edward VII, was
nearing the end of an unhappy three-month military training stint at the
Curragh Camp, near Dublin. An ill-conceived postscript to Prince Albert's
rigorous scheme of education for his son, the course was designed to fit Bertie
within one month for the command of a battalion, thus justifying his
honorific promotion to the rank of colonel. The Prince was as glum as his
commanding officer, Colonel Percy, and indeed his mother the Queen, when
by the end of the third month he still fell short of requirements. When Victoria and Albert paid a visit of inspection, their son suffered the humiliation
of performing a mere subaltern's duties in his colonel's uniform. 'You are
too imperfect in your drill, sir,' Colonel Percy told him. 'Your word of command is indistinct.'

History might tactfully have forgotten this miserable episode, had it not
been for one eventful summer night that August. The Prince's brother
officers, through curiously mixed motives of charity and mischief, smuggled
into his quarters a young actress whose company they had all enjoyed, one
Nellie Clifden. Thus was Bertie expertly initiated in a subject distinctly not
on Prince Albert's curriculum.

It is the fate of kings and princes to have this, perhaps the most private
moment of their lives, trumpeted to posterity as gleefully as their other, more
public conquests. Most, happily, are spared it in their own lifetimes. For
Bertie, however, the incident proved disastrous. As Queen Victoria noted

painfully in her diary, Nellie Clifden 'bragged' after the encounter had become an affair. The story was soon a favourite in the gentlemen's clubs, and was thence brought to court by a new lord-in-waiting, Lord Torrington, described equally painfully by Victoria as 'one of the great gossips of London'. Prince Albert travelled to Cambridge to remonstrate with his son, and returned home with the subject closed, the transgression forgiven. He also returned home, however, depressed and exhausted. Within a week he had collapsed with what was diagnosed as typhoid fever, and twelve days later he was dead. Victoria, distraught, immediately blamed the loss of her beloved husband on the 'fall' of their eldest son. 'Oh, that boy,' she wrote to her daughter, the Crown Princess of Prussia, 'much as I pity, I never can or shall look at him without a shudder.'

In the century since Bertie's 'fall', social attitudes in the loftiest circles have altered as much as in society at large. But one of the lasting, distinctive qualities of the English upper classes is their discretion about each other, a code of self-preservation which has kept them cohesive during the drift towards a classless society. In the exuberant Prince of Wales-ship of Edward VII, once Nellie Clifden had launched him on his way, his many and varied affairs were well known and discussed throughout high society, whose members were outlawed only if they gossiped beneath themselves. By the 1930s and the brief, heady youth of the future Edward VIII, princely dalliance was an accepted and well-guarded secret long before he met Wallis Simpson. His friendships with Lady Furness and Mrs Freda Dudley Ward were the talking-point only of his own charmed circle, the same well-born élite which has since changed its outward show but not its inward dealings.

Certain members of today's aristocracy could, if they chose, noise abroad salicious details of the present Prince of Wales's private life, notably of those country week-ends which do not appear in the Court Circular. Those gentry who occasionally open their gates to the public these days are careful to shut them more firmly than ever the rest of the time. But Prince Charles is the first Prince of Wales to have grown up in the era of the rampant mass media, when the Royal Family as much as anyone else has had to adapt to insatiable public curiosity about its private life. On more than one occasion in the late 1970s a senior member of the royal circle felt free, in what he thought the Prince's best interests, to talk of Prince Charles 'popping in and out of bed with girls'. But the present Prince of Wales is by nature less of a libertine than either of his immediate predecessors. Unlike Edward VIII, he would not contemplate abandoning his public duties, let alone his crown, for a woman. Unlike Edward VII, he will not contemplate taking mistresses after he has taken a bride. Prince Charles's religious and moral convictions on the sanctity of marriage are firmly held.

Paradoxically, it is the major common factor of his and Bertie's lives which most distinguishes them. That dauntingly long wait in the wings, as understudy to a longeval and revered sovereign, earns Prince Charles all the parental indulgence denied his great-great-grandfather. He intends to marry in the next few years; he would not wish to be too old a father to his children, and his own happy family background is the single most important component of his life so far. But only his duty to breed heirs will compel him to marry in his thirties. Until that day the Prince's amorous exploits may cause the occasional family row, and earn the avuncular disapproval of his former private secretary, but they are scarcely likely to change the course of history. Elizabeth II may have wished her son had married younger; she hopes, and has on one occasion attempted to ensure, that he can find someone of royal blood to love. But she has always behaved more as his mother than his Queen.

Nevertheless, the Prince of Wales regards it as something of an achievement that he reached the age of thirty unmarried. Throughout his twenties, the pressures on him to choose the nation and the Commonwealth its future Queen – constant from the press and public, intermittent from those close to him – were almost as daunting as the family precedents. His parents married when his father was twenty-six, his mother twenty-one. His grandfather, King George VI, married at twenty-seven; his great-grandfather, George V, at twenty-eight; his great-great-grandfather, Edward VII, at twenty-one. Of Charles's own generation of the Royal Family, the Duke of Gloucester married at twenty-seven, the Duke of Kent at twenty-five, and his sister Anne at twenty-three.

The history of his office proved even more formidable. Apart from his immediate predecessor, whose eventual choice of bride led him to renounce the throne, Charles is the only Prince of Wales to have reached thirty unmarried since James Stuart, the Old Pretender, in 1718 – and he took a wife the following year. Of those Princes of Wales who became Kings of England, only Henry V and Charles II were unmarried at thirty. But each remained so only two more years; and each, already on the throne, had had a singularly busy youth.

Prince Charles had no Agincourt, no exile from a republican government to occupy his twenties. He had time on his hands. Despite his Service career, there was leisure enough to be seen escorting the eligible, the well-born, the well-connected, the merely attractive, even the not so suitable – beauties all, most from the requisite top drawer. There was, moreover, his strong romantic streak. He falls in love easily, and has by his own confession done so 'on countless occasions'. Throughout his twenties, the attentions of the press had cramped his style, and alienated the affections of several girls, but he had at least once come close to a proposal. Why then did he disappoint matrons and tantalize maidens the world over by delaying?

The reasons are many and varied: personal and public, domestic and constitutional. For no other man in the world, perhaps, is the choice of a bride so complex, so fraught with pitfalls, so hedged with restrictions. Few other men, meanwhile, are so much in need of a paragon among women, prepared to be privately loving and supportive, the sole confidante of a man with many confidences to share, as well as publicly conscientious – prepared, in short, to sacrifice her life entirely to his. When still only twenty, Prince Charles showed himself more than aware of his plight:

> It's awfully difficult, because you've got to remember that when you marry, in my position, you're going to marry somebody who perhaps one day is going to become Queen. So you've got to choose very carefully.... The one advantage about marrying a Princess, for instance, or somebody from a royal family, is that they do know what happens. The trouble is that I often feel I would like to marry somebody English. Or Welsh.... Well, British, anyway.

So it is in his choice of bride – if not, before that day, in his quest for one – that Prince Charles's accident of birth perhaps most restricts his life. By the Bill of Rights of 1689 (enshrined in the 1701 Act of Settlement, through which his legal claim to the throne is established) he is forbidden to marry a Catholic – which rules out half the princesses of Europe and, more to his chagrin, many an otherwise suitable English rose. Under the Royal Marriages Act of 1772 – introduced, ironically enough, by King George III, the 'much maligned monarch' whose reputation he has so struggled to rehabilitate – he is effectively barred from marrying without the consent of his mother or both Houses of Parliament. As he will on accession become head of the Anglican Church, there could be no question of his marrying a divorcee or ever himself being divorced.

Any or all of these choices Prince Charles, the British citizen, could of course make. But marrying a Catholic, a divorcee, or anyone vetoed by the sovereign or Parliament, would force him to renounce his right to the throne. His entire upbringing, and all his own personal inclinations and beliefs, militate against his becoming a second Duke of Windsor. He will not, like Edward, he has said privately, 'become a martyr to the cause'.

The Prince's own lifetime has seen only one royal relaxation of the rules. In 1955 his aunt, Princess Margaret, was persuaded not to marry the divorced Group Captain Peter Townsend; in 1978, however, she was at length permitted to divorce Lord Snowdon. But Princess Margaret was never heir to the throne, nor ever likely to be after Charles's birth in 1948. The Prince saw it as a happy precedent when his sister married a commoner,

Captain Mark Phillips, in 1973; but again Princess Anne was always freer to choose, with her three brothers (and any male offspring they may have) between her and the throne.

It is possible that Elizabeth II's lifetime may see the repeal of both the laws restricting royal choice, but scarcely before Prince Charles marries, and scarcely anyway to an heir's advantage. The Queen has it in mind to persuade a Prime Minister to do away with the Royal Marriages Act, which has long outlived its purpose. George III introduced it in an attempt to curb his sons' erratic sexual behaviour, and thus ensured that it affected all those in direct line of succession. In 1978, therefore, the sixteenth in line, Prince Michael of Kent, had to renounce all rights to the throne to wed a Roman Catholic, Baroness Marie-Christine von Reibnitz, whose previous marriage had been annulled. The Pope refused them permission to marry in church, which prompted the Prince of Wales to make a bold public protest about the 'needless distress' caused by doctrinal dispute among Christians. But the Act had already been proved unrealistic, in the latter half of the twentieth century, by Princess Margaret's divorce, and the divorce and remarriage of the Queen's cousin, the Earl of Harewood.

The 1689 Bill of Rights is less easily disposed of, outmoded though it is in an age of greater religious tolerance. In 1977, when the nation was briefly convinced that the Prince of Wales was about to marry the Roman Catholic Princess Marie-Astrid of Luxembourg, there was much discussion of dropping the ban on Catholic consorts. But although the Archbishop of Canterbury was meeting the Pope in Rome that very month, there was little sign of the spirit of ecumenism infecting the Church of England's attitude to its monarch and titular head. Plans that such a couple might raise their sons as Protestants and their daughters as Catholics drew sniffs of distaste from the Anglican establishment, and outright condemnation from the Vatican. The debate was reopened late in 1978, when a curiously-timed speech from Enoch Powell, the Ulster Unionist MP, declared that such a marriage 'would signal the beginning of the end of the British monarchy'. The Prince, though puzzled by Mr Powell's motives, was glad of the leading articles he provoked, which again called on the churches to settle their differences on this score at least. But again the indignation of laymen fell on dead ears; more heat was generated in Mr Powell's direction for stirring jingoistic anti-Catholic feelings in Ulster, for reasons of purely party political advantage.

'If I marry a Catholic, I'm dead,' the Prince told a friend. 'I've had it.' He better than anyone knew the law, but he saw no reason why it should meanwhile inhibit his bachelorhood. As these checks and balances began to assert themselves on his early public romances, another equally striking reason for delay emerged. By the age of thirty this slightly awkward, fundamentally shy figure, still in some ways young for his years, publicly noted for his weak chin and jug ears, had developed an extraordinary ex-officio power over women. It took him by surprise, and he began rather to enjoy it.

By his late twenties, the Prince of Wales had become a besieged sex symbol wherever he went. At his approach girls would giggle and scream as if he were a pop star, lunge forth with kisses as if he were a matinée idol, fight to touch him as if he were divine. For once, moreover, their mothers warmly approved. It started during his tour of Wales in the summer of 1969, in the wake of his investiture at Caernarvon; confronted in the flesh by the image etched on their television screens, girls quite literally fainted away. It climaxed eight years later, during his 1977 tour of Australia, the main feature of which was the number of girls daily launching themselves out of a crowd towards the royal cheek, even the royal lips. By this time, he had mustered sufficient self-confidence occasionally to return the compliment.

By the time he left the Navy, in November 1976, Prince Charles was of a mind to prolong his independence. It was perfectly possible to separate the public accounts of his love-life from the private truth. But his newfound power was not, alas, without responsibility. He must exercise self-denying care in his choice of all friends, but immeasurably more so in his selection of female intimates. Of all the many girls he has dated only one, Lady Sarah Spencer, has been tempted into talking to a journalist, and that under somewhat harassed conditions. She was careful to insist, after a skiing holiday with the Prince in 1978, that their relationship was platonic. Contrary to popular belief, he did not 'drop' her immediately after the incident; indeed she was a guest of the Queen at Sandringham, in Prince Charles's company, during January 1979. He was, in fact, more hurt than annoyed by one remark she made: 'I am not in love with him . . . and I wouldn't marry anyone I didn't love, whether it was the dustman or the King of England. If he asked me, I would turn him down.'

Lady Sarah, however, was very much the exception that proved the rule. She was so excited to be among the Prince's known escorts that she preserved every press cutting about their meetings in a scrapbook. Otherwise, his girl friends have thrown a blanket of remarkably loyal discretion over Prince Charles's amorous exploits, doubly remarkable in view of the amount of money any one of them could receive for even a mild indiscretion. His public consorts, however, have all been to the manner, if not the manor, born. Society girls, most with aristocratic backgrounds, they regard the Royal Family with even more awe than the rest of its subjects, to the extent of swallowing their feminine pride in Prince Charles's company. They call him

'Sir', even when alone with him. They will walk a pace or two behind him when protocol requires it. They know, with very few exceptions, that it is he who issues the invitations, he who makes the phone calls. Whatever the feelings in their heart, they are not allowed to forget the privilege his company bestows on them.

The Prince, for his part, is an otherwise chivalrous suitor. He is concerned lest his friends suffer from being seen with him. For some girls, a weekend with the Prince has been followed by a week of pressmen camped on their front doorstep. 'It's very hard on them,' Prince Charles has said. 'I have layers to protect me, but they are not used to it. It tends sometimes to put the really nice ones off.' He takes pains to warn them of the strains of appearing in public with him, and urges them to call on his staff for assistance in emergencies. His greatest hidden asset, however, is that they know the slightest word out of place would signal the end of the affair.

Some, who remain close friends after passion has cooled, are prepared to do him even greater favours. They will contentedly escort him to Ascot, to the theatre or wherever, to be photographed, gossiped about and restored to the newspapers' royal marriage stakes, while offstage he woos another unheard of by the waiting world. Prince Charles has become quite expert at raising smokescreens and laying false trails. His male friends will occasionally 'lend' him a girl friend with whom to be seen in public, to distract attention from a more discreetly conducted romance. In 1977, for instance, the popular press grew very excited about the Prince's friendship with Penelope Eastwood, a twenty-two-year-old graduate of the London School of Economics, the daughter of a wealthy army officer retired to Majorca. She was in fact the girl friend (now the wife) of the Prince's old Gordonstoun chum Norton Knatchbull, grandson of Lord Mountbatten. When the deception was discovered, vengeance was extracted – and the rumours prolonged – in the form of stories about the Prince 'pinching' his friend's girl.

He is also self-confident, even vain enough to enjoy mild public flirtations with the famous and fashionable: pop stars such as the Three Degrees, the all-female black soul trio who sang at his thirtieth birthday party, and film stars such as Susan George. They must, of course, be unattached. Given that he should not be photographed in the arms of married women, and given that some of the world's most desired women are intent on being photographed in his arms, the Prince has had to develop politely tactful skills. He had to disentangle himself, for instance, from the headlong embrace of Farrah Fawcett-Majors, whom he met in Hollywood in 1977, and who flew hotfoot to London soon after for a charity show in his presence, confiding her admiration in copious newspaper interviews. Then at the height of her fame as, appropriately enough, one of television's Charlie's Angels, she was equally well-known to be the wife of Lee Majors, television's Six Million Dollar Man. Similarly the revelation in 1979 of Mrs Margaret Trudeau, estranged wife of the Canadian Prime Minister, that Charles had once 'looked long and hard down my cleavage' was treated with right royal disdain.

The unattached, however, he has been known to telephone, late at night, after a casual meeting at a party or a film première. He can entertain in complete privacy, at his own home or that of a friend. His two regular detectives, who have to accompany him even on such private sorties, would scarcely breathe a word of them even to each other; but their occasional reliefs, who take over their duties in holiday periods, have been known to complain of long, boring waits outside private houses in assorted London suburbs. These excursions are kept to a minimum, as the Prince is well aware of the risks involved. Besides, his quarters at Buckingham Palace are completely self-contained, and an invitation there from the Prince of Wales is scarcely likely to be refused.

Such invitations can, however, lead to surprises. For at least one girl, an evening alone with the Prince meant listening to a catalogue of his conquests. Like any other hot-blooded male, he can make the mistake of trying to boast his way into a lady's affections. He can also behave in somewhat cavalier fashion: months can go by without a word, just when our heroine thought she had won a place in her Prince's heart. This, of course, is partly of necessity; any escort of the Prince of Wales must prepare herself for the daily shock of seeing someone else in his company in the morning's news-papers. The requirements of rank are a great provider of explanations.

For the most part, it is his tenderness and concern which win hearts, just as they remain the qualities most mentioned by other friends. They are evident in his few public pronouncements on the subject of marriage:

> I think an awful lot of people have got the wrong idea of what it is all about. It is rather more than just falling madly in love with somebody and having a love affair for the rest of your married life. Much more than that. It's basically a very strong friendship. . . . I think you are very lucky if you find the person attractive in the physical *and* the mental sense. . . . In many cases, you fall madly 'in love' with somebody with whom you are really infatuated. To me marriage, which may be for fifty years, seems to be one of the biggest and most responsible steps to be taken in one's life.

At the age of twenty-seven, he told an interviewer that he thought thirty 'about the right age for a chap like me to get married'. He regretted the remark, naturally enough, on his thirtieth birthday, when it was flung back in his face with a vengeance. But the popular British press has been marrying

off Prince Charles since he was three. Immediately after his mother's accession, the first of countless subsequent lists of eligible brides appeared, casting
its net around all the European Royal Houses as well as the country homes of
England. Many in both categories have since become unavailable – a fact of
life which Prince Philip, who otherwise brings very little pressure to bear
on his son in these matters, has occasionally mentioned in jocular fashion.
'You'd better get on with it,' he'd say, 'or there won't be anyone left.'

Bertie, Prince of Wales, was nineteen when Nellie Clifden introduced him
to one of his life's lasting pleasures. Prince Charles was just the same age,
and also a Cambridge student, when he too embarked upon his first serious
romance. The Master of Trinity, Lord Butler, was at the time writing his
political memoirs, *The Art of the Possible*, and had engaged as his research
assistant a young history graduate, the daughter of the then Chilean Ambassador to London. At twenty-three, Lucia Santa Cruz was three years older
than Charles, and considerably more experienced in the ways of the world.
The phrase *in loco parentis* can rarely have had a more resounding ring than
it did at that time for Butler, who was aware of all the disadvantages: the
girl was a foreigner, a Catholic, and much the more sophisticated of the
two. But she was also intelligent, vivacious and, for what it was worth, well-
connected; and the couple were anyway separated after dark by the Trinity
curfew, which locked the gate at night between a student and his girl friend.
The Master disapproved of the system, and was in the process of reforming
it. In the meantime, he felt it his duty to help the Prince enjoy the dwindling
days of as private a life as he would ever know. Lord Butler 'slipped' Lucia
a key to the Master's Lodge. 'The Prince' he remembers, 'asked if she might
stay in our Lodge for privacy, which request we were very glad to accede to.'
    Charles's feelings for her appear to have been the kind of puppy-love most
men experience in their teens. Until he met Lucia, his circumstances had
prevented the adolescent adventures all too familiar to lesser mortals. Any
conversation with any girl had been inflated by the press into romance: a
bashful encounter at a Gordonstoun social evening had led one Sunday
paper to declare he was being sent to school in Australia 'to break up the
affair'. But Prince Charles, on the threshold of his twenties, was wholly innocent, wholly inexperienced. It was at Cambridge, contemporaries testify,
that he 'discovered' girls. Lucia Santa Cruz is now married to a Chilean
lawyer, and living in South America; Prince Charles is godfather to their
first child. She remained a good friend to the Prince for several years after
their Cambridge days; her occasional week-end visits to Balmoral invariably
renewed rumours of romance, long after their respective affections had
moved on. Whatever she meant to him at the time, since that first friendship

with Lucia Prince Charles has never been without at least one steady date in his life.

At Cambridge he soon took up with Sybilla Dorman, daughter of the Governor-General of Malta, with whom he spent those two holidays on the island after his investiture in 1969. Both were reading history, and Sybilla shared Charles's enthusiasm for amateur dramatics. He collected her for dinner in a mud-stained Sandringham Land-Rover – 'I'd expected the MG, at the very least,' she complained – and was popularly supposed to have climbed the walls of her college, Newnham, with other party guests who had outstayed the curfew's welcome. Journalists who pursued the couple to Malta watched quivering as she applied the Prince's sun-tan oil. But it was the first of innumerable false trails. Charles was soon escorting another girl, one of the daughters of Prince Philip's naturalist friend Aubrey Buxton, to a Trinity May Ball. Sybilla is one of Prince Charles's many former girl friends who have since married someone else.

The list of the Prince of Wales's escorts, over the ten years to his thirtieth birthday in 1978, is impressive, not least as a *Who Was Who* among the debutantes of the 1970s. More than half have since married; some remain good friends, others no more than acquaintances, seen rarely, but seen with pleasure. A few, despite popular rumours to the contrary, were never more than that in the first place.

Some of the first rumours surrounded Rosaleen Bagge, the daughter of a retired major living near Sandringham, who exchanged letters with the Prince while he was at school in Australia in 1966. Then came Cambridge, Lucia Santa Cruz, Sybilla Dorman and the Buxton girls. For the next ten years, the Prince of Wales was quite clearly playing the field. His turnover was high; and there was scarcely one among his many companions without a drop of blue blood.

The roll-call, complete with pedigrees, included: Lady Leonora Grosvenor, daughter of the Duke of Westminster (now married to the Earl of Lichfield, better known as Patrick Lichfield the photographer); her sister Lady Jane Grosvenor, now the Duchess of Roxburghe; Lady Victoria Percy, daughter of the Duke of Northumberland, a Roman Catholic, now married to John Cuthbert, a wealthy landowner; her sister Lady Caroline Percy; Bettina Lindsay, daughter of the Conservative politician Lord Balniel, now Mrs Peter Drummond-Hay; Lady Cecil Kerr, daughter of the Marquess of Lothian, now married to Donald Cameron of Lochiel; Lady Henrietta Fitzroy, daughter of the Duke of Grafton; Lady Charlotte Manners, daughter of the Duke of Rutland; her cousin Elizabeth Manners; Angela Nevill, daughter of Prince Philip's private secretary, Lord Rupert Nevill; Lady Camilla Fane, daughter of the Earl of Westmorland; Lord Astor's daughter, Louise; Georgiana Russell, daughter of the diplomat Sir John Russell, now Mrs Brooke Boothby; Rosie Clifton, a colonel's daughter, now married to the Prince's polo-playing friend Mark Vestey; Caroline Longman, daughter of the wealthy publisher, the late Mark Longman.

Through the interminable catalogue of speculation, three girls genuinely did enjoy close and lasting friendships with the Prince. A regular companion still, despite her momentary indiscretion, is Lady Sarah Spencer, goddaughter of the Queen Mother, and daughter of the Queen's old friend, Earl Spencer. Red-haired, vivacious, an ideal public escort, Sarah suffered from *anorexia nervosa* when first she met Prince Charles at Ascot, but his companionship seemed to speed her full recovery and they were soon indulging their mutual love of outdoor sports. A skiing holiday with the Duke and Duchess of Gloucester in February 1978 led to press innuendo about the number of bedrooms in their Klosters villa, but it was after this that Lady Sarah insisted their friendship was platonic. A year later, she was out shooting with the Royal Family at Sandringham.

Before Sarah, there was Davina Sheffield, the soldier's daughter, blonde, ex-debutante, his love for whom Prince Charles could not disguise even in public. After their first few meetings she took herself off, somewhat dramatically, to Vietnam, where she worked in an orphans' hostel during the last stages of the war; forced by the Viet Cong advance to flee, she returned home to more tragedy: the brutal murder of her mother by raiders in their Oxfordshire home. She turned to the Prince for solace, and by the end of the year, 1976, was publicly arm in arm with him again. But she was to fall prey to the artificial standards by which he must live. On a discreet surfing expedition to Bantham, a quiet Devon cove frequented by Prince Charles and his friends, she was said to have been discovered naked in the men's changing room. There was scarcely time for the denials to be issued before a greater misfortune befell Davina: her former fiancé chose to let it be known that they had once lived together – enough to preclude her being seen again with the heir to the throne, let alone remaining a candidate for Queen. A similar fate befell Fiona Watson, daughter of the Yorkshire landowner Lord Manton, whom the Prince had been seeing on occasion until noisy complaints from her boy friend led to the discovery that she had once revealed her startling 38–23–35 statistics in full colour across eleven pages, to readers of *Penthouse* magazine.

But there was, above all, Lady Jane Wellesley, daughter of the eighth Duke of Wellington, who in a highly competitive field has remained probably the closest and most enduring of Prince Charles's female friends. They had known each other since childhood – Jane had attended some of those sprightly early birthday parties at Buckingham Palace – but had not taken more than usual notice of each other until some twenty years later. She was the first of the Prince's true loves who was also an eminently suitable candidate for Queen. Daughter of one of England's proudest noble families, she was quite at ease at court; she shared the mischievous nature of his youth, but was prepared to behave with due decorum when necessary. One of the prettiest of all the girls who have passed through Prince Charles's life, she is undoubtedly also the brightest, and one of the few who actually enjoys earning her own living.

Her father, moreover, owned ancestral estates in southern Spain: 30,000 acres at Molino del Rey, near Granada, won for the family by the Iron Duke's peninsular campaign. They made an ideal retreat. On one of the first of many sojourns there, during a break from his duties aboard HMS *Minerva* in 1973, the Prince became so exercised by the rapaciousness of the press that, for one rare moment, he behaved like his father and swore at them, thus adding strength to their convictions. Lady Jane, they reported home, had been observed pulling the Prince of Wales's hair, and 'playfully throwing melons at him'. He apologized for his bad language through the sterner of his private detectives, Inspector Paul Officer: 'They are just two young people relaxing with friends for a few days. The publicity their friendship has raised has not made it easy for them.' But Officer saw the newshounds off with a few words of his own:

> I can definitely state that there is no romance. The whole affair has been built up from a molehill to a mountain. It is just not on – the two are just very good chums. The Prince will not be a party to deception. That is why he has refused to be photographed with Lady Jane.

Nobody believed a word of it. The more curt and irritated the Duke of Wellington's protests, the more Britain grew convinced its Prince had chosen his future Queen. Later that year, when Jane attended Sunday morning service at Sandringham as a week-end guest of the Royal Family, 10,000 defied both royal denials and a petrol shortage to turn up and watch. Even Davina Sheffield, who was once reduced to tears at Heathrow Airport by the harassment of the press and excited onlookers, had suffered nothing like this. Jane Wellesley braved phalanxes of reporters outside her Fulham home to go to work each morning; after refusing all comment to those who telephoned her at her office, she would leave for home to see newspaper placards announcing MY LOVE FOR CHARLES – JANE TELLS ALL. The irony was that she was a journalist herself, chairman of her union branch, soon to be a member of the national executive.

Friends of Prince Charles are surprised that he did not marry Lady Jane years ago, and they place the blame on him for dithering. It has been sug-

gested that she turned him down, not wishing to make so incomparable a
surrender of her freedom. It has also been suggested that insufferable press
attention destroyed their friendship. The truth lies elsewhere; Prince
Charles had most nearly contemplated marriage at a time when his Service
career took him away too much for it to be possible, and would continue to
do so for several years. By the time he left the Navy, he had a taste for
seeing more of life before settling down. But Jane Wellesley remained a
better friend than most, despite the Prince's penchant for teasing her mercilessly.

Throughout 1973 and 1974 British bookies quoted Jane as firm favourite
in the royal marriage stakes. They seemed about to pay up when she accompanied the Queen Mother and Princess Alexandra to the 1974 royal film
première, a public sign of family approval. Later that year, however, her
odds lengthened briefly when a glossy American blonde was among the dignitaries in the Strangers' Gallery of the House of Lords to hear the Prince
of Wales make his maiden speech. She was Laura Jo Watkins, the daughter
of an American rear-admiral, whom the Prince had met that summer when
HMS *Jupiter* called at San Diego, California. Throughout the week she
popped up at various smart functions, and newspapers were already waxing
lyrical about an unmarried Wallis Simpson when she just as suddenly disappeared again. Unusually large crowds converged on Cowdray Park that
Saturday to see the Prince's weekly polo game, but they were disappointed.
'You don't think I'm such a bloody fool as to bring her here today, do you?'
he laughed. And that, it seemed, was that – until four years later, in the
summer of 1978, when Guy Wildenstein flew her over to Deauville as a
present during Prince Charles's annual polo visit.

By this time he had also had his long awaited, almost obligatory, encounter
with the glamorous Princess Caroline of Monaco, daughter of Prince Rainier
and the former Grace Kelly. It was an undisguised mutual sizing-up operation, and it was not a success. Caroline was forty-five minutes late for their
first rendezvous, at which both discovered they had little in common. A
second meeting was cancelled, and in 1978, pleading pressure of work,
Charles regretfully refused his invitation to Caroline's wedding to Philippe
Junot, a French businessman.

The available European princesses, their names annually trotted out by
the women's magazines, were becoming somewhat thin on the ground. The
Queen, however, is known to hope that her son will marry royalty; such
is his duty, she feels, to the Blood Royal of the House of Windsor. Even
the otherwise *laissez-faire* Prince Philip has said: 'People tend to marry
within their own circles ... there is a built-in acceptance of the sort of life
you are going to lead.' Buckingham Palace has always looked askance at the

suggestion, but both Elizabeth II and her husband clearly had a hand in the *événements* of 1977, when what would to the Queen have been an ideal match for her son was finally frustrated. Prince Charles, for his part, appears to have been ready to consider his mother's proposition: that he should marry Princess Marie-Astrid of Luxembourg.

The Queen is an old family friend of the Princess's father, Grand Duke Jean, and is said to have returned from her state visit to Luxembourg in November 1976 'enchanted' by the Princess, and with hopes of persuading her son to take an interest in her. The following month, on 8 December, HMS *Bronington* docked at Ostend, and the Prince drove to Laeken Palace in Brussels for lunch with King Baudouin and Queen Fabiola of the Belgians, and Prince Philip, who was in Brussels for a meeting of the International Equestrian Federation. Princess Marie-Astrid is King Baudouin's niece; she and her sister Margaretha were at the time sharing an apartment in the Belgian Royal Palace, while Marie-Astrid worked at an Antwerp Hospital. Few believe Buckingham Palace's denial that she too was at the lunch. Also attending was the Belgian primate, Cardinal Joseph Suenens, friend and adviser to both the Pope and Bishop Jean Hengen, head of the Luxembourg Church.

It was the month he was due to leave the Navy – an optimum moment for the Prince of Wales to become engaged. Princess Marie-Astrid was a demure and intelligent, if unexciting, twenty-three-year-old: a qualified nurse, who had attended the Prince's investiture in 1969 and visited Britain to learn English in 1974. The problem, of course, was that the Luxembourg Royal Family is Catholic.

The comings and goings of the next few months, as churchmen met to discuss matters ecumenical, have always been declared wholly insignificant by the Royal Family's official spokesmen. Prince Charles during this period had separate meetings (both routine, he insists) with the Archbishop of Canterbury and Cardinal Hume of Westminster. The Archbishop, indeed, was to meet the Pope in Rome that June.

Before that meeting could take place, however, any chance of such a marriage was suddenly and spectacularly killed off. News of the Palace activity leaked – via a member of the Royal Family – and on Friday 17 June the *Daily Express* announced CHARLES TO MARRY ASTRID – OFFICIAL.

> Prince Charles is to marry Princess Marie-Astrid of Luxembourg. The formal engagement will be announced from Buckingham Palace on Monday. The couple's difference of religion will be overcome by a novel constitutional arrangement: any sons of the marriage will be brought up according to the Church of England, while daughters will be raised in the Catholic faith.

It was Ascot week, and Prince Charles's friends and relations were assembled in strength at Windsor Castle, where he came down to breakfast to much royal mirth at his expense. Himself far from amused: he had at midnight already, for the first and only time in his life, issued a formal, personal denial – significantly through the Queen's then press secretary, Ronald Allison, rather than his own. It read: 'I am authorized by His Royal Highness the Prince of Wales to make the following statement. There is no truth at all in the report that there is to be an announcement of an engagement of the Prince of Wales to Princess Marie-Astrid of Luxembourg.'

The wording, Charles's own, was cautious to the point of ambiguity. The *Express*, who had not taken such a flier without excellent evidence, remained unconvinced; in a cartoon next morning (p. 246), a royal coronet hung on the editor's hatstand. Other newspapers began to take the statement apart word by word, concluding, not unreasonably, that it did not altogether rule out the engagement, only its imminent announcement. Prince Charles told his own press secretary, John Dauth, to go further, which he did in style:

> They are not getting engaged this Monday, next Monday, the Monday after, or any other Monday, Tuesday, Wednesday or Thursday. They do not know each other, and people who do not know each other do not get engaged. The Royal Family do not go in for arranged marriages. If the Prince and Princess have met at all, then it has been briefly at official functions.

This, of course, left the way clear for an engagement on a Friday or Saturday. But it also hedged its bets: 'They do not know each other.... If the Prince and Princess have met at all ...' Well, *had* they met? Yes, it transpired, apparently after a rummage through the files. On perhaps two occasions. But the Prince, somewhat ungallantly, said he could not remember the first thing about the Princess. Thus, with scant ceremony, was she consigned to a footnote of British history.

Princess Marie-Astrid had suffered the same fate as nearly befell Prince Philip thirty-six years earlier: premature public certainty precluding a future royal possibility. In 1941, when Princess Elizabeth was fourteen and Prince Philip of Greece and Denmark nineteen, Chips Channon wrote in his diary that they were to marry. Philip spelt out the danger to his biographer, Basil Boothroyd: 'It had been mentioned, presumably, that "he is eligible, he's the sort of person she might marry".... Inevitably, I must have been on the list, so to speak. But people only had to say that for people like Chips Channon to go one step further and say it's already decided, you see what I mean?' The implication is startling: had Chips Channon's diaries been published in the 1940s rather than the 1960s, or had Channon indeed worked for the *Daily Express*, Prince Philip might not even have made history's footnotes.

Since Marie-Astrid's dramatic exit from the scene, no new contender for the Prince's hand has emerged publicly, although as he himself puts it: 'I've only got to look twice at someone, and next morning I'm engaged to her.' Which happens not infrequently, as the Prince undoubtedly has a roving eye. The diffident, awkward youth of twenty, a late developer sexually as in other ways, has at thirty all the self-confidence of a man who knows he is the most eligible bachelor in the world. He says he has not yet met the right girl, and might only have added 'at the right time'. He confesses 'I often look at someone and think "I wonder if I could marry her?",' but his views on the institution of marriage, uncluttered and chauvinist though they are, severely limit his powers of decision:

> Whatever your place in life, when you marry you are forming a partnership which you hope will last for fifty years. So I'd want to marry someone whose interests I could share. A woman not only marries a man; she marries into a way of life – a job. She's got to have some knowledge of it, some sense of it; otherwise she wouldn't have a clue about whether she's going to like it. If I'm deciding on whom I want to live with for fifty years – well, that's the last decision on which I would want my head to be ruled by my heart.

Or, even more simply: 'Creating a secure family unit in which to bring up children and give them a happy, secure upbringing – that's what marriage is all about. . . . I hope I will be as lucky as my parents, who have been so happy.'

Lord Mountbatten, an inveterate matchmaker, will continue to make helpful noises. The Queen will continue to exert a gentle pressure, and the Duke of Edinburgh to treat the whole business with relaxed bonhomie. But Prince Charles will make his own decision, and make it soon.

16

Prince of Wales, Superstar

His prodigious talents in the arts, in sport, in academic life make him perhaps the most accomplished young man in Britain ... rich, handsome, intelligent and eligible – the twentieth-century Renaissance man who has done everything, been everywhere, met everyone that matters ... he is actor, sportsman, pilot, musician, artist, orator, academic, wit, sailor and future King.

BRITISH WOMEN'S MAGAZINES tend to get a bit carried away on royal birthdays. Prince Charles at thirty was an accomplished young man, more so than a nation might reasonably expect of one born to his position, but scarcely the prodigy painted by *Woman's Realm*. He could, perhaps, justifiably captain the England polo team (he had already captained Young England). He is a better-than-average amateur skier, fisherman and shot. He has a natural aptitude for flying helicopters. He could probably hold down most of the jobs in which his Oxbridge contemporaries, in their early thirties, are beginning to make their names. But he has long since given up the cello, and is unlikely ever to join the National Theatre Company. He is not in line for an Olympic gold medal, an Oscar or the Nobel Prize. Of all the roles set out for him above, the one for which his accomplishments most fit him is, as it should be, future King.

Curiously enough, his breathless admirer forgot to hail Charles the television star. He is the first Prince of Wales to have grown up in the era of mass communications, and he has taken pains to master its dominant medium. With a growing list of credits behind him, he is quite at ease in front of the cameras, whether conducting the viewer around Canterbury Cathedral or skateboarding with deprived kids in the slums of London. He has made a programme with Alistair Cooke about the 'much maligned'

George III, interviewed anthropologists for the 'World About Us' series, *Face Values*, and broadcast an all-channels fund-raising appeal to the nation at the time of Elizabeth II's Silver Jubilee. From his first TV appearance in 1969, the pre-investiture interview, through his own six-hour spectacular at Caernarvon a week later, to the sequence he himself directed for *Pilot Royal*, he has proved himself a more natural performer than either of his parents. The Queen is still ill at ease in her annual Christmas broadcasts; Prince Charles likes using television to promote his own multifarious activities, and enjoys watching himself on the video cassettes he keeps of all his appearances.

Regular TV performers pay tribute to his skills: those characteristic, awkward gestures – the concertina-playing arms, the interlocked, restless fingers – look remarkably cool and professional onscreen. It is through television that he has broadened the popular lustre attaching to any youthful Prince of Wales, traditionally an icon of postage stamps, medallions, picture-postcards and biscuit tins. Add television and T-shirts, and you have, if not twentieth-century Renaissance Man, a twentieth-century superstar.

In an age of short-lived, one-dimensional popular heroes, the Prince of Wales is an enduring, ex-officio superstar. By continuing to expand the realms of his endeavour, he seeks to justify the attention paid to him merely because of his office. He is a born and determined achiever, with more than a streak of *machismo*, loving any challenge to his masculine powers. 'I like to see if I can challenge myself to do something that is potentially hazardous, just to see if mentally I can accept the challenge and carry it out.... I'm one of those people who don't like sitting and watching someone else doing something.' He does not, for instance, share his mother's enjoyment of race meetings: 'I'd rather be riding the horses myself.'

It is, of course, royal understatement to say that a way with horses runs in the family. Ben Jonson would have approved. Princes, he wrote, learn no art truly but the art of horsemanship: 'The reason is, the brave beast is no flatterer. He will throw a Prince as soon as his groom.' Prince Charles is a naturally skilled horseman, though not as expert as his sister, who was European Three-Day Event champion in 1971 and a member of the British team at the 1976 Olympic Games in Montreal. After initial indifference, he has grown to enjoy hunting more and more, whilst well aware of the widespread public hostility to blood sports. A boar-hunting expedition to Liechtenstein in 1978 earned him the accolade of 'Hooligan of the Year' from the Royal Society for the Prevention of Cruelty to Animals, and the Prince has determined that hunting is the one activity he would give up if ever he felt a majority of popular opinion required it of him: 'You can't have everything you want, even if you feel it does no harm. People's susceptibilities count.' For the present, his hunting dates are among his most closely guarded secrets; when he joins the Belvoir, the Cotswold or the Duke of Beaufort's pack, it is usually well after they have moved off, out of public view.

A recent counterpoint to hunting is cross-country riding, which Prince Charles took up early in 1978 after finding its skills and dangers exhilarating. Teams of four race across rugged country terrain punctuated by alarmingly difficult fences. 'Good practice for parachuting,' he laughed off one afternoon with more than its share of ugly-looking falls. The Prince now has two teams of his own, the Duke of Cornwall's chasers and the Earl of Chester's chasers. With its bolder horsemanship, and its lack of sacrificial fox, cross-country riding could in time prove a happy alternative to the Prince's love of the chase.

But of all his various mounted pursuits, the one with which he is most associated, and which indeed gives him most personal excitement, is of course polo. Whatever else is going on, and wherever he is in the world, Prince Charles will be disappointed if he doesn't fit in one, often two, games a week during the polo season. He started playing under his father's tuition at the age of sixteen, won his half-blue at Cambridge, and is now one of the country's better players – handicap three. But he is not quite in the international class. His coach, Sinclair Hill, believes that Prince Charles has even more natural ability at the game than Prince Philip in his heyday – and his handicap was five (the higher the better). But Charles, according to his teammates, does not treat his ponies with sufficient brutality to be world class. Nor does he have enough time to practise, or indeed maintain enough ponies, to make the grade in this extremely expensive pastime. The Prince owns a string of six polo ponies, whose upkeep is estimated at some £12,000 a year – neither statistic high enough for those who would like to see him representing, perhaps captaining, his country.

Like most aristocratic pursuits, polo is as obsessive to those who play it as it is tedious to those who spectate. Aficionados among the nobility express outrage that the Prince of Wales's other duties intrude on his single-minded pursuit of polo excellence. His years in the Navy slowed his development as a top-class player; in 1977, after he had left the Services, he improved so rapidly that a special meeting of polo's governing body, the Hurlingham Association, had to be convened to revise his handicap upwards. From the nation's point of view, the Prince of Wales's indulgence in the game is quite obsessive enough. Many a lady friend has spent many a cold afternoon at Smith's Lawn, a captive audience to rugged displays of manliness.

Dismounted, the Prince is an equally skilled shot and fisherman. The present Royal Family's experts at shooting and fishing were once, respectively, the Duke of Edinburgh and the Queen Mother. But Prince Charles has bettered them both. Prince Philip, often cited by Sandringham guests as one of the best shots in the country ('which means', they add in awed tones, 'the world'), is now equally lavish in praise of his son. The Queen Mother, who taught her grandson the art of angling from his childhood, was as impressed as the hardy Balmoral ghillies by his feat in the dry summer of 1976. The River Dee, which winds through the royal estate, was too low to be thought worth fishing, but the Prince scooped out seven salmon in one day. Another challenge more than adequately met.

In the passage outside the dining-room at Sandringham, rack after rack of royal shotguns testify to more than a century of princely slaughter. Since Prince Albert bought the house in 1861, as a country home for the too metropolitan Prince of Wales, the Sandringham game book has recorded some fearsome carnage (the record bag in one day being 3,114 pheasants on 14 November 1896). For each Prince of Wales, it seems, it has become a matter of pride to outdo the feats of his predecessor or parent. 'I love shooting more than anything else,' the future Edward VIII wrote to his father, George V, in 1912, '& it was very kind of you to allow me to shoot so much here while you were away. I have had some splendid practice, & feel that my shooting has very much improved.' In later life, when Duke of Windsor, he could still remember the best days: 'A good day's bag was a thousand head, but two thousand was not uncommon on the larger estates.'

There were days, however, when even George V said: 'Perhaps we went a little too far to-day, David.' On 18 December 1913, at the Beaconsfield estate of Lord Burnham, then owner of the *Daily Telegraph*, all royal records were broken. The Duke of Windsor recalled:

> My left arm ached from lifting my gun, my shoulder from the recoil, and I was deaf and stunned from the banging. . . . When in the late afternoon the carnage stopped, almost 4,000 pheasants had been killed. The bright, limp carcasses were laid out in rows of 100; the whole place was littered with feathers and spent cartridges. My father had shot over 1,000 birds; I had even passed the 300 mark. He was proud of the way he had shot that day, but I think that the scale of the bag troubled even his conscience. . . .

The days of such excess – 'I always suspected', added the Duke of Windsor, 'that in addition to the birds raised on the place, a good many hundred pheasants were brought in and released for the King's benefit' – are happily long gone. Just as well, for there was public outcry when Prince Charles shot his first stag at Balmoral at the age of thirteen, and it has continued ever since. The slaughter of thousands, however, tends to cause revulsion even among sportsmen these days. A good bag by contemporary standards is a few hundred birds, grouse at Balmoral, pheasant and partridge at Sandringham. When the Prince of Wales is holidaying at either, he will be out with his shotgun at least three days a week. Strangely enough, he has never sampled the excellent shooting to be had on his own private estate at Chevening, in Kent, where a private consortium has now sub-contracted the rights.

It is hardy and energetic outdoor pursuits with which the popular imagination probably most identifies the Prince of Wales. Apart from his hunting, shooting, fishing and polo, they have seen him water-skiing, scuba diving, wind-surfing, skiing – all rather solitary pursuits, those of the man wishing to pit himself against the elements. But in the best traditions of Juvenal and Kurt Hahn, he does not neglect matters of the mind. Apart from his painting and music – again somewhat solitary, introspective pastimes – he reads as much as he can, and if a particular enthusiasm seizes him he can become positively bookish. Having read history at Cambridge, he has become by far the best-informed member of the Royal Family about his forbears, and is particularly partial to new historical biographies. For a man so written about, with such decisive views on what is said and the way it is put, he is not averse to turning his own hand to the occasional preface, the odd review.

In 1971, at the age of twenty-two, the newly graduated Prince first developed his passionate views on history's treatment of King George III, after reading books, pamphlets and learned correspondence (in the *Times Literary Supplement* and the *British Medical Journal*) on the subject of his 'madness'. Browsing through the Royal Archives at Windsor one day, he met the historian John Brooke, who had been granted access for a biography of George III he was then writing. They fell into conversation, in which, the Prince recalled, 'we both agreed that George III had been unfairly maligned by historians and the writers of textbook history'. Finding a kindred spirit, intent on portraying the King as a gracious, cultivated and dutiful monarch, Prince Charles agreed to write a foreword to the book. It is worth quoting in some detail.

If the average schoolchild remembers anything about history after leaving school, then he will remember that George III was mad. If he is American as well, then madness is often given as the reason for the 'irrational' behaviour of the King towards the Colonists, making it necessary for them to declare independence. George III's cardinal error was that he 'failed' in history – he failed to retain the American colonies, and in the search to find a scapegoat for this national disaster the King became the obvious target....

Much has been written by learned scholars to the effect that George III was manic depressive, and suffered from sexual frustration, a difficult wife, and hideous family problems – all acting upon an inherently unstable character which finally gave way under the strain. If this was so why didn't the King 'go mad' far earlier than 1788? In that year he celebrated his fiftieth birthday and had apparently solved his long-standing political problems, with Pitt established firmly in the nation's confidence. Not only that. The Prince of Wales' debts had at last been settled and it was three years since the traumatic experience of finding that the Prince, in defiance of Acts of Parliament, had contracted a marriage with Mrs Fitzherbert – enough to crack any remotely unstable character. George III's illness does not appear to correspond to mania or hypomania. . . .

Brooke's theory was that the King had porphyria. Prince Charles did not entirely agree.

The recurrent toxic and confusional states suffered by the King could have been due to other physical causes such as infectious and metabolic disturbances. The observation of purple urine by itself is not sufficient proof; indeed, medical experience has shown that most cases of modern porphyria are precipitated by barbiturates. . . . There is no evidence that he was schizophrenic, or depressive, or that he suffered from syphilis of the central nervous system which, when untreated, is steadily progressive. Only in the last ten years of his life when between the ages of seventy and eighty, deaf, blind, deserted by his family, surrounded only by 'mad doctors' and apothecaries who tied him up in straight waistcoats at the slightest sign of opposition to their will and banished him to the North side of Windsor Castle, did he show signs of mental decay associated with natural senility.

I think there can now be little doubt that George III suffered from periodic attacks of a metabolic illness . . . there was nothing wrong with his brain *before* the onset of the illness.

The stigma of madness attaching to the King had persisted far too long.

It is high time that the veil of obscurity stifling the King's true personality, known and loved by his contemporaries, should be lifted. . . . It was, after all, in George III's reign that the office of Prime Minister gradually evolved – thereby reducing the power of the Crown to the role of influential adviser.

He had been, in short, a King 'almost over-dedicated to duty' . . . 'the father of his people'.

The Prince did not discuss George's attempts, for a time successful, to control Parliament through bribery, or the merits and demerits of his alliance with Bute against Pitt on the American question. Medical matters, and George's neglected reputation as a patron of the arts, were his prime motive; the disastrous conduct of the war with the American colonies, and later the King's ill-timed anti-Catholic prejudice (from which Prince Charles himself still suffers under the Royal Marriages Act), became the acts of a well-intentioned idealist. George III became an obsession, and cropped up wherever the Prince had a chance to sound off about him.

In 1976, with Alistair Cooke, he made a TV film entirely devoted to reha-bilitating the 'Much Maligned Monarch'. He told Cooke: 'He was a complete idealist and moralist. Either a thing was right or wrong. I am determined to clear his name. It's very unfortunate if one is misunderstood in history. I personally would hate to be misunderstood.'

A clue to his strength of feeling? Does the Prince of Wales already have a weather eye on posterity? Certainly his interest in history has always stemmed from an acute awareness of his own ancestry. His Cambridge supervisors remember his approach as anecdotal, even to the extent of 'Oh yes, he was a splendid chap. I remember my mother saying her father had told her ...'

The vein of continuing royal self-justification can be most clearly seen in the opening of a book review by Prince Charles, also in 1976, for *Books and Bookmen* magazine. Although Queen Victoria's sense of humour was the subject for discussion – he was reviewing Alan Hardy's *Queen Victoria Was Amused* – George III again defiantly enters the argument in advance of his imperial great-niece:

It seems to be one of the curious quirks of human nature that members of our great-grandparents' generation and earlier are invariably regarded as 'his-torical' creatures who displayed few of the normal human characteristics we associate with our contemporaries. Wherever monarchs are concerned this quirk is magnified tenfold and popular impressions of past sovereigns often reach the realms of the ridiculous, remaining firmly imbedded in the minds of successive generations of schoolchildren. The vulgar view of King George III is quite simply that he was mad and, to make matters worse, that he also succeeded in losing the American colonies. The fact that he had wide and civilized interests, was a great patron of the arts and sciences and devoted a vast quantity of time to affairs of state has been conveniently neglected. '... the good is oft interred with their bones'.

As far as my great-great-great-grandmother is concerned...

Two years later, in a foreword to a collection of cartoons of royalty (proceeds to the Queen's Silver Jubilee Appeal), he is still the royal public relations officer *par excellence*:

This book comprises an intriguing collection of 'royal' cartoons mostly from the past 25 years, and shows the changes which have taken place in that period in both style and approach to the subject. Looking at them I cannot but reflect on how politely we have been treated, compared to the way in which King

George III and his family, for instance, were treated by the 18th and 19th century cartoonists, such as Rowlandson...

There are, however, subjects which simply won't accommodate the Hanoverians. One was the first novel of the Welsh entertainer Harry Secombe, a friend of the Prince (known to him as 'Ned of Wales'), a former Goon, made a Commander of (the Order of) the British Empire in 1963. Prince Charles reviewed the book for *Punch* magazine in 1974, shortly after carving his initial in the celebrated Punch table. His first paragraph is a deft, and not uncharacteristic, *de haut en bas* rebuke to the magazine's literary editor, Miles Kington:

'We would be delighted if you would write a review of Harry Secombe's first novel, *Twice Brightly*,' was what the man from *Punch* said. 'It doesn't have to be a comic masterpiece,' (what does he mean, it doesn't have to be a comic masterpiece? People have wandered feet first into the Tower for less than that...) 'nor is it really necessary to cause a literary sensation,' the letter continued. What does that leave me with? Presumably a model of memorable mediocrity – but after reading this compendium of Welsh wit and thespianism I humbly beg to submit that mediocrity would be difficult to achieve.

Prince Charles's honorary role as public relations officer for the Goons also produced, at Peter Sellers's suggestion in 1973, a preface to a Christmas volume of Goon Show scripts. Declaring himself 'one of their most devoted and dotty supporters' (despite such cryptic *lèse-majesté* as 'Eccles for King' in Secombe's contribution), the Prince hailed their 'mental slapstick and imaginary cartoonery'. He went on:

It has always been one of my profound regrets that I was not born ten years earlier than 1948, since I would then have had the pure, unbounded joy of listening avidly to the Goons each week. I only discovered that the Goon-type humour appealed to me with an hysterical totality just as the shows were drawing to a close.
      Then I discovered the Ying Tong Song in record form and almost at once I knew it by heart – the only song I do know by heart. I plagued everybody with its dulcet tones and 'Solo for Raspberry Blower' to such an extent that when my small brothers heard a recording of the Goons for the first time, they thought it was their elder brother.

A love of the absurd, however jejune, is a handy asset in a man whose job constantly brings him up against it. The rest of his literary output, however, is rather more sober: forewords or contributions to books on wildlife preservation, anthropology, royalty's love of aircraft, underwater diving and his grandmother, Queen Elizabeth. Only on special occasions does he unbend: in 1978 he contributed his favourite recipe – for bread-and-butter pudding – to a book called *Chevening Cookery*, published to raise money for the restoration of the parish church near his country house.

The extra-curricular interest which he is most intent on developing, however, is his love of opera. As both Patron and President of the Friends of the Royal Opera House, Covent Garden, he starred in 1979 in a fund-raising film in which he realized every amateur musician's dream: conducting the Covent Garden orchestra (in the overture to Mozart's *Magic Flute*). But he is aware that his knowledge is as yet very limited. He surprised Humphrey Burton of BBC-TV in April 1979 by the confessions he made in an interview to introduce BBC-2's Opera Month: his favourite opera was *La Traviata* and his favourite composer Verdi, but he had never heard *Macbeth*. He liked Bellini, and had seen *Norma*, but he had never heard any Puccini, Wagner or Strauss.

> I've got a lot to learn ... one of the things I really enjoy about being Patron of the Royal Opera is having the chance to see as many operas as I can and to find out more about it.... I like to think I can go whenever I want to, at short notice – turfing people out of the Royal Box so I can get a seat!

The Queen Mother has said of her grandson: 'If there was anything left to discover in the world, Charles would have been an explorer.' An earlier verdict, in a *Times* critique of an earlier biography, was that the Prince would have made 'an excellent schoolmaster'. In the book under review, *To Be A King* (1968), Dermot Morrah wrote: 'No British Prince since the Stuarts has cared more sincerely for the things of the mind and the spirit.' Several previous Princes of Wales, notably Charles's protégé George III, might justly feel abused by the claim, especially as it was made when the Prince was barely nineteen years old. But he has developed and maintained a great respect for learning, a genuine love of music, and a deft and generous hand for forewords. A biographer of the last Prince of Wales, rashly predicting a glorious reign, added one caveat: 'Unfortunately, among the young people of England Edward does not know the idealists.' Prince Charles, by deliberate example, will seek to lead them.

'Royal Action Man', as he has been called, has plenty of time for introspection. It may be the privilege of his position to dive beneath the Arctic ice, explore Caribbean coral reefs, wind-surf off Cowes, hunt wild boar in Liechtenstein, play polo in all five continents. It is also his lot, however, to be forced consistently into solitude, read books about his ancestors, write lectures on spiritual values ('a subject on which I have rather strong views'), meditate upon his curious fate. By the time he graduates from the biscuit tins to his coronation plates, this Prince of Wales should have behind him a spread of accomplishment befitting the first Master of Arts to ascend the

British throne. The appeal of bachelor youth will have given way to a more sober, cosy domesticity, but the Prince will wish to be thought a twentieth-century man for all seasons. Outside his official duties he will remain ever active in a curiously assorted world of parachutes and cave paintings, opera seats and wet suits, polo sticks and paint brushes, beagles and books, guns and Goons.

17

The Ambassador

The whole idea of these visits is for me to meet as many
people as I can, so they can see for themselves that I'm a
pretty ordinary sort of person.

IN THE PAST hundred years, Princes of Wales have forged their early reputations as much abroad as at home. In the 1870s and 1880s, the mid period
of his long decades of unemployment, the future Edward VII went on
protracted, swashbuckling tours of India, Egypt, Europe and the USA,
occasionally travelling incognito, always taking a huge and costly retinue,
invariably free to enjoy himself with even more abandon than at home.
In like fashion, immediately after the First World War, the future
Edward VIII embarked on tours through Canada and the United States,
New Zealand and Australia, and later Africa; success after success was
reported in the British newspapers, his ability to draw huge crowds anywhere in the world only serving to increase his popular glamour back in
England.

The world travelled by the present Prince of Wales has shrunk immeasurably. The age of exotic, prolonged continental tours is gone, and jet travel
makes a week to ten days the comfortable length for a crowded schedule
half-way across the globe. Apart from which, solo tours on the grand scale
still lie ahead of Prince Charles. His busy programme in the United
Kingdom makes him reluctant to leave it for too long at a time; the six weeks
he spent in the Far East, Australia and Canada early in 1979 was, apart from
school and Service attachments, the first time in his life he had been away
for so long. But he is an ardent collector of new sights and experiences, as
acquisitive as most of us about the exotic stamps in his passport.

Heir to the most travelled monarch in British history, he knows the years
ahead will provide almost any opportunity he cares to seek, although it was

only in his late twenties that he began to venture beyond Europe and the Commonwealth. He is eager to visit the Soviet Union. But the major unknown quantity remains the People's Republic of China, which, like his mother, he would dearly love to see. As Elizabeth II, however, recently told a London orchestral player just back from a tour of China: 'I don't think they're too keen on Queens out there, are they?'

Sending the Prince of Wales abroad is a complex, protocol-ridden and costly business. In Commonwealth countries, whether monarchies or republics, he travels as a member of the Royal Family, and Buckingham Palace bureaucrats must be careful not to tread on the toes of his local hosts. Elsewhere he travels in official pursuit of the British Government's foreign policy, and Buckingham Palace must make it clear to his hosts that the usual diplomatic courtesies are the very least he expects. Official visits are pencilled into the schedule as much as a year in advance, sometimes more; conditions, political or otherwise, both at home and in the country to be visited often dictate postponements, as of the Prince's cherished plans to tour India, put off until 1979 because of the political upheavals of 1975–8. Once the dates are secure, an advance party sallies forth to reconnoitre.

A month or so before the Prince's departure, his private secretary, press secretary and detective travel out to set things up in the minutest detail. They base themselves, wherever possible, at the British Embassy or High Commission, as it is British diplomats abroad who bear a heavy share of the considerable burden. In consultation with host diplomats, they will then inspect every inch of the ground to be travelled by the Prince. The detective will discuss security with his local counterpart; the press secretary will ensure that local journalists understand the nature of their prey – no spot questions, no undue familiarity, perhaps a press conference but no political questions – and that the British press travelling with the Prince will have ample facilities to transmit the good news home. Above all, the British Ambassador and the private secretary will ensure that the programme is appropriate.

There must, for example, be official receptions on both sides, hosted respectively by the British Ambassador and the head of state or his representative, at which the Prince will be guest of honour; there must be a chance for the local British community to meet him; there must be visits to industry, especially any with British connections; there must be visits to the local armed forces (a chance for the Prince to don his uniforms); there must be private talks with the President, Prime Minister, Foreign Minister or their equivalents (Mayors, etc., when outside the capital). Tree-planting and plaque unveilings are tolerable, but should be kept to a minimum. There must be guards of honour for his inspection on arrival and departure, and at all appropriate points between; the Prince's personal flag must fly along-side that of the host country on his car at the head of each motorcade, and so on *ad infinitum*. Hospitals and specialists are alerted at points along his route; his medical records are sent out in advance. Menus and accommodation are inspected; guest lists are screened; modes of address, seating plans, who enters which room in what order, who wears what decorations when – all requirements are painstakingly spelt out by the Prince's representatives.

Even Princes are human, and it must be ensured that life's most fundamental facilities are regularly available. The Duke of Windsor once quoted 'the two best pieces of advice my father ever gave me: never refuse an invitation to take the weight off your feet, and seize every opportunity you can to relieve yourself'. Above all, nothing must be unscheduled. Thus itineraries become inordinately crowded, containing anything from six to twenty engagements a day. Sightseeing, if the hosts wish to cram it in, is optional. The Prince is not too keen on it.

On trips of ten days or more, as many as fifty items of baggage travel out under the supervision of the Prince of Wales's baggage master. The author once found himself sharing the hold of an RAF Hercules with the Prince of Wales's luggage, flying up the Amazon in advance of the smaller aircraft carrying the Prince and his eight staff. Half the aircraft's bulk was a wonderworld of pleasantly battered red trunks bearing the Prince's name and insignia; old-fashioned hat boxes marked 'straw' and 'top'; trunk after trunk of military, naval and air-force uniforms, none required by the schedule but all on hand just in case. Leather cases bearing polo sticks protruded through the netting holding it all in place.

Thirty suits and uniforms were being carried, though his valet could not persuade him to venture beyond a choice of six grey suits, which – to the photographers' chagrin – all looked exactly the same. Safari suits were ready, as would be snow suits in other climates. Prince Charles also takes a full set of mourning clothes wherever he goes, in case of a royal death back home; black-edged notepaper is even on hand to continue, in such an event, the flow of thank-you letters. There are crates of gifts: a few gold cuff-links bearing the Prince of Wales's insignia, more signed photographs, graded by the quality of their frame to the rank of the recipient.

He will be escorted on any overseas excursion by his private secretary, his press secretary, his private secretary's secretary, a detective, an air attaché (if travelling by air), his valet, a typist, a baggage master and often an equerry. Occasionally there will be a special adviser, such as Sir Fitzroy Maclean on the Prince's visit to Yugoslavia in October 1978. The British Ambassador will receive him on his arrival, and remain with him around the country until his departure. The staff of the British Embassy are at his disposal. The flow of red boxes continues, and each day brings a Central Office of Information digest of the British newspapers. Constant contact is maintained with Buckingham Palace.

If the host country is much more than 1,000 miles away, the first-class section of a scheduled aircraft, preferably the British carrier for that route, is reserved for the Prince and his staff. Usually a bed will be installed for his use. On long-haul flights across the Atlantic or down to Australia, he will perform the Heathrow handshakes in a suit, and change out of it immediately after take-off. He will turn down the first-class champagne, but enjoy an in-flight movie, however insipid. (After a scheduled Air Canada flight to Calgary in 1977, the Prince confessed that he had stuck out a 'dreadful' film called *Logan's Run* because he was 'rather partial' to Miss Jenny Aguter.) By the time he re-emerges, with a few friendly words for the economy passengers who have gradually grown aware of his presence – the escort of fighter jets is a good clue – he will be back in his suit again, pleasantly rested.

On shorter trips he will pilot himself there in an Andover of the Queen's Flight – antiquated but conspicuously safe aircraft which he likes for a number of reasons. Successive Captains of the Queen's Flight have tried for years to up-date their small fleet, in the last decade hoping for BAC 111s, but have always been frustrated by the fear of public outcry at yet more royal expense. Prince Charles and his father are quietly rather pleased. The Andover, which dates from 1955, travels slowly enough to allow them respite from official duties, and to clock up many more flying hours (a matter of some personal pride). They ensure, therefore, that even on far-flung official visits, an Andover travels out for their use around the interior. In South America as in Yugoslavia, both examples from 1978, local dignitaries' first glimpse of the heir to the British throne was through a cockpit window: an aquiline profile obscured only by headphones, at the controls of a quaintly antique, somehow very British, aircraft. His personal standard flutters aloft, thrust through a flap in the roof, as he taxies the gleaming red and silver aircraft to the reception area.

To be ready for his use around Brazil, where he travelled by British Caledonian Airways, the Prince's Andover had flown a four-day journey from London, hopping up to Greenland and then down through North America; a back-up Hercules had more simply flown in from Belize. The Andover was dutifully polished each day by the Queen's Flight crew as it seethed with heat on tarmac reflecting 100-degree sunshine. Occasionally the Prince's staff wished that they, like others in the party, had opted for a ride in the RAF support plane. In São Paulo, Wing Commander the Prince of Wales landed the Andover on one wheel, earning 'nought out of ten' from a white-faced aide; his next landing, in Belo Horizonte, was perfect, prompt-ing a spontaneous outburst of applause from his relieved passengers.

Rather to Prince Charles's annoyance, the Andover became something of an issue during his foreign travels in 1978, especially the tour of Brazil and Venezuela in March. His official visits abroad can achieve little but good-will – a commodity valued highly enough by the British Foreign Office, which pays his way out of a fund set aside for royal tours. But the Prince is anxious to extend his role in the only non-political direction he can: to-wards becoming a trade ambassador for British exports. In Brazil of all countries, therefore, a huge tract constantly criss-crossed by extremely wealthy businessmen, why was he not flying himself around in a British-made executive jet, perhaps the Hawker-Siddeley 128? His acclaimed pre-sence in the country, set off by the even more dashing figure he would have cut in the cockpit, must have ensured a few dozen sales.

He could not himself, of course, answer an essentially political question. But the truth of the matter was made clear, ironically enough, during that same visit to Brazil, when back in London the *Daily Express* announced all over its front page that the Prince of Wales had accepted an offer from a consortium of British businessmen to become a £50,000-a-year roving sales rep. Amid the angry denials telephoned home to the Buckingham Palace press office was an assurance that he could never accept hire and salary from individual British companies. A few days later, again by chance, he was able to show what he *can* do. By fortunate timing, his presence in Brazil coincided with the finalization of a huge investment by British banks in a steel-mill complex near Rio, expected to yield a profit of some £11 million. A little delicate blurring at the edges, and the Prince could be said to have 'clinched' the deal. As his ten-day trip had cost the British taxpayer some £11,000, it showed an equally neat 1,000-1 return on investment.

It was on his first solo official visit abroad, to Japan in April 1970, after touring Australia and New Zealand with his parents, that Prince Charles genuinely did pull off just such a royal coup. Visiting Expo 70 in Tokyo, he met the president of the Sony electronics conglomerate, and learnt of their plans to build a plant somewhere in Western Europe. 'Why not try Wales?' suggested its Prince, less than a year after his investiture at Caernar-von. Two years later Prince Charles was able to open the new Sony plant in Bridgend, Glamorgan, which had created several thousand jobs in an area of acute unemployment.

In the wake of his investiture and twenty-first birthday, and thus of his emergence into public life, Charles clocked up his heaviest year of foreign travel in 1970. After the 1954 visit to Gibraltar, to greet his parents' return from their coronation tour of the Commonwealth, he had made only five foreign trips in the next ten years, all private: to visit his father's family in Germany, to attend King Constantine's wedding in Athens, to go skiing in Switzerland and Liechtenstein. During 1966 he was at school in Australia, returning via the Commonwealth Games in Jamaica, and 1968 took him on his archaeological excursion to France and Jersey. Between the two, in December 1967, he joined the then Prime Minister, Harold Wilson, and the Opposition Leader, Edward Heath, in setting a modest aviation record: their round trip to Australia in an RAF VC10, for the funeral of Prime Minister Harold Holt, was completed in 82 hours 19 minutes, a record for that class of aircraft.

'Who's representing the family, Ma'am?' Wilson had asked the Queen at his weekly audience. 'Well,' she replied, 'Charles has expressed some interest.' Wilson met the heir apparent, just turned nineteen, by the lift. 'Fancy a trip to Australia? All right, go and get your bags packed, then.' It was the first occasion on which the Prince of Wales had officially represented the Queen. In Perth the Prime Minister grew concerned about the attempts of various Australian politicians, as they jockeyed for the dead man's shoes, to exploit the Prince's presence. They would ask him round for tea and photographs, to show the electorate they had royal endorsement. Charles was too young to cope. Before leaving England, Wilson had asked the Queen's private secretary, Sir Michael Adeane, how he should behave towards the Prince. 'Treat him like your son,' said Adeane – and Wilson took the advice very literally. After the funeral he whisked the Prince of Wales off to Perth to spend the day with forty-three close relatives, the Australian branch of the Wilson family. When Prince and ex-Prime Minister repeated their excursion together eleven years later, for the funeral of Sir Robert Menzies, Charles made a point of greeting them all again, including Wilson's eighty-nine-year-old maiden aunt.

His post-investiture holiday in Malta in July 1969, as guest of the island's governor, Sir Maurice Dorman, led to a return visit later that year to inaugurate the new campus of the Royal Maltese University. Here he received an early lesson in royal aplomb, remaining impassive during the ceremony as students exploded stink bombs (having earlier stolen a plaque he was due to unveil), and taunted him about his friendship with Sir Maurice's daughter, Sybilla. He proved he had maintained his humour at a banquet that evening, when he reminded his audience of Princess Elizabeth's visits to Lord Mountbatten's villa during the Duke of Edinburgh's naval service in Malta: 'I am told many Maltese believe my future appearance was determined whilst my parents were in this island.'

Apart from a skiing holiday with Prince (now King) Carl Gustav of Sweden, and attending his aunt the Margravine of Baden's funeral in Germany, both also in 1969, that was the sum total of the Prince of Wales's foreign adventuring before his twenty-first birthday. In 1970 it was more than doubled. The year began with a trip to Strasbourg with Prince Philip, to attend the Council of Europe's Conservation Conference, and was to end with President de Gaulle's memorial service in Paris. In between, while winning his university degree, Prince Charles circled the globe three times.

In Australia and New Zealand that March, touring with his parents and his sister, the Prince of Wales, for the first but by no means the last time, occasionally upstaged his mother. The dashing, eligible young Prince, his magic aura enhanced by fresh televisual memories of his investiture, stole Elizabeth II's headlines. In New Zealand a thousand Maoris danced, it was said, for him alone, though he was sharing the platform with the sovereign. It was his visit to a hospital in Dunedin, exchanging operation scar stories with women patients, which led reports of the day the Queen visited the University of Otago. In Auckland a square-dance by the Prince of Wales was the high-light of the Royal Family's visit. And so it continued through Australia, where Prince Charles even stole his father's habitual thunder by allowing a few unguarded words to stir controversy. After surfing at dawn on St Kilda beach, near Melbourne, he declared that it had been 'like swimming in undiluted sewage', prompting one local Mayor to say he deserved 'a good thump under the ear'. Three Melbourne Mayors were challenged to try the water for themselves, and did so one morning in the photogenic company of a bikini-clad young lady. The Mayor of St Kilda itself, Councillor Jim Duggan, was sufficiently moved to return the abuse. 'When that young crank came here,' he barnstormed, 'he didn't have the brains to tell us he was going to St Kilda or we would have cleaned the place up. He's the guy who stirred up this idea of pollution and now everyone is running around worrying about it. Pollution has become the in-thing, and I'm fed up, sick and tired of the whole business.' The Prince's aspersion on his beach was 'the kind of inane remark you'd expect from an inane person'. Councillor Duggan was forced to retract his remarks equally gracefully – 'The Prince is the son of his father' – after a fellow-councillor rose to declare: 'Who does this young crank think he is? The future King of England?'

The Prince, alas, missed the merriment as he had already left his parents and gone on alone to Japan. Twenty-one Expo 70 pavilions in one morning was a typical item on his agenda, while more unguarded remarks about the comfort of airline seats – 'I don't know why I'm the one who gets all these long flights; they should have an asylum waiting for you at the end of them' – earned him a much-publicized back massage from a geisha girl. Japanese girls, quickly warming to a by now intercontinental theme, jumped up and

down squealing when he passed by – the characteristic reception they normally reserve for pop stars.

He had been abroad for most of March and half of April, but by July, after
taking his Cambridge Finals, Prince Charles was travelling again. A
two-week trip through Canada was completely upstaged by its *commedia dell'*
arte aftermath: three days in Washington with Princess Anne as guests at the
Nixon White House. The visit had been announced a year ahead, and
America had been anticipating it for months. Memories were revived of the
American forays of two other recent Princes of Wales.

In 1860, aged only eighteen, Prince Bertie had chosen the US, where civil
war was already looming, for his first official visit abroad. Under the name
of Lord Renfrew, which fooled no one, he travelled from Detroit to Chicago,
through St Louis, Cincinnati, Pittsburgh and Baltimore to Washington and
New York. President James Buchanan, as whose guest he stayed at the White
House, personally escorted him to George Washington's grave at Mount
Vernon, where George III's great-grandson performed a profoundly sym-
bolic act by planting a chestnut sapling at America's national shrine (while
writing home to his father: 'The house is, unfortunately, in very bad repair
and rapidly falling into decay'). When he attended the opera in Philadelphia,
the audience spontaneously rose to sing 'God Save The Queen'; when he
attended a ball at the Academy of Music in New York, where his reception
had been tumultuous, the dance floor collapsed under the weight of the
crowd preparing to greet him.

In 1919 the twenty-five-year-old Prince Edward, travelling as Lord
Chester, was the guest of the ailing President Wilson. He visited Mount
Vernon in his grandfather's footsteps, and received a ticker-tape welcome
in New York, where the excitement caused by his arrival could be measured
by the twelve columns devoted to it in the *New York Times*. Five years
later he returned on a more private visit, a whirlwind round of dances and
parties which had his staff wondering each night where he had got to, and
the comedian Will Rogers declaring: 'The Prince is a good kid. Too bad
I can't afford to carry a guy like that around with me. I'd have a swell act
if I could.' Rarely in bed before 5 or 6 a.m., spending his afternoons at polo
games and race meetings, he was preceded home by American headlines
such as PRINCE GETS IN WITH THE MILKMAN. King George V forbade any
of his sons ever to visit America again.

Nearly fifty years later, as the arrival of a new, if less exotic, Prince of
Wales became imminent, America positively quivered. The White House
issued a long list of instructions for those whose paths young royalty might
cross. 'You don't talk to royalty unless they want to talk to you. . . . Prince
Charles should be addressed as "Sir" and Princess Anne as "Ma'am", but

a murmured "How do you do, Your Royal Highness" will suffice. A hand should be shaken only if it is first extended by Royalty.' Mrs Nixon's staff director, Connie Stuart, ventured to suggest that the Nixon children 'would probably be accorded the privilege of being allowed to call them Charles and Anne'. (They weren't.) 'And', she went on, 'our young people will be quick to respond "Please call me Tricia, Julie and David."' Further White House announcements revealed that a bicycle had been made ready for Prince Charles's use, and that the brass had been polished on his four-poster bed in the Lincoln Room of the White House. *Life* magazine advised its readers not to tire the Princess with questions about her hats – 'although she will be receptive to chat about tanks and sub-machine guns' – and to discuss drama rather than football with Prince Charles.

The President's press secretary made it clear that although Mr and Mrs Nixon would greet the Prince and Princess on their arrival, their daughters and son-in-law would be the official hosts at all the functions. The Nixons' younger daughter Julie was by then already married to David Eisenhower, son of the former President; her elder sister, twenty-four-year-old Tricia, was still unattached. American newspapers quickly began to emulate the speculation of their transatlantic cousins. And soon after his arrival by heli-copter on the White House lawn, Prince Charles felt a strong sense of unease that the President was trying to pair him off with his daughter. 'My wife and I will keep out of the way,' said Nixon, 'so that you can really feel at home.' Seating plans constantly had Charles and Tricia side by side, while the programme had them spending all of each day together, even to being left alone in rooms. Tricia was quick to remind Charles that she had repre-sented her father at his investiture the previous year, where – ironically enough, in view of later events – she had sat next to Princess Marie-Astrid of Luxembourg. The Prince, his sense of his position not receiving its accus-tomed deference, was distinctly annoyed by the episode. So much so that on his next official visit to the United States, after President Nixon's resigna-tion and disgrace, he was to describe Tricia Nixon with uncharacteristic cruelty as 'artificial and plastic'. Her sister Julie, by contrast, he had found 'a bright, warm personality'.

Quite as vivid a memory of that trip was his private chat with President Nixon in the Oval Office. Scheduled to last ten minutes – and on tightly planned royal (let alone presidential) schedules that *means* ten minutes – it went on for eighty, longer than most official State visitors had been granted by the President. Nixon gave Charles a broad account of the then world as he saw it, waxing expansive about his own foreign policy. As the con-versation moved onto Anglo-American relations, environment, youth and population problems, the Prince began to give as good as he was getting – all of it, he has assumed since the revelations of the Watergate affair, immortalized on tape. Prince Charles had made 'a very good impression', said Nixon, somewhat patronizingly, afterwards. 'We had a very good talk.'

In a recent letter to the author, Mr Nixon recorded his memories of the meeting:

His visit came during a very busy period, shortly after I had ordered the attacks on Communist sanctuaries in Cambodia. While my staff had allowed only fifteen minutes for what was supposed to be only a courtesy call, I found him so impressive that I extended it to an hour and a half with the result that we arrived late for a dinner in the residence.

From news accounts in the British and American press I expected to meet a rather callow, superficial youth with no particular interest in or understanding of world affairs. His conduct completely dispelled that image.

He was serious without being dull, dignified without being pompous, respectful without being deferential. We discussed the whole range of East–West relations, NATO, the Third World countries, and the attitude of young people toward Government in the US and Britain.

His perception and knowledge with regard to developments in the Commonwealth nations was greater than that of many State Department professionals. Without crossing the line of interfering in British governmental policies, he expressed agreement with my long-held conviction that Britain must continue to play a role on the world stage – particularly in NATO and in those nations in Africa and Asia where the legacy of the British parliamentary system and the common law is so essential if ordered freedom is to survive.

I told Mrs Nixon after our meeting that the British and American media greatly underestimated him as a student of world affairs and as a man. . . . Should he some day become King, he will assume that responsibility in the very best tradition of the British Royal Family.

For the rest, it was a 'cookout' at Camp David; visits to assorted museums and monuments, including the now ritual homage at Mount Vernon; a tour of the Capitol building, during which the Senate minority leader, Hugh Scott, said of a gilt mirror on his office wall: 'That is the mirror Dolley Madison rescued from the White House when your ancestors were burning it up'; a meeting with Neil Armstrong, first man on the moon; a river trip in the Presidential yacht, *Sequoia*; a baseball game; and a 'young people's dinner-dance' at the White House, where the arrangements decreed that the Prince of Wales would lead off the dancing with Miss Tricia Nixon.

Throughout the three days Prince Charles received ecstatic praise in the American press for his 'outgoing nature, his dashing charm, his intelligent interest', while Princess Anne was rapped over the knuckles for appearing 'sullen, ungracious and plain bored' throughout the proceedings. The *New York Times* conceded that she was 'a young woman of noted independence', but went on: 'She made no effort to conceal a mood of incredulity and vague discomfort.' Remarked the *Washington Daily News*: 'The Prince is full of pep, the Princess acts pooped.'

Matters were not helped by an incident on the last day, when the royal pair were for some reason taken to the Patuxent Wildlife Refuge, near Washington, to witness the dissection of a bald eagle which had died from organic pesticides. When the Prince asked why the bald eagle had been chosen as America's national symbol Princess Anne remarked that it was 'rather a bad choice'. That capped it for the American newspapers. 'Something about our national bird,' mused the *Washington Post*, 'and nobody's quite sure what, was bugging our Royal visitors from Great Britain.' The Princess later explained that she had been upset and irritated by the constant attentions of the press, which her brother had long since learnt to take in his stride. 'Every time I turn round,' she said, '20 million reporters are on my heels, and I can't get used to it.' Nor had she been too pleased by the welcome accorded 'England's Royal siblings' in the *New York Sunday News*. 'Good ole Charley Windsor,' it enthused, somewhat mysteriously, was 'a young feller who's really as common as a new shoe'. Princess Anne, meanwhile, was described as an impatient girl. 'She has a 35–25–37 figure and likes to display to good advantage the maximum amount of leg.'

After an unusually heavy summer of engagements at home, October 1970 saw the Prince of Wales undertake his first extended foreign tour in his own right. He had been disappointed to miss Tonga on his parents' Commonwealth tour that spring: by way of compensation, the Queen had promised him Fiji, to whose independence celebrations he flew via Bahrain, Singapore and Darwin on 8–9 October. A strong draught of the narcotic local brew, *kava*, greeted his late arrival; as other engagements were cancelled, he insisted on driving slowly into the capital, Suva, through the huge crowds which had been waiting for him all day. Next morning he watched the formal hauling down of the Union Jack, the first of many such ceremonies he would attend in the coming years. In the following week there was much criticism that the visit had been planned by old-style colonialists, despite its purpose; the Prince was rarely able to mingle with the people, spending most of his time sandwiched between dignitaries on platforms. His one moment of relaxation, a fishing trip in a flat-bottomed boat, was marred by a sudden storm whipping up the treacherous South Pacific surf. The Prince, drenched to the skin and bailing furiously, was offered a ride ashore by anxious British officials aboard an escort launch, and recorded his first father-like 'Go to hell'.

Five more days amid the Pacific islands, stop-overs in Fiji and Tahiti, a night in Acapulco, and he was in Bermuda for the 350th anniversary of the island's Parliament. Riots had marked his approach, and the ceremony at which he formally opened the new session was boycotted by the opposition Progressive Labour Party. A British frigate, the *Grenville*, hovered in Hamilton harbour during the three days of festivities, but the promised demonstrations never materialized. Charles had disarmed many with, in the circumstances, a somewhat risqué joke in his speech to Parliament: 'Bearing in mind I am the first Charles to have anything to do with a Parliament for 350 years, I might have turned nasty and dissolved you.' And there were, as everywhere, the girls, whose Bermudan greeting was to shower him with pink oleanders.

The only tricky moment of the entire tour came, less expectedly, at his next port of call, Barbados, where the twenty-three-year-old president of the University's student union, Victor Alexis, chose to greet the Prince of Wales with a Black Power salute. The Prince, rather revealingly, did not know what it meant. Alexis kept his right fist clenched, stunning the Prince into momentary silence, before grabbing Charles's hand, palms across. 'Do you always shake hands like that?' asked his visitor. 'This is Black Power,' replied Alexis, who then struck his chest with his clenched fist and raised it aloft again. A Government statement next day said that Prince Charles had been 'deeply concerned' by his meeting with Alexis, who had apparently told him he was studying law so as to defend 'all the black people against all the white people'. The twenty-one-year-old Prince, who otherwise carried off official duties with grave maturity, had for a moment displayed one of his several chinks of innocent naïvety.

Over the next six years, Prince Charles's Service career was to take him back many times to this part of the world, including more independence celebrations in the Bahamas and Papua New Guinea. Apart from a trip via India to Nepal in 1975, for King Birendra's coronation, he made no new landfalls until March 1977, when he had his first extended taste of Africa. His Kenyan safari with Princess Anne in 1971, during which a rhinoceros had menaced him as he lay helpless in his sleeping-bag, had left him with a taste for another. Before undertaking official tours of Ghana and the Ivory Coast, therefore, he set off once more into the bush, camera in hand, to emerge ten days later apparently aware of reports that he had taken a 'mystery blonde' along with him. They were, alas, untrue; but he was sufficiently amused to present the reporter who had started it all with a home-made stuffed bird, complete with blonde wig, labelled 'mystery bird'.

A few days later he was on official duty again, being installed as Naba

Charles Mampasa, honorary Chief of Bolgatana, capital of Ghana's remotest and most impoverished region. In the steps of his great-uncle fifty-two years before, he had spent several days paying courtesy calls on tribal chieftains around the country. For those accompanying the Prince, staff and pressmen, the trip was an arduous mixture of extreme heat and administrative chaos. Developing countries tend to be the most punctilious about Royal protocol, while not always the most effective at carrying it out. As the Prince's Andover came in to land at Bolgatana's remote airstrip, the commander of the 150-man guard of honour chose to order his men to take up position across the runway. The aircraft had to overshoot and circle again. The Prince of Wales, for once, was not at the controls, though in the co-pilot's seat beside the then deputy captain of the Queen's Flight, Squadron Leader Derek Lovett. He asked to be allowed to make the second landing, to avoid causing offence to the embarrassed Ghanaians. Feeling that conditions on the ground remained unpredictable, Lovett (though outranked) brusquely took command, and ordered the Prince out of the cockpit.

Four days in the Ivory Coast gave the Prince another chance to wax lyrical about British exports to an emergent nation with a rapidly developing economy. The fact that President Houphouet-Boigny's ruling Democratic Party, the State's only political party, had distributed flags and costumes bearing the Prince's face, and transported people into the capital from all over the country, only added to the Prince's astonishment when more than a million people lined his route into Abidjan from the airport. He repaid the compliment by delivering a stylish impromptu address in their native French.

It was the beginning of a very heavy year of travel. That summer saw him installed, again in a tradition set by his great-uncle, as a Red Indian chieftain by the Kainai tribes of Alberta, Canada. His Royal Highness Prince Red Crow, only recently photographed in the striped robes of an African chieftain, was giving his attendant photographers their best year yet: in full Red Indian regalia, complete with head-dress blowing in the wind, he donned warpaint and joined enthusiastically in a Kainai war dance, only to reappear next morning in stetson hat and cowpoke gear, astride a nut-brown non-bucking bronco, to open the Calgary Stampede. By October, he was crossing the United States, taking in eleven cities in twelve days, even by his standards the most arduous schedule he has undertaken. Between his civic reception in Chicago, and a gala dinner with the stars in Hollywood (at which he sat between two glamorous TV cops, Angie Dickinson and Farrah Fawcett-Majors), he lost a stone in weight. He braved Irish demonstrators in San Francisco before flying onto another ten-day swing round Australia, marked mainly by the number of kisses he gave and received. Where

American matrons had slyly placed their daughters next to him at interminable dinners, Australian girls simply threw themselves at him. One who greeted him at Adelaide airport, and made sure her revealing T-shirt was not obscured from the cameras when she launched her lips at his, turned out to be a blue-movie star.

1978 brought pastures new. In March he visited Brazil for the first time, and consolidated his reputation as a dancer by joining in a samba with almost hysterical enthusiasm. His party had reached Rio too late for the Mardi Gras carnival, so a mini-carnival was specially staged for the Prince's benefit in the grounds of the Mayor's residence. After watching from a balcony as the exotic throng threaded its way round and round the residence garden, the Prince came down to dance in his dinner jacket with a young Brazilian female in a few slithers of silver tinsel and little else.

He was able to enjoy some polo with South America's finest players – and a secret night out at São Paulo's top night-club, the Hippopotamus – before flying on for a rather more staid few days in Venezuela. At his departure point from Brazil, Manaus, he found himself, by complete coincidence, in the same hotel as Lord Snowdon, returning from a photographic assignment for *The Sunday Times* magazine. It was a time of high speculation about Snowdon's marriage to Princess Margaret, which was to end in divorce before the year was out. The two friends had a drink in the Prince's suite, but it was not thought appropriate for them to be seen dining together.

The year ended, just before the Prince's thirtieth birthday, with his first visit to a communist country: an easy initiation in non-aligned Yugoslavia, at the invitation of President Tito, a particularly close friend of the British Royal Family. The tour was remarkably low-key, as communist states do not announce such visitors in advance. But Prince Charles had a chance to explore the Adriatic coast, visiting those very fleshpots where King Edward VIII had taken his famous cruise on the *Nahlin* with Mrs Simpson. Over a lavish lunch at the President's Adriatic retreat, Tito gave Charles an elder statesman's run-down on the state of the nation. The Prince, according to those present, 'gave as good as he got'.

With a visit to NATO and SHAPE headquarters in Brussels, and long tours of Australia and India in 1979, the Prince of Wales approached the 1980s a seasoned ambassador for his country, more than capable of carrying off the ritual diplomacy required of him. It was not always thus. Visiting the Wellington estate in Spain in 1972, he admired the Moorish Palace of the Alhambra in Granada rather too much. 'It's so marvellous,' he said, 'I can't understand why tourists don't take it away stone by stone,' prompting a Spanish politician to remind him: 'The Prince should remember how his countrymen carried off another Spanish stone, a rather larger one called the Rock of Gibraltar.' Before visiting the Arctic in 1975, he said he was 'off to rub a few noses', causing predictable offence to his Eskimo hosts. He has since learnt that of such asides are diplomatic incidents born, and has grown ever more cautious in the supposedly off-the-record cocktail-parties thrown for the journalists accompanying him.

It is another of the frustrations of his position that such vigilance must be, exercised. But his last few foreign sorties, into more exotic and controversial lands, have also made him more aware of other limitations to his role. There were fewer opportunities than he had hoped for trade initiatives, even fortuitous, cosmetic ones such as that in Brazil. There was a growing frustration about his political muzzle: in Brazil he could say nothing about human rights, in Yugoslavia he could make no public comment on his first glimpse of life according to Karl Marx. There was also a growing sense of isolation: in Rio he had to view Copacabana beach from his hotel room, in Split he could not join his staff for an early morning swim in the Adriatic. To travel abroad with the Prince of Wales is to see more of the restrictions than the perks of his job. He may not have to worry about air connections and lost baggage, but nor can he drown such worries in a few gin slings beside the hotel pool.

As he grows into middle age, swaps his youthful glamour for domestic stability, adds substance and *gravitas* to his young intelligence, such disadvantages should evaporate. His skill at present is to duck political questions; in time it will be to answer them in broad humanitarian tones. As he learns more of international commerce, of which his current notions are at best sketchy, he will add more than his mere presence to British markets overseas. When he travels abroad as King, it is already clear that he will want more positive duties than looking at things and being looked at. He shows all the promise with which Edward VIII excited his countrymen as Prince of Wales, and all the conscientiousness which Edward turned out to lack. The 1970s, abroad as elsewhere, have been his training ground.

18

The Social Worker

I believe it best to confine myself to three basic aims at the
start: to show concern for people, to display interest in them
as individuals, and to encourage them in a whole host of ways.

ON 15 JUNE 1977, at the height of Elizabeth II's Silver Jubilee celebrations,
the Prince of Wales paid a visit to the Moonshot youth centre in the heart
of South London's slumland. It was to be a routine inspection of the kind
of place which might receive a grant from the Silver Jubilee appeal, of which
the Prince was chairman. But twenty-four black youths from the Lewisham
area had recently been arrested on mugging charges, and Moonshot
members were among a group of anti-police demonstrators who greeted the
Prince's arrival. As he stepped from the royal Rolls, his eye fell first on
one of the noisiest young protesters, who sported a lapel badge declaring
'Stuff the Jubilee'.

Not for the first time in his life, Prince Charles decided against the soft
option of walking straight past. 'I must go across and see them,' he said,
to counter-protests from his staff and police escort. The Prince headed
straight for the lapel badge, whose owner turned out to be Kim Gordon,
secretary of the Committee To Free The Lewisham 24, and a full-time
official of Flame, the black section of the Socialist Workers Party. Gordon
recounted the group's grievances against the police, and the Prince called
over Commander Douglas Randall, head of P Division of the Metropolitan
Police, whose men had made the original arrests. A small, somewhat tense
conference ensued, which the Prince cut short by declaring: 'Well, I'm sure
there's some truth on both sides. Couldn't you come together and discuss
it?'

Next day he was in trouble. The Prince of Wales had intervened in a
matter which was *sub judice*. Some police voices told him, in effect, to mind

his own business; Kim Gordon blithely accused him of naïvety. But a meeting *was* held, a week later at Buckingham Palace, at which Commander Randall got together with youth and community leaders from the area, for a discussion chaired by the Prince himself. Those involved testify that a great deal of good emerged. Tension in the Lewisham area was eased and more regular meetings organized. Justice, naturally, proceeded on its due course: in time, nineteen of the youths were brought to trial and all were convicted, seven having pleaded guilty. The Moonshot Club itself, meanwhile, benefited in unexpected ways.

It began to receive a series of cash grants from the Prince's Trust, with which it has improved facilities and been able to attract many more young members in an area notoriously short of such meeting-places. The club remains in regular communication with the Prince, by way of the reports its members send him about how they have used the money. Before that day in June 1977, few people in Lewisham knew of the existence of the Prince's Trust. To this day many more all over the country still don't. It is one of four charitable organizations to which the Prince devotes a great deal of time, and one of two which he has himself set up. They receive very little publicity: typically, his intervention that morning outside the Moonshot Club was front-page news the following day, while the subsequent follow-up work was never reported. A huge central chunk of his time and interest, which he regards as perhaps his most valuable work as Prince of Wales, has hitherto gone more or less totally unrecorded.

The Moonshot incident was perhaps evidence of a certain naïvety, as the Prince had laid himself open to charges of manipulation by a revolutionary political group. He had also, from the police's point of view, publicly helped undermine their authority in an already very difficult operational area. But it was greater evidence of deep-seated good intent. The Prince's concern for deprived and disadvantaged youth, especially ethnic minorities, was well known privately, but in public remained little more than rather bland and innocent Lord Bountiful-type pronouncements. In fact, for several years, Prince Charles had already been organizing practical assistance for many such groups all over the country – and most of them had never known where the money was coming from.

One afternoon in December 1972 George Pratt, deputy chief probation officer for London, was surprised to receive a telephone call from Buckingham Palace. Pratt had been making a series of TV and radio appearances to launch a new scheme of community service for young people in trouble with the law; on the line was David Checketts, to say that the Prince of Wales had seen one of his broadcasts, and was wondering if there was anything he could do to help.

Pratt was flattered but dubious. As a professional, he knew that any new community service schemes tended to complicate existing ones, and that layer after layer of bureaucracy had to be consulted, informed, cajoled and convinced before new projects could be launched. He would, he said, think it over and come back with a suggestion. A month later, he had organized a discussion meeting at Buckingham Palace.

Around the table were representatives of the probation service, the church, the social services, welfare organizations and the police. From the chair the Prince, just twenty-four, made an impassioned speech about Gordonstoun and Kurt Hahn, mountain and air sea rescue work; he said how impressed he had been by young Army NCOs taking on responsibilities beyond their years. Surely there was some role the heir to the throne could play in helping disadvantaged or delinquent youth?

More study meetings were organized and the group, as Pratt had feared, grew larger. It was thought prudent to co-opt officials from the Department of Education, the Home Office, social scientists, representatives of the Welsh and Scottish Offices. Prince Charles was gently steered away from all notions of traditional youth work, with which it was thought he should not be seen to interfere. Nor was an incentive scheme like his father's, the Duke of Edinburgh's Awards, deemed appropriate. That was designed to inspire the already motivated to greater heights of accomplishment; Pratt was anxious that any scheme to be launched in the Prince's name should somehow motivate the unmotivated.

But was it to be in the Prince's name? The Prince thought not, even when large initial cash donations were made by the Drapers Company and one anonymous individual (who, because of the intense secrecy surrounding his or her identity, is thought to be someone very close to Prince Charles). The royal involvement was therefore kept under wraps when the first few trial projects got under way.

The police and probation services teamed up to find groups of wayward youngsters who could be persuaded, by small cash grants, to do something useful within their community. A local policeman from Cornwall reported that a group of reprobate kids were plaguing his life; if they formed themselves into a life-saving team, they were told to their astonishment, the police would pay all the necessary fares and expenses. They did so; and they were made to feel that the initiative had been their own, with the police servicing rather than supervising them.

In London, a group of school drop-outs who had been before the juvenile courts expressed a wish to go camping. The request filtered back through the system. They were given £37.50 to cover their rail fares. Buckingham Palace obtained a tent and some pots and pans from the Army, and their

The cadet: receiving his wings at Cranwell, and in the passing-out parade at Dartmouth, both in 1971

'Bat' in hand: guiding a helicopter aboard HMS *Jupiter*

Butterflies: the first royal in history
to make a parachute jump

Sub-Lieutenant the Prince of Wales
shows his mother round HMS
Norfolk

Left: The bearded commander of
HMS *Bronington*, looking uncannily
like his great-grandfather, King
George v

Above: Last day in the Navy:
farewell to *Bronington*, with a
lavatory seat slung round his neck

An unhappy visit: the Nixon White House, 1970

Paired off with Tricia Nixon at a baseball game in Washington

On safari: Kenya, 1971

Naba Charles Mampasa, honorary
Ghanaian chieftain

An occupational hazard in Fiji

Children dance for the Prince in the Ivory Coast, where more than a million
people turned out to greet him

One day an Indian chieftain, the next a rodeo cowpoke: with Prince Andrew in Canada, 1977

Natural rhythm: an exotic samba in Rio, 1978

Left: The world's most eligible bachelor: with Lady Jane Wellesley, the bookies' favourite

Above: In his Aston Martin with Davina Sheffield

With Lady Sarah Spencer at the Windsor horse trials

Laura Jo Watkins: a Yankee at the court of Prince Charles

The meeting that went wrong: with Princess Caroline of Monaco

JEAN ROOK Centre Pages **DAILY EXPRESS**

No. 23,940   Friday June 17 1977   Weather: Dry: Sunny spells   8p

Express Exclusive **Engagement next week**

Sons will be Protestant, daughters Catholic

CHARLES TO MARRY ASTRID

—Official

By JOHN WARDEN

PRINCE CHARLES is to marry Princess Marie Astrid of Luxembourg. The formal engagement will be announced from Buckingham Palace next Monday.

The couple's difference of religion — she is a Roman Catholic — will be overcome by a novel constitutional arrangement: any sons of the marriage will be brought up according to the Church of England, while daughters will be raised in the Catholic faith.

The Queen and Prince Philip have assented to this procedure, which also has the approval of Church leaders.

Prince Charles, who is 28, first met 23-year-old Astrid about a year ago.

Although their association has been kept secret a friend said last night: "They fell for each other at that first meeting."

Astrid — who will become Princess of Wales and eventually Queen—is the daughter of the Grand Duke of Luxembourg. Her mother, the former Princess Josephine Charlotte, is the daughter of the former King Leopold and Queen Astrid of the Belgians.

● Last night Buckingham Palace denied there was to be an announcement of an engagement.

Above: The *Daily Express* front page, 17 June 1977

Right: The Queen with Princess Marie-Astrid of Luxembourg: matchmaking?

Overleaf: 'A plug too far': in a promotional T-shirt, with friend

teacher lent them a camera. A few weeks later an illustrated account of the expedition turned up on Prince Charles's desk, with the news that they were all back at school. He also learnt that a young South London gang of bicycle thieves had undergone a miraculous transformation into a bicycle repair unit.

The Prince was in mid-naval career at the time, but every application for a grant was sent to him in the diplomatic bags which pursued him around the world. He would return them all to Pratt, with copious comments scribbled in the margin. As the scheme got going, the reports filed by enthusiastic teenagers were also sent on to him. He personally selected all the original beneficiaries, and followed their progress through the system. Few of them knew who it was that had helped them. But after the scheme had been going nearly three years, word began to get around. Shoals of letters began arriving at the Palace thanking him for what he was doing.

This put him in something of a dilemma when it was decided, in the spring of 1976, to regularize the aid programme into a charitable trust. Prince Charles was still against the use of his name, while keen on remaining actively involved. But Pratt's views had changed. Now that the Prince had begun meeting groups of youngsters who had received money from the trust, he could see the effect of the royal presence on the enthusiasm with which they went about things. Charles was serving on HMS *Hermes* in mid-Atlantic when a decision had to be made. After a long discussion on the ship-to-shore phone he told Pratt: 'OK, let's call it the Prince's Trust.'

The Queen's permission was obtained to use as the Trust's motif his personal insignia – the large letter C which would have been his emblem had he not been Prince of Wales. Regional committees were established in the seven areas where he had titular connections which gave a satisfying spread around London and England, Wales, Scotland and Northern Ireland. Bishops, chief constables, youth and social services directors, probation officers and police were co-opted to run them. Three years later, early in 1979, there were fifteen regional committees, and the Prince hopes that his Trust will eventually cover the whole of the country. All those who co-ordinate its work, including the director of the Prince's Trust, George Pratt, are voluntary, unpaid workers.

By 1978, some £35,000 was being distributed each year to about 250 separate projects. At the Prince's wish, applicants are not usually given the entire sum they request, but a percentage of the total as an incentive to raise the rest. The Trust smiles with especial favour on original or innovative ideas: one group, for instance, has developed a new type of two-seater canoe, in which the able-bodied can take handicapped people for river rides, even shooting rapids. Prince Charles makes a point of including a visit to Trust beneficiaries in every regional tour he makes around Britain. After a fund-raising carol concert in Westminster Cathedral during Christmas 1978, he said his farewells and made his formal departure through the main door, then slipped back in through a side entrance to talk for ninety minutes to young Londoners who had undertaken projects with money from the Trust.

Also in 1978 he was asked to become patron of Operation Drake, a two-year circumnavigation of the globe by 250 young people from all over the world in a British barquentine, *Eye of the Wind*. The Prince is patron of many organizations, but does not like to be merely a name on a letterhead. He turns down all such requests unless there is an active role he can play. The only reason, for instance, he made his second parachute jump that same year was that he had just become Colonel-in-Chief of the Parachute Regiment, and felt he should do something to merit the title. When approached by Operation Drake, he laid down conditions. He would lend his support if the organizers would allot four places to disadvantaged children. Most young people on the voyage were being sponsored, at considerable expense, by their parents, their firms or other charitable organizations; the costs of maintaining the ship, and flying children around the world to join it for their three months on board, were not likely to attract the underprivileged. As a result of Prince Charles's stand, four young people who had been before the Magistrates Courts – including a member of the Moonshot Youth Club – were taken onto the strength of Operation Drake.

By stipulating that all applicants must be under twenty-five, that grants would be made only to individuals rather than organizations, and that those individuals must have no other prospect of assistance, the Prince's Trust established new ground rules in the often muddled world of the social services. Prince Charles himself also tried to see to it – though it could not, of course, be laid down as a condition – that the majority of grants were made to young people who had found themselves brought before Juvenile or Magistrates Courts. For him, as for many who worked with him, it was a new direction, which he attempted to promote publicly in his second speech in the House of Lords. Not a single newspaper noticed what was really rather a good story.

In his maiden speech to the Lords, in June 1974, the Prince had made an impassioned plea for more government money to be spent on the nation's leisure time – 'to remove the dead hand of boredom and frustration from mankind'. He called specifically for the appointment of a Minister of Leisure, to expand the responsibilities of the newly designated Minister of Sport. Because it was his maiden speech, the text was widely quoted; but because it was a familiar theme, royalty harping on about how people should make better use of their off-duty hours, it was quickly forgotten. Two years later he returned to the same theme in the House, and announced in the process that he had been raising money to promote recreational activities for those who might otherwise drift into crime. The formation of the Prince's Trust – a unique event in recent royal history – was specifically mentioned. But few readers of the official text got beyond his first few paragraphs on good intentions and worthy royal works.

Even in Jubilee Year, when Prince Charles expanded these activities as Chairman of the Silver Jubilee Appeal, few really grasped what was going on. He launched the Appeal with a television and radio broadcast from Chevening, put out on all channels and watched by the majority of the nation. As usual the words Outward Bound, air sea rescue and other such appeals to hairy-chested idealism, showing once again the Royal Family's great dependence on the precepts of Kurt Hahn, proved a huge turn-off. The Prince's speech, even so, had been rewritten; the original version was even more remote from popular values, with lofty sentences about the joys of service and of the great outdoors, and had been gingerly thrown back at him by the Appeal's youth committee. The Prince's staff were horrified by such high-handedness, but the Prince himself was more than willing to listen. David Checketts attempted to intervene as one hapless committee member, delegated by less courageous colleagues, told the Prince what was thought of his draft. 'No, it's my bloody speech,' he told Checketts, 'let them say what they want.' They suggested a new version, which he asked them to draft. He inserted his own familiar personal touches, and the compromise version was that eventually broadcast.

Then came the euphoria of summer 1977, the street parties around the nation, the memories that communities had never felt so united since the blitz. In May 1978, in the Music Room of Buckingham Palace, the Prince was able to announce that more than £16 million had been raised – an astonishing sum from a nation of some 56 million people. Almost half a million pounds had been sent to Prince Charles personally at Buckingham Palace, in grubby £1 and £5 notes – much of it from people who could scarcely afford the price of the stamp. The money would go, at the Queen's request, 'to help young people help others'.

In 1935 Edward, Prince of Wales, had launched a similar scheme to mark the Silver Jubilee of his father, King George v. 'For Youth' was the simple slogan of that campaign, which raised £1 million from a country in the grip of the depression. In 1978 the two funds united, under the joint name of the Royal Jubilee Trusts, with Prince Charles as chairman of the administrative council. Their joint investment income yields almost £1 million a year for distribution to youth and community projects – with every application again personally vetted by the Prince of Wales, in the chair at grants meetings four times a year.

The work of the Jubilee Trusts had to be distinguished from that of the Prince's Trust. With their much larger resources, the Jubilee Trusts began to make grants to larger-scale, continuing projects, while the Prince's Trust continued to assist small, one-off bursts of individual idealism. Even so, the largest single grant made by the Jubilee Trusts was of £20,000 to the Trident Trust, an organization which provides industrial training for young people who might otherwise never have such a chance. Most grants are much smaller, and at the Prince's request go primarily to help ethnic minorities, to assist those from broken or deprived homes, to combat urban violence, and to improve life on large, bleak housing estates. Heady ideals indeed, with which the Government's social services departments have been struggling for years. But by concentrating as much as possible on specific, well-argued applications from individuals, the Prince of Wales believes the Trusts provide a valuable support to the State-financed projects they complement.

Elizabeth II's Silver Jubilee Year has thus had some bizarre repercussions. Few Londoners realize that the murals painted on the vast concrete wastes beneath their urban motorways, designed and executed by teenagers in their spare time, were financed by the Royal Jubilee Trusts. One group was granted money for a collection of tandems, on which the sighted have been able to take blind people for bicycle rides. A Derbyshire family received £100 to buy musical instruments, with which they have formed a cabaret act to tour old people's homes.

'Let's help young blacks,' said Prince Charles to the Jubilee Trusts' director, Harold Haywood, after his Moonshot experience. 'Let's help the young help the old. All that goes without saying. But do you think there's anything we can do to help in Northern Ireland?' Haywood went to see. The Prince of Wales, to his chagrin, was prevented by the security services from going himself. But after he had considered a number of ideas, money was provided for such items as the purchase of a seaside holiday home, to be shared by Protestant and Catholic children.

Nationwide, BBC TV's early evening news magazine, filmed the Prince among North London kids who had benefited from Jubilee Trust money. At one point – to the nation's subsequent delight – the Prince of Wales took to a skateboard. But this, the film's best moment, was nearly consigned to the cutting-room floor. A meeting had been hurriedly called at the BBC on the morning of transmission. Prince Charles had not been wearing a helmet while skateboarding – an unforgivable royal example to the nation's youth. The film, thought his staff, could not be shown. At which point HRH himself stepped in, and re-recorded his voice-over commentary: 'Had I known I'd have the chance to try a skateboard, I would of course have brought my helmet with me. . . .'

When the Trusts had taken over the Jubilee Appeal's work, still under the chairmanship of the Prince of Wales, there had been criticism that the membership of executive committees was too old and mandarin. The Prince thought it justified, and began to make his own appointments. Black faces, at last, began to appear at meetings discussing the problems of black youth. A friend of the Prince's from his undergraduate days at Trinity wrote to offer his services; he had now become a social worker, and would be happy to do what he could. The Prince asked for a discreet check – 'You can never,' he told George Pratt, 'be too careful' – and Anthony Kerwin became a valued committee member of both the Prince's Trust and the Jubilee Trusts, adding a touch more youth to the proceedings. Other younger people, from industry, public relations, the police and local government were pleasantly surprised to be asked, after chance meetings with Prince Charles, to join the work of the Jubilee Trusts.

Both enterprises are now launched to last beyond the Prince's lifetime, and officials of each expect his contributions to continue as long. Across in Wales the same hopes are held by the staff of the Prince of Wales' Committee, the third of his charitable preoccupations, and the second he has himself initiated and developed.

In 1968, two years before European Conservation Year, the Prince of Wales agreed to be chairman of the Welsh steering committee. In this role, in Cardiff on 10 December 1968, he took the chair of a meeting for the first time in his life, and made his first public speech. The nation was faced, he told the Countryside in 1970 Conference, with 'the horrifying effects of pollution in all its cancerous forms'. The cost of many conservation exercises was 'fiendish'. But the cost of inaction might be even greater. He took the chance to announce the Prince of Wales's Countryside Award, green and white metal plaques to mark individual enterprise in protecting the environment: 'They had great trouble trying to design something which is vandal-proof. I am told that if anyone tries to shoot airgun pellets or .22 bullets at this, they will ricochet back and clobber them.'

Throughout 1969, the year of Aberystwyth and his investiture, the Prince encouraged conservation work during his progress around Wales. By the end of 1970, the year of internationally co-ordinated efforts, a great deal had been done, and a great many projects begun which suddenly faced extinction. Prince Charles announced that he was forming a new environmental committee to carry on the good work, to be known as the Prince of Wales's Committee – or, perhaps more appropriately, Pwyllgor Tywysog Cymru. Its chairman would continue to be Ei Uchelder Brenhinol Tywysog Cymru, KG KT PC GCB.

For a decade now, the Prince of Wales's Committee, operating on similar lines to the Prince's and Jubilee Trusts, has raised money, invested it and awarded grants to conservation schemes around the principality. Many, as again decreed and personally selected by the Prince, are small-scale projects dearly cherished by local communities: schoolboys marking out a town trail through the urban wasteland of Splott, in Cardiff; an historic oak tree saved from the encroaching sea by a new sea wall at Picton Ferry, near Haverfordwest; duckboards laid across a marshy footpath by comprehensive schoolchildren from Pontypridd; the conversion of disused railway lines into footpaths and picnic sites; the rescue of the Great Western Railway signal box at Penmaenpool from demolition, and its conversion into an information centre and observation post for the Royal Society for the Protection of Birds. A group of secondary schoolchildren researched the history of a Napoleonic War cannon and built a carriage for it, after the Prince himself had airlifted it by helicopter from an inaccessible hilltop. In Aberfan, where the mining community was devastated by a coal-tip collapse in 1966, the Prince of Wales's Committee joined forces with the World Council of Churches to sponsor an international work camp, whose members – of many different nationalities and creeds – landscaped the derelict sites left by the disaster. Prince Charles and the committee's director, Brian Lymbery, have persuaded the Variety Club of Great Britain to raise £400,000 towards their most ambitious project: the complete restoration of the abandoned Montgomery Canal. The first three miles of one of Wales's most pleasant waterways has already been reopened to small craft and barges. High up Snowdon, meanwhile, volunteers funded by the committee have restored unsafe paths and rebuilt a causeway across a mountain lake, shortening the emergency rescue route by more than two miles.

With these three home-based charities steaming ahead on full throttle, the Prince of Wales in 1978 spread his philanthropic wings much further afield. His great-uncle, Lord Mountbatten, was retiring as president of the United World Colleges, a group of multi-national, multi-racial sixth-form colleges around the world, in whose foundation a major role had been played by the inevitable Kurt Hahn. A non-profit-making, charitable organization, the colleges aspire to develop world understanding, by breaking down racial prejudice and national barriers. Another time-honoured ideal, and a daunting one. But by simply implementing Hahn's thesis, that prejdices evaporate in disciplined communities facing constant challenges and occasional stress, the UWC system aims to raise generations of 'multipliers' to spread the gospel through the world.

Students at the three colleges already established in Wales, Singapore and Canada have been drawn from more than 120 countries. Some 1,750 sixth-formers nominated and financed by their governments are already in the system at any one time – 350 at the United World College of the Atlantic at St Donat's Castle in South Glamorgan, 200 at the Lester B. Pearson College of the Pacific in Victoria, British Columbia, and 1,200 at the United World College of South East Asia in Singapore. A two-year residential course leads to the International Baccalaureate, an exam pioneered by these three colleges, now used in more than 100 schools around the world and accepted by 400 universities including Oxford, Cambridge, the Sorbonne and the United States 'Ivy League'. A broad-based diploma covering six areas of specialization – from maths, languages and literature to the arts, the 'experimental sciences' and 'The Study of Man' – it has been described by its advocates as 'an international A-level'.

No entrance exam, by contrast, is required. Students are selected by interview, on academic merit and 'personal qualities'. Family or financial circumstances are irrelevant. No one can buy his way into a United World College, although the international committee are aware of charges that they are out to produce a world-wide élite. They prefer the term 'meritocracy', which is their unashamed aspiration. The Prince of Wales – a little disappointed that Gordonstoun has not abandoned the A-level for the International Baccalaureate – expressed as he became president 'a really deep and personal conviction of the intrinsic merits of the UWC concept'.

He now devotes a great deal of his time abroad to promoting it. It is no exaggeration to say that he has specifically convened meetings of former UWC students in every country he has visited since 1977. Plans are now afoot to establish United World Colleges in Italy (near Trieste), India and the Bahamas. Negotiations with the government of Iran were well advanced when the fall of the Shah early in 1979 forced their abandonment. Longer-term goals include adapting existing schools to the system in Africa and South America.

When Prince Charles visited Venezuela in March 1978, he spent some time touring regional farms and agricultural plants, where the constant complaint – the kind of localized special pleading all too familiar to royal ears – was the lack of training opportunities in a country so dependent on the land. The Prince had already had his statutory meeting with the President, Carlos Andrés Pérez, but now he asked for another. He spent some time explaining the UWC ideals before offering the President a bargain: you put up the money for an agricultural college, and we will help import international experts and a proportion of non-Venezuelan pupils. Thus Venezuela would not only become agriculturally streamlined, but house an international centre of research and development. Within a year, and despite a change of government in Venezuela, initial agreements had been signed by agriculture ministers on both sides.

Before the Prince undertakes any foreign visits these days, the director-general of the United World Colleges, Sir Ian Gourlay, will brief him on UWC connections in the area. If there is no college to visit, or proposal to advance, there will be a network of ex-pupils with whom a meeting will be arranged. The same is true of his three British-based trusts. The director of each receives the Prince's monthly schedules, and will look for chances to advance activities in the areas to be visited. Immense sheaves of paper flow between their offices and the Palace: applications for grants or college places, reports on work completed, minutes of meetings, ideas for fund-raising activities and promotional speeches. The Prince likes to see to this work himself. Each of the four directors is a regular caller at Buckingham Palace.

But none of these visits appears in the Court Circular. It is impossible to compute the amount of time Prince Charles devotes to his 'social work', but it must consume something approaching one-third of his working hours. And yet, he complained consistently in the late 1970s, after leaving the Services, most of the nation thought he hadn't got a job. Very few, moreover, were aware of the existence of these charities, or at least of his connection with them. In February 1979, when the author was in the offices of the Prince's Trust, its director received a telephone call from the Home Office. The Home Secretary had to go to Wales, to present some Prince of Wales's Awards, and 'he hadn't a clue what the hell they were'. He hadn't even managed to telephone the right place.

Two particular achievements satisfy the Prince of Wales. A Glasgow hoodlum, straightened out by community work financed by the Prince's Trust, has now become a Glasgow policeman; and another young offender, who has been working for the mentally handicapped, hopes soon to join the executive committee of one of the Prince's charities. It is the kind of work which does not always make for exciting reading, which is why it will probably continue to go largely unpublicized, but the Prince of Wales regards it as perhaps his most important contribution. Many a previous heir apparent would have preferred other ways of spending his time.

Prince Charles's ideal accomplishment, while he remains Prince of Wales, would be to rescue a young drop-out from the Juvenile Courts, give him some money to start a youth club, finance him to save a few lives at sea or up mountains, award him a plaque for greening the Welsh landscape, educate him at a United World College, and appoint him to the staff of the Prince's or Jubilee Trusts. It may yet happen; but if it does, we'll probably never hear.

19

The Prince and the Press

It's when nobody wants to write about you or take a photograph of you that you ought to worry in my sort of job. Then
there'd be no great point in being around.

IT IS 14 NOVEMBER 1978, the Prince of Wales's thirtieth birthday, and
he is cutting a large cake in the unlikely setting of a London clothes store,
surrounded by civic dignitaries, shop assistants, journalists and tailor's
dummies. From outside in Regent Street, whose Christmas lights he has
just switched on, the cheers of a large, lingering crowd waft gently in through
the windows. As he samples his cake, the Prince spots a familiar journalist,
responsible for one of the week-end's many birthday assignments. 'Liked
your piece on Sunday,' he calls out. 'But did you see the *Sunday Telegraph*?'
It had said he possessed a squint. 'I knew my eyes were close together, but
not as close as that.'

The Prince of Wales is an avid reader of his own press cuttings. Which
is saying something, for he can confidently be declared one of the most consistently publicized men in the world. Prime Ministers and Presidents come
and go, sports and showbiz stars have their hour, but a Prince is a Prince
from cradle to throne, when the attentions of the press are scarcely likely
to diminish. For once, it is true to say that everything he does makes news.
He doesn't, in fact, even have to *do* anything; a picture of Prince Charles
in the most everyday pose – entering a building, shaking a hand, unveiling
a plaque, leaving a building – will normally make the British press. His daily
movements are chronicled in the Court Circular. If he has a cold, it rates
a front-page paragraph in *The Times* and the *Telegraph*. He sells newspapers.

So it may seem surprising that he has only one press secretary – and a
diplomat at that, rather than a professional public relations man. The assistant press secretary to the Queen (at the time of writing John Dauth, an

Australian) handles press liaison for both Prince Charles and Prince Philip, with the support of Buckingham Palace's small but efficient press office. It is a job assigned to a Commonwealth diplomat for two years at a time, and the duties are arduous: organizing press facilities at each of the Prince's public appearances, dealing with the conflicting demands of short-tempered reporters and photographers, processing countless requests for interviews, photo sessions, accreditation and sundry other facilities, handling mountains of paperwork on the Prince's behalf, sifting fact from fiction when one newspaper's speculations start all the others ringing up. So constant is newspaper attention that Buckingham Palace press staff are the only members of the Royal Household to have been issued with 'bleepers', which can find them anywhere in London, day or night.

The quality of these diplomat-press officers has fluctuated wildly in recent years, many devoting their energies much more to the suppression than the release of facts. This may be to the liking of the Palace, but it is counter-productive in Fleet Street. It is also the reason why one man can control an apparently enormous and complex operation. There is a strictly limited dossier of biographical 'nuts and bolts' he can make available to any journalist new to 'Charles-watching', but even as he does so he knows it is less than enough. A great deal of the press acreage devoted to the Prince is quite simply fabricated, in the certain knowledge that Buckingham Palace very, very rarely issues formal denials. Disraeli's old adage 'Never complain, never explain' has, with very rare exceptions, been the Royal Family's instruction to its press staff. Such a position can lend a certain dignity to the proceedings, but it also leaves royal reputations at the hands of fantasists.

Elizabeth II's unspoken policy on her press, apart from continuing the hallowed tradition that the monarch is above granting personal interviews to anyone, has been to sit back and let the tide of invention, myth, innuendo and speculation wash over her and her family. There are times it hurts, of course, and there are times a Prince's rage has to be contained by a joint effort of family and staff. (Prince Philip was as annoyed as his son by the suggestion that there might be a squint somewhere in the royal genes.) But more often it amuses. The fantastical inventions of the continental press have long since fallen into this category: Queen Elizabeth To Abdicate, Elizabeth And Philip To Separate, Charles Proud Father Of Love-Child, Andrew Secretly Married, and so on. One of the few jokes on record from Princess Anne dates from a few months after her wedding, when a distinguished French visitor called at the Palace. 'Am I', she asked him, 'divorced yet?' The only British publication which falls into this category is *Private Eye*, the satirical fortnightly magazine, which nicknames the Queen 'Brenda', Prince Charles 'Brian', and Princess Margaret 'Yvonne'. Although naughtily enjoyed by many household and domestic staff, *Private Eye*, they will tell you, rarely finds its way 'upstairs'.

Palace 'spokesmen' frequently on their own account dismiss press reports about the Prince, but have lacked some credibility since 1972, when they denied rumours of romance between Princess Anne and Captain Mark Phillips only months before their engagement was announced. Prince Charles has reason still to be angry that such denials were ever issued.

But the 'Asty' affair – the *Daily Express*'s incorrect 'official' announcement of his engagement to Princess Marie-Astrid of Luxembourg – remains the only occasion on which the Prince has attached his own name to a statement of refutation. It was a particularly vivid error, as the *Express* added the tag OFFICIAL to its headline CHARLES TO MARRY ASTRID, and confidently stated that a Palace announcement would be forthcoming the following Monday. But the incident also signalled a period of disenchantment with the British press's unremitting speculation on his marriage prospects. What had been a source of innocent amusement, which he had been at least partly guilty of encouraging, had suddenly become a tedious, rather unbecoming irritant. At the age of twenty-four, after a long summer of rumour about his friend-ship with Lady Jane Wellesley, he had felt relaxed enough to joke about it when addressing a luncheon of the Parliamentary Press Gallery:

> I have read so many reports recently telling everyone who I am about to marry that when last year a certain young lady was staying at Sandringham a crowd of about 10,000 appeared when we went to church. Such was the obvious conviction that what they had read was true that I almost felt I had better espouse myself at once so as not to disappoint too many people.

Two years and countless other rumours later, he had had enough. King Edward VIII, like Prince Charles an unmarried thirty-year-old Prince of Wales, was never subjected to such a barrage of invention and innuendo. If Prince Charles, indeed, were to form a relationship with an American divorcee, it is difficult to imagine contemporary British newspapers agreeing to a conspiracy of silence on the subject.

For one with so many years' experience of the press, the Prince's attitude to it is a strange combination of shrewdness and naïvety. He can 'use' it quite as cunningly as the most seasoned politician. In July 1978, for instance, he knew full well what would be the effect of his remark to a Salvation Army congress that doctrinal argument among Christians caused 'needless dis-tress': a healthy row among churchmen, and a fortnight of 'Letters to *The Times*' (under the gratifying headline 'The Prince and the Pope'). Coming after Pope Paul's refusal to allow a church wedding to Prince Michael of Kent and his divorced Roman Catholic bride, Baroness Marie-Christine von

"Do stop snivelling. Emma. Prince Charles will even get around to you—the way he's going!"

MEANWHILE, BACK AT THE DAILY EXPRESS...

"The Palace demands to know the source of this scurrilous farrago of lies!"

Reibnitz, the Prince's unspecific remark had an immediately specific context. While appearing to make a vague, humanitarian statement, he had in effect attacked the Pope, provoking an argument as much in his own marital interests as those of his cousin. By the end of the week, with Buckingham Palace still expressing blithe surprise on his behalf, the Vatican was accusing the Prince of 'sheer impertinence'. He meanwhile had cunningly flown himself off to Norway for King Olav's seventy-fifth birthday party, leaving the controversy behind him on automatic pilot.

At the same time, however, he can display a touching innocence of news values. He chose to play down his thirtieth birthday in 1978, instructing his press officer to turn away all requests for interviews, and asking him to promote instead the tenth anniversary in 1979 of his investiture as Prince of Wales – scarcely a news editor's dream. A give-away trace of vanity meanwhile crept in : as he turned down the personal interviews sought by virtually every British publication, he gave one (albeit written answers to written questions) to *Time* magazine, so pleased was he to be a *Time* cover story. British complaints were loud and not unjustified.

The decision was also a conscious snub to the British press, an indication of the Prince's impatience with its preoccupations. Given unremitting public interest, the most trivial details remain the most sought after. In the handful of formal, on-the-record interviews he has given, Prince Charles has refused to answer only one question (put to him by Douglas Keay for *Woman's Own* in 1975): 'What, if anything, do you wear in bed?' (This seems to be a perennial poser for Princes of Wales; on his return from the US in 1924, Prince Edward found his father, George V, muttering 'Fancy their saying this about you!' as he fingered an American newspaper cutting headlined OH! WHO'LL ASK H.R.H. WHAT HE WEARS ASLEEP?)

Popular newspapers have been known to devote an entire front page in recent years to an urgent, lavishly illustrated debate on whether the Prince of Wales is losing his hair. His weight, chest and waist measurements are kept up to date in a Buckingham Palace file, though he has baulked at revealing his inside leg measurement. On one of his recent foreign tours, a red mark on the Prince's nose (in fact caused by the sunglasses he wore while flying his aeroplane) was the subject of heated argument between journalists and the Prince's staff for several days. Had he fallen off a horse? No? Then someone must have thumped him? A girl friend ... ? Attention was diverted only when a four-year-old English girl, held aloft to greet the Prince by her proud parents, bit the royal finger. Front-page news.

The Prince's sourness was understandable. In his late twenties, after leaving the Navy, he was occupied on more committee work than ever, notably running the Queen's Silver Jubilee Appeal, and he was concerned to be seen

performing a constructive role. To news editors, of course, this was worthy
but dull stuff, not rating a mention unless something went interestingly
wrong. To Prince Charles, it was evident denial of those same newspapers'
criticisms that since the end of his Service career he had been 'out of a job'.
He had already put his views on press 'sensationalism', in more general
terms, to the Parliamentary Press Gallery:

> The Press has a responsibility not to let its comparative freedom degenerate
> into cheap sensationalism. I cannot accept the argument that says 'Oh well,
> it's a sign of the times' or 'We must keep in touch with present trends of
> readership demand.' That is nonsense, and simply leads to a vicious circle
> of unnecessary and sometimes dangerous trivia.

He had been talking in broad terms of the state of the nations, but now
his own arguments were rebounding on himself.

The problem, from the Prince's point of view, is that he has always been
the property of the so-called 'popular' (i.e. mass circulation) press. The
'heavier', 'quality' newspapers have rarely taken much interest in anything
but the most public and respectable aspects of his life. The daily diet
of princely trivia has meanwhile become a full-time occupation for several
Fleet Street reporters and a full posse of globe-trotting photographers.
They are a colourful crew, in whose company it is a pleasure to travel. But
they are not always as beloved of Prince Charles as they would like to
think.

He enjoys better relations with the press than any other member of his
family, largely through force of circumstance: they surround him wherever
he goes, more consistently than they do his sister and brothers, more informally than they do his parents. He knows it is in his interests to be affable.
Thus those who dog his footsteps receive many a chummy greeting, which
can all too quickly go to their heads. Like anyone with a glancing acquaint-
anceship with royalty, pressmen in their cups will set themselves up as intimate friends. At the same time, they grow unduly familiar. The Prince dislikes being hailed by photographers as 'Charlie'; he likes even less being
embarrassed in front of punctilious hosts.

During his tour of Yugoslavia in 1978 the travelling cameramen, denied
their accustomed access to the Prince by over-zealous State authorities, at
one point conspicuously laid down their burden. The Prince of Wales had
the unnerving experience of entering a building through an arcade of silent
photographers, their cameras lying on the ground at their feet. 'What's this?'
he asked. 'You on strike?' 'Yes.' 'What, *again*?' Nervous laughter. 'Are you
going home then?' 'No, sir. We ain't got no pictures, and we're staying here
till we do.' Leaving his press secretary to smooth things over, the Prince

registered extreme annoyance and felt obliged to apologize to his Yugoslav hosts.

Later that day, a slow news day, he was surrounded by the same posse of now desperate photographers on a bleak, windswept Yugoslav hilltop. The scene of a famous resistance by Second World War partisans, the peak was capped by a bizarre contemporary sculpture, shapeless, ineffable, with whose creator the Prince was engaging in polite, if halting conversation. 'Is it', he asked rather desperately, 'made of concrete or stone?' As the sculptor's reply wound its way through the interpreter, up piped a photographer: 'No, it's made of polystyrene, and it's gonna blow off that cliff in a moment.' General hilarity, except on the part of the Prince. The sculptor was offended, and Queen Victoria's great-great-great grandson was not amused.

Such episodes are a measure of the extreme seriousness with which he takes his role as the Queen's representative overseas. They are also a measure of his complete impotence in the face of the handful of men and women who are responsible for his public reputation. They are a motley crew, constantly in dispute about the Prince's attitude to each of them, more than usually jealous of any scrap of information any of them turns up. The reporter who has chased Prince Charles more devotedly and more outlandishly than any other is James Whitaker of the London Express group's new newspaper, the *Star*, formerly of Rupert Murdoch's (London) *Sun*. He also writes for other publications under the name of Jeremy Slazenger; it was Whitaker, for instance, who reported the Prince's 1978 skiing holiday with Lady Sarah Spencer for the *Sun*, Slazenger who interviewed Lady Sarah for a women's magazine. Since 1974, the majority of Whitaker's life has been spent in royal pursuit, staked out for weeks on end around Sandringham dale or Balmoral glen in the certain knowledge that sooner or later the Prince will come his way. Whitaker is a fine distillation of British attitudes to the heir to the throne: he is a passionate monarchist – believing, for instance, that the Prince was guilty of dereliction of duty for failing to marry by his thirtieth birthday – and at the same time considers it his right to make every possible invasion of the Prince's privacy. If challenged by a member of the royal staff, he will say his duty to his family comes before his duty to his Queen. He is, unsurprisingly, not the Prince's favourite journalist (though it should be said he strives heroically for accuracy). One advantage in such a life, which Whitaker is fond of quoting, is that there is no law of trespass in Scotland. This did not help him and his photographer, Arthur Edwards, at Balmoral in the summer of 1978, when they clandestinely watched the Prince corner a stag he had been stalking for a week. Up popped Edwards's camera, and off popped the stag. As the royal ghillie saw the offenders off the estate, Edwards attempted to make amends. 'I think I've got a *picture* of the stag, if that might be of any consolation to His Royal Highness?' The ghillie's answer is not on record.

A Prince must expect such occupational hazards. Wind-surfing off Cowes the same summer, Prince Charles afforded newspaper readers and television viewers much innocent enjoyment by falling into the grey, cold briny several times. Only those present could know that a launch hired by two photographers from national newspapers had hugged him so closely, criss-crossing his path several times, that their wake was bound to sink him. Whether or not this was deliberate – it certainly made for better pictures – is a matter for the photographers' consciences. The Prince of Wales knows what he thinks. His press secretary tried to refuse one of the offenders' request for accreditation to the Prince's next overseas tour; he turned up all the same, under a different name.

Given such harassment, Prince Charles is remarkably long-suffering. He has taken trouble to find out how newspapers work, and has a shrewd understanding of what those familiar faces around him are after.

> I look at it from the newspaperman's point of view; he's got a job to do – I've got a job to do. At times they happen to coincide, and compromise must occur, otherwise misery can so easily ensue. I try to put myself in their shoes, and I hope they try to put themselves in mine, although I appreciate that is difficult. . . .

He has never, like his father, turned a hose on the press, and only rarely, like his sister, shouted abuse. But he defends her for that:

> If you are doing something competitive in public, especially in the top international class, you are inevitably keyed up. To have a lot of people with cameras pursuing you, and possibly frightening the horse, is annoying to say the least; and it is easy to become irritable and to feel that it is only when things go wrong and you fall off that the gentlemen of the press are interested, that it is only when you are upside-down or half-way up a tree that photographs appear in the papers or on TV.

The Prince's most spirited escapade dates from 1964 – between the Cherry Brandy Incident and the Affair of the Missing Exercise Book, a time when his view of newspapers might justifiably have been a trifle jaundiced. The fifteen-year-old Prince, during the school holidays from Gordonstoun, was in Athens for the wedding of his cousin King Constantine (to Princess Anne-Marie of Denmark, one of the eligible Europeans the British press had lined up for its own Prince). After the ceremony he and Princess Anne, with some of their German cousins and Crown Prince (now King) Carl Gustav of Sweden, were sunbathing on rafts at the Astor Club in the nearby resort of Vouliagmeni. Greek naval police, patrolling in paddle-boats, formed a protective cordon, but three French photographers managed to pick their way through and approach the young Royals. What happened next has been analysed in some detail by previous biographers, as next morning the French newspapers exploded with indignation that their staff had been ducked by 'precocious sprigs of British and Swedish royalty'. The truth of the matter is that it was one of Prince Charles's cousins who won the race to the enemy raft, and helped its already lopsided load – cameras and all – into the water. But the Prince of Wales was not far behind, and still wishes he had got there first.

His early youth was regularly punctuated by such moments of unwelcome attention, at a time when he was least able to cope with it. The Duke of Windsor wrote of his own childhood:

> I recall with wonder and appreciation the ease with which we were able to move about in public places. The thought occurs to me that one of the most inconvenient developments since the days of my boyhood has been the dis-appearance of privacy. I grew up before the age of the flash camera, when newspapers still employed large staffs of artists to depict the daily events with pen sketches. This artistic form of illustration seldom achieved the harsh or cruel accuracy of the camera lens, nor could it match the volume and mobility of the present-day photographer dogging his unsuspecting victim or waiting in ambush for a candid shot. Because our likenesses seldom appeared in the press, we were not often recognized on the street; when we were, the saluta-tion would be a friendly wave of the hand or, in the case of a courtier or family friend, a polite lifting of the hat.

Compare that to Prince Charles's own childhood, when his nannies were forced to abandon their walks around St James's Park because of the atten-tions of photographers and sightseers. Or to the Prince's Bavarian skiing holiday in January 1963, when the *Weekly Tribune* of Geneva wrote: 'It was like a snow scene from a Keystone Cops movie, as impatient voices bawled suggestions in English, French, Italian and German, their cars revv-ing madly, wheels spinning, as they leaped, slithered and bumped into each other in a frantic race for the best positions behind the speeding sleighs.' When finally cornered, the young Prince deftly turned his own 35 mm camera on the exhausted and dishevelled photographers, thus effectively obscuring his own face.

Such scenes are now a commonplace to him, although his detective and his press secretary would these days be likely to insist on some vestige of order and decorum. (Royal reporters have recently taken to preceding Prince Charles on his now annual January visit to Klosters – for skiing lessons. He skis so fast, indeed so recklessly – in January 1979 he badly bruised his thigh, then declared 'We Britons must ski on' – that they reckon they need to approach competition standards to have a hope of keeping up.) Given the competitive nature of journalism, it is from such attempts at keeping order that the worst chaos usually develops. A happy exception was the Prince's tour of the North-West Territories of Canada in 1975, when the ordeal of pursuit through such arduous terrain led the press corps to compose a song for the Prince, complaining about the difficulties of keeping up with him 'across the ice floes'. He responded in kind: next day Prince Charles, his equerry, his private secretary and his detective performed a ditty he had written himself, appropriately enough to the Welsh hymn tune 'Immortal Invisible':

> Impossible, unapproachable, God only knows
> The light's always dreadful and he won't damn well pose,
> Most maddening, most curious, he simply can't fail,
> It's always the same with the old Prince of Wales.
>
> Insistent, persistent, the press never end,
> One day they will drive me right round the bend,
> Recording, rephrasing every word that I say:
> It's got to be news at the end of the day.
>
> Disgraceful, most dangerous to share the same plane,
> Denies me that chance to scratch and complain.
> Oh where may I ask you is the monarchy going
> When Princes and pressmen are in the same Boeing?

Those pressmen who regularly shadow Prince Charles believe he has a moral duty to give them every facility. There is a general feeling that something of the royal presence brushes off on the royal press: it is unseemly to be scrambling and fighting for position, as is always the way, on so smart an assignment. Despite such good-natured episodes as the Prince's 'witty ditty' (his own name for it), the relationship has grown more tense of late. Especially on tour abroad, where press and Prince are often cheek by jowl in the same hotel, if not the same Boeing, he feels a constant need to withdraw; and the accompanying press corps tend to resent this rather than understand it. In Rio de Janeiro, where Prince and press alike stayed at the Copacabana Hotel, the first day of the royal tour in 1978 was spent recuperating from mild jet-lag, the press in 100-degree heat beside the hotel pool, the Prince cocooned in his top-floor suite. The photographers offered to put away their cameras if he wanted to come down for a swim. 'He couldn't do that,' said one of his staff. 'There'd be a bloody riot.'

The Prince, for his part, has tired of the trivia which co-operation with the press invariably produces. As he has grown out of his youth, so he has grown more aloof. The boyish enthusiasm, the shared humour of each absurd situation, are on the wane. At the start of each royal tour, a private, strictly off-the-record cocktail-party is thrown for all travelling journalists to meet the royal personage – which obviates the need for him or her to speak directly to them again during the trip. Prince Charles's exchanges at these increasingly formal occasions have become much briefer. His guard is never down. He has had some bad experiences: in Australia his off-the-record remarks about 'the creeps and Mafia types' with whom Frank Sinatra surrounded himself were published all over the world next day. But it is not only the danger of indiscretion which now makes the Prince keep his distance; those press who travel with the Prince of Wales have had to learn to know their place.

The dilemma is that of any public figure: while reluctantly dependent on the press for popular repute, how to nudge it in the direction one wants it to go? Royalty has a head start at home, for it can expect little short of arrant sycophancy from all British newspapers. But Prince Charles is still too vulnerable a person to have developed the imperviousness so needed by one in his position. Addressing the assembled editors and proprietors of Fleet Street in 1978, when presenting the annual British Press Awards, he put in the time-honoured plea for more good news:

> Regrettably, it does not make news to know that fifty Jumbo jets landed safely at London Airport yesterday, but it does make news if one doesn't. I still believe, however, in the necessity every now and then of reminding people, metaphorically, that vast numbers of Jumbos *do* land safely – for the simple reason that we are all human, and the maintenance of our morale needs careful consideration.

They were heartfelt words. Alas for the Prince, news values about Jumbo jets, let alone about Princes of Wales, do not appear to be in danger of imminent realignment. The calm prose of a newspaper page will always be produced from a happy carnival of chaos, in which the subject of that prose is bound to find himself caught up. And the fascination of a constitutional monarchy to its people will always be less to do with a Prince's role in society than with what, if anything, he wears in bed.

THE LIFER

PART V

King Charles III

20

Winning his Spurs

There is no set-out role for me. It depends entirely what I
make of it ... I'm really rather an awkward problem.

09.25: the executives of Lansing Bagnall Ltd, of Basingstoke, Hampshire, manufacturers of fork-lift trucks, suppliers of industrial trucks to Her
Majesty the Queen, By Appointment, tidy their desks and straighten their
ties. They are to be visited today by the Prince of Wales, who is due to
arrive at 09.30. They hover nervously in the corridor, grown men of the
world suddenly become excited schoolchildren. One straightens the portrait
of Prince Philip in the boardroom; another tidies the bottles of apple juice,
so that their labels all neatly face the front; a third anxiously scans the bleak
industrial horizon, hoping Front Gate has remembered the drill.

At 09.50 they are all still waiting. To reassure themselves, they put it down
to the weather. They do not know that the Prince's day has begun a little
later than usual, though with his customary jog round the Windsor estate.
The Queen and the Duke of Edinburgh are away, on a three-week tour of
the Gulf states; Prince Charles, in their absence, is a Councillor of State,
empowered to hold Privy Council meetings and sign Acts of Parliament –
even to make peace or declare war. In reality, the job is rather less dramatic.
Last night after an eight-hour day touring a metal factory in Wembley, he
was kept up late by the chores of royal paperwork, and this morning has
left Windsor a little behind schedule. Punctuality may be the politeness of
Princes, but this one arrives at Lansing Bagnall twenty-five minutes late.

It is the third fork-lift truck factory he has recently visited, as part
of a scheme devised at his request by 'Neddy', the National Economic
Development Office, to familiarize him with the current state of British
industry. He has attended the Neddy working parties on this sector
of industry, and is becoming something of an expert on fork-lift trucks. In

Scotland he has seen them being manufactured by an American-owned multi-national, Hyster (Europe) Ltd; last week he was in the Midlands to see more, at the Coventry Climax plant. As he listens to an extremely dry twenty-minute lecture on the business from Lansing's chairman and governing director, Sir Emmanuel Kaye, the Prince knows rather more about the opposition than Sir Emmanuel realizes.

The chairman is pushing his luck a little. 'And this, sir, is the building we would like you to open.' 'Oh really? I wasn't told anything about that.' 'Well, very informally, of course.' 'You mean you want me to drive a fork-lift truck through the wall?'

When he gets there he finds a plaque on the first floor saying it was opened by Mr Hugh (now Lord) Scanlon, president of the Amalgamated Union of Engineering Workers, last year. The Prince's plaque is more conspicuously positioned downstairs, by the front door. 'Well,' he surmises, as he obligingly pulls the drapes, 'presumably you built the upstairs first.'

The royal motorcade processes in incongruous splendour, some 300 yards, along the plant's dowdy by-ways. Then into an enormous, empty warehouse, for 'a demonstration of a broad range of our products'. Inside, over the door, against an artificially lit blue sky, a Union Jack is fluttered by an artificial breeze. Canned music strikes up; a sales executive, invisibly microphoned, is spotlit; and the Prince and his party, with mounting incredulity, watch a broad range of fork-lift trucks demonstrate their skills at formation dancing. HRH, unlike the rest of his party, is obliged to keep a straight face.

As the display ends, the press, who had been tidied away after his arrival at the factory gates, suddenly trickle in from the wings. There is a request from the executive microphone – not on the programme, this – that the Prince might graciously consent to be photographed aboard a Lansing Bagnall fork-lift truck of his choice. Hard to turn down, with the chairman on one side and the TV cameras on the other. His private secretary looks anxiously towards him; at the slightest sign, he would demur on the Prince's behalf. But the Prince is as anxious for the British public to see him touring industry as are Lansing Bagnall to have a picture of him endorsing their product. He climbs aboard. To general euphoria, he wants to drive the thing. His mastery is instantaneous; he is quickly bobbing and weaving to the amplified strains of some martial film music. But he has forgotten the protruding forks. As he spins round deftly, he comes within an inch of slicing the chairman's leg off at the ankle.

The royal progress is still twenty minutes behind schedule, so the severe timings allotted the Lansing Bagnall training centre and apprentice school, the parts and service division, Product Engineering, the labs, design department and testing facilities are each discreetly trimmed by a few minutes. As he glides from one to the next, the Prince stops to talk to anyone who looks receptive. 'What exactly are you doing?', 'Keep you busy here, do they?', 'Pay you enough, do they?', are oft-repeated questions. Each group giggles furiously after he has left it, and cannot remember a word he has said.

Two pleasantly unrehearsed moments occur. In each department, union shop stewards are wheeled forward to shake the royal hand; in one he asks if they've agreed to settle within the Government's pay guidelines. The chairman steps forward anxiously, but industrial relations at Lansing Bagnall are not a problem: 'No, we haven't,' says the senior convenor, 'but perhaps we'd better not talk about that now, eh?' In the training centre, a middle-aged woman in an overall is holding a collection box: an apprentice is getting married. The Prince motions to his detective. Prince Charles does not carry money. Chief Inspector Paul Officer fishes a £1 note out of his wallet, and hands it to the Prince, who passes it to the delighted collector. He also, rashly in the view of his staff, agrees to sign the list of contributors. Royalty is not supposed to sign anything like that. You never know what it says on the other side.

Lunch at last. The Board of Directors' Gents is guarded while under royal occupation; upstairs, the executives wait nervously, their names attached to their lapels. The Prince is motioned to the buffet immediately he enters, past a portrait of his mother taken some twenty-five years ago. 'I'd rather have a drink, if I may.' He's just like us, think the executives, and not afraid to show it. He moves from group to group, talking of the problems of British industry. In conversation with the chairman, he has already revealed a few pockets of ignorance; he did not know, for instance, that an unquoted company could not be taken over. 'What, not even by the Government?' 'Well, yes, sir, they can take over anyone they like.'

Now he asks everyone about the travails of the British motor industry. It may seem incongruous in such an efficient fork-lift truck factory, he agrees, but his dilemma is that no one will enlighten him. All the factories he has toured, thanks to NEDO, have outstandingly good industrial relations. When he travels abroad as an unofficial British trade ambassador, he comes up against charges that industrial relations in the UK are the worst in the world, that British firms will fail to meet delivery dates, that they have inadequate quality controls, that they are inferior in every way to the Germans, the French, the Japanese. He is unable to answer these charges, as no one will let him visit such places as British Leyland. He would have thought that a visit from him would be just the sort of shot in the arm those chaps needed? His voice grows quite animated, and the rest of the room falls silent.

Once again the chairman intervenes. He wishes to mark the Prince's visit by making a small presentation: a specially commissioned sculpture in gold, an abstract shape representing perpetual motion, or the finding of solutions to every problem, or remedies to every fault, or something like that. A helter-skelter of gold leaf circles around a central maypole, ending in a sharp, thrusting arrow. 'Thank you very much,' says the Prince. 'I'll have to think carefully whose chair to leave it on. . . .'

Such is the stuff of royal tours of industry. The insights gained barely rival those of a visiting party of sixth-formers. Prince Charles's attempts to discover more about the current state of British industry are as well-intentioned as everything else he does, but they can never – as he himself is the first to admit – do more than scratch the surface. Yet a week after his morning at Lansing Bagnall the Prince made a speech geared for the front pages, blaming management for the woeful state of British industrial relations. Communication, he declared, was the problem, then reminisced about his 'Neddy' tour. There was one manager he had met who 'breezed in every morning with a pipe clenched firmly between his teeth, never bothering to acknowledge people and giving instructions to everyone. When he had a problem, they all told him to get stuffed.'

The manager in question was, of course, easily identified, and thus considerably embarrassed in the following morning's newspapers. Management organizations – the Confederation of British Industry, the Institute of Directors, the Engineering Employers Federation – tactfully expressed the wish that the Prince might spend a little more time becoming a little more closely involved with industry before making such sweeping statements. What most surprised those who know the Prince well, however, is that in private he is an inveterate and impassioned union-basher. His political views on this, as on most economic and industrial issues, are considerably to the right of centre.

In the Commons there were dark hints that the Prime Minister had put him up to it. Prince Charles had in fact lunched twice with James Callaghan shortly before his speech, at the beginning of an election year (1979) marked by an especially damaging round of strikes. The inactivity of dustmen, ambulance and lorry drivers, hospital workers, civil servants and even grave-diggers had sent the Conservative Opposition's popularity in the polls to unprecedented heights. Callaghan would certainly not have thought the Prince's speech ill-timed.

It is also true that Callaghan was the first Prime Minister with whom the Prince of Wales had been able to enjoy a mature working relationship. In October 1978, during his official visit to Yugoslavia, the Prince had been annoyed by a particular development of economic policy of which he read in the Cabinet papers flown to him in Belgrade. He sat down that moment to write a strongly-worded note to the Prime Minister, which his staff – to a man – advised him not to send. But he insisted, and on his return received a note from Callaghan expressing his appreciation and inviting him to lunch. Prince Charles had scarcely altered the course of government policy, but he had injected a dash of his own brand of conservatism into a Labour Government's approach to a long winter of industrial unrest. His helpful speech followed in late February, just a week after he had spent a day at the Prime Minister's side, observing the workings of Number Ten Downing Street and the peculiar rituals of Prime Minister's Question Time in the House of Commons.

Any such collusion would, of course, have been highly unconstitutional. No Prince of Wales has better expressed the limitations on the role, and the frustration they cause, than the Duke of Windsor in his memoirs. A former King uniquely free to express his reservations about the institution of monarchy, he wrote:

> Like the Parliamentary system, the constitutional Monarch who stands aloof from and above politics is a British invention. As a device for preserving the Crown as a symbol of national unity while divesting it from abhorrent forms of absolutism, it is a remarkable example of the British genius for accommodation. But one effect of the system, which is perhaps not so well understood by the public, is the handicap imposed upon a Prince, who, while obliged to live and work within one of the most intensely political societies on earth, is expected to remain not merely above party and faction, but a-political.

Edward when Prince of Wales never took the opportunity to speak in the House of Lords, though he did – as we have seen – later use the privilege of his office to appeal to the consciences of politicians. King Edward VII, when Prince of Wales, spoke and even voted in favour of an Act in which his family had a special interest (to legalize marriage with a deceased wife's sister) and served on the Royal Commission on the Housing of the Working Classes, for which he toured the slums of London in disguise. Prince Charles has hitherto confined his two speeches in the Lords to the wholly uncontroversial subject of welfare work for the young, and has otherwise been an extremely rare attender. A hundred years ago, in 1879, the future Edward VII attended debates in the Lords on nineteen occasions.

Elsewhere, however, Prince Charles has felt free to emulate his father by discoursing on the problems of contemporary British society, including those in the economic and industrial fields which are far from a-political. He is generally saved by the fact that his remarks are wholly innocuous; nevertheless, they are open to a wide range of interpretation by party or faction.

In times when party ideologies, if not day-to-day policies, are anyway sufficiently blurred, this is perhaps innocent enough. A more important question, to the Prince as to his future subjects, is whether Charles will ever be able to use his unique position to more positive ends.

In pursuance of the heir's a-political role, Prince Charles has already developed all the skills of a politician to avoid the appearance of being one. He is adept at ducking questions which might tempt him across the sacred divide, and usually a skilful judge of how far he can go in speeches on quasi-political subjects. As Britain saw in the aftermath of the February 1974 election, the monarch still has a political role to play in moments of national crisis. Had Edward Heath chosen to persevere in his attempts to retain power through a coalition with the Liberal Party, and Harold Wilson as leader of the majority party chosen to challenge his right to do so, Elizabeth II would have had the final say between them. It very nearly came to it. Prince Charles, by the time he becomes monarch, will have had more than adequate preparation for what Harold Macmillan has called 'the last great prerogative of the crown': to agree to or refuse a Prime Minister's request for a dissolution of Parliament – 'of vital importance', as Macmillan wrote, 'at a time of national crisis'. But can he meanwhile use his expertise in roles other than that of the effective 'Viceroy' he will inevitably become?

Much that he already achieves is admirable: his social work, his visits abroad in pursuit of British foreign policy, his increasing efforts to become guardian of the national morale. But he is faced for the indefinite future with the daunting prospect of continually biting his tongue on subjects about which he is uniquely well informed. His visits to industry, it is true, can never be more than a well-intentioned democratic gesture, and his view of the world from the windows of the royal palaces is scarcely a realistic one. But he sees all Cabinet papers, and discusses contemporary issues with politicians of every party in complete confidence. Many of his letters are from the disadvantaged or the deprived, whom he can help. But many more seek a lead from him on political or commercial matters in which, however much he may want to get involved, he must stay his hand. He is doomed, it seems, to remain a repository of problems rather than a source of solutions.

Or is he? There is, as was said of the last Prince of Wales, 'no doubt of the young man's capacity for goodness'. But there is, perhaps, doubt of his capacity for boldness and imagination. On his thirtieth birthday, the otherwise glowing tribute in one of the 'quality' Sunday newspapers made an intriguing suggestion. If the Prince were so anxious to develop his non-political role, to alleviate unemployment and assist the British export drive, why did he not himself go into industry? What about 'HRH Electronics'? It was a time when Britain was dragging its feet in the electronics markets of the world, when British scientists had joined the 'brain drain' to the United States and elsewhere to develop the silicon chip and other such innovations likely to revolutionize modern technology, if not society itself. A royally-sponsored company could pioneer other exemplary innovations, such as worker participation in management and equal profit-sharing; it would help the monarchy prove its heavy State subsidy cost-effective; above all, it would provide the Prince of Wales with a clearly identified and dynamic role of his own. His two younger brothers could take over some of the ritualistic public duties of royalty for which he would be less free. Was it not time the monarchy dropped its inhibitions and rolled up its sleeves?

The writer of the article received a letter from the Prince of Wales's press secretary, thanking him for his kind words, but passing on the Prince's view that the piece as a whole was 'tendentious'. To be fair, it *had* contained a highly tendentious section suggesting that Prince Charles, footloose and fancy-free at thirty, was about to go the way of the Duke of Windsor. But the notion of HRH Electronics had clearly incurred princely disapproval. There had been no suggestion of any personal profit motive: all profits could be ploughed back into the business, or even go to charity. But the twenty-first century monarchy, it seems, is not about to besmirch its name and ancient dignities by lending them to the commercial market. Still less will the family business, whose assets, investments and other finances remain a closely-guarded secret, ever 'go public'.

Prince Charles himself has said that he wants 'to change the old, remote image of Royalty'. Yet he seems intent on preserving the gulf between the Crown and its people, the illusion that divinity doth hedge a King. The British Royal Family has always been somewhat sniffy about the more democratic gestures of its contemporaries around Europe, seeking to maintain the prestige of its position at the head of the royal league table. The Scandinavian monarchs, for instance, are known to them as 'the bicycle Kings'; British subjects are never likely to enjoy the chance of greeting their monarch on a casual stroll through St James's Park. But to preserve this mystique, as the maturer Prince Charles seems intent on doing, could prove a foolish lack of enlightenment towards the end of a turbulent century.

'In these times', he has said of the monarchy, 'this sort of organization is called into question. It is not taken for granted as it used to be. In that sense one has to be far more professional than I think one ever used to be.' Britain is in no immediate danger of a republican upsurge, though the Royal Family may be forgiven a certain paranoia on the subject as it watches the gradual disappearance of other monarchies, most recently that of Iran, around the world. But it should not, perhaps, be forgiven for thinking more 'professionalism' the answer to a less class-ridden society. If anything has underlined the irrational nature of a constitutional monarchy in recent years, and posed any longer-term threat to its survival, it has been the improvement in the conditions of the working classes, and the rapid rise in the political power of the trade unions. The Royal Family's traditional professionalism, however twentieth century the current brand, has meanwhile served rather to preserve, even strengthen class distinctions. These are the countervailing forces with which the twenty-first century King Charles III will have to contend. At present, however, he appears to aspire to a reign more of entrenchment than innovation.

The latest evidence can be found in his recent appointments. The keynote has been caution. In Edward Adeane he has found himself a private secretary young enough to have hopes of one day becoming private secretary to the King, and thus the most powerful single figure beside the monarch himself in royal policy-making. Adeane is not a radical thinker. His expertise is legal, and his instinct deeply conservative. It was his great-grandfather, Lord Stamfordham, who suggested the name 'Windsor' to King George V in 1917 (when everything from York, Lancaster and England to Fitzroy and D'Este were under consideration). It was his father, Sir Michael (now Lord) Adeane whom Lord Altrincham described in 1957 as the leader of 'an unimaginative, second-rate lot, simply lacking in gumption'. The latest Adeane to serve the Royal Family has not yet had time to win a more generous judgement; but in certain private matters he has already steered the Prince along the safest, most traditional paths.

In 1978 Lord Altrincham, now plain John Grigg but still a staunch monarchist, saw no reason to alter his judgements of 1957: 'Unfortunately, much of what I wrote about the Royal Household twenty-one years ago still seems to apply. The Royal Family's "official" family is still nothing like socially or racially representative of the community. Still less is it representative of the Commonwealth, of which the British monarch is Head.'

There is, for instance, still not one black face anywhere in the royal entourage, for all the Prince of Wales's frequently voiced and palpably sincere concern for greater racial understanding. It is the kind of public example, however specious, for which the Royal Family exists, and which a young and popular Prince of Wales is ideally placed to make. His many public panegyrics of the Commonwealth make it an even more extraordinary omission.

In these as in other matters, such as his own marital prospects, he has shown an understandable wish not to be hurried. He is still, to a large extent, feeling his way. But this Prince of Wales will have in time to make some radical gestures to win his spurs. He will have to take the Crown into new, more pragmatic roles. He will have to integrate it more fully into the economic working life of its people, if at the expense of some of that cherished mystique. He has so far shown few signs of being willing to do so.

Charles's parents have shown themselves sound, if cautious, royal innovators, not least in the decisions behind his own upbringing. But it will fall to him to see the monarchy into a new millennium, which will call for new directions as momentous as the times. Conscientiousness and deep-seated good intents may not, for once, be enough. He will be required, as will those in whose advice he places his trust, to demonstrate radicalism of a kind they now conspicuously shun. The prognosis, for the present, does not sparkle.

In the years ahead much will depend on how far he can liberate himself from the influence of his parents, who still place stern restraints on his public behaviour. After his 'anti-Vatican' speech in 1978 a member of his staff was sent to Heathrow, ostensibly to greet his return from Norway; in fact he had been delegated to ensure that the Prince talked to no one, least of all the press, before arriving home to a carpeting. Unless Charles can win himself more freedom to take such stands, he may, like his great-great-grandfather, simply grow bored and resentful. 'I don't mind praying to the eternal father,' Bertie, approaching sixty, told the archbishop who conducted Queen Victoria's diamond jubilee service, 'but I must be the only man in the country afflicted with an eternal mother.'

21

Vivat Regina

There once was a man who said: 'Damn!
It is borne upon me that I am
    An engine that moves
    In predestinate grooves,
I'm not even a bus, I'm a tram.'

Michael E. Hare

ON 18 APRIL 1977 the Prince of Wales dined privately at Chequers with the Prime Minister and half a dozen members of the Labour Cabinet. The evening was long and convivial, and the exchanges increasingly frank. Prince Charles, by one account, grew somewhat morose as he listened to a discussion of political power by those, unlike him, in a position to wield it. At length he told them the story of the Quantas air hostess who not long before had summoned the *chutzpah* to say to him: 'What a rotten, boring job you've got!' The Cabinet laughed politely. 'But you don't understand,' complained the Prince, 'she was right!' At which one of the most senior politicians present, deep in his cups, is said to have tweaked the heir apparent gently on the cheek, and remarked: 'Well, you shouldn't have taken the job, then, should you?'

The joke, for once, was on Charles. But the monotony of his life, coupled with its frustrations, could in time prove ever harder for him to handle. Walter Bagehot, discussing the prospects of Bertie, Prince of Wales, in the 1867 edition of *The English Constitution*, declared that the ideal monarch would be one who is 'willing to labour, superior to pleasure and ... begins early to reign'. Prince Charles's early introduction to affairs of State, as Elizabeth II's logical antidote to what she herself called the 'Edward VII situation', could over the years quicken his impatience to occupy the centre-stage. And the longevity of recent royal females suggests that he *will* be at least as old as Edward VII when he inherits the throne; his own children, as yet figments even more of the public imagination than of his own, will probably themselves be parents before King Charles III is crowned. The Queen Mother, as Prince Charles entered his thirties, was as old as the century and still going strong; George V's widow, Queen Mary, lived to be eighty-five and Edward VII's widow, Queen Alexandra, to be eighty. Queen Victoria died at eighty-one.

The present Queen is a shrewd and sympathetic mother, who understands only too well the grim prospect facing her son. The need to provide him with a more positive and specific role – at first a Governor-Generalship, later perhaps that of an executive 'vice-president' to an ageing and less active monarch – will become more and more pressing. There will be ever more frequent discussion of the pros and cons of Elizabeth II's abdication.

In 1978, when the Queen was only fifty-two, an Opinion Research Centre poll for *Woman* magazine showed as many as a third of young people in Britain in favour of a hand-over to Prince Charles 'before too long'. The figure dropped to a quarter among the over-sixty-fives, typical among whom was an elderly woman who said: 'We want the Queen and I'd hate to see her go!' A younger voice added: 'Let her decide for herself when she's had enough.'

Abdication will remain a perennially vexed question around the land, but the answer will grow increasingly simple. The Queen recognizes the logic of handing over the central role to her son before his time, before he is past the height of his powers. As a private woman, she would be only too happy to retire to the country homes, the family life and the animals which occupy her most natural affections. But of late the question has been less frequently raised in royal circles. There was a time she would discuss it quite freely. As long ago as 1965, at the dinner party to plan Prince Charles's higher education, the Queen herself tried to start a debate among the select group of family, political and ecclesiastical intimates at her table. 'It might be wise', she said, 'to abdicate at a time when Charles could do better.' 'You may be right,' said her husband light-heartedly, 'the doctors will keep you alive so long!'

But the subject was not on the agenda, and Prince Philip's joke deflected further serious discussion. In the intervening years, Elizabeth II has changed. In Silver Jubilee Year, 1977, she was not averse to boasting that she had already been served by seven Prime Ministers. Gladstone once said of Queen Victoria: 'Parliaments and Ministers pass, but she abides in lifelong duty and she is to them as the oak in the forest is to the annual harvest in the field.' In 1977, those close to Elizabeth II suddenly perceived her vision of advancing to Victorian venerability. The older and more experienced a monarch she becomes, the greater the affection and respect she will command among her people. However much she may wish as a woman to quit the public scene, she will grow stronger in her determination as a constitutional monarch that it can never be done.

Since 1936 the very word abdication has sent a collective shudder through Buckingham Palace, and still does. Though the circumstances would be very different, a hand-over of the office would be thought to devalue it, to reduce the British monarchy to the ranks of its junior European counterparts – who believe, as two British royal ladies sneered of two Dutch after Queen Wilhelmina's abdication in 1948, that the Crown is a pensionable job like any other, to be tossed lightly aside at the age of sixty-five.

Abdication would also, as has happened in Holland, create an irresistible precedent. Prince Philip was once tempted by a newspaper proprietor's advice that he should hold regular press conferences, but eventually abandoned the idea for fear of committing his heirs to continuing the tradition. Prince Charles himself – he will be forty-two, an ideal age for accession, when the Queen reaches sixty-five – would be the first to defend this principle: that an abdication, however honourable its intentions, would be a mortal blow at the monarchy's foundations, the beginning of the end of its survival in its present form. He has said on several occasions, and is the only member of the Royal Family to have put it publicly on record, that the Queen will not abdicate in his favour. He would not wish her to.

Those who advocate abdication fail to understand the nature of the British monarchy's popular appeal. Its majesty lies in its antiquity; its prestige, its dignity, its pre-eminence as the fount of all wisdom are based on continuity and tradition, on apparently infinite experience. A Prince is hailed as King in the very minute of his parent's death; the chain of succession, renewed rather than broken by mortality, is a lingering contemporary echo of the divine right of Kings.

Irrational, of course, but so is the monarchy's sustained hold over its people. Britons revere it as a symbol of Christian qualities of which they have long since made light in their own personal lives. In his book *Crown and People*, based on the reports of all manner and class of British subject to the social studies group Mass Observation, Philip Ziegler made the same point about the success of Elizabeth II's Silver Jubilee: 'It was striking in 1977 how many tributes were paid to her conscientiousness and dignity, to the way in which she embodied qualities such as decency, respectability, family loyalty, which were often represented as being out of fashion ...'

In this context, both the Queen and Prince Charles recognize the importance of his establishing a family life of his own, both to provide the nation with more royal infants to coo over, and to continue the tradition of domestic virtue which is the contemporary monarchy's mainstay. Elizabeth II would of course remain matriarch of the Royal Family, but the nation will grow restless unless Prince Charles's junior circle is soon built around her grandchildren and heirs. In all the furore over Edward VIII's abdication, both in 1936 and thereafter, the one central issue was neatly pinned down at the time by J.H. Thomas, the trade union leader and socialist politician, who told George V's biographer, Harold Nicolson: 'And now 'ere we 'ave this obstinate little man with 'is Mrs Simpson. Hit won't do, 'Arold, I tell you that straight. I know the people of this country. I *know* them. They 'ate 'aving no family life at Court.'

Philip Ziegler went on to suggest 'the British people like their monarchs either old, wise and paternal or young and hopeful'. A sixty-year-old King Charles III would be neither. The logical conclusion, he said, was for the Queen to hand on the Crown to a grandson of twenty or so years old. 'The Golden Jubilee of 2002 might be a suitable occasion.'

Ziegler was gracious enough to acknowledge that this might constitute something of a waste of the present Prince of Wales, requiring as it would his 'premature disappearance ... the need for which he might reasonably consider inadequately proven'. But it is an eery coincidence that the first sons of monarchs have fared less than happily this century. Both George V and George VI were second sons, the one promoted by a death, the other by default. (The Duke of York's unsuitability for kingship led in 1936 to serious consideration within the Royal Family as to whether the throne should pass instead over the then Duke of Gloucester to his youngest brother, the then Duke of Kent, who was better equipped for the role and already had a male heir. Had the plan gone ahead, the Duke would presumably have been kept back from active service in the Second World War, which saw his death in an air crash in 1942; the present Duke of Kent would now have been either Prince of Wales or King, and Prince Charles would at best be Duke of somewhere considerably less profitable than Cornwall.)

Hence perhaps the continuing anxiety about Prince Charles's *penchant* for risking his neck to prove himself a royal he-man. Both George V and two of his Prime Ministers, Stanley Baldwin and Ramsay MacDonald, attempted for the same reason to talk the future Edward VIII out of his love of reckless steeplechasing, which more than once involved him in dangerous falls.

Prince Andrew, moreover, has yet to prove himself a worthy next-in-line. There has been ill-disguised concern in the Royal Family recently about the abandon with which he has embarked upon the princely life, and his early reputation as a ladies' man. When her children were young, Elizabeth II decreed that members of the Royal Household should call them by their Christian names until they reached the age of eighteen, when they were to be more correctly addressed as 'Sir'. Significantly, on Prince Andrew's eighteenth birthday in 1978 the Queen instructed her staff that the rule need not yet be observed.

The way ahead may seem to hold no dangers for Prince Charles. Polls consistently acclaim him the Royal Family's most popular member apart from the Queen herself; the most recent, the ORC survey for *Woman* in 1978, awarded him 61 popularity points out of 100 to the Queen's 73, with Prince Philip third on 56, the Queen Mother – surprisingly – fourth on 52, and Princess Anne and Princess Margaret bringing up the rear with a mere 30 and 29 respectively.

But closer analysis shows that the Prince's popular appeal is strongest with age-groups older or younger than his own, and that this has remained a constant throughout his adolescence, youth and early manhood. His adherence to the values of his parents' generation rather than his own, and his outspoken rejection of many of his contemporaries' values, have both grown more marked in recent years. They are in danger of losing him the sympathy, even the interest, of many Britons his own age.

Though it is too early to pass fuller judgement on his younger brothers, he will always compare favourably with his sister, Princess Anne, whose constant public surliness serves only to underline Prince Charles's self-denying devotion to duty. In 1976 she moaned to the British Airways in-flight magazine *High Life*: 'We've never had a holiday. A week or two at Balmoral or ten days at Sandringham is the nearest we get.' Going out and about, moreover, was 'purgatory ... either too many people or too many press'. The first sentiment was palpably untrue, the second scarcely regal. It was left to Prince Charles, a few months later, to mend his sister's fences in another interview with the same magazine: 'Britain has indulged in far more self-indignation than is good for her. There are millions of people who work incredibly hard and achieve magnificent things without any recognition whatsoever.'

Charles is becoming a master of such populist rhetoric – British Airways' motto, 'Fly the Flag', could be ripe for princely adoption – but his future will need to be made of sterner stuff. Whatever role is found for him, he will need to prove himself of more substance in those areas which still occasionally expose his naïvety. He will need to prove himself more in touch with the progressive thinking and relaxed life-style of a large proportion of his own age-group, who approach the seats of power quite as remorselessly as he approaches the throne. It is the greatest irony of the many innovations in his upbringing, and the many royal 'firsts' he has himself achieved, that they have combined to produce the most conventional young Prince of Wales of modern times.

When the future King Edward VIII was but a few days old, the Scottish radical and socialist leader Keir Hardie rose in the Commons to make a dire prediction:

> From his childhood this boy will be surrounded by sycophants and flatterers by the score, and will be taught to believe himself as of a superior creation. A line will be drawn between him and the people he might be called to rule over. In due course, following the precedent which has already been set, he will be sent on a tour round the world, and probably rumours of a morganatic marriage will follow, and the end of it will be that the country will be called upon to pay the bill.

Remarkably prophetic words in that instance, they will always hold true of any Prince of Wales. Prince Charles knows he would have to do something utterly drastic to lose his *ex officio* popular glamour. He is by definition a jet-setter, even if he prefers a more stately progress by turbo-prop. He has already established his own racy permutation of the annual royal routine: skiing at Klosters in January, polo at Deauville and fishing in Iceland in August, amid the familiar Sandringham winters, Balmoral summers and Windsor week-ends. Around his travelling circus, in time, as his mother grows into an elderly, revered, perhaps more retiring monarch, a glittering junior court will gather. A place at his table will be the most sought after in the land.

The magic attending his presence in a room will not diminish; tides of humanity will continue to ebb and flow around him; enthusiastic crowds will always wait hours for the merest glimpse. Yet it is a very twentieth-century irony that probably the most publicized Prince of Wales of all time is perhaps the most misunderstood. Whatever the efforts made on his behalf, his people will always regard him as a swashbuckling, hard-living extrovert Prince rather than the kindly, hesitant, very vulnerable man he really is. The popular imagination will always picture him astride a polo pony, where he in fact spends very little of his time, rather than toiling at his desk, where he spends a great deal.

In the summer of 1978 the director of one of the Prince's charitable trusts arrived at Buckingham Palace for a routine meeting. He was due to have a few words with the Prince before escorting him into committee, but HRH was nowhere to be found. Eventually a footman said he had last seen Prince Charles in the garden, sitting under a tree, writing a speech. The director waited patiently as the Prince was summoned, then heard a door close at the far end of the vast Palace corridor. As he watched the distant, solitary figure advance towards him, head hung in preoccupation, he wondered: 'What sort of a life is this? What are we doing to this young man?'

Prince Charles has more natural intelligence than most previous heirs apparent, and a more conscientious spirit than a nation has any right to expect of one born to such a fate. Britain, in this respect, has been lucky. Or, in the words of the Prince's great-uncle, Lord Mountbatten, closest personal friend of three British monarchs this century: 'It's not luck at all. It's a bloody miracle.'

Yet these, Charles knows, are the public bones he must make flesh. It will not be easy. The monarchy is not the most adaptable of institutions, but ahead lie times with which it must change. As Prince of Wales, and one day as King Charles III, he will have to see to it that he subtly alters both offices, rather than they him.

It says a good deal for Charles's record so far that his future subjects wish this idealistic young Prince well in the unenviable years ahead. His enthusiasm for making the most of his birthright, more than many of those who have gone before him, is one of his greatest assets. An even greater one is his modesty in knowing that he is not yet fully equipped for the task, that there is still much to learn.

During his coast-to-coast tour of the United States in 1977, the most arduous itinerary he has yet undertaken abroad or at home, an awe-struck American journalist remarked: 'My God! That guy works so hard you'd think he was running for office.'

In a way, he is.

APPENDICES

APPENDIX A

Curriculum Vitae

Members of the Royal Family are above individual listings in *Who's Who*; they have their own dignified, cursory mention at the front. If the Prince of Wales did have his own individual entry, it would read something like this:

WALES, 21st Prince of, *cr* 1301; His Royal Highness The Prince Charles Philip Arthur George (Mountbatten-Windsor), KG 1958; KT 1977; GCB 1975 (Great Master of the Order); PC 1977; Prince of Wales and Earl of Chester, Duke of Cornwall and Rothesay, Earl of Carrick and Baron Renfrew, Lord of the Isles and Great Steward of Scotland; heir to the throne of the United Kingdom; *b* Buckingham Palace, London, 14 November 1948; *es* of Her Most Excellent Majesty Elizabeth II of The United Kingdom of Great Britain and Northern Ireland and of Her Other Realms and Territories, Queen, Head of the Commonwealth, *er d* of His late Majesty King George VI and Queen Elizabeth The Queen Mother; and His Royal Highness The Prince Philip (Mountbatten), Duke of Edinburgh, Earl of Merioneth and Baron Greenwich, *os* of HRH the late Prince Andrew of Greece and Denmark and HRH the late Princess (Victoria) Alice Elizabeth Julia Marie of Battenberg.

Educ: Hill House School, London; Cheam School, Hampshire; Gordonstoun School, Morayshire; Geelong Grammar School, Melbourne; Trinity College, Cambridge (MA); University College of Wales, Aberystwyth. Served in Royal Air Force 1971, and Royal Navy 1971–76. Flight Lieutenant, RAF Cranwell, 1971; Wing Commander RAF, 1976. Royal Naval College, Dartmouth, 1971; Sub Lieutenant RN, 1971; Lieutenant, 1973; Commander, 1976. Served aboard HMS *Norfolk*, 1971–72; HMS *Glasserton*, 1972; HMS *Minerva*, 1973; HMS *Fox*, 1973; HMS *Jupiter*, 1974; HMS *Hermes* (with 845 Squadron, the 'Red Dragons'), 1975; Commander, HMS *Bronington*, Jan.–Dec. 1976.

Personal ADC to Queen Elizabeth II, 1973–. Prince Charles of Edinburgh, 1948–52; Duke of Cornwall, 1952; *cr* Prince of Wales, 1958. Invested Prince of Wales at Caernarvon, 1969, took seat in House of Lords, 1970. Chairman: Elizabeth II's Silver Jubilee Appeal, 1977.

Colonel-in-Chief The Cheshire Regiment (1977), The Gordon Highlanders (1977), Lord Strathcona's Horse (Royal Canadians) (1977), The Parachute Regiment (1977), Royal Australian Armoured Corps (1977), Royal Regiment of Canada (1977), Royal Regiment of Wales (1969), 2nd King Edward VII's Own Gurkha Rifles (The Sirmoor Rifles) (1977), Royal Winnipeg Rifles (1977). Colonel, Welsh Guards (1975); Hon Air Commodore, RAF Brawdy (1977); Air Commodore in Chief, Royal New Zealand Air Force, (1977); Colonel-in-Chief, Air Reserve Group of Air Command in Canada (1977).

Grand Cross, Order of the Dannebrog, Denmark (1974); Grand Cross, Order of the White Rose, Finland (1969); Grand Cordon, Supreme Order of the Chrysanthemum, Japan (1971); Grand Cross, Order of the Oak Crown, Luxembourg (1972); Grand Cross, Order of Ojasvi Rajanya, Nepal (1975); Grand Cross, Order of the House of Orange, Netherlands (1972); the Order of the Seraphim, Sweden (1975); Hon Member, the Order of the Wapiti, USA (1969). Queen Elizabeth II Coronation Medal (1953); The Queen's Silver Jubilee Medal (1977).

President: Bach Choir (1976), British Sub Aqua Club (1974), Cambridge University Polo Club (1975–79); Commonwealth Youth Exchange Council (1977–80), Council for National Academic Awards (1977–), Devon County Agricultural Association (1979), Friends of Covent Garden (1977–), Highland Society of London (1978), The Lord's Taverners (1975–76), The National Rifle Association (1977–82), Peterborough Royal Foxhound Show (1978), Prince of Wales's Company Club (Welsh Guards) (1975–), Printers Charitable Corporation (1977), Royal Aero Club (1975–80), Royal Agricultural Society of England (1978), Royal Bath and West Show (1977), Underwater Conservation Year (1977), Wells Cathedral Appeal Trust Fund (1976–), Welsh Committee, European Architectural Heritage Year (1972–75), Welsh Environment Foundation (1971), Youth and Music (1977–80).

Vice-President: Society of the Friends of St George's and the Descendants of the Knights of the Garter (1968–).

Chairman: Canterbury Cathedral Appeal Fund (1974–79), King George's Fund for Sailors (1977–), King George's Jubilee Trust (1974–78), Prince of Wales's Committee for Wales (1970–), Queen Elizabeth II's Silver Jubilee Appeal (1977), Steering Committee for Wales 'Countryside in 1970' Conference (1968–70), The Royal Jubilee Trusts (1978–).

Patron: Abbeyfield Society (1978–), British Deer Society (1978–83), Bath Preservation Trust (1973–78), British Flight Team (1977–79), British North Pole Expedition (1977), British Surfing Association (1978), City Arts Festival (1978), Council for British Archaeology (1978–83), Elgar Foundation (1975–80), English Chamber Orchestra and Music Society (1977–82), Friends of Brecon Cathedral (1974–), Game Fair (1975–80), Joint Services Expedition to the Elephant Island Group (1970–71), Joint Services Expedition to the Chagos Archipelago (1978), League of Venturers (1974–), Men of Trees Society (1978–), National Ski Federation of Great Britain (1978–), Old Cranwellian Association (1978–), Operation Drake (1977–78), Royal Anthropological Institute of Great Britain (1972–78), Royal Opera House, Covent Garden (1975–80), Royal Asiatic Society (1972–), Royal Cornwall Yacht Club (1977–), Royal Tournament (1978), Royal Regiment of Wales Officers' Dining Club (1969–), Royal Regiment of Wales Regimental Association (1969–), Society for the Promotion of Nature Reserves (1977–), Society of Friends of Royal Naval Museum, Portsmouth (1977–), Somerset County Federation of Young Farmers Clubs (1973–76), Thames Angling Preservation (1974–81), United Nations Organization 25th Anniversary, 1970, National Co-ordinating Committee (1969–75), Wales In Bloom Campaign (1970–75), Welsh Association of Male Voice Choirs (1977–), Wiltons Music Hall Trust (1971), York Archaeological Trust (1977–80), Transglobe Expedition (1979–).

Member: Air Squadron, Armed Forces Benefit & Aid Association (USA), Army and Navy Club, Association of Royal Naval Officers, Aston Martin Owners Club, Athenaeum, Automobile Association, Blue Seal Club (Household Divisional Dining Club), Boodles, British Automobile Racing Club, British Deer Society, British Horse Society, Buck's Club, Cambridge Open Regatta, Cambrian Archaeological Association, Cavalry and Guards Club, Cerce de Deauville, Cheam School Association, Circolo Della Caccia, Confrerie des Chevaliers du Sacavin, Cornish Club, Country Gentleman's Association, Cowes Corinthian Yacht Club, Cambridge Union Society, Faculty of Advocates, Fleet Air Arm Officers Association, Fly Dressers Guild, Friends of St Michael the Archangel Church (Mere), Game Conservancy, Gilde Royale St Sebastian, Gordonstoun Association, Ham Polo Club, Hawaii Polo Club, Helicopter Club of Great Britain, Highland Brigade Club, High Peak Hunt, Honourable Artillery Company, Imperial Service Club (Sydney), Institution of Electronic Radio Engineers, International Variety Club, Island Sailing Club, Leander Club, Les Ambassadeurs Club, Lincolnshire Constabulary, Lloyd's Register of Shipping, Lord's Taverners, Magic Circle, Marylebone Cricket Club, Melbourne Cricket Club, Mounted Infantry Club, National Equestrian Centre (Stoneleigh), Naval and Military Club (Melbourne), Naval Club, New Club (Edinburgh), Norfolk Club, Order of the Road, Other Club, Oxford and Cambridge Rifle Association, The Parlour, Punch Table, Royal Air Force Club, Royal Air Forces Association, Royal Automobile Club, Royal British Legion, Royal Dart Yacht Club, Royal Forestry Society, Royal Fowey Yacht Club, Royal Institution of Chartered Surveyors, Royal Institution of Navigation, Royal London Yacht Club, Royal Naval Bird Watching Society, Royal Naval Club, Royal Brighton Yacht Club (Melbourne), Royal Motor Yacht Club, Royal Thames Yacht Club (Commodore), Royal Naval Saddle Club, RNVR Club (Scotland), Royal Ocean Racing Club, Royal Yacht Squadron, Surrey County Cricket Club, St David's Society of New York, Singapore Polo Club, Ski Club of Great Britain, Society of Merchant Venturers, Students Union Society (University College, Cardiff), Taupo International Fishermen's Club, Tiger Club, Traveller's Club, Trinity House (Elder Brother), Turf Club, United Oxford and Cambridge University Club, United Service and Royal Aero Club, Variety Club International, Variety Club of Australia, Zoological Society of London.

Freeman: Worshipful Company of Fishmongers, Worshipful Company of Shipwrights, Worshipful Company of Drapers. Member: Honourable Artillery Company, Honourable Company of Master Mariners.

Hon Fellow: Institute of Water Pollution Control, Institution of Mechanical Engineers, Royal College of Physicians, Royal College of Physicians (Edinburgh), Royal Fellow of Royal College of Surgeons of England, Society of Antiquaries of London; Master of the Bench, Society of Gray's Inn.

Hon LL.D.: The Citadel, The Military College of South Carolina (1977), Cleveland State University (1977), University of London (1974). Hon D.Litt.: University of Wales (1972), Council for National Academic Awards (1976). Chancellor, University of Wales, 1976–. Hon D.Eng.: Stevens Institute of Technology (1977).

A Freeman of the Cities of Cardiff, Chester, London, Montgomery, Portsmouth, Windsor. High Steward: Royal Borough of Windsor and Maidenhead. Honorary

Citizen of Chicago and Oklahoma. Companion Rat in the Grand Order of Water Rats.

Publications: contributions or forewords to numerous books, including King George III (1972), Captains and Kings (1972), The Living World of Animals (1970), The Puffin Annual No 1 (1974), More Goon Show Scripts (1973), The World Underwater Book (1973), The Country Life Book of Queen Elizabeth the Queen Mother (1978); occasional journalism (*Punch, Books and Bookmen, Gordonstoun Record, Varsity, Triton*, etc).

Recreations: hunting, shooting, fishing, polo, skiing, flying, painting, reading, listening to music, jogging.

Addresses: Buckingham Palace, London SW1; Windsor Castle, Berkshire; Balmoral Castle, Aberdeenshire; Sandringham House, Norfolk; Palace of Holyroodhouse, Edinburgh; Chevening, Sevenoaks, Kent; Tamarisk, St Mary's, Isles of Scilly.

APPENDIX B

*Chronology of Principal Events in Prince Charles's Life, 1948–79,
Including Foreign Visits*

1948
Nov. 14   Born at Buckingham Palace
Dec. 15   Christened at Buckingham Palace

1950
Aug. 15   Birth of Princess Anne

1952
Feb. 6   Becomes heir apparent and Duke of Cornwall on death of his
              grandfather, King George VI, and accession of his mother as
              Queen Elizabeth II

1954
April 22–   Visits Malta, Libya (Tobruk) and Gibraltar to greet his
May 11   parents home from coronation tour of Commonwealth

1957
Jan. 28   Joins Hill House School as day-boy
Sept. 23   Joins Cheam preparatory school as boarder

1958
July 26   Created Prince of Wales and Knight of the Garter

1960
Feb. 19   Birth of Prince Andrew

1962
April 1   Leaves Cheam School
April 11–14   Visits relatives in Germany with Prince Philip
May 1   Joins Gordonstoun School

1963
Jan. 9–19   Skiing holiday in Switzerland (guest of Prince Ludwig of
              Hesse)

1964
March 10   Birth of Prince Edward
July   Passes five GCE O-levels
Sept. 14–15   Private visit to Germany (Langen) en route for
Sept. 15–20   Athens for wedding of King Constantine
Dec. 29   Visits Paris with Prince Philip and Princess Anne en route for
Dec. 30–   Skiing holiday in Liechtenstein
Jan. 8

1965

Nov. 26	Plays Macbeth in Gordonstoun school play
Dec. 20	Wins Duke of Edinburgh's Silver Award
Dec. 28–	Skiing holiday in Liechtenstein
Jan. 9	

1966

Feb. 2	Joins Timbertop, country annexe of Geelong Church of England Grammar School, Melbourne, Australia, for two terms
May 12–31	Visits Papua New Guinea and tours Australia during school holidays
Aug. 1–3	Visits Mexico en route from Australia to
Aug. 3–16	Commonwealth Games in Jamaica
Nov. 14	Eighteenth birthday. Made Councillor of State. Now eligible to succeed to throne in own right

1967

Jan.	Made head boy at Gordonstoun
April 20–21	Private visit to France (Nice)
July	Passes two GCE A-levels
Oct.	Joins Trinity College, Cambridge, to read archaeology and anthropology, later history
Oct. 31	Attends first State Opening of Parliament
Dec. 20	Visits Melbourne for funeral of Prime Minister, Harold Holt

1968

March 8	Contributes article to *Varsity* magazine
March 25–	Archaeological expedition to France and Jersey
April 1	
June 9	Wins half-blue for representing Cambridge at polo
June 14	Awarded a II,1 in Part One of Cambridge Tripos
June 17	Invested as Knight of the Garter at Windsor
July 2–10	Holiday in Malta as guest of governor, Sir Maurice Dorman
July 11	Attends first Buckingham Palace garden party
July 30	First flight (familiarization)
Dec. 10	Chairs first meeting (Steering Committee for Wales, 'The Countryside in 1970' Conference, Cardiff). Also occasion of first public speech

1969

Jan. 14	First solo flight
Feb. 25–	Takes part in Cambridge revue *Revulution*
March 3	
March 2	First sound radio broadcast: interview with Jack de Manio (13.15 hrs, BBC Radio 4)
March 21–30	Skiing holiday in Sweden (guest of Crown Prince – now King – Carl Gustav)
April 20	Arrives for one term at University College of Wales, Aberystwyth

June 11	Inauguration ceremony for Royal Regiment of Wales, of which he is Colonel-in-Chief. Receives freedom of City of Cardiff
June 26	First television appearance. Interview with Brian Connell and Cliff Michelmore
July 1	Investiture as Prince of Wales at Caernarvon Castle
July 2–5	Tour of Wales
July 7–14	Holiday in Malta (guest of Sir Maurice Dorman)
Oct. 23	Germany: funeral of Margravine of Baden
Nov. 21–25	Malta: inaugurates new campus at Royal University

1970

Feb. 8–9	Strasbourg: Council of Europe's European Conservation Conference
Feb. 11	Takes seat in House of Lords
March	Obtains Grade A private pilot's licence
March 12– April 8	Tours Australia and New Zealand with Queen and Prince Philip
April 9–14	Tours Japan (Expo 70)
June	Graduates BA (Hons) from Cambridge
July 2–15	Visits Ottawa, then joined by Queen and Prince Philip for tour of Canada
July 16–18	With Princess Anne, guest of President Nixon in Washington
Oct. 1–4	France: private visit (Paris–Amiens)
Oct. 9–15	Fiji: independence celebrations
Oct. 15–19	Gilbert and Ellice Islands
Oct. 20–22	Bermuda: 350th anniversary of parliament
Oct. 22–25	Barbados
Nov. 11–12	Paris: funeral of President de Gaulle
Nov. 29– Dec. 4	Germany (private visit)

1971

Feb. 6–20	Kenya: safari with Princess Anne
Feb. 25–27	Germany: visits Royal Regiment of Wales at Osnabrück
March–Aug.	Flight Lieutenant in RAF. Trained at RAF College, Cranwell
Sept.–Oct.	Acting Sub-Lieutenant in Royal Navy. Six-week course at Royal Naval College, Dartmouth
Nov. 5	Gibraltar: to join HMS *Norfolk*. Promoted Sub-Lieutenant

1972

–July	Serves aboard HMS *Norfolk*
May 17–18	Joins Queen and Duke of Edinburgh on State visit to France
July	Shore courses at HMS *Dryad*, Portsmouth. Familiarization flying with RN and Queen's Flight
Oct. 29–31	Berlin: military and civic engagements
Oct. 31– Nov. 3	Spain: private visit as guest of Duke of Wellington

Nov. 22–24   Holland (private)
Nov.   Served with HMS *Glasserton*, coastal minesweeper

1973
Jan. 25–6   Visits Royal Regiment of Wales in Germany
Feb. 12   Leaves Portsmouth aboard HMS *Minerva*, aboard which he
               serves until September. (Gains bridge watch-keeping and ocean
               navigation certificates. Promoted Lieutenant)
June 1   St Kitts: opens newly restored Prince of Wales's bastion
July 6–11   The Bahamas: independence celebrations
Oct.   Completes shore courses for divisional officer
Nov. 4–5   Luxembourg: guest of Grand Duke
Nov. 14   Wedding of Princess Anne and Captain Mark Phillips
Nov. 20–25   Spain: guest of Duke of Wellington

1974
Jan.–Aug.   Serves aboard HMS *Jupiter* as communications officer
Jan. 2   Flies to join *Jupiter* at Singapore
Jan. 29–   New Zealand: joins Queen and Duke of Edinburgh for
Feb. 6   Commonwealth Games
Sept.–Dec.   Royal Naval Air Station, Yeovilton, for helicopter conversion
               course
Sept. 4   New Zealand: funeral of Prime Minister, Norman Kirk
Oct. 8–12   Fiji: represents Queen at independence celebrations
Oct. 12–30   Australia: inaugurates Anglo-Australian telescope; visits
               Tasmania

1975
Jan.   Returns to Yeovilton for advance flying training
Feb. 20   Visits Delhi en route for
Feb. 22–26   Nepal: coronation of King Birendra
March–June   Serves aboard HMS *Hermes*, commando ship, with 845
               Squadron ('Red Dragons'). Visits Caribbean
April 11–20   Bahamas: guest of Lord and Lady Brabourne at Eleuthera
April 20–30   Canada: tours North-West Territories
Aug. 3–9   Iceland: fishing holiday as guest of Lord and Lady Tryon
Sept.–Dec.   Lieutenant's course at Royal Naval College, Greenwich
Sept. 14–19   Papua New Guinea: represents Queen at independence
               celebrations
Sept. 19–21   Indonesia (private visit to Bali)
Nov. 9–11   Germany: visits Royal Regiment of Wales in Berlin
Dec. 21–22   Netherlands: private visit as guest of Prince Bernhard

1976
Feb.–Dec.   Commands HMS *Bronington*, minehunter, based at Rosyth.
               (Promoted Commander in RN and Wing Commander in RAF
               on leaving Services in December)
July 23–25   Canada: private visit to Olympic Games in Montreal
Aug. 2–8   Iceland: fishing holiday as guest of Tryons

1977
March 6–16   Kenya: safari holiday
March 17–25   Ghana: official visit
March 25–28   Ivory Coast: official visit
April 1–10   Bahamas: private holiday
April 26–28   France: skiing holiday (Isolo)
April 28–29   Monaco
May 9   France (Bordeaux)
July 5–9   Canada (Alberta): official visit. Made Red Indian chieftain;
              opened Calgary Stampede
Aug. 3–16   Iceland (fishing holiday with Tryons)
Aug. 20–22   Deauville: polo
Oct. 18–30   USA: official visit
Nov. 1–11   Australia: official visit
Nov. 17–18   Germany: visiting 1st Battalion, Welsh Guards

1978
March   Brazil, Venezuela: official visit
May 18–19   Australia: funeral of Sir Robert Menzies
July 1–2   Norway: King Olaf's seventy-fifth birthday party
Aug.   Fishing in Iceland with Tryons and polo at Deauville
Aug. 31   Kenya: funeral of Jomo Kenyatta
Oct. 22–27   Yugoslavia: official visit
Nov. 14   Thirtieth birthday
Nov. 30–31   Brussels: official visit to NATO and SHAPE headquarters
Dec. 1–4   Spain: private visit as guest of Duke of Wellington

1979
March–April   Visits Hong Kong, Singapore, Australia and Canada
Nov.   Visits India and Nepal

APPENDIX C

Prince Charles's Descent

In August 1977, at the age of ninety-two, Mr Gerald Paget of Welwyn Garden City, Hertfordshire, published his first book: in two volumes costing £60, containing nearly 1,000 pages and weighing 13 lb., it is entitled *The Lineage and Ancestry of HRH Prince Charles, Prince of Wales*. Mr Paget's introduction opens with the rare and enviable sentence: 'This book had its origin about seventy-five years ago....'

It was in Queen Victoria's diamond jubilee year, 1897, that the schoolboy Paget first became interested in genealogy. G.W. Watson's work on the ancestry of King Edward VII, published in *The Genealogist* some ten years later, gave him the idea of tracing the pedigrees of various European monarchs. With the birth of Princess Elizabeth in 1926 he decided to explore her ancestry, hopefully as far as William the Conqueror; but he was still immersed in his project twenty-two years later, when Princess Elizabeth gave birth to Prince Charles. So Paget, then sixty-three, decided to start afresh and pursue the new Prince's ancestry, though the introduction of Prince Philip's lineage of course doubled his work-load. Had he stuck to his original intent, to trace Prince Charles back to William the Conqueror, the theoretical number of ancestors would have risen to the astonishing figure of 1,073,741,824. He decided to call a halt in the fourteenth and fifteenth centuries, at the eighteenth generation. Even so, his monumental publication leaves only some forty thousand ancestors untraced out of a total of 262,142.

These two paragraphs are by way of tribute to Mr Paget's life work, without which this appendix could scarcely have been written. I must also acknowledge a debt to an excellent two-part review of his work, in *Books and Bookmen* (vol. 23, nos 7–8), by the genealogist Sir Iain Moncreiffe of that Ilk, Albany Herald. Sir Iain's voluminous knowledge of his subject was able to detect a few minor errors, and add some intriguing new dimensions; he has also had a large hand in the compilation of this appendix. As he himself says: 'HRH's breeding is the most important in the world ... he is heir to the world's greatest position that is determined solely by heredity.'

Through cousin marriages many of the ancestors traced by Paget, more than a quarter of a million of them, are of course the same people. The total number of individuals is thus greatly reduced, which is as it should be. The Blood Royal is proportionately the purer.

In Prince Charles's veins runs the blood of emperors and kings, Russian boyars, Spanish grandees, noblemen of every European nation, bishops and judges, knights and squires, and tradesmen right down to a butcher, a toymaker and an innkeeper. Readers curious for more detail than this appendix can provide should turn to Mr Paget's work. His discoveries include the fact that Prince

Charles is a cousin or nephew, in varying degrees, of all six wives of Henry VIII; that he has many descents from the Royal Houses of Scotland, France, Germany, Austria, Denmark, Sweden, Norway, Spain, Portugal, Russia and the Netherlands. Many of his ancestors died bloodily, in battle or by the axe, especially in the Wars of the Roses and the reigns of the Tudor sovereigns.

The most significant of Prince Charles's forebears fall into three categories. First there are those who were historic figures in the British Isles, the immediate realm. Secondly, there are similar figures, especially royalty, in the rest of Europe from which emigrants have gone out in such numbers to the Old Commonwealth. And thirdly, there is a leaven of solid British stock of all classes: just enough to keep HRH down to earth, but not enough to dilute his royal blood unduly, or to give him too many inconvenient near-relations among his family's subjects.

In England, he descends over and over again from the Anglo-Saxon, Norman, Plantagenet and Tudor kings, indeed from every English king who has left descendants (even including Henry IV), except Charles I and his sons. He descends from the non-royal Protectors of England, Edward Seymour, Duke of Somerset and John Dudley, Duke of Northumberland (but not from Cromwell; curiously enough, HRH does not take sides genealogically in the Civil War). Other famous characters abound in his ancestry: Alfred the Great; Hereward the Outlaw (better known, incorrectly, as the Wake) hero of the Anglo-Saxon epic, together with the King Harold slain at Hastings *and* their foe William the Conqueror; Simon de Montfort, Earl of Leicester, the first Parliamentarian; Harry 'Hotspur', Lord Percy, hero of the Ballad of Chevy Chase; Warwick the Kingmaker; and the great Elizabethans Essex, the Queen's favourite, Sir Frances Walsingham and William Cecil, Lord Burghley.

Thanks to the lineage of Queen Elizabeth the Queen Mother (born Lady Elizabeth Bowes-Lyon, daughter of the 14th Earl of Strathmore), the blood of some of England's noblest houses runs in the Prince of Wales's veins: including de Vere, Earl of Oxford; Courtenay, Earl of Devon; Percy, Earl of Northumberland; Talbot, Earl of Shrewsbury; Stanley, Earl of Derby; Clifford, Earl of Cumberland; Cecil, Earl of Salisbury; Howard, Duke of Norfolk; Russell, Duke of Bedford, and Cavendish, Duke of Devonshire. Queen Anne's chief minister Robert Harley and the prime minister Portland were direct ancestors; Sir Philip Sidney and the 'Iron Duke' of Wellington his ancestral uncles; Charles Darwin, and – through the relationship of the Hastings, Earls of Huntingdon, to the Ardens – probably Shakespeare, were the Prince's ancestral fifth cousins.

In Wales, the present Prince of Wales descends from such renowned characters as Davy Gam and such historic families as Morgan of Tredegar, but above all from the great Owen Glendower (Owain Glyndwr), proclaimed 'Prince of Wales by the Grace of God' during the last Welsh rising. Moreover, he descends many times over from Llewelyn the Great, Prince of Wales, and all Welsh kings and princes by way of Hywel Dda back to Cunedda and Old King Coel himself, who reigned in the fifth century, soon after the Romans left Britain.

In Scotland, the Prince derives his title of Great Steward of Scotland from his ancestors the Stewart kings. Through George VI and Prince Philip he descends *twenty-two times over* from Mary Queen of Scots, and he has more than two hundred direct lines of descent from King Robert Bruce and thus from the ancient

Celtic kings of the Picts and Scots. Through the Lyons of Glamis, most of the historic Scottish houses contributed to his lineage: the 'Black Douglas' Earls of Douglas and the 'Red Douglas' Earls of Angus; the 'lightsome' Lindsay Earls of Crawford; the 'handsome' Hay Earls of Erroll; the 'gey' (which means ferocious, not gay in any sense) Gordon Earls of Huntly; the 'proud' Graham Earls of Montrose. A rather surprising ancestor was Cardinal Beaton, the murdered archbishop of St Andrews.

On the Borders his forebears included the Homes of Wedderburn, the 'bold' Scotts of Buccleuch and their foes in many a ballad, the Kerrs of Fernihurst. In the far North, through the 1st Sinclair Earl of Caithness, he comes from the old Norse jarls of Orkney. In central Scotland, the Prince springs from the Lords Drummond and the Murrays of Tullibardine, the Moncreiffes of that Ilk and Stirlings of Keir, and the Stewart Earls of Atholl. Elsewhere in the Highlands, through his descent from the Grants of Grant and the 10th Chief of Mackintosh, the Prince has Hebridean blood of the mighty Clanranald – and in the West, too, he descends not only from the MacDougall chiefs of Dunollie and the Campbell Earls of Argyll, but above all (as befits the present Lord of the Isles) at least two dozen times over from the paramount Macdonald chiefs who were the original Lords of the Isles.

In Ireland, Queen Elizabeth the Queen Mother has brought Prince Charles the most distinguished Irish ancestry, the blood of the Dal Cais and Eoganacht dynasties of Munster and that of the Ui Neill high kings. Among his ancestors were the O'Brien Earls and Kings of Thomond (including the high kings Brian 'Boru' and Toirdhelbhach); the McCarthy Reagh chieftains of the line of King Cormac who built the famous chapel at Cashel; the O'Donnells of Tyrconnell; the MacDonnells of Antrim (including 'Sorley Boy'); the wild Burkes of Clanricarde; the FitzGerald Earls of Kildare and Desmond, and the Knights of Glin; the Butler Earls of Ormonde; and, above all, Red Hugh O'Neill, Earl of Tyrone, the last native King of Ulster, who died in exile in Rome in 1618.

To turn to the continent of Europe: Prince Charles, through his father, is Danish, in the direct male line of the Royal House of Denmark, which still reigns in Norway. He descends father-to-son through Christian IX, King of Denmark (1863–1906) from Christian I, King of Denmark, Norway and Sweden (1448–1481). Among his celebrated Viking ancestors were King Sven Forkbeard of Denmark and King Harold Haardrade of Norway, but he also springs from the ancient 'Peace-Kings', whose vast grave-mounds can still be seen at Uppsala in Sweden. King Canute was his ancestral uncle. So too were Gustavus Adolphus and Charles XII of Sweden, for his Scandinavian ancestry is octopoid, taking in the Royal House of Vasa as well as such locally historic names as Oxenstierna and Sture, Sparre and Gyllenstierna, Banér and Konigsmark, Bonde and Bielke.

In Russia, he is descended through Czar Nicholas I from both Catherine the Great and Peter the Great. He also has innumerable descents from the Grand Princes of the House of Rurik, who originally founded 'All The Russias', among them St Vladimir of Kiev, who Christianized the Russians; Yuri Dolgoruky, celebrated as the founder of Moscow; and St Michael of Chernigov, executed by the Tartars for refusing to kneel to a statue of Genghis Khan. In Poland, he descends from the original Piast dynasty and from the Jagiellons up to King

Zygmunt I (d. 1548). His Lithuanian ancestry goes back to Gedimin, last pagan
sovereign of Lithuania (1316–1341). His Byzantine imperial blood flows from the
Angeloi and Comnenoi emperors of the East, and through the House of Savoy
from the later Emperors Michael VIII and Andronicus Palaeologue.

In Bohemia, the Prince descends from all the kings who have left descendants,
from the original Czech house of Premsyl (the family of Good St Wenceslas) down
through the House of Luxembourg to Anne of Bohemia, wife of the Emperor
Ferdinand I. So his ancestors include the 'Blind King' slain at Crécy, the Emperor
Charles IV who founded the University of Prague, and above all the popular Hus-
site elected King George of Podiebrad. Other historic Czech names in the Prince's
ancestry are Lobkowicz and Sternberg, and Ulric 'the lame lord' of Rosenberg.
In Hungary, he similarly descends from all the kings (who left issue) of the original
Royal House of Arpad; moreover, the famous King John Szapolyai was his
ancestral uncle. Also, through his great-grandmother Queen Mary, the blood of
many Magyar noble families, including several of the Bathory voivodes of Tran-
sylvania, flows in his veins. In Romania, by way of Queen Mary's ancestry, he
descends from Vlad Dracul, Voivode of Wallachia (father of the original Dracula)
and thus from the Bassarab dynasty who were very possibly derived from Genghis
Khan himself.

In what was the Holy Roman Empire, he descends over and over again from
Charlemagne and Frederick Barbarossa and all the great dynasties, Habsburg and
Hohenstaufen, Guelph and Hohenzollern, Bavaria and Saxony, Hesse and Baden,
Mecklenburg and Württemberg, Brunswick and Anhalt, the Electors Palatine and
other Wittelsbachs, plus many of the historic houses such as Hohenlohe and Galen,
Moltke and Sickingen, Schwarzenberg and Trauttmansdorff. Otto the Great and
Phillip of Hesse were his direct forefathers. Frederick the Great and the Emperor
Charles V were his ancestral uncles.

In Portugal, the Prince descends from the marriage of the son of King John I
of Aviz, Alfonso, Duke of Braganza, to Beatrix, daughter of the Blessed Nuño
Alvarez Pereira, the 'Holy Constable'. The equally celebrated infante Henry the
Navigator was an ancestral uncle.

In Italy, his forefathers include the Dukes of Savoy and the Emperor Frederick II
'Stupor Mundi' and the medieval Kings of Sicily, as also the Orsini of Rome
(Pope Nicholas III was his ancestral uncle), the Visconti of Milan, della Scala
of Verona, Doria of Genoa and Gonzaga of Mantua (besides the great *condottieri*
Colleoni and Hawkwood); in Spain, they include Ferdinand and Isabella (who
financed Columbus's discovery of America) and thus El Cid himself. In France:
the Carolingian, Capetian and Valois kings up to Charles VII (the Dauphin of
Joan of Arc fame), among them St Louis many times over, and such historic names
as Montmorency and Rohan, Polignac and La Rochefoucauld and La Tour d'Au-
vergne. In the Netherlands: through his wife Charlotte of Bourbon, none other
than William the Silent, Prince of Orange and founder of the Dutch Republic.
In the Low Countries, too, Prince Charles bears a remarkable likeness to portraits
of Charles the Bold, Duke of Burgundy, who was his direct forefather.

HRH's immemorial roots of course go back far, far beyond the generations
covered by Mr Paget's monumental work. The Prince's Anglo-Saxon and Danish
royal forefathers sprang from Dark Age kings who incarnated the storm-spirit

Woden (after whom Wednesday is named), and among his pagan Celtic royal fore-fathers were King Niall of the Nine Hostages and the dynamic Iron Age sacral kings of Tara, the great sanctuary of ancient Ireland. Through the Lusignan cru-sader kings of Cyprus, titular kings of Jerusalem, Prince Charles descends a mil-lennium further back from King Tiridates the Great, the first Christian monarch of all (under whom Armenia was converted in AD 314, before even Rome itself), and thus from the divine Parthian imperial House of Arsaces (247 BC), which reigned over Persia and Babylonia and was in its time the mightiest dynasty in the Ancient World.

Finally, down to earth. In 1779 Mr George Carpenter, of Redbourn in Hertford-shire (writes Sir Anthony Wagner, Garter King of Arms, in his *English Genealogy*) 'had the plumber down from London to repair the roof of his house. With the plumber came his daughter, and both remained at Redbourn some time. Mary Elizabeth Walsh, the daughter, was then eighteen years of age, and Mr Carpenter upwards of sixty, yet notwithstanding the disparity of their ages and positions he married her. Their daughter married the 11th Earl of Strathmore' – the Queen mother's great-great-grandfather. The Prince of Wales is thus eighth in descent from that plumber, John Walsh. There are many other plain English names in his ancestry; but it is through the plainest of them all, John Smith, that Prince Charles is one of the nearest living relations of George Washington, first President of the United States.

APPENDIX D

Prince Charles's Surname

History decrees that princes do not have surnames. In modern times, however, when even those of such exalted rank occasionally have to fill in forms which require one, it has become the fashion for royalty to lay claim to a 'hidden' surname from somewhere in their family history. When Prince Philip became a naturalized British subject in 1947, dropping his Greek and Danish titles, he had to borrow a surname from his mother's side of the family: Mountbatten, the Anglicized version of Battenberg. Through the Prince of Wales that name has now, in the wake of complex legal argument, become enshrined in past and future British history.

For the first few years of his life, Prince Charles made do without a surname. On his mother's accession to the throne in 1952, however, the brows of genealogists clouded over. English law dictates that a child born in wedlock takes the name of his father. But this child was the eldest son of the Queen, the only woman in the land to outrank her husband. It would not do for Prince Charles to make use of his father's name. The law would have to be changed. Thus – on the insistent suggestion of her Prime Minister, Winston Churchill – the Queen issued an Order in Council on 9 April 1952, barely two months after her accession:

> It is my Will and Pleasure that I and my children shall be styled and known as the House and Family of Windsor and that my descendants, other than female descendants who marry and their descendants, shall bear the name of Windsor.

Thus, for bureaucratic purposes, he became Charles Windsor.

In the ensuing years, however, the Queen looked back on her decree with mixed feelings. On 22 February 1957, in recognition of his ten years of public service to the country, she gave her husband the style and dignity of Prince of the United Kingdom (which most of the nation thought he already bore). The 1957 Order, she felt, unfairly ignored his contribution to the country's future. She changed her mind, and on 8 February 1960, issued another Order in Council:

> It is my Will and Pleasure that, while I and my children shall continue to be styled and known as the House and Family of Windsor, my descendants other than descendants enjoying the style, title or attribute of Royal Highness and the titular dignity of Prince or Princess and female descendants who marry and their descendants, shall bear the name of Mountbatten-Windsor.

It didn't help much. The Queen's aspiration was that her son, who had been born Charles Mountbatten and had in 1952 become Charles Windsor, should now be known as Charles Mountbatten-Windsor. But the clause excluding Princes and those of the rank of Royal Highness had everyone, including the genealogists, confused. It was a gesture to history, reasserting the constitutional view that Princes are too grand to bear surnames. If ever he *has* to use a surname, she was trying to say, I want it to be Mountbatten-Windsor.

But whoever drafted the Order for the Queen had made matters worse. She was compelled to issue an explanatory statement: 'The Queen has always wanted, without changing the name of the Royal House established by her grandfather, to associate the name of her husband with her own and his descendants.'

Even that didn't really help much, either. Writing in the *Daily Express* the then editor of Debrett's, Cyril Hankinson, tried to explain.

> It is most unlikely that there will ever be a Mountbatten-Windsor dynasty. But this is how it could come about. If the Queen's third baby were a Prince [it was: Prince Andrew, born on 19 February 1960, less than a fortnight after the Order in Council].... If that Prince married and had a son who was created a Duke and the son then had two sons.... The elder son would then take one of his father's secondary titles and would not then need a surname, but the younger son would be a Mountbatten-Windsor.... If the line of the Prince of Wales became extinct.... If the Mountbatten-Windsor's elder brother died without issue ... then the Mountbatten-Windsor would succeed to the Throne. It is as remote as that.

Even the editor of Debrett's had got it wrong. The House of Windsor would remain the House of Windsor, even if the Queen's third son's second son became King – though as King, of course, he would be entitled to change the dynasty's name to whatever he liked. The point was that the Queen wanted her children to acknowledge their father's name as well as hers, despite her precedence. A constitutional lawyer, the late Edward Iwi, attempted to put matters straight in the 18 March 1960 issue of the *Law Journal*:

> Reading the words of the Declaration and message together, as we are entitled to, and bearing in mind that they were given out on the same day and only eleven days before the birth of the infant Prince [Andrew], we may well feel that the Queen intended the name Mountbatten-Windsor to be in the lineage of her children, not merely to be given to her great-grandchildren and their descendants. To give the Royal children the name of Mountbatten-Windsor – even if they never use it – is in keeping with the idea that it is the birthright of every legitimate child in a Christian country to be identified with its father ...
>
> Reading the Queen's Declaration in conjunction with the contemporaneous message and in the light of the surrounding circumstances, the writer feels that the conclusion is patently clear. While sympathizing with the difficulties of cautious presentation felt by the draughtsman, working perhaps at speed, it is yet natural to interpret the Declaration simply as intimating that Her Majesty's real intention was to confer upon each of her children what has been, so the writer believes, properly described as a 'hidden' surname ...
>
> The common man using his common sense will arrive at the same conclusion as most lawyers. They will understand the 1960 Declaration to be that the Queen's House and Family is named Windsor; that of her children if they ever use a family name after their Christian names would be Mountbatten-Windsor, and it is that name which they will pass on to their descendants and which will be used by those descendants when the use of a surname becomes necessary.

Iwi had judged the Queen's intention correctly, but it was still far from clear whether her Declarations had achieved the legal and constitutional effects she desired. She consulted successive Lord Chancellors, who discerned the simple heart of the matter: whatever the monarch says goes. Thus it was that Princess Anne, when she married Mark Phillips on 14 November 1973, signed the Westminster Abbey register as Anne Mountbatten-Windsor. Prince Charles, said a statement from Buckingham Palace, would sign as Charles Mountbatten-Windsor 'at such a time as he needs to use a surname'.

For now, he sticks simply to Charles, not even using the suffix of P (for *princeps*) to which he is entitled. Perhaps he always will. When he becomes King Charles III, his mother's Declarations ensure that the dynasty will still be known as the House of Windsor – unless King Charles III chooses to start issuing more Declarations of his own.

With which in mind, it is worth pointing out that he is under no obligation to call himself King Charles III. He likes the name, despite its inauspicious historical associations, so he probably will. But he is equally entitled to call himself King Philip, King Arthur II, King George VII, or indeed any other name he cares to choose. His first constitutional act on becoming King will be to announce the name by which he wishes to be known.

APPENDIX E

Previous Princes of Wales

ENGLISH PRINCES OF WALES SINCE AD 1301

		Date created
Edward of Caernarvon (Edward II), son of Edward I	1284–1327	1301
Edward the Black Prince, eldest son of Edward III	1330–1376	1343
Richard (Richard II), younger son of Black Prince	1367–1400	1377
Henry of Monmouth (Henry V), eldest son of Henry VI	1387–1422	1399
Edward of Westminster, only son of Henry VI	1453–1471	1454
Edward of York (Edward V), eldest son of Edward IV	1470–1483	1472
Edward of Middleham, son of Richard III	1473–1484	1483
Arthur of Winchester, eldest son of Henry VII	1486–1502	1489
Henry of Greenwich (Henry VIII), second son of Henry VII	1491–1546	1503
Henry Frederick, eldest son of James I and VI	1594–1612	1610
Charles (Charles I), second son of James I and VI	1600–1649	1616
Charles (Charles II), second son of Charles I	1630–1685	1630
James, the old Pretender, son of James II	1688–1766	1688
George Augustus (George II), son of George I	1683–1760	1714
Frederick Louis, eldest son of George II	1707–1751	1727
George William Frederick (George III), son of Frederick Louis	1738–1820	1751
George Augustus Frederick (George IV), son of George III	1762–1830	1762
Albert Edward (Edward VII), eldest son of Queen Victoria	1841–1910	1841
George (George V), second son of Edward VII	1865–1936	1901
Edward (Edward VIII, later Duke of Windsor), eldest son of George V	1894–1972	1910
Charles Philip Arthur George, eldest son of Elizabeth II	1948–	1958

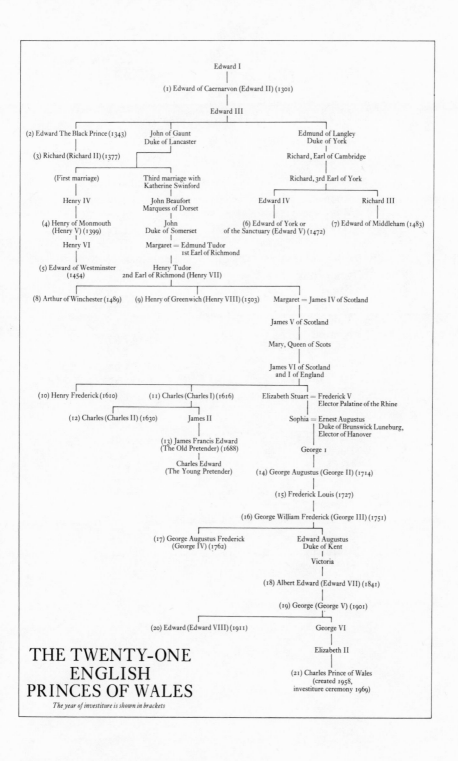

Edward I
|
(1) Edward of Caernarvon (Edward II) (1301)
|
Edward III

(2) Edward The Black Prince (1343)   John of Gaunt   Edmund of Langley
| Duke of Lancaster   Duke of York
(3) Richard (Richard II) (1377)   Richard, Earl of Cambridge

(First marriage)   Third marriage with   Richard, 3rd Earl of York
                          Katherine Swinford
Henry IV   John Beaufort   Edward IV   Richard III
| Marquess of Dorset | |
(4) Henry of Monmouth   John   (6) Edward of York or   (7) Edward of Middleham (1483)
(Henry V) (1399)   Duke of Somerset   of the Sanctuary (Edward V) (1472)
Henry VI   Margaret = Edmund Tudor
| 1st Earl of Richmond
(5) Edward of Westminster Henry Tudor
(1454)   2nd Earl of Richmond (Henry VII)

(8) Arthur of Winchester (1489)   (9) Henry of Greenwich (Henry VIII) (1503)   Margaret = James IV of Scotland
|
James V of Scotland
|
Mary, Queen of Scots
|
James VI of Scotland
and I of England

(10) Henry Frederick (1610)   (11) Charles (Charles I) (1616)   Elizabeth Stuart = Frederick V
| Elector Palatine of the Rhine
(12) Charles (Charles II) (1630)   James II   Sophia = Ernest Augustus
| Duke of Brunswick Luneburg,
(13) James Francis Edward   Elector of Hanover
(The Old Pretender) (1688)   George I
| |
Charles Edward   (14) George Augustus (George II) (1714)
(The Young Pretender)
|
(15) Frederick Louis (1727)
|
(16) George William Frederick (George III) (1751)

(17) George Augustus Frederick   Edward Augustus
(George IV) (1762)   Duke of Kent
|
Victoria
|
(18) Albert Edward (Edward VII) (1841)
|
(19) George (George V) (1901)

(20) Edward (Edward VIII) (1911)   George VI
|
Elizabeth II
|
(21) Charles Prince of Wales
(created 1958,
investiture ceremony 1969)

THE TWENTY-ONE
ENGLISH
PRINCES OF WALES

The year of investiture is shown in brackets

APPENDIX F

The Prince of Wales's Flying Hours
(at the end of 1978)

Andover	95.15
Wessex	28.05
Hawk	1.15

TOTAL SUMMARY BY TYPE UP TO 31 DECEMBER 1978

Chipmunk	80.25
Basset	92.50
Spitfire	.35
Vulcan	3.00
Nimrod	7.05
Phantom	2.00
Gannet	1.05
Jet Provost	123.35
Hunter	1.05
Wessex	338.15
Andover	248.30
Harrier T4	2.05
Buccaneer	1.45
Hawk	1.15
	903.30

SUMMARY OF GROUPS

Single engine	209.00
Multi engine	356.15
Helicopter	338.15
	903.30

BIBLIOGRAPHY

Any biographer of the present Prince of Wales will always owe a considerable debt to the late Dermot Morrah's book, *To Be A King*, an account of the Prince's early life and education made possible by the express approval and co-operation of the Queen. This biographer is no exception. Other books consulted, or which would provide the reader with more detail in specialist areas, include:

ARNOLD-BROWN, ADAM, *Unfolding Character; The Impact of Gordonstoun*, Routledge & Kegan Paul, 1962.

BAGEHOT, WALTER, *The English Constitution*, Chapman & Hall, 1867; Longmans, Green, 1915.

BEATON, CECIL WALTER HARDY, *Photobiography*, Odhams Press, 1951.

BEAVERBROOK, WILLIAM MAXWELL AITKEN, Baron, *The Abdication of King Edward VIII* (edited by A.J.P. Taylor), Hamish Hamilton, 1966.

BIRCH, NEVILLE HAMILTON and ALAN BRAMSON, *Captains & Kings*, Pitman, 1972.

BOOTHROYD, JOHN BASIL, *Philip: An Informal Biography*, Longman, 1971.

BRERETON, HENRY LLOYD, *Gordonstoun: Ancient Estate and Modern School*, W. & R. Chambers, 1968.

BROOKE, JOHN, *King George III*; with a foreword by H.R.H. the Prince of Wales, Constable, 1972.

CATHCART, HELEN, *Prince Charles: The Biography*, W.H. Allen, 1976.

CHANNON, SIR HENRY, *'Chips': The Diaries of Sir Henry Channon* (edited by Robert Rhodes James), Weidenfeld & Nicolson, 1967.

CHARLES, PRINCE OF WALES, 'Legend and Reality', a review of *Queen Victoria Was Amused* by Alan Hardy, *Books and Bookmen*, November 1976.

CHARLES, PRINCE OF WALES, Review (unheadlined) of *Twice Brightly*, a novel by Harry Secombe, *Punch*, 6 November 1974.

COOLICAN, DON and LEMOINE, SERGE, *Charles: Royal Adventurer*, Pelham Books, 1978.

COUNIHAN, DANIEL, *Royal Progress*, Cassell, 1977.

CRAWFORD, MARION, *The Little Princesses*, Cassell, 1950.

DONALDSON, FRANCES LONSDALE, LADY, *Edward VIII*, Weidenfeld & Nicolson, 1974.

DORAN, JOHN, *The Book of the Princes of Wales, Heirs to the Crown of England*, R. Bentley, 1860.

DUNCAN, ANDREW, *The Reality of Monarch*, Heinemann, 1970.

EDGAR, DONALD, *The Queen's Children*, Arthur Barker, 1978.

EDWARD VIII, King of Great Britain, *A Family Album* by the Duke of Windsor, Cassell, 1960.

EDWARD VIII, King of Great Britain, *A King's Story: The Memoirs of H.R.H. the Duke of Windsor*, Cassell, 1951.

FISHER, GRAHAM and HEATHER, *Charles: The Man and the Prince*, Hale, 1977.

GORE, JOHN, *King George V, A Personal Memoir*, John Murray, 1941.

INGLIS, BRIAN, *Abdication*, Hodder & Stoughton, 1966.

IWI, EDWARD, 'Mountbatten-Windsor', *The Law Journal*, 18 March 1960.

LACEY, ROBERT, *Majesty: Elizabeth II and the House of Windsor*, Hutchinson, 1977.

LAIRD, DOROTHY, *How the Queen Reigns; An Authentic Study of the Queen's Personality and Life Work*, Hodder & Stoughton, 1959.

LANE, PETER, *Our Future King*, Arthur Barker, 1978.

LIVERSIDGE, DOUGLAS, *Prince Charles: Monarch in the Making*, Arthur Barker, 1975.

MAGNUS, SIR PHILIP, *King Edward VII*, John Murray, 1964.

MARPLES, MORRIS, *Princes in the Making; A Study of Royal Education*, Faber and Faber, 1965.

MARTIN, KINGSLEY, *The Crown and the Establishment*, Hutchinson, 1962.

MASTERS, BRIAN, *Dreams about H.M. The Queen and Other Members of the Royal Family*; illustrated by Michael Ffolkes, Blond and Briggs, 1972.

MILLIGAN, TERENCE ALAN, *More Goon Show Scripts*, written and selected by Spike Milligan; with drawings by Peter Sellers, Harry Secombe, Spike Milligan, Woburn Press, 1973.

MORRAH, DERMOT, *To Be A King*, Hutchinson, 1968.

NICOLSON, HON. HAROLD GEORGE, *King George the Fifth; His Life and Reign*, Constable, 1952.

PAGET, GERALD, *The Lineage and Ancestry of H.R.H. Prince Charles, Prince of Wales*, 2 vols, Skilton, 1977.

PEACOCK, IRENE CYNTHIA, Lady, *The Queen and Her Children; An Authoritative Account*, Hutchinson, 1961.

PEEL, EDWARD, *Cheam School from 1645*, Thornhill Press, 1974.

PINE, LESLIE GILBERT, *Princes of Wales*, Herbert Jenkins, 1959.

POPE-HENNESSY, JAMES, *Queen Mary, 1867–1953*, G. Allen & Unwin, 1959.

RÖHRS, HERMANN, *Kurt Hahn*; from the German edition. English edn, with additional material; edited by H. Röhrs and H. Tunstall-Behrens; preface by the Duke of Edinburgh; Routledge & Kegan Paul, 1970.

ST JOHN-STEVAS, NORMAN, *Walter Bagehot*, published for the British Council and the National Book League by Longmans, Green, 1963.

SIDNEY, THOMAS, *Heirs Apparent*, Allan Wingate, 1957.

SKIDELSKY, ROBERT JACOB ALEXANDER, *Hahn of Gordonstoun*, Penguin, 1969.

STEWART, WILLIAM ALEXANDER CAMPBELL, *The Thirties and Gordonstoun*, Macmillan, 1968.

TALBOT, GODFREY, *The Country Life Book of Queen Elizabeth the Queen Mother*, Country Life Books, 1978.

WAKEFORD, GEOFFREY, *The Heir Apparent: An Authentic Study of the Life and Training of H.R.H. Charles Prince of Wales*, Hale, 1967.

WARREN, ALLEN, *Nobs and Nosh*, Leslie Frewin, 1974.

WHITAKER, JAMES, *Prince Charles*, City Magazines Ltd, 1978.

ZIEGLER, PHILIP, *Crown and People*, Collins, 1978.

INDEX

Queen Elizabeth II and the Prince of Wales are abbreviated to QE and W respectively

THE ROYAL HOUSE
OF WINDSOR

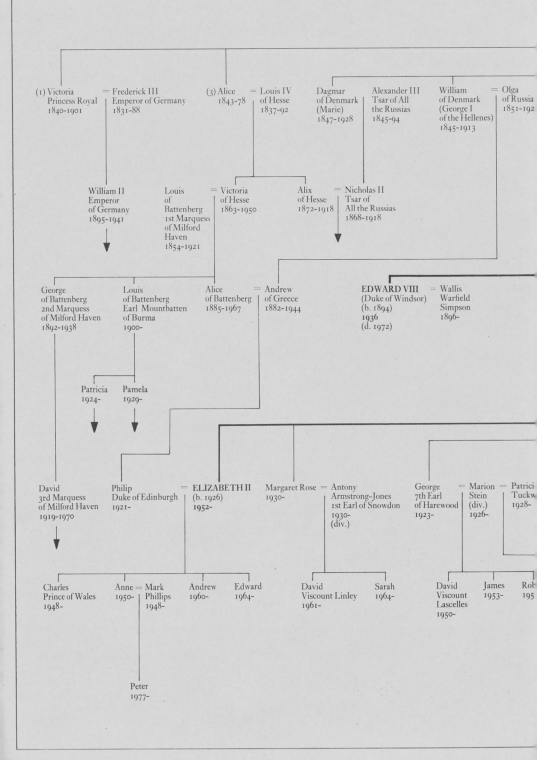

(1) Victoria
Princess Royal
1840-1901

= Frederick III
Emperor of Germany
1831-88

(3) Alice
1843-78

= Louis IV
of Hesse
1837-92

Dagmar
of Denmark
(Marie)
1847-1928

Alexander III
Tsar of All
the Russias
1845-94

William
of Denmark
(George I
of the Hellenes)
1845-1913

= Olga
of Russia
1851-192

William II
Emperor
of Germany
1895-1941

Louis
of
Battenberg
1st Marquess
of Milford
Haven
1854-1921

= Victoria
of Hesse
1863-1950

Alix
of Hesse
1872-1918

= Nicholas II
Tsar of
All the Russias
1868-1918

George
of Battenberg
2nd Marquess
of Milford Haven
1892-1938

Louis
of Battenberg
Earl Mountbatten
of Burma
1900-

Alice
of Battenberg
1885-1967

= Andrew
of Greece
1882-1944

EDWARD VIII
(Duke of Windsor)
(b. 1894)
1936
(d. 1972)

= Wallis
Warfield
Simpson
1896-

Patricia
1924-

Pamela
1929-

David
3rd Marquess
of Milford Haven
1919-1970

Philip
Duke of Edinburgh
1921-

= **ELIZABETH II**
(b. 1926)
1952-

Margaret Rose
1930-

= Antony
Armstrong-Jones
1st Earl of Snowdon
1930-
(div.)

George
7th Earl
of Harewood
1923-

= Marion
Stein
(div.)
1926-

= Patrici
Tuckw
1928-

Charles
Prince of Wales
1948-

Anne
1950-

= Mark
Phillips
1948-

Andrew
1960-

Edward
1964-

David
Viscount Linley
1961-

Sarah
1964-

David
Viscount
Lascelles
1950-

James
1953-

Rob
195

Peter
1977-